Psychotherapy

Current Perspectives

D1370023

Psychotherapy

Current Perspectives

edited by
Thomas J. Cottle
and Phillip Whitten

NEW VIEWPOINTS
A Division of Franklin Watts
New York   London

New Viewpoints
A Division of Franklin Watts
730 Fifth Avenue
New York, New York 10019

Library of Congress Cataloging in Publication Data
Main entry under title:

Psychotherapy, current perspectives.

Includes bibliographies and index.
1. Psychotherapy—Addresses, essays, lectures.
I. Cottle, Thomas J.   II. Whitten, Phillip.
RC480.P825   616.8'914   79-9426
ISBN 0-531-05411-X
ISBN 0-531-05625-2 pbk.

5 4 3 2 1

FOR
KAY COTTLE AND
GAYLE JOHNSON WHITTEN

Contents

Preface

As with many areas of study in the social sciences, the body of literature pertaining to psychotherapy is rich, varied, and in some respects highly disorganized. This is hardly surprising, however, as so many people—both lay observers and people in the profession itself—write about psychotherapy. If one scans the literature, one finds myriad references, some of them so technical only a handful of professionals would comprehend them, others so faddish that only a few might take them seriously. In between these extremes lies a vast collection of materials, which, when properly arranged in an anthology, provides the reader with a good and substantial sense of what psychotherapy, in terms of theory, philosophy, and practice, is all about.

In light of the enormity of the literature on psychotherapy, one wonders why there should be a paucity of informative anthologies. Possibly it is because the literature is always changing, with new materials and perspectives replacing old ones. Possibly it is because the biases anthologists bring to their task prevent them from doing justice to forms of psychotherapy alien to their own approaches. Or perhaps only a few anthologies exist because there is too much on the subject to consider; hence, the idea of putting together a viable collection seems hopeless. Whatever the reasons, we strongly felt that such a book might prove valuable for lay readers, prospective professionals, and active professionals alike.

The purpose of this volume is to present the major issues, purposes, and styles of practice in psychotherapy. In the following pages we explore some of the philosophical principles underlying the theory and practice of psychotherapy, and look as well at the various styles of psychotherapy that have evolved—from classical psychoanalytic psychotherapy to the more modern forms of group psychotherapy, sex therapy, bioenergetics, and family therapy. In addition, we will examine psychotherapy as it pertains to adults and children, and as it is practiced in private offices, as well as in hospital and community settings. Finally, we will consider a sample of the findings about human behavior that derive from psychotherapy, and explore relationships among political, economic, and social variables on the one hand, and the theory and practice of psychotherapy on the other.

In order to cover these topics adequately, we found it necessary to study the works of European and American psychoanalysts, psychiatrists, psychologists, social workers, counsellors, so-called para-professionals or mental health workers, as well as interested lay observers and researchers. It was also necessary to pursue articles published in the more popular journals and magazines. The problem in designing such a book was to give ample coverage to as many topics and perspectives as space would allow, for the field has its conceptual as well as political and parochial disagreements. We felt it essential to do justice to highly conflicting viewpoints and orientations. After all, we found psychoanalysts refusing to recognize the value of behavior therapy, as well as behavior therapists rejecting the value of more contemporary therapeutic techniques. The danger then, in compiling the selections for this volume, was to fall victim to the cant, dogmatism, and self-interest existing in the literature. The point of the present anthology is not to convince people of any one viewpoint, or dissuade them from adopting some perspective. Rather, we wish to inform readers of various aspects and fields of psychotherapy so that they may have a more substantial understanding and feeling for the area of psychotherapy generally.

Apart from the problems and dangers inherent in putting together such a book, the challenge for us was to create something useful to people who know little about the field, as well as to those who are fully engaged in it. And let us not forget that all readers will bring their biases and prejudgments to every article. To meet this challenge, we selected articles which we believe not only cover a particular topic, but are written with such thoughtfulness and intelligence that no one can readily dismiss them. Just as we have tried to eschew cant and rhetoric, we have tried to include dispassionate and at times erudite, but hopefully not highly technical, articles. A host of professional and lay people not practicing psychotherapy actively study the field. These include dentists, pediatricians, lawyers, historians, theologians, sociologists, social psychologists, and teachers. In addition, we find that group of people known as para-professionals engaged in full-time and part-time work directly related to psychotherapy, as, for example, family and sex counselling, community problem centers, human growth movements, and the like. What characterizes almost all the people who work in these areas is a willingness to examine thoughtful and non-dogmatic material that will help them to evaluate their own work and orientations, and enhance their understanding of the value to a society as well as to its individual members, of theories and techniques of psychotherapy. In this vein, we hope the present volume will prove worthwhile.

We would like to express our appreciation to William Harris, Oliver W. Holmes, and Viviette Reynell for their able assistance. Sally Makacynas, as always, did a marvelous typing job. And, of course, our special thanks must go to the contributors to this volume, who generously allowed us to reprint their work and without whom this book would not have been possible.

Part One

Philosophical Issues

We begin our exploration of the process called psychotherapy by examining the three aspects of a context in which psychotherapy sits. By selecting the articles that appear in this first section we are making explicit the point that psychotherapy is fundamentally a cultural phenomenon, by which we mean that it is in great measure defined by the culture and in turn serves the culture in some manner. The issue here is a complicated one and requires a bit of explanation.

To begin, psychotherapy can be said to derive from various conceptions of man and woman, conceptions that the culture perpetuates both in its popular forms and in its more creative or artistic forms. On the one hand, psychotherapy is aimed at helping people adjust to various strains in their public and private lives, and, on the other hand, it serves to enhance people's search for personal meaning. Thus psychotherapy has a more practical quality, helping people merely to get on with their lives, as well as a philosophical or creative quality—namely, helping people to express their creative propensities or indeed create new forms of living, new life-styles, or new definitions of privacy and public encounter. Given these two sometimes disparate qualities, it is not difficult to see how psychotherapy must address itself to both the literal and the metaphorical or even imagined readings of reality. Immutable reality and boundless fantasy become the common strands of the psychotherapeutic process if only because cultures and societies deal with the facts of immutable reality and the expressions of boundless fantasy, in terms of dreams, literature, art—even madness.

The point we are stressing, therefore, is this: One must not view psychotherapy strictly as some medical intervention or even temporary form of human encounter. It is both a social process and a personal engagement of human beings shaped by cultural and societal forces, customs, and conventions, many of which we will be exploring in later sections. As process and encounter, psychotherapy invokes critical readings of reality in the form of how people perceive and react to real and fantasized events and experiences. To understand this process-encounter we must explore not only those social psychological mechanisms extant in the theory and practice of psychotherapy, but in addition we must begin to appreciate the delicate process called imagination, which presumably contains the substance of our memories and expectations. To gain some insight into the act of fantasizing as well as the nature of imagination we turn to the psychology of literature, where we find both explicit and implicit descriptions of human imagination, as well as the products of human imagination and creativity. We then seek to make connections between creativity as found in the products of artists and writers, and creativity as found in the products, if you will, of psychotherapy. Both forms of creativity demonstrate a person's rendering of his or her experience in both literal and metaphorical terms. But this is not surprising, for when we deal not only with the facts of our experience but our feelings as well, it is only natural that we would lapse into metaphorical or analogical modes of thought. Some feelings and experiences, after all, are barely capable of being verbalized, much less conceptualized. In fact, as we proceed to tell someone of an experience, or an intense emotion, we are barely able to discern whether or not we are re-experiencing the experience or undergoing a wholly new experience. And if real life should produce these confusions of the literal and metaphorical renderings of experience, then imagine what effect a process and encounter like psychotherapy would have on these renderings. After all, the process of psychotherapy must also be perceived and reacted to by the people engaged in it, and hence their reactions and perceptions will, like the culture in which they live, influence the form and process of the psychotherapeutic engagement.

These, then, are some of the issues to be addressed in this first section. But there is one additional point to be made. Whether or not the actual practice of psychotherapy proceeds in reality-bound terms or highly imaginative and free-floating terms, it will inevitably be encountered in moral terms. That is, the fundamental influence of the culture on what we have called the process and engagement of psychotherapy will emerge in the form of a morality imposed upon the participants. Indeed, it could be said that one of the most intriguing products of psychotherapy is the form of morality generated in the actual process. Said differently, psychotherapy invokes values of the culture while establishing so-called guidelines for the participants in their private as well as public dealings. In this manner, a form of moral order is born that inevitably shapes not only the style of engagement practiced in psychotherapy, but the style of engagement and personal reflection that participants carry (or ought to carry) with them outside the therapeutic encounter. In a word, there are deeply philosophical issues—being, thinking, and acting—that underlie that process and engagement we call psychotherapy. In this first section we address but a few of these issues.

1

Psychotherapy and Moral Culture: A Psychiatrist's Field Report

FRED A. BLOOM

The increasing social prominence in this century of psychological theory and psychotherapies can hardly be accounted for by the influence of psychotherapy on the relatively few people for whom it is a formal treatment. Psychotherapeutic formulations dominate thought in areas far removed from the formal treatment relationship, and increasingly pervade social relations and conceptions of the self. A social worker, for example, reports that she divorced her husband because they were not "helping one another grow as people," betraying a therapeutic conception of marriage that would have surprised Freud. Grade-school children are advised that professionals are waiting to help them should they have "problems," so that, from an early age, children learn to see themselves as potential patients of professional psychotherapists. Leaving "special problems" aside, teachers are trained to regard normal children as having "normal problems," and to pride themselves on their sensitivity to the needs of their students, which they conceptualize as therapeutic needs, while at the same time corporation executives explore T-groups and various quasi-therapy services for their management personnel, to improve staff relations or morale.

The accumulated images of father attending T-groups at the office, mother going to women's consciousness-raising groups at the church, the children taking their "problems" to the school counselor, and the grandparents, at the senior citizens' luncheon, receiving talks from more "professionals" on death and dying, as if it were a

Reprinted by permission from *The Yale Review*, LXVI (March 1977), 321–346. Copyright © 1977 by Yale University.

new fad, compose a general view of life organized around a dialectic of the problematic and the therapeutic, and of the person as a patient from the cradle to the grave.

As psychotherapeutic thinking becomes a general feature of the way in which the culture mediates the needs and trials of the individual, what was first derived as a body of psychological theory and a rationale of therapy reappears in general discourse as moral philosophy. ("My husband does not help me to grow.") We find ourselves in a culture increasingly dependent on a psychological analysis of man and his social relations for the terms on which life can be felt to have meaning, a development described by Philip Rieff as "the emergence of psychological man." This puts psychotherapists and their patients in a sensitive social position analogous to the orders of monks and clergy in the Middle Ages whose ascetic disciplines stood for an ideal of character for the culture as a whole, though it was practiced in rigorous form only by the few. Similarly, while only a few people receive formal psychotherapy, increasingly it serves as a paradigm from which the meaning and validity of many diverse social activities are derived: teaching, ministering, mothering, or even marriage. The main social issue then in psychotherapy is its relation to culture generally.

In one sense psychotherapy appears as a prototype for the future institutions of culture, an avant garde of the future society. But the emergence of Rieff's psychological man is not predicated on the invention of psychotherapy or even its efficacy as therapy, but on the ascendance of psychotherapeutic logic to the position of a validating principle of life. Psychological man is the character type for whom the hope of self-achievement is now the highest form of inspiration. He makes the rationale of therapy into a rationale of life. A therapist would be content to see his patient leave therapy having achieved selfhood, but would hardly regard that achievement as the final moral task of life. Beyond therapy and beyond self-involvement there is a moral life of broader scope. Psychological man is thus not the product of psychotherapy as such, but of the failure of the traditional moral fabric of culture to hold. Far from being the avant garde of this process, any nondecadent psychotherapy must fall victim to it. The emergence of psychological man creates a cultural climate in which a valid psychotherapy can no longer occur, and in its place the psychological man demands and dispenses a new therapy on a radically altered premise. To psychological man the psychoanalytic therapy of Sigmund Freud seems an instrument of oppression, while the therapy of liberation advanced by this new man would have been regarded by Freud as an attempt to legitimize the essential illness.

In my own day-to-day attempt to provide a meaningful psychotherapy, I find myself increasingly thwarted by the reality outside the therapy, by the social and material culture of the patient and the therapist, the ambience, the setting, the milieu in which the therapy takes place. We know that the world outside the therapy is important to the therapeutic process in that it provides the material for the therapy: the conditions of his life are what the patient brings to the therapist. We understand little, however, of how the external reality influences and shapes the therapeutic process itself, how it defines the form and the nature of therapeutic change, or how it may enhance or diminish the possibility of a therapeutic experience.

A drug advertisement in a psychiatric journal depicts a psychiatrist's office with a fireplace, white walls, large black leather chairs, a primitive soapstone carving on the mantel, and a photograph of Freud on the wall. It is an elegantly appointed office, even to the smoking pipe and the rosewood humidor beside the doctor's chair. No people are pictured. During my training years at the Sheppard and Enoch Pratt Hospital, where such appointments were ubiquitous and taken for granted, I would have hardly noticed the ad or dismissed it as an appeal to snobbery and elitism, which no doubt it is. But after I began work at a mental-health center where I was seeing patients in a windowless room furnished with a steel desk and two straight-backed chairs, I became fascinated with the ad and unable to restrain the terror and alienation it inspired. It made me feel like an outcast, under siege, as though behind enemy lines or strayed from my own kind; disinherited; abandoned. It was like looking through time at a lost age or a forgotten language. Beyond the appeal to snobbery in the ad was a subtler, more menacing, appeal to nostalgia. The beautiful room represents a commonly shared and richly meaningful cultural milieu which creates the possibility, the "space," for depth of meaning in what goes on between the doctor and the patient. For the purpose of the ad, this possibility is associated with the drug, as though giving this drug would make that kind of "space" available. What is implied by an image of a cultural milieu, the psychiatrist's office, is a possibility of relationship which is not suggested, for example, by an ad showing a worried patient, in a work shirt, clutching the iron bedpost of a barracks-style bed while the doctor in the background looks on, concerned; or by an ad showing a patient standing with his suitcase ready to leave the hospital, in front of a table at which a doctor sits writing a prescription. In the latter two examples, the patient is a problem that the doctor worries about and feels vaguely threatened by. He seems to be a stranger to the doctor, personally and socially. There is no suggestion of a longstanding involvement with the patient. The doctor and the patient seem to meet across a social gap, either of class or "background." There is no implication that the patient is invited to talk to the doctor or to express himself as an individual other than to make known his complaints. This is in contrast to the social closeness and comfort in the doctor-patient relationship implied in the image of the psychiatrist's well-appointed office. That patient would appreciate the art on display, the good taste shown, and would recognize Freud's portrait. The person in the easy chair opposite that doctor is the object of compassion and empathy, rather than worry. His relationship with the doctor is intimate, longstanding, and complex, and he is clearly invited to speak his mind fully and at leisure. It was the realization that these values could be represented in the furnishings of an office that focused my interest on the cultural milieu in which therapy takes place; and it was the move from an environment relatively rich in these cultural artifacts, the 80-year-old, 400-acre, Sheppard-Pratt Hospital, to a relatively more modern and impoverished environment, that showed me how much I had taken for granted. Once a patient had driven through the stone gatehouse of Sheppard-Pratt, and through its wooded property and over the expanse of well-kept lawns, to the dignified Gothic edifice of the hospital, and seated himself in the tastefully appointed office that had been provided for my use, a great deal had already been accomplished. The patient knew that he was entering an institution which placed a value on beauty, on dignity, and on the high purpose of its work, so that even before I spoke he could be fairly certain that I would treat him humanely, that I could be more or less trusted not to be brutal, and that he could regard me as an important person by virtue of my association with an institution which he could regard as important. In contrast, the patient who enters the mental-health center, a one-story cinder-block building, cold and functional, with a large sterile public waiting room and tiny offices partitioned off with prefabricated vinyl walls, is being treated to an entirely different kind of experience. His associations with what he sees are the social security office, the welfare office, or an army induction center. He has no reason to think that he will not be brutalized by me because the building is already brutalizing us both.

I recall sitting with a patient in a sunlit room at Sheppard-Pratt Hospital where the summer breeze carried sounds of splashing and shouting from the swimming pool outside. The patient, sprawled across a wicker couch smoking cigarettes and sipping Coke, would attack and berate me mercilessly for my brutality and my insensitivity, and would rage against the hospital as though it were his prison. I would listen in silence, contemplating the toes of my shoes against the ceramic-tiled floor; and eventually would begin to hear, through the attacks on me and the hospital, the cries of anguish at the deeper hurts that could not be expressed directly.

Had the same patient been sprawled across a wooden bench in the corner of a state hospital ward, and had he attacked me and the hospital over the sound of slamming steel doors, my silence would have been simply a tacit complicity with the brutality of the real situation. The psychotherapeutic event becomes possible only when the therapist can listen to the patient's complaints in benign and compassionate silence, in the full knowledge that the patient has every reason to believe that he is held in regard by those who are treating him.

In the absence of a cultural milieu in which the values of personal dignity and respectability are consistently reaffirmed in the available artifacts, such as the Sheppard-Pratt gatehouse, or the sunlit room, or the leather chairs in the psychiatrist's office, the affirmation of those values becomes a difficult, self-conscious, and time-consuming program in the psychotherapy itself.

I find myself sympathetic now as I never had been with the missionary in the first scene of The African Queen who doggedly finishes the last stanzas of "Rock of Ages" in his grass-hut church deep in the jungle despite the commotion and dispersion of most of the congregation at the sound of the whistle which signals the arrival of the mail boat outside. My new-found sympathy was for the missionary's necessity, as he saw it, to be in his own person, and in isolation, the Church of England, in a cultural milieu in which no one could have imagined the existence of Canterbury Cathedral. The missionary feels that he has been exiled, and that his fate now is to be a church where there is no church; to be this church, he abandons who he is as a person and thinks of himself as an institution. He cannot permit himself to admit to his own excitement at the arrival of the mail boat. There is no choice for him but orthodoxy.

There are times when the psychotherapist in the modern-day situation feels a similar destiny, and tends to turn himself into an institution, but the missionary mentality is a trap because of the rigidity and orthodox devotion it demands. In fact, the missionary in *The African Queen* is an irrelevant appendage to the community life of his village because, by institutionalizing himself, he and his values remain aloof and detached; his attention is occupied with empty formality rather than the living reality around him, and his devotions become merely self-serving.

The values embodied in the traditions, the texts, the artifacts, and the conventions of an institution such as the Church, or the institution of psychoanalytic psychology, provide the context for meaningful personal responsiveness; but the institutionalized values are not and can never be the spontaneous and complex personal response itself. They only make such a response possible. Orthodoxy and tradition are never the substance of a creative exchange, whether religious or therapeutic. When the missionary finishes the last stanzas of "Rock of Ages," or when I, to take another example, use a word like "symbiosis" or "sublimation" when I know that it will not be understood, we are each insisting that we will go on acting as though the context were still there. If the context were there, however, our own responses would certainly be more complex and richly personal. The missionary, if he were preaching in a little church in the English countryside, where he could assume that his congregation understood and respected the decorum of the service, could easily feel free to betray his own excitement upon the intrusion of a happy distraction such as the mail boat, and even to end the service early without fearing the collapse of tradition as a result. Similarly, if I were not, insanely, trying to recreate the hallowed halls of psychoanalysis in the busy traffic of a mental-health center, I would be less bound to the conventional language of psychoanalytic thinking and free to use more down-to-earth language.

To the extent that the values of the psychotherapist become increasingly alien to the values of the culture in which he practices, the problems and responsibilities of the missionary become increasingly relevant to him. To represent his values as a person requires of the therapist that he be much more personal with his patients, for example, by offering opinions about books, music, or art, not as a rejection of conventional psychoanalytic techniques but as a means of establishing that there are commonly held esthetic and moral values between them. I find that suggesting to a patient that he might be interested in a particular book or a movie is a way to communicate to him that I respect his intelligence and his sensitivity, and that in psychotherapy my object is to share my knowledge with him as an equal rather than to administer to him from above. This personal "offering" of the therapist is simply an attempt to create a common cultural space with the patient, a space which already exists and thus needs no special attention in the sunlit room at Sheppard-Pratt Hospital or in the psychiatrist's office in the advertisement.

In some cases this need for a common cultural space becomes a major issue in the therapy. For a man who had been hospitalized in a state institution for the mentally defective for a suicide attempt at age thirteen, and had since been treated in other brutal and inhumane inpatient and outpatient programs, it took months of patient reassurance that I had respect for his mind, that I did not regard his perception of the brutality of his experience as "sick"or "psychotic," before he could entertain the notion that I could consider him an equal. After weeks of silent procrastination and agonizing doubt, he trusted me with information given him by another patient that a professional colleague had engaged in obscene activity in this patient's presence. The fact that I treated the information with respect, held it in confidence, and did not automatically dismiss it as insane raving helped him to feel that I did not regard his mind as "inferior" because he was a patient. It was only then I learned that he had always assumed that he would never be accepted into a medical school or graduate school in psychology because of his "record" as a mental patient, an attitude that would logically grow out of his previous "treatment" as a patient. He was initially totally incredulous about my suggestion that a school might consider his personal experience with mental illness and its treatment an asset rather than a disgrace. One day after I had given him a ride to his appointment, he said, sitting in my cramped office with noise outside the door, that he would just as soon have therapy in my truck as in this "goddamned office." I felt that it was an essential part of his therapy to damn the office, as a repudiation of the degradation he had experienced, and that, to be effective as a therapist, I must accept his need to dissociate me from the mental-health establishment which had brutalized him by agreeing that the office was an insult to the importance of the work we were engaged in. This was my only way to give him some substitute for the stone gatehouse and well-kept lawns that were missing, to allow the emergence of a common cultural space in an otherwise alienated and culturally inadequate milieu.

To the extent that the Sheppard-Pratt situation is the more anachronistic and the mental-health center the more modern setting, we recognize the difference between the two as an historical development of sorts. Understanding that development means looking at psychotherapy in the context of the larger culture in which it is practiced.

Pschotherapy occurs in history. It exists and evolves in a specific time and place uniquely and in relation to the complex social and cultural forces of the changing scene. It is not the hothouse flower of some pure intellectual pursuit, and one cannot assume that it is determined only by its own internally rational development.

We must not assume that a history of psychotherapy, with "advances" in therapy, new theories or techniques, represents a rational or progressive development in the sense that quantum mechanics represents a progressive development from Newtonian mechanics. It is possible for psychotherapy to develop in regressive or degenerate forms as well as progressive ones. Psychotherapy is a phenomenon of culture, with complex origins and relationships. It has ties to medicine in its primitive and its scientific traditions, to art and to religion as sources of meaning in culture, and to politics as an agency of social control and of social criticism. To assume that psychotherapy is any less complex than this, or that it can be studied in isolation and out of context of the culture in which it is practiced, is more an ideological assertion than a scientific premise.

A comparison of Freud's office in Vienna, with its brocade, Persian rugs, and collection of primitive sculpture, to a modern mental-health center building of cinder blocks, steel desks, Muzak, and California landscape posters with mottos like "Today is the First Day of the Rest of Your Life," reveals something relevant to what has happened in the history of psychotherapy from its original form as daily psychoanalytic sessions to its present dispersion into the various tendencies and techniques of brief therapy, behavior therapy, desensitization therapy, transactional therapy, reality therapy, etc. The comparison of rooms is obviously one of esthetic values, yet it is in these that the culture which is the context of psychotherapy is represented and revealed.

Psychotherapy is a part of our cultural life. Developments and tendencies in therapy reflect and manifest similar tendencies in the morality and ideology of the time. To become conscious of this content the psychotherapist must be a self-conscious moralist who will not accept at face value the manifest therapeutic rationale of a therapy as the only moral content of the actual therapeutic exchange, but will analyze critically the therapeutic experience itself specifically for its "latent" moral content. For example, to tell a patient that his "illness" is caused by a "biochemical defect" over which the patient has no control is not only to present a scientific theory, but in the context of therapy is to advance a moral doctrine of predestination and human nonaccountability, and to deprive the patient of the moral option to regard himself as responsible for and potentially master of his fate. Even if it were to become empirically evident that patients improve when presented with this theory (presumably because they are given a release from the burden of responsibility), the moral issue could not be decided on the basis of empirical outcome alone.

To take another example, the use of first names by psychotherapists is usually justified by the rationale that it expresses the equality of the patient and the therapist, that it rejects the so-called "medical model," and that it is a way of being personally "open" with the patient. A critical look at examples will show that use of the first name can also be a means of evading responsibility and a subtle form of mystification.

My initial impression of the names on the row of mailboxes behind the receptionist's head in the waiting room of the mental-health center (Wendy, Cindy, Rick, Rob, or Debbie, nicknames from a generation of "April Love," *Peter Pan*, and *South Pacific*) was that it seemed more like roll call at a summer camp than the roster of a professional staff. I suppressed my impulse to take offense partly because it seemed an esthetic judgment merely, or worse, that I was feeling threatened with loss of status. Was it not after all more democratic to be Fred than to be Dr. Bloom?

My experience has shown since that informality, rather than making the patient feel more equal to the therapist, can instead be a subtle insult if the informality is not a mutual agreement to put aside the conventions of respect and respectability that are in common social use; and is rather an imposition by the therapist of an ideological stand on the patient and on the therapeutic relationship. A grey-haired gentleman from a conservative, religious, working-class community told me that his therapist walked into his group-therapy session on the first day without introducing himself, slipped off his shoes, put his feet on the coffee table, folded his hands on his chest, and treated the group to a broad grin. His communication is not that all are equal. Nobody else has his feet on the table, and if other members later add their feet to the table it is clearly under the therapist's auspices and his mandate that they do so, not through a mutual agreement to suspend customary formality.

Insistence that people be immediately and uniformly on a first-name basis, or that they put their feet on the table, is a refusal to acknowledge that formal conventions of address and decorum constitute the social language by which people confer on one another the freedom to remain at a distance, that is, to decline intimacy. An ideology of intimacy and familiarity denies that choice, and defines anyone who refuses to accept it as rejecting health and wholeness of personality, when what is being offered and rejected is neither health nor wholeness, but a code of behavior which negates the difference between strangers and intimates, and a language of first names which obliterates that distinction.

A variation on this use of first names is the instance of a group therapist, let us call him Richard Smith, whose patients call him "Dr. Rick." Dr. Rick, by insisting relentlessly on his equality through such devices as the first name, wearing Levis and leaving shirttails out, and justifying this insistence on ideological grounds (nonelitism, shared humanity, being a "real person"), also evades the uncomfortable fact that he exercises authority in the life of his patients; and insofar as this is not reciprocated (and to my knowledge none of our patients has ever invited one of our staff on "an adventure of self-discovery") the situation is not equal. The patient puts his trust in someone he assumes to be a responsible professional who will accept authority for his treatment, but is told that for such authority to exist would be elitist, undemocratic, etc. The professional person becomes just "Rick," de-professionalized, and not accountable. Yet "Rick" no more accepts real equality with his patient than he expects to go out repairing televisions with him the morning after the group meeting, if real equality means that Rick and the patients make sense together out of what they are doing, and develop a common understanding and rationale of their task which would be open to criticism on both sides. To retain the title "Doctor" then serves, along with the rest of the paraphernalia and jargon, to mystify and impress so as not to have to answer and explain. Dr. Rick is a healer in short pants, a shaman in sneakers and football jersey. He is so intimidating with his degree and his jargon, and is such a down-to-earth nice guy, that he is invulnerable.

Therapies which operate on empty mystification and evasion of responsibility, in which the therapist indulges himself in cheap charismatic heroics, and in which the accepted forms of social interchange in the patient's community are ridiculed, could easily be called anti-therapy on moral grounds alone, irrespective of the empirical outcome of treatment.

As technicians and specialists exercise increasing authority over the lives of individuals, the influence of technical ways of thinking on social relations and on the ways in which we conceptualize our experience correspondingly increases, so that not even the most technical procedure can be passed off as morally neutral. Technicians preempt the moral authority of tradition, church, family, and of the individual responsible person on the grounds of special expertise or technical competence. The social categories of health and sickness, for example, become defined by medical diagnostic and therapeutic technologies, so that health is measured in a laboratory profile rather than experienced by the individual as an internal state of well-being. Diagnostic technology in this case becomes the method of social certification to which the individual's claims to health or sickness are subjected. The moral authority for the social definition of health and sickness becomes assimilated into a set of technical functions. Similarly, the social definition of knowledge and education becomes that which is taught in mechanized schools by technically trained teachers and which can be tested by mechanized examinations. The moral authority for the social definition of knowledge and folly becomes assimilated into the technology of schooling and testing.

The psychotherapist, in his modern role as the technical engineer of personality, also indirectly assimilates a social function. This is the crucial meeting point of psychotherapy and culture. The psychotherapist is the unique focus for the social expression of our changing notion of what constitutes human nature. The forces shaping our view of human nature achieve articulate social expression in the theory and practice of psychotherapy. The theories that psychotherapists use are the current cultural forum in which the issues of man's essential nature are debated.

The transfer of this forum from religion and from the domain of social criticism (Marxism, utopian socialism, etc.) into the domain of psychotherapy is partially due to the ascendance of science and technology, the ideological mainstays we believe in, so that in our single-minded reliance on expertise we turn to the scientific psychologist to discover the nature of man. But it is also due to the relative decline of Judeo-Christian dogma as a metaphysical voice that can still be vital for us, and the relative absence of critical social theory in a society in which the thorough isolation of the individual from his archaic communal ties and his reintegration into the interdependent industrial world, always potentially unstable on a mass scale, creates the necessity for immediate accommodation to and neutralization of social criticism. What remains is the individual sick soul, the individual suffering person, who can only see himself as sick because he can no longer see himself as spiritually bereft, a lost soul, or damned, and can no longer see himself as socially or politically oppressed. The responsibility for sustaining a meaningful existence falls on this individual isolated personality and becomes redefined as the achievement of personal adjustment, which is now the domain of psychotherapy.

The emergence of psychotherapy in this century as the available mode of transcendence is associated with a specific narrowing of the conceptualizing of the transcendent possibility inherent in human nature. Transcendence in the religious sense is the integration and reconciliation of the individual with a total universe which is perceived to be alive with spiritual and moral meaning. It is the resolution of a state of alienation with respect to nature, to mankind, to the forces of creation, and to the spiritual order of the cosmos. In religious activity men bring themselves into harmony, into oneness, with the whole. The moral order within is continuous with the moral order on the scale of creation. Utopian social theory abandons the hope for total oneness with the universe but retains the vision of integration and reconciliation on the scale of the total human community. In psychotherapy we retreat further to an enclave in the individual personality and hope for the individual to achieve integration and reconciliation only with himself. In a sense it is a last stand. The moral ground of any psychotherapy is therefore not in its theory of psychopathology or its rationale of treatment, but in its vision of the best that the individual person can be.

This is not to say that therapy is simply a form of moralizing. It would be a rejection of psychology as such not to go beyond moralizing to an understanding of the determinates of behavior or character. Without such understanding there could be no rational therapy other than moralistic exhortation. Psychological analysis, whether it be of behavioral, social, biochemical, or psychodynamic "causes," puts aside moral judgment in an attempt to explain personality. But whatever rationale is used, whether the "cause" of the patient's difficulties is found in his infantile experiences or his biochemical endowment, the patient himself must retain the potential for authentic action and responsibility in the moral realm. That is, he must retain a potential for integrity. If therapy has any meaning it is in relation to that potential: to expand the domain of responsibility, authenticity, and integrity in the life of the patient. It is a process of unification and integration of the personality under the dominance of the responsible, authentic person.

A therapy which increases mastery over life's trials, its crises, its daily events, even over the biochemistry or the behavioral conditioning of the individual, can only broaden the basis for responsibility and integrity in the adult. Whatever theory describes the pathological failure of responsibility, moral categories must be preserved as the psychological categories appropriate to nonpathological adult life. The end point of a psychotherapy of personal integration is personal integrity. A therapy which invites the patient to imitate a social role and thereby ignore his inner experience also betrays the possibility for an integration of that inner experience into an authentic life; it betrays the possibility of integrity. Mystification of the patient, even if it changes his behavior for the better or makes him feel better, still deprives him of his need to recognize in his therapist an authentic person and further alienates him from himself.

There are therapies then which undermine rather than affirm the authentic, integrated individual. Is this a degenerate form, a failure of therapy to meet its task, or do these therapies in reality fill a social role other than to foster the integration of the individual? Has the necessity for people to perform their various alienated social roles become so pervasive that personal integrity becomes a handicap rather than an asset to social adjustment? It may be that as pseudo-intimacy becomes a general condition in society and life takes place more on the surface and out in the open, as the intimacy of the suburban living room becomes infused with the "intimate" talk of the Johnny Carson Show, the therapy of the time becomes the social pablum of a hopelessly content public. In this therapy of sham and mystification, which obliterates integrity and substitutes glib and facile pretenses, more practical in an alienated world than a therapy of the authentic self?

A clinical example of a physician who had been practicing for many years prior to seeking therapy will illustrate the erosion of the cultural basis of a therapy of personal integration by the general acceptance of fakery and deceit as valid social forms. The patient sought treatment because he wanted to run away with a girlfriend, but found himself unable to leave his wife and son. I had a report from another psychiatrist who had seen the patient, prior to this affair, because of marital discontent, but felt that he had been unable to help him other than to reassure him that there was nothing wrong with him and that the circumstances of his unhappiness were certainly due to the wife's infantile ways; her demanding, her petulance, etc. With me, as with the previous psychiatrist, he told tales of the miseries he suffered at the hands of his infantile wife and pleaded to know what he might be overlooking in his own behavior that would allow him to see his wife as less than totally to blame. What he was overlooking, of course, was that he had stayed with his wife through twelve years of this torment, and still would not or could not leave, even for a brilliant, beautiful, and understanding paramour, despite the fact that he obviously had no moral scruples about being unfaithful to his wife.

It was clear that the beginning of therapy would be in the recognition that he goes from psychiatrist to psychiatrist, to his colleagues and to his friends, asking to be reassured that there is nothing wrong with him. At the same time, he thinks that his life is a sham and a fraud, so when he succeeds in getting his reassurances, he is filled with contempt for the person he has fooled. While he is asking for insight, he covertly makes his alibis and rationalizations impenetrable. He consciously withholds self-incriminating information about how he baits and provokes his wife, partly not to be humiliated by self-exposure, but also simply to bamboozle; partly to enlist the psychiatrist as an ally, to be liked, but also to lead the psychiatrist through a matrix of fabrication and half truth, to reduce the therapy to triviality and pretense. Because the patient is looking for reassurance that irresponsibility and inauthenticity are general facts of life and not a personal moral failing, he must convince himself that therapy, his therapist, and the world at large have nothing to offer which is less trivial and less a pretense than he feels his own life to be.

The transference neurosis is a model of the patient's disturbed view of the nature of the therapeutic process. Insofar as that model derives from the patient's past experience in being reared, provided with growth and maturational or therapeutic experience, it is also a model of past relationships, but this only secondarily. First of all it is the disturbed aspect of a creative striving in the present for what the patient believes to be his cure, or more correctly, it is a consolidation of the contradictory unconscious programs the patient has invented for his cure.

For this patient, the "cure" consists of gaining the reassurance that to be the "bullshit artist" he believes himself to be is not essentially abnormal, and therefore that nothing is wrong with him. To do this he puts himself to the test of daring the psychiatrist to see through him, to call his bluff. He asks to be called to task on some deeper level than he presents himself, by a psychology that will penetrate beyond his own pseudo-psychological presentation of reality, which he knows is an empty fabric of rationalization. If the psychiatrist is fooled and the therapy reduced to triviality, the triviality of two people commiserating over the impossibility of one of their wives, the patient is reassured that all psychology is empty rationalization. There is no deeper reality or higher validity than appearance.

The compulsive need to bamboozle, to gain allies to his own illusions, derives from the patient's need to convince himself that no one else is any more substantial than he is, that all men are fakes, and that nothing means anything. Whatever he can manipulate becomes immediately worthless and he is reassured that his sense of meaninglessness and fraudulence is a universal condition, not a personal failing. In this way, even though his life has little meaning, at least he is not missing anything. In contrast to the sociopathic personality, this for him is a moral struggle against his deeper need to confer respect upon his therapist, the object of his confidence game.

His persistent returns to treatment reveal this deeper contrary need, which corresponds to the wish that the therapy make possible for him a reality and an authenticity that he now lacks; and corresponds to the wish that the therapist be an incorruptible and unfoolable moral authority. So the patient's dilemma over whether or not he can allow therapy to mean anything to him, to be real for him, reflects a basic conflict in his life between authenticity and façade.

At crucial points along the way he has clearly chosen to continue a fraud rather than to ask the ultimate questions, just as we all choose to act with integrity or to capitulate at various crucial junctures. But can we really accept the notion that my patient must flee therapy because he has sold himself down the river too often? Perhaps a man can be too much corrupted or too much compromised by social expedience to be able to use a therapy of personal integration. But is therapy not the legitimate way out of that corruption and toward responsibility? The prohibitive social cost of his therapy and the reason he finally quits is not the necessary confrontation with his own corruption in the past; it is the pain and alienation of a life of integrity in the future. If his cure, instead of returning him to a station of respect in a community of honorable men, should make him a stranger to his colleagues and render his whole personal and professional life suddenly problematic, if he should awaken to moral responsibility, like Jonah, in a land and a time which has no use for it, then, like Jonah, he will flee his awakening.

In a sense psychotherapy presupposes the moral life of the patient and the therapist, in that they must each be striving after integrity and responsibility. But it also presupposes a certain integrity of the ambient cultural climate, in which the patient's therapeutic gains can be seen as a cure of a corrupted and alienated state and a return to the moral community, rather than a climate in which therapeutic gains would be perceived as painful moral burdens to be borne in isolation and sorrow.

It makes sense, then, to ask what happens to therapy as culture moves toward 1984, that is, as integrity becomes more hollow, as contradictions become neutralized, as compromise and corruption become universal, as reality is identified with appearance. Under such circumstances therapy moves closer to theatre; not the theatre of the ritual enactment of sacred drama, but the theatre of entertainment, of diversion, of self-delusion, of illusion for its own effect, bedazzlement, mystification, delight, turn-on; theatre which is circus. Or else, in opposition to the reign of meaningless performance, therapy assumes the task of establishing meaning and moral certainty, which drives it toward a religious purpose.

Psychotherapy can be judged on a basis totally different from the empirical determination of outcome of therapy, and yet with criteria that are still perfectly objective; for example, in terms of the degree to which the therapy affirms or undermines the authenticity of the patient as a moral agent. Psychoanalysis could be objectively compared with transactional analysis or gestalt therapy in this respect. A therapy is valid when it preserves and enriches the cultural possibility of knowledge of ourselves as we are, in depth, and knowledge of ourselves as having depth; when it makes a position of honesty and integrity available to us. The alternative is one-dimensional man administered with Valium and a teaspoon of group therapy.

We have seen that the dynamics of the modern individual can be viewed as an elaborate defense against real experience; the frantic fabrication of pretense and façade protects the individual from confronting himself as compromised and sold out. In the mental health industry—among the college youth studying social work, among medical students going into flashy psychiatric residencies, among high school students going into "mental-health technology"—precisely this same dynamics will invariably reject psychoanalysis in favor of transactional analysis, just as it would reject any serious psychotherapy in favor of any pretense to one. Our annihilation and our holocaust will not be imposed from without, but will arrive as an inner compulsion. The modern mind is bent on that final liberation and cultural death in which appearance equals reality. A professional psychologist signals our demise when he says to his students, in a lecture on transactional analysis, "Let me give you a quickie way to think about this..."

The scientific conceit that psychological theory and psychotherapy can be "objective" and morally "neutral" pursuits must give way to a recognition that social and cultural values are intrinsic to psychotherapies and, reciprocally, that a psychotherapy is an intrinsic feature of the moral structure of the society that adopts it.

In another instance, two psychotherapists plan to act as co-therapists in an experiential group of the "human growth movement" type. The group will operate on the premise that the leaders meet with the participants on an equal footing and together make a commitment to "complete self-disclosure." Here the manifest purpose is the realization of the authentic individual by allowing the self to emerge in a group setting that will be tolerant to it. The social mask is to be stripped away by means of an ideological commitment to democratic nakedness in which the therapists no less than the participants must be "who they really are." Apart from the dangerous equation such a therapeutic rationale makes between social reserve and dishonesty, there is the assumption that the alienation of the individual is enforced by no more sinister agency than social convention, so that by merely changing the ground rules of social exchange in the group, the deeper self will spontaneously emerge.

The two psychotherapists, a man and a woman, are in fact having an affair. Since each is married and has a family, they decide that their "self-disclosure" will include everything about themselves but the fact that they are lovers. Therapy is in this way reduced to theatrical performance and the authentic self degenerates into an empty social role. Simply leaving out the fact that the therapists are lovers on their lunch hour makes all mannner of self-exposure and "deep" revelation immediately possible, even easy. But it is the intimacy of the husband who will tell his wife about everything but his mistress. The essential truth always escapes into the one detail withheld. In this case that essential truth is precisely that there are things that one does not easily expose. The "real self" exposed after first deciding to hide the one essential fact is in reality the highest expression of the real façade, the most successful hiding.

The decision to withhold information which could prove damaging from a group of strangers is in itself perfectly legitimate. It is the pseudo-commitment to "complete self-disclosure," the implication that an intimate, chest-baring performance represents a valid strategy or ethic of therapy, or learning, or self-realization that is fraudulent. It equates the appearance, acting the role of self-disclosure, with the reality, self-disclosure in fact. The need for secrecy and privacy and the difficult contradictions of the therapists' lives are hidden from the group. The content of the therapists' immediate experience is betrayed by the therapeutic performance. Similarly, for the participants, a loyal pretense of gallant self-exposure becomes inevitably a betrayal of immediate experience. Certainly no participant is any more prepared to abandon his refuge in privacy than are the two therapists. A compromise of integrity becomes a premise of the therapeutic activity.

If, from the outset, the therapists were to admit that there were some things that would not be revealed because they were too dangerous, the group would begin on a more authentic basis. The problem then of real self-disclosure, with its risks and dangers in the real social world, would be fairly confronted. What would be lost, however, would be the false glamour and charisma of the leaders. The mask of the drama would drop. The actors would find themselves on stage out of costume. The curtain would rise on real people.

As a substitute for integration of the personality we are presented in this type of therapy with the image of the "together" person, the person without conflict, without doubt or shame, with no need for secrecy or for reserve, for whom emotion and the drama of "gut feelings" are greeted with sporting good humor, in the same way that *Playboy* magazine turns eroticism into a sporting pastime for sophisticates and connoisseurs. In both cases an imago is being peddled. The reader of *Playboy* purchases not an idealized sexual object, but an image of himself, a persona in whom sterilized erotic fantasies can range conflict-free. The imago of the psychologically liberated man functions in a similar way in this therapy to advance an ideal character type for the conflict-free discharge of drives and pent-up feelings. Allowing the mask to fall from the *Playboy* image, to photograph a varicose vein or a soiled bedsheet, would dissolve the basis of its appeal. In a self-disclosure therapy group, to expose the conflict-ridden person behind the "together" persona would similarly dissolve the basis of the therapeutic impact.

Making therapy identical to learning a new social role undermines the conception of the potential in the human personality for experience which has depth and which carries the individual into irrevocable moral commitment. If therapy is the replacement of one social mask for another, there is no authentic person.

The experience of a person performing in a lie is qualitatively different from the experience of that person confronting his most immediate and direct experience and being understood and confirmed by others in that. Integrity in this context can be seen as a dimension of psychological experience. More than moral position, integrity is a state of mind, a relationship between the self and inner experience different from the benign well-being of the compromised man. The description of that difference would require a metapsychology of the moral sense which could distinguish between a state of inspiration which derives from authentic action, from the willingness to live in an uncensored reality, and from the discovery of allegiance or commitment to some domain of responsibility outside the needs of the self, and a state of excitement which derives from the discharge of drives in association with release from commitment, with distraction from the uncomfortable complexities of reality, played out under assumed personae. Inspiration, on the one hand, is a source of energy, it increases attentiveness, it is satiating, self-limiting, and it carries with it a sense of commitment. Excitement, on the other hand, is energy draining, distracting (decreasing attentiveness), insatiable, addictive, and easily repudiated. These two dimensions of moral experience are made more or less available in a particular culture. It is in this sense that psychology can be viewed as a science of the internal structure of moral form, and it is in this sense that the meaning of the therapeutic event derives ultimately from the culture.

Sexual liberation, for example, which is perceived as a moral triumph in the modern world, would have been perceived as exactly the inverse, a spiritual debauch, in medieval times, not because psychology has changed, or because the medieval world was backward or ignorant psychologically while we moderns are smart and progressive, but because the internal moral structure of culture, from which the healthy personality derives, has become inverted.

The dilemma which faced my patient, the physician, was that I offered him a therapy of integrity for a life situation which demanded the flexible adaptation to numerous empty performances. My therapy would have made him that much more rigid, that much more unfit, for that life. He would either have had to reject the tenets of the therapy as such or effect a revolutionary moral transformation reaching every aspect of his life. In this sense what I offered him was not therapy but conversation. For the patient to proceed in therapy, large areas of autonomous, i.e., nonconflictual, nonproblematic areas of ego functioning would have had to become problematical, and would have had to submit to transformation. In fact, his therapy was characterized by a constant struggle on his part to limit its scope to the problematical, which meant that he constantly retreated from the logical extension of "the problem" into critical thinking about his facile self-assurance and his sucessful career. He came to treatment not because he was unable to make an authentic commitment to his marriage, but because he was not able simply to walk away from it. My treatment offered to make it only that much more difficult to walk away. A therapy like the self-disclosure group just discussed could teach him styles of self-deception that would solidify his alienation from his need for a moral standard, which he regards, to the extent that he is conscious of the need, as an archaic cultural remnant, like an appendix. In self-disclosure therapy he could disabuse himself of the moral relics of the Age of Reason which disturb his life. Authentic moral action would be transformed into role playing and performance. The need for commitment to some domain of moral authority, from which inspiration is derived, would be transformed into the indulgence in some domain of appetite, from which excitement is then derived. The Freudian attitude of acceptance and non-judgment as a strategy for the inhibited and guilt-ridden patient has subtly been transformed into a strategy of permission and license for the insatiable and nihilistic patient.

Psychotherapy is, more and more, an institution which sanctions direct satisfaction of appetites. It is becoming a training ground in inauthenticity, perverting the need for integrity and integration by the sanctioning of suprastimulation and ultraindulgence. The proliferation of game and play words in the theoretical language of psychotherapists reflects this development.

The strategy of this modernized psychotherapy is to invite the patient to adopt a role which he can act with impunity, because it is a role, because it is specifically sanctioned, and because it is in a therapeutic setting. When the patient attaches some affect to his performance, it is hailed as self-discovery, and the actor is sent away to play his part on the stage of life. I participated in a training session in which a medical resident played the role of the doctor, a hospital social worker played the role of the patient with a sexual problem, and the others observed through a one-way mirror. The resident launched with impunity into detailed questions about the patient's masturbation techniques and the adequacy of her "vaginal lubrication" while the "patient," with blithe disregard for the embarrassment a "real" person might have felt in the situation, answered him with the bravado of a GI, while confounding his efforts to understand her problem. In the discussion that followed, a "psychological analysis" was applied to the interchange as though it had been a real event; that is, as though a doctor and patient had been discussing a real problem. The discussion perpetuated the verisimilitude of the role-playing, as though we were all now to play the role of analysts of what we pretended was an event, as opposed to a pseudo-event. What insights does such an analysis produce? While it might make sense for one to play a role in order to elicit fantasy, one can hardly assume that in the role-playing the deepest self is represented or that the unconscious plays along in a supporting role. It is precisely that what is being "analyzed" is the persona of the role-player, rather than the person playing the role, that allows the discussion to flow so good-naturedly through the rocky psychological depths. Self-disclosure is easy so long as it involves only the persona and never the person. What remains "unconscious" is the immediately available reality that would appear if the personae were dropped: the medical resident anxious to appear well-informed and effective before his colleagues and teachers is facing a female social worker who too often feels inferior and subservient to male doctors and is anxious to show them that she is not to be outdone on her home territory, particularly, that she will not accept the role of the embarrassed woman receiving sexual aid from the male doctor. The interview thus becomes a covert competition to exhibit the most sexually liberated attitudes. Remarking on this in the discussion would be like turning on the house lights before the final curtain.

The discussion is a pseudo-analysis because it will not penetrate to the real event. Instead it remains a commentary on a prearranged and preconceived scenario. The resident was always expected to be anxious, so his anxiety is discussed; he is expected to have difficulty with the open discussion of sexual issues, so that is discussed, even though he has clearly demonstrated a willingness, indeed, a compulsion, to discuss everything. It is as though the one-way mirror had failed to allow a view into the other room, but instead reflected back to the observers only their own expectations.

We see in this role-playing exercise a fundamental betrayal of the analytical mind. The reality of the objective world is both serious and unknown, and the task of reason is to penetrate into that outer thing. When the other person ceases to remain essentially unknown to the observer of human behavior, the observer is then observing only his own system of persuasion. The mind, intent on the frontier of its understanding, is always aware that understanding has its frontier, beyond which the other person remains separate and objectively mysterious. When all things are categorizable and therefore "known," human behavior becomes mail to be sorted rather than a text to be studied. It follows that an analytical mind preserves the authenticity of the observed person, his objective status as something separate from the system of observation. When the observer knows that he has nothing to discover, that it all comes down to "parent-adult-child" or some such thing, we have a system which is both functionally efficient because it simplifies and routinizes interaction, and murderous of the deeper person. The system of observation determines whether the observed person may discover himself through the eyes of the observer, or merely learn the set of social roles and personae he is expected to adopt.

The broader relevance of the role-playing exercise is that, in mistaking persona for identity, it obscures the essential task of identity formation, which is an integrative one: the synthesis of conflicting and incompatible fragments of identification and their integration with already established identity structures. Thus we train people to play the role of a doctor in preference to teaching them to be doctors. This preference derives from the culture.

The problem of identity must be circumvented in a culture which demands the ready adoption of numerous, fragmented, and contradictory social performances. The numerical order of hypocrisies must eventually overwhelm the integrative capacity of the isolated individual, so that integration itself begins to appear anti-adaptive, rigid, an unrealistically idealistic and saintly pursuit, while compromise and a "healthy" cynicism become the therapeutic virtues of a decadent modernity.

An integrative psychotherapy, one which addresses itself to the individual in depth, cannot be expected to survive the death of integrity as a social possibility. If psychoanalysis can be viewed as the social form of the nineteenth-century death of God, then the death of psychoanalysis in the therapeutic abandonment of reason and analytical thought, and the ascendance of the "new therapy," would mark the twentieth-century death of moral culture, the replacement of the morally integrated individual of the Age of Reason with the totally adaptable psychological man.

2

Understanding Persons As Persons

IRWIN SAVODNIK

American psychiatry has tended to divide into two camps—one seeking to understand persons as bodies, and the other seeking to understand them in terms of a mechanistic mental life. Both these approaches, while rewarding in certain respects, fail in the quest of understanding persons as persons. Since psychiatry is rooted in this type of understanding, it is unfortunate that the division within its ranks should be along lines which confuse the major issue of psychiatry and obstruct the development of a systematic understanding of persons which is the major task of psychiatry.

> . . . we do not observe the existence of any subject which more immediately acts upon our soul than the body to which it is joined, and that we just consequently consider that what in the soul is a passion is in the body commonly speaking an action; so that there is no better means of arriving at a knowledge of our passions than to examine the difference which exists between soul and body in order to know to which of the two we must attribute each one of the functions which are within us.
>
> Rene Descartes[1] (1596–1650)

Human beings understand and deal with one another in a variety of ways. We relate to one another through friendship, economics, family structure, intellectual interests, and so forth. Each type of relationship involves a particular mode of understanding of each other which helps to define the peculiarity of that relationship. In my relationship to the banker, I feel relatively confident in depositing my money with

Reprinted by permission from *Psychiatric Quarterly*, 48 (1974), 93–108. Copyright © 1974 by Human Sciences Press, 72 Fifth Ave., New York, N.Y.

him because I know that his activities are tied up with people who want their money to be held in a secure and minimally productive manner. His behavior in the sphere of banking is something of which I have at least a faint grasp. With relatives, I have a knowledge of their personal histories, even their genealogies, in some cases. I understand them in a manner quite different from the one in which I understand the banker.

Psychiatrists also have a particular type of relationship with a class of people called patients. We must ask ourselves, as psychiatrists, what is the nature of the understanding which characterizes our relationships with patients. Unlike some other cases, an agreeable answer to this question is not easily brought forth. There are those who will characterize the relationship along classical psychoanalytic grounds, using such language as transference, counter-transference, resistance, and the like. Others will speak of a relationship between a specialist in problems of life and his client.[2] An understanding of the relationship insofar as it is peculiar to psychiatry is an understanding of the contractual agreement between the two individuals. Still others will view the relationship between therapist and patient as essentially political, and the language employed to describe the way the two interact will involve references to power, leadership, and charisma. Finally, there are those who assert that the relationship ought to be one between a specialized physician and his patient. Psychiatric problems, in this view, are disorders of the *soma* and are to be treated as such. The language which characterizes the way in which the psychiatrist understands his patient in this context is the language of neurophysiology, biochemistry, and related disciplines. The psychiatrist speaks in terms of endogenous bioamine metabolism, drug half-life, and neuronal circuits.[3]

While there are numerous other ways of people coming to understand other people, there is, in American psychiatry, a division between two groups of individuals which needn't exist and is related to the manner in which understanding human beings is actually conceived. There are in one camp those who state that psychiatry ought to strive for the type of understanding of people which physics has of the natural world. Natural science is given as the paradigm case of human understanding and is, therefore, viewed as the ideal toward which we all should strive, be we historians, biologists, or psychiatrists. In the other camp are those who assert that since psychiatry deals with people and their problems, it ought to speak in a language which refers to the manner in which people find themselves in the situations they do, and what they can do to help themselves. Instead of biochemical formulations, wishes, dreams, and aspirations are spoken of. It is of interest to understand just how these two camps often find themselves regarding each other as enemies. This interest is both theoretical and practical since it involves patient care and the education of psychiatrists. The entire problem turns about the way in which persons conceptualize how other persons are to be understood.[4,5] The question is: How do I understand another person *as a person?* In the final portion of this paper a more systematic explanation of the concept "person" will be offered. While it in no way can be regarded as complete, it will suffice for the purposes of this paper.

One way to approach this question is to note the way we ordinarily understand each other—i.e., note the way we speak of each other. When I consider the situation of the other fellow, I think of him in terms of his goals, intentions, character, and features of his reality such as whether or not a particular end has been realized by him. For ordinary purposes, this sort of understanding is quite sufficient. Most of us understand each other enough so that a minimum degree of success and gratification is yielded from our interpersonal relations. We often note, in fact, that there are those of us who are especially keen with regard to understanding other persons, and we are led to ask just what the nature of their understanding is. This ability which we all have to greater or lesser extents is usually regarded as a desirable one for a person to exercise. To be able to know the feeling of another, to see the world as he does, seems on the surface at least, to be desirable. We call this ability empathy. This peculiarly human capacity enables me to understand the other as a person. Empathy is not among the lesser of human capabilities. It is regarded by many people as being one of the highest functions of the human animal. Certainly, other animals, for all their abilities, do not demonstrate any empathetic understanding for their associates. We often note that animals suffer pain as do humans, have emotions like those of men, and even show some cognitive abilities. But in no way is empathy a trait which is regarded to be possessed by animals. It is the case that animals will care for one another in health and disrepair, but it would be hard to make the case that these activities are empathetic in nature.

An understanding of other persons as persons, in the light of what has been said, can only be had by other persons. It is significant to note that psychiatry pays particular attention to those people with whom other persons have difficult times empathizing. While the work of psychiatry is not merely empathy, it is properly said that it begins with a consideration of its possibilities. The language of this sort of understanding involves "actions," "intentions," "feelings," "desires," "imagination," "memories," and "perceptions." When we account for another person, we use these terms to explain his uniqueness as a person with regard to his relationships to others. It is because we have the same sorts of experiences that we can understand other persons. Setting a goal, feeling sad, remembering a past experience, are all experiences which enable us to empathize with another. For this reason, we look upon experience as educational since it broadens and deepens our capacity to understand other persons.

Psychiatry has its roots in this ordinary understanding of persons. Just as people seek to understand one another in order to know how to act with each other, so psychiatry tries to understand persons in order to know how to act in its special way towards them. The understanding which psychiatry seeks, however, is a deeper, more systematic one than that in use ordinarily. It is also oriented for the person so that the relationship between psychiatrist and patient is often referred to as therapy. Psychiatrists often speak of theories of behavior and psychopathology, and in this way reveal that their search for a deeper understanding is considerably more involved than what may be required in everyday life. Hence, they speak of "psychodynamics" as if it were something to be studied like theoretical mechanics. Many psychiatrists feel confused on this subject. On the one hand, they want to have a clear and systematic understanding of human interaction and behavior, while on the other hand, they want to comprehend their subject matter in ordinary terms which empathetic understanding employs.[6]

This problem is dramatically seen in psychoanalysis. Freud's early development reveals the elements of just such a struggle. His deep positivist and determinist influences derived from the 19th century *weltanschauung* are in sharp contrast to the deeply personal understanding of his patients and himself. Those writings produced around the turn of the century illustrate the tension within Freud. In *The Interpretation of Dreams*,[7] the second through sixth chapters are a deeply personal, often moving account of how Freud translates dream language into everyday discourse. When one reaches the seventh chapter, it is almost as if that part of the book were written independently of the rest. Here is Freud the formulator, the scientist. A mental architecture is constructed which will accommodate all of what has been said in the preceding chapters. Today, it is often this chapter that is read most frequently by people training to be psychiatrists, while the rest of the book is ignored. Such neglect is true folly for those wishing to understand Freud, since the dream work is what is primary and expressed in the language of its original experience. The final formulations in the seventh chapter can never demonstrate the depth or the value of the analyses.

As Freud progresses in his subsequent work, his thought seems to be less and less "scientific." In *The Three Essays on the Theory of Sexuality*,[8] Freud certainly couches his thoughts in a quasi-scientific language, but it is clear that his method is not very scientific at all from the point of view of, say, a Mach. The recurrent question is: Where does he get his information from, and how can he be so sure that he is correct in his assertions? The answer is well known to most psychiatrists. Freud places supreme value on the individual case. Just as Socrates pictures the search for truth in individual dialogue, so Freud sees the individual case as the basis for his insights. There need be very few cases for him. Instead, his confrontation with another person yields great stores of information as the relationship between the two develops. Freud realizes that his understanding of the patient as a person and not merely as a scientific object involves different procedures. Experimentation as it is found in the physical and biological sciences is out of the question. Rather, knowledge emerges out of the relationship which grows between two persons. If this is scientific understanding, then it is a new science which has been born, as Freud indicates in *The Question of Lay Analysis*.[9] Psychoanalysis, from our point of view, is a method of engaging another person so that one may achieve the deepest knowledge of him and for him. It is a continuing search for personal enlightenment. This enlightenment is expressed in ordinary language using terms like wishes, dreams, love, and so forth. The more technical idiom of psychoanalysis is truly parasitic upon these primary terms. This element of parasitism is quite important in this context, for it tells us that Freud's basic insights are an extension of the insights gained through an ordinary understanding of other persons. This point is revealed to us many times in the writings of Freud and, on occasion, there is a great poignancy to the manner in which he indicates the relationship between his technical terminology and his own ordinary language. For example, the first chapter of Breuer and Freud's *Studies in Hysteria* is entitled "The Mechanism of Hysterical Phenomena." In this early work, the "scientism" of his 19th-century heritage is clearly present. Yet, even then he recognizes that a technical language is not necessary for certain aspects of what he is saying. Indeed, it may even obscure the issue. Freud seems to struggle with the problem of the best way to let the reader know of what he is thinking. He settles on the ordinary usage to express the root problem of hysteria and states: *"Hysterics suffer mainly from reminiscences."*[10] The poignancy of this statement lies in the fact that Freud expresses a well known fact to which ordinary language is quite well suited.

Later in his career, Freud recognizes quite explicitly the value of using ordinary linguistic locutions in explaining complex dimensions of human behavior. Contrasted with works such as the *Ego and the Id*,[11] in which the language is highly technical and filled with a host of stipulative terms, are his various studies on a multitude of human problems. These works are clearly couched in lucid and simple terms which lead us to the central elements of these various issues. Consider the following passage Freud wrote in 1923:

> Cases of demoniacal possession correspond to the neuroses of the present day; in order to understand these latter we have once more had recourse to the conception of psychic forces. What in those days were thought to be evil spirits to us are base and evil wishes, the derivative of impulses which have been rejected and repressed. In one respect only do we not subscribe to the explanation of these phenomena current in medieval times; we have abandoned the projection of them into the outer world, attributing their origin instead to the inner life of the patient in whom they manifest themselves.[12]

What Freud has done here is to interpret an aspect of human experience in a way which is relieved of any technical vocabulary. Instead of the language of demonology, we find the language which we commonly use to account for other persons. The "inner life of the patient" is a simple, non-technical locution which is introduced in order to shift the emphasis from the external realm of a complicated world replete with spirits et al to an internal one. This latter is understood by us all in terms of wishes, fantasies, dreams, and the like. Freud is acknowledging to the reader that the way to understand a person as a person is through the ordinary understanding which we all cultivate in ourselves and which is reflected in our language. That our language is aptly suited for the expression of the most subtle modes of human experience is pointed out clearly by Austin.[13] One of the chief values of psychoanalysis, then, is that it seeks to understand persons in the manner in which other persons ordinarily do.

Certainly, the manner in which psychoanalysis proceeds is problematic. The step which is taken from the one case to all men is often questioned. Its justification lies in the reply, "See for yourself!" That is all that can be said. It is at this point that the two camps that divide psychiatry emerge. One asserts that such a reply is empty and opposed to what men have held to be the paradigm case of human understanding. The other points out that this is a case of understanding not covered by that paradigm situation. How are the two camps to be reconciled with one another? To begin with, let us look at the way the opposing camp views its task in psychiatry.

One of the ways in which we can speak of another person is to speak only of his body. This approach has the advantage of dealing only in observable entities. By not referring to states of mind, feelings, intentions, and so forth, the psychiatrist eliminates the danger of asserting propositions which have *no means* of verification or falsification. Since everything in his system is visible, his statements about patients are statements which are conceptualized in terms of objectifiable entities. This hard scientific approach deals with behavior—i.e., with the clearly visible movements of the organism. It does not deal with action—i.e., with intentional activity. To deal with the latter, one would have to make reference to intentions, and such a move is ruled out by the boundary conditions initially set up for investigation. The adoption of such a posture with regard to the study of the human animal is quite rewarding. Through this stance, such things as anthropomorphism and individual interpretation are reduced to a minimum. In a certain sense, the methodological maxim which dominates this approach is: "John is John's body." In some more restricted contexts, one might say: "John is John's brain."

The result of this viewpoint is that certain disturbances of personal life are viewed as derangements in the biophysical condition of the body. Schizophrenia is understood in terms of serotonin metabolism and endogenous hallucinogenic substances, while the problem of anxiety is formulated in terms of lactic acid concentration and muscle tension. The need to understand the "psychodynamic" basis of these various behavioral patterns is seemingly minimized or completely eliminated. Why speak of interpersonal circumstances which might predispose an individual to an acute psychotic episode when one can isolate with considerable precision a specific substance which is correlated with the clearly visible bizarre behavior of the patient?[3, p 85]

The major implication of this point of view is that the manner in which we ought to deal with a problem such as schizophrenia is essentially via the *soma*. If we can simply adjust the working of the body so that the inherent defect is corrected or minimized, then we shall have treated the schizophrenic patient. To a significant extent, somatic alteration is a powerful method of dealing with the schizophrenic or even, in principal, the neurotic. The advent of the phenothiazines, for instance, represents something of a revolution in psychiatry. Hospital stays are shorter, people are more productive, and psychiatrists are more pleased with their results. There is, however, a significant negative dimension to the introduction of such a set of armaments. I want to compare phenothiazine therapy with analytic geometry, since an investigation into their similarities will prove to be of considerable interest.

The development of analytic geometry in the 17th century was obviously of enormous value to the subsequent growth of mathematics and physics. After Descartes had presented his work on the application of algebraic techniques to classical synthetic geometry, the integral and differential calculus was born. The calculus needed the tools of analytic geometry for its own conceptualization; without them there could be little possibility of it ever developing. Theoretical physics used both the new geometry and the calculus and expressed its obvious debt to both these branches of mathematics in its every turn. But there was a significantly negative effect which this new development had which could not be foreseen.

With the rise of a new way to deal with the problems of geometry, the traditional techniques were largely abandoned. It was thought that they had reached their maximum utility and had nothing more to offer. With their abandonment, the entire geometrical imagination which gave birth to them was also left to decay. What more could the old geometry tell us? What most men did not realize was that the most powerful aspects of this abandoned imagination were yet to be expressed. It was not until the 19th century that the development of non-euclidean geometries signaled the rebirth of this manner of thinking. The influence which this renaissance in mathematics exerted is well known. Poincaré suggests the lesson to be learned in the following passage:

> If Tycho had had instruments ten times as precise we would never have had a Kepler or a Newton, or Astronomy. It is a misfortune for a science to be born too late, when the means of observation have become too perfect.

Joseph Woodger states the point quite clearly:

> We are thus furnished with data of great abundance, and interpretations of great complexity, just as Kepler would have been had he possessed Michaelson's interferometer. We are, therefore, in danger of being overwhelmed by our data and of being unable to deal with the simpler problems first and understand their connection[14]

The introduction of phenothiazine therapy into the mainstream of psychiatric treatment is an analogous development to the development of analytic geometry in the sphere of mathematics. In the case of psychiatry, the need to understand human action is seemingly minimized since drug therapy helps individuals return to their former, less disturbed states. As our knowledge of psychopharmacology increases, the temptation is to abandon the old type of imagination for this new one. Perhaps we have reached the end of this way of thinking. Perhaps it has yielded all it can and further pursuit is wasteful. There are several points which militate against this point of view. In the first place, if we learn from history at all, then here is a case in which our knowledge can be put to use. In the second place, we must recognize that the understanding involved in the "old" imagination is of a different order from the new. It is not going too far to say that the two modes of comprehending deal with different subject matters. They do not intersect and cannot contradict one another. The language of the *soma* and the language of the *psyche* are quite disparate and independent. If either manner of understanding is taken as sufficient for the task of psychiatry, then the view of man which emerges will be truncated and not very satisfying for the purposes of contemporary psychiatry.

To see man *merely* as a biological animal is not to see him as a person. Whatever it is that constitutes a person, it is certainly more than biological makeup. It is not cells, molecules, or synapses that have desires, fears, and phobias, and an understanding of one does not entail an understanding of the other. We can isolate all the hallucinogens we want to from the blood of different individuals, but that which makes that individual a person cannot be so collected. If we are to understand human beings as persons, then we must use the original imagination with which we developed our ordinary understanding of each other. It is this very same imagination which is at work in psychodynamic psychiatry. When I confront another person, I do not ordinarily see him as a network of cells, molecules, and plasma. Rather, I view him as a being with human qualities. Insofar as I understand him as a person, I empathize with him.[4]

Investigation of various states of the brain in an attempt to understand what certain mental states are all about is worthwhile and fruitful in certain restricted ways which need not be spelled out. But there are severe limitations imposed upon this sort of approach to man, and it is because of these limitations that an understanding of persons can never result from this sort of methodology alone. Take, for example, the case of pain. As a neurophysiologist I can monitor John's brain so that I will learn just what the state of his nervous system is when he is in pain. Assume, for the sake of simplicity, that John's pain is associated with the firing of a single neuron in his cerebral cortex. I can study that neuron in every imaginable way so that I know how rapidly it fires, what neurons it connects with, and when it fires. But no matter how much I study that single cell, I will not be able to understand what John's experience of pain is like. The neuron does not have the pain; John does. In this respect, the maxim, "John is John's brain," falls short of our goal. To think that we can understand what it is for John *as a person* to experience pain of one sort or another by studying his nervous system is to fool ourselves. Such an understanding is a function of the empathetic imagination and cannot be had through neurophysiological investigations. Furthermore, John is not apt to feel consoled by me when I inform him that I have located the neuron that is causing the pain. He may be gratified if I can stop the neuron from firing, but if I cannot, my information is of no help to him. Also, if I inform him that I understand the dynamics of how the pain causes him anxiety, he will not in all probability express any relief as a result. Neither approach is sufficient for my dealing with John and his pain.

To pursue one course to the exclusion of the other is a dangerous step for American psychiatry. Treating the person as a biological machine, in principle, negates his existence as a person. Dealing with him strictly in mental terms ignores his somatic existence. No mere amalgamation of the two is sufficient for a proper psychiatric confrontation with another person.[15] What is the basis for this claim? The answer lies in the viewpoint that a person is not to be conceived in a Cartesian dualistic manner as a combination of body and mind. Such a framework is quite misleading and has been shown to be so.[16] To say that one concentrates on the body to the exclusion of the mind in understanding a person involves a twofold distortion of the problem. In the first place, the dichotomy between mind and body is a non-existent one in that there are not two separate substances—mind and body—which constitute man. In the second place, a concentration on one aspect or dimension of a person will necessarily fall short of a full understanding. There is a further, more subtle problem which emerges when such a stance is assumed. When the person is conceived of being one-half of the body-mind dichotomy, the investigator will frame his hypotheses as if the only factors bearing upon his problem can be expressed in the language of that particular side. Consider, for example, the following passage from Erickson:

> In every field there are a few very simple questions which are highly embarrassing because the debate which forever arises around them leads only to perpetual failure and seems consistently to make fools of the most expert. In psychopathology such questions have always concerned the location and the cause of a neurotic disturbance. Does it have a visible onset? Does it reside in the body or the mind, in the individual or in his society?...Such simple contraposition now seems long outdated. In recent years we have come to the conclusion that a neurosis is a psycho- **and** somatic, psycho- **and** social, and **interpersonal**.
> More often than not, however, discussion will reveal that these new definitions too are only different ways of combining such separate concepts as psyche and soma, individual and group. We now say "and" instead of "either-or," but we retain at least the semantic assumption that the mind is a "thing" separate from the body, and society a "thing" outside of the individual.[17]

This is an interesting passage. Seemingly, Erickson is telling us to pay attention to both parts of the person, psychic and somatic. But his conception of a person is deeply Cartesian and misleading. He views the person as being constituted of something called the mind and another thing called the body. When the two get together, there is an individual person formed. Such an attitude is a regression back into the 17th century and is not the direction that psychiatry should be taking. Ryle paints the picture quite accurately:

> Since, according to the doctrine, minds belong to the same category as bodies and since bodies are rigidly governed by mechanical laws, it seemed to many theorists to follow that minds must be similarly governed by rigid, non-mechanical laws. The physical world is a deterministic system, so the mental world must be a deterministic system.[16, p 20]

Suffice it to say that where the dichotomy of mind-body is operative, a correct understanding of persons is thwarted. The unfortunate situation in contemporary American psychiatry is that sides have been taken along the lines of this false dichotomy. Most psychiatrists fall into one of two camps: students of the body or students of the mind. They are opposed to one another because they see their "part" of the person which they are studying as being more important or fundamental than the other. It is one thing to fight over realities; it is quite another to duel over misconceptions.

The question now arises as to just what it means, in an operational sense, to treat a person *as a person*. It we cannot do some minimal justice to this problem, then the above criticism loses a great deal of its impact since there may be no other paths for psychiatry to follow than the ones just outlined. Clearly, there are other uses of this term which are important and may even bear on the problem at hand. Nevertheless, the restriction to a single use of the term should be sufficient to make the point necessary for the purposes of this paper.

The concept of a person has been given considerable attention in the philosophical literature.[18,19] In philosophy (as in the current attempt in psychiatry) the theory of persons has been introduced in order to avoid the difficulties of materialism and dualism.[20] The major emphasis of various theories of the person lies in the notion that the entity which we sometimes refer to in materialistic terms and at other times refer to in mentalistic ones is not to be conceived as being either one or the other exclusively. In the same sense that something may have orange in it and not be orange, so something may have physical attributes and not be purely physical. Clearly, the same assertion is made with respect to mental attributes. The "person," then, whatever a full elucidation of that concept may entail, requires a different sort of language to account for the nature of its existence. How, then, are we to speak of persons in a meaningful way which does not fall into the traps mentioned above?

One way of getting to a preliminary answer to this question is to observe the manner in which persons ordinarily speak of and to one another. From such observations we may begin to conceptualize the framework of understanding which underlies the ordinary understanding revealed through everyday discourse. Let us take, for example, an instance of a person, say Jones, cashing a check. Suppose we are asked to explain what Jones is doing to someone who is not familiar with such a procedure. One way of speaking might be strictly in terms of the bodily movements and sounds that Jones makes. In speaking this way we would be describing Jones' *behavior*. On the other hand, we could speak of Jones' intentions and expectations in the context of describing his movements. In a rather broad sense we would be describing Jones' *actions*. The distinction between behavior and action is quite crucial here since it is via the latter that our ordinary understanding of persons obtains. Bodily movements do not suffice to explain what it is that people do for the purpose of understanding persons as persons. It may be necessary to speak of the intentions, desires, wishes, expectations, imaginings, etc., in order to account for another person in his daily life.

One problem that arises immediately, however, is that the introduction of concepts like intentions, wishes, and desires precludes the possibility of a systematic comprehension of human activity, because such terms refer to private events which are excluded from the sphere of objective investigation. We would be well advised to speak in a language which did not have to make reference to such concepts while at the same time did not revert back to purely mechanistic descriptions. We can accomplish this goal if we look at human action and interaction in terms of rules. The thesis here is that insofar as human beings act in a manner that is understandable to others, they do so in accordance with various rules.[21] The concept of a rule necessarily involves the notion of following or obeying it. For example, when we speak in the English tongue we generally follow the rules of grammar. Yet were we asked to elucidate these rules we would be hard pressed to do so. Indeed, the perfect grammar has yet to be written. Following a rule, then, does not imply the ability to state that rule. In actuality, when we act we do not usually state the rule of action to ourselves first and then perform. For the most part, the rule is not even conscious at the time of acting.

Furthermore, the concept of disobeying a rule is clearly related to that of obeying one. If a child who is totally unfamiliar with the game of chess were to sit down and randomly move the pieces about the board, we would hardly say he was disobeying the rules of the game. Rather, he is not thought of as playing the game of chess at all. In order to disobey a rule one would have to be able to act in accordance with that rule. In the sphere of moral responsibility we do not hold children responsible for their actions much of the time because they have not yet learned the rules according to which persons usually act.

The notion of following a rule is also contextually bound. That is, the rule is understood and followed by the large number of people with whom we interact. A chess game is a context which supplies the rules which are to be followed if the game is to be played. There are rules of the market, of the school, of the church, and of play—all of which are different contexts in terms of which the rules which people follow are understood. In each of these different contexts we have different expectations of people and the reason for this is that there is implied in these different situations a different set of rules. These different expectations are reflections of the different *roles* which people play in different contexts. Each role a person plays carries with it a different set of expectations which may or may not be evoked in another person within the same context. If one does not understand the particular context of human action (e.g., a foreigner visiting a strange land for the first time), then he does not understand the rules according to which the people act and roles which they play that are characterized by these rules.

The point here is that it is persons who follow rules—not bodies and not minds. When a psychotherapist speaks with a patient, he is confronting a person and not a machine or a disembodied spirit. On an operational basis, the manner in which the therapist deals with the patient is suggested by the above discussion. The patient is understood as a person in terms of the rules which characterize his behavior. Person-language is the language of the rules that characterize human action and the roles that people play in the diverse activities of their lives. Neither bodies nor minds follow rules and play roles. Only persons do. Insofar as psychiatry recognizes this point, it changes its level of discourse and concern from that of mechanics (either physical or mental) to that of persons. Since the proper endeavor of psychiatry is the understanding of persons as persons, it is not unreasonable to assert that the language one speaks ought to reflect this endeavor. Furthermore, the assumption of such a mode of discourse reflects a manner of dealing with people and patients which is more properly in line with the central task of psychiatry.

REFERENCES

1. Descartes, R.: The Passions of the Soul, p. 332, E. E. Haldane and G. R. Ross (editors), Dover, New York. 1955.
2. Szasz, T.: The Ethics of Psychoanalysis, pp. 81–92. Dell. New York. 1965.
3. Denber, H. C. B.: Can psychopharmacology advance? Psychosomatics, 9: 85–89, 1970.
4. Graham, David T.: Health, disease, and the mind-body problem: Linguistic parallelism. Psychosom. Med., 29: 59–71, 1967.
5. Serban, G.: Freudian man vs. existential man. Arch. Gen. Psychiat., 17: 598–607, 1967.
6. Laing, R. D.: The Divided Self, pp. 17–26. Penguin. Baltimore. 1965.
7. Freud, S.: The Interpretation of Dreams, trans. by James Strachey. Standard Edition. Vol. VI. Hogarth. London. 1953.
8. _____: The Three Essays on the Theory of Sexuality, trans. by James Strachey. Standard Edition. Vol. VII. Hogarth. London. 1953.
9. _____:The Question of Lay Analysis, trans. by James Strachey. Standard Edition, Vol. XX. Hogarth. London. 1959.
10. _____:Studies in Hysteria, trans. by James Strachey. Standard Edition, Vol. II., p. 7. Hogarth. London. 1955.
11. Freud, S., and Breuer, J.: Ego and the Id, vol. XIX, 1961.
12. Freud, S.: A Seventeenth Century Demonological Neurosis, trans. by James Strachey, Standard Edition, Vol. XIX, p. 72. Hogarth. London. 1961.
13. Austin, J. L.: A plea for excuses. Proceedings of the Aristotelian Society, LVII, 1956–1957.
14. Woodger, J.: Biological Principles. Routledge and Kegan Paul. London. 1929.
15. Chertok, L.: Psychosomatic medicine in the west and in eastern European countries. Psychosom. Med., 31: 510–521, 1969.
16. Ryle, G.: The Concept of Mind. Barnes and Noble. New York. 1950.
17. Erickson, E.: Childhood and Society, p. 20. Norton. New York. 1950.
18. Strawson, P. F.: Individuals, ch. 3. Methuen. London. 1959.
19. _____: Persons. Essays in Philosophical Psychology. pp. 377–403. Donald F. Gustafson (editor). Doubleday. New York. 1964.
20. Shaffer, J. A.: Philosophy of Mind, pp. 52–57. Prentice-Hall. New Jersey. 1968.
21. Melden, A. I.: Action. Essays in Philosophical Psychology, pp. 58–76. Donald F. Gustafson, (editor) Doubleday. New York. 1964.

3

On Our Clinical Fantasy of Reality

JEAN SANVILLE

If we accept the definition of the philosophers that reality is the sum of all that is real, absolute, and unchangeable, then since almost no phenomena with which we deal clinically can be seen as absolute and unchangeable, we might conclude that we do not address ourselves to "reality" at all. The unsatisfactory state of the science of psychology is artistically treated by the poet, Wallace Stevens, in a number of his poems. We clinicians are all like his "Man with the Blue Guitar," who is accused by those to whom he plays:

> ... "You have a blue guitar,
> You do not play things as they are."

> The man replied, "Things as they are
> Are changed upon the blue guitar."

> And they said then, "But play, you must,
> A tune beyond us, yet ourselves,

> A tune upon the blue guitar
> Of things exactly as they are."

Reprinted by permission from *Clinical Social Work Journal*, 4 (Winter 1976) 245-251.
Copyright © by Human Sciences Press, 72 Fifth Ave., New York, N.Y.

I cannot bring a world quite round,
Although I patch it as I can.

I sing a hero's head, large eye,
And bearded bronze, but not a man,

Although I patch him as I can,
and reach through him almost to Man.

If to serenade almost to Man
Is to miss, by that, things as they are,

Say that it is the serenade
Of a Man that plays a Blue Guitar. (1964, p. 165–166)

Although we try we always miss "things as they are," for our beliefs about the nature of human nature leave us inevitably biased.

In fantasy, however, the realm of vivid imagination, depictions in pictures and words, we abundantly deal. We utilize myths to represent commonly recurring clinical syndromes—such as of Oedipus, or of Narcissus. Recognizing that no patient exactly conforms to these primordial types we try to correct the illusions, the erroneous perceptions of "reality" into which our categorizing has led us. We discard labels and look at and listen to the patient himself, and we observe data that are unexplained. Some of us then push our myths back to even more fundamental, more inclusive versions, such as the stories of pre-Oedipal Oedipus or of the infancy of Narcissus. Others are declaring that we should do away with myths and metaphors altogether, and simply use language that describes clinical phenomena, the facts perceptible to our senses. The title of this Biennial, "The Art and the Science of Clinical Social Work," suggests that we award a place both to the poetic and to the empirical.

Freud, in The Future of An Illusion (1927/1961), noted that we call belief an illusion when wish-fulfillment is a prominent factor in its motivation. If we concede that it is an omnipresent wish of human beings, including clinicians, to know, to perceive not only with the senses but with the mind, then, in a basic sense, we must regard all our beliefs as mental inventions which are never revealing of ultimate truths. We must suspect ourselves whenever we become so overly invested in our theoretical constructs that we do not readily admit new data. If we can, on the other hand, play with our ideas, we may then constantly move toward more satisfactory depictions of our ever-shifting realities, striving for what the poet Stevens called "the supreme fiction" (1964, p. 380). This demands taking our artistic creations, our "scientific ideas," at once seriously and lightly. If we can do that, we may accomplish ever-closer approximations to "truth" via a dialectic process: applying our theoretical abstractions as far as they will usefully go, suspending them a bit to attend to the facts at hand, modifying theory to accord with our observation, trying new formulations on for size, so to speak—again, out of our discontent, returning to "original" data and so on. Sometimes we find that our old theories develop so many contradictions that, as Hegel described, they pass over into their own negation.

This spiralling dialectic process occurs throughout the development of any given professional person. The novice starts with a situation in which he or she is confronted by "facts," raw clinical data, people with complaints and problems. But this novice already has, by virtue of living some twenty years or so, some "ideas" about these facts, perhaps even a rudimentary science. Applying these "lay" theories he or she finds them inadequate both as bases for understanding and as bases for treatment. So, if that novice does not harbor too many intrapsychic obstacles, he opens himself up to new concepts, including a concept of self as observer, and with these, freshly observes the "facts." He tries out these new ideas in his clinical practice. With them he finds that he can observe that which was perhaps there before but which he did not, could not, see. He confirms his new knowledge by experiencing what it will enable him to understand and to do. Recognizing the limits of his learning, he returns to absorb more of that body of systematized knowledge already acquired by those before him. (Of course, we must note that there are some who do not return to original sources, professing to discard that which in fact they never had.)

Inevitably, there comes a time when, as seasoned clinicians, we feel that we have experimented with the teachings and writings of the seminal thinkers and their models of practice yet still find ourselves not knowing enough, not skilled enough, although we may have pushed our theories to their limit. In Steven's words, we have reached "a point beyond which thought could not progress as thought" (1964, p. 403).

Therefore, we attempt to suspend theory, to return to the "primary," the patient, attempting to impose nothing. We wish to discover and we know that to impose is not to discover. Bion (1970) has suggested that the clinician should approach each session unencumbered by memory or understanding. I think we do that only in a "make-believe" sense, for as adults, we find that there is no real return to the "first idea." We can pretend to erase our labels and our theories, but they will still influence our perceptions. We cannot erase our words, our language, and as Sapir (1921) has affirmed, language is the sieve in which we catch our thoughts. The human mind always perceives reality through categories that it has laid down in advance, and always misses data other than that provided for in its code of classifications. Nevertheless, it is an important exercise, an important phase of the dialectic, to attempt at times the erasing of our fictions.

As usual, I find that the poets give words to this perhaps better than we. Wallace Stevens has prescribed:

> .... to find the real
> To be stripped of every fiction except one,
> the fiction of an absolute—Angel,
> Be *silent* in your luminous cloud and *hear*
> The luminous melody of proper sound. (1964, p. 404)

But Stevens also observes that there comes "a point, beyond which fact could not progress as fact" (p. 402). The advance of knowledge depends also on the imagination, the creation of new hypotheses, thus art is itself inherent in science.

In his "Notes Toward a Supreme Fiction" (1964, p. 380–408), Stevens proposes three requirements which we might well apply to a critique of our own science: it must be abstract, it must change, and it must give pleasure.

In regard to the first, that our theories are always abstractions, Stevens comments:

> The major abstraction is the idea of Man
> And major Man is its exponent, abler
> In his abstract than in his singular. (p. 388)

We well recognize his message: that no individual ever fits that major abstraction. Individuals change, and change even in general ways, from culture to culture, and from one historic period to another. Science can describe only general laws. As scientists, we, like Freud, must use theory to direct the systematic search for new information, to lay out our biases and thus make it easier to disavow them when they are found inadequate. Out of the "dangling data" we then find it necessary to construct new hypotheses.

Innovators often claim to have seen the light, to have the final answers. Especially do they claim to have found the way when their innovations are gimmicks, over-simplified notions which do not contribute toward the fuller understanding of humankind. When, however, the practitioner is willing to test out the limits of usefulness of a new theory, he or she comes sooner or later to experience a "fluctuation of certainty," and again sees the need to modify it, or perhaps even discard it.

This brings me to Stevens' second point, that our ideas must always be in flux.

> .... The distaste which we feel with this withered scene
> Is that it has not changed enough. (p. 390)

One of the tests of any theory, ergo, is its flexibility, its openness to new data. And there is much new data to be absorbed and assimilated, both from the biological side, and from the sociological side. These require new "imaginings," which in turn will alter what we regard as "real." In Stevens' words:

> Two things of opposite natures seem to depend
> On one another, as a man depends
> On a woman, day on night, the imagined
> On the real. This is the origin of change.
> Winter and Spring, cold copulars, embrace
> And forth the particulars of rapture come. (p.392)

The potential danger, to which we may be alerted at this biennial, is that, under the guise of "standards" and "accountability," we could freeze our art, our practice. This could hamper our getting at new knowledge and newly reordering the old.

Stevens' third point, that our "fictions" must give us pleasure, is well known to clinicians. It is exhilarating, heady wine when we glimpse a new order, new "truths." It is rewarding when we see the results in our practice, or art, of our new concepts, and exciting when we are joined with others in agreement with our new beliefs and practices. Stevens reflects on our joy when we come

> To be crested and wear the mark of a multitude
> And so, as part, to exult with its great throat. (p. 398)

Anna Freud, at the International Psychoanalytical Meetings in London in the summer of 1975, spoke of the "elation" of her time, the "adventure" felt by the second generation of psychoanalysts as they widened the scope of their science, applying it not only to neurosis, but to character problems, to perversions, to delinquencies, and even to psychosis. These extensions, plus the inclusion in practice of children and adolescents, necessitated modifications in theory and in technique. The result, she noted, was "a springing up of rivals," with ideas and methods quite divergent from those which had preceded.

The very label "rivals" brings into existence a climate of hostile opposition which seems to me unnecessary if we maintain the perspective of the spiralling dialectic process. Over time, and within any clinical session, this involves applying our present concepts as far as they are useful, playing at erasing them for awhile when they do not seem to help us understand, then perhaps experimenting with other, even opposite notions. Thus, we have discovered that psychoanalytic theory in its classical form did not adequately explain many emerging "facts." It did not enable us to deal with patients whose problems did not fit "Oedipal" theory. An artist, Melanie Klein, then came on the scene, and her imaginings were about a realm in which there were few facts, the realm of infancy, the period before words began. Her followers, in their zeal, have sometimes made her theories gospel, overthrowing the father and overemphasizing the mother. Like the early Freudians, they have sometimes seemed to impose their fantasies on the patient, and have appeared to be overly invested in their own fictions. Many of them may be at a phase of the dialectic spiral in which mental invention is utilized instead of phenomena. However, we might predict that, in carrying their notions to extremes, they will discover new data and, in all likelihood, ultimately they too will make modifications.

A diametrically opposite stance to theirs can be recognized in the present eagerness for "the experiential," in the rejection of all theoretical constructs, in the swing back to phenomena: to each individual's thinking and feeling and doing, to "what works." That too is a response to impatience with old ideological concepts, a reaction to the pain of not knowing enough, not being competent enough. If we regard these "experiential experiments" as a necessary phase, the manifestation on a large scale of that suspension of abstraction which we may attempt in any given clinical hour, it will fit well into our dialectic spiralling. But if we cannot, or do not, use words and concepts to distil from the experience new hypotheses to be tested, we may stultify our science, and become only a technology.

Unlike the International Psychoanalytic Congress in London last July, our Biennial is fortunately not set up for polemics. In London, that polarizing had the observable effect, we noted, of further dividing a profession into camps, and of fostering rather than diluting dogma. As Theordore Reik (1951) used to point out, heresy is the parent of dogma. When new ideas are treated as heresy, dogma is born. And so we shall cherish our stubborn rebellious spirits who are willing to point out exceptions to our general rules, "facts" which do not permit interpretation by old schemes, syndromes which do not yield to old methods.

Our biennial can be part of the dialectic growth of our profession. New notions will be brought here for presentation to peers, for their examination, discussion, and criticism. Perhaps we will detect in ourselves some of the phases I have been describing. We come with certain preconceptions, which we will suspend for awhile to hear of and entertain new ideas. As we savor the new we may become aware of both anxious and pleasurable body sensations and emotional and intellectual responses. We will be asking ourselves and our colleagues: Does this new theory or method afford us hope of filling gaps in our knowledge and practice? Will it enable us to see that which has eluded us, to move beyond the former impasse? Throughout, we will be exchanging, meeting with others, and perhaps noticing that not everyone is equally excited by this new idea. In our dialogue with others, we will try to comprehend why not, and throughout, we will continue to tune into our own inner worlds, and one of the questions we may well ask is, "Could this enhance our own lives?"

Social workers have tended in the past to be epigons, that is, second-rate imitators or followers, selecting and applying from the heritage of predecessors, in our case mainly psychoanalysts. I would propose that in former years the "institutionalization" of social work rendered its practitioners inclined to think it was presumptuous that they should contribute to theory. Conferences such as this Biennial suggest that to the extent that we see ourselves as independent practitioners and not simply as satellites of other professions, we will offer valuable input toward improving our science and our art. The social-historical context in which we find ourselves will enable those of talent and courage among us to suggest fresh insights into the nature of the human psyche—superior theories, superior modes of practice. We shall ask only, "Is the enthusiast ready to participate in the process of refining the supreme fiction, the science which underlies our art?"

REFERENCES

Bion, W. R. *Attention and interpretation: A scientific approach to insight in psychoanalysis and groups.* New York: Basic Books, Inc., 1970.

Freud, S. The future of an illusion. *Standard Edition*, Vol. XXI, (1927). London: The Hogarth Press, 1961, pp. 5–56.

Reik, T. *Dogma and compulsion: Psychoanalytic studies of religion and myths.* New York: International Universities Press, 1951.

Sapir, E. *Language.* New York: Harcourt Brace & Co., 1921.

Stevens, W. *The collected poems of Wallace Stevens.* New York: Alfred A. Knopf, Inc., 1964.

Part Two

Psychiatry and Psychotherapy

While historically, psychotherapy hardly begins with that field of medicine known as psychiatry, it nonetheless seems logical to commence our discussion of psychotherapy by turning to psychiatry. If for no other reason, psychiatry is the parent of contemporary psychotherapy because of its legitimate standing as one of the healing arts. Indeed, these last two statements say a great deal about psychiatry, and while the following selections take up these issues in greater detail, a few words of introduction seem appropriate.

By the time psychiatry had taken its position in the panoply of medical disciplines, administrators and practitioners alike had taken a very major step in helping form the so-called mental health sciences. Psychiatry, after all, while basing some of its work on fundamental physiological and biochemical processes, also has advanced some rather less scientific styles and notions. Surely the form of treatment many psychiatrists offer is hardly compatible with the forms of treatment offered by other physicians. Still, the argument psychiatrists offered could not be ignored by those who worked in the more organic, rather than psychogenic, forms of illness: We deal with sick people and we seek to make them well. A fair enough statement, to be sure, but on closer inspection almost every one of these words is open to debate. Are the people, for example, who seek out psychiatrists properly labeled ill? Indeed, do we rightly address them as patients, in contrast with, say, clients? Furthermore, does psychiatry make these people well? Is cure, in fact, an appropriate goal? After all, many would allege that not only is the typical psychiatric patient not ill, but he or she is only being helped by the psychiatrist to adjust to certain past or present circumstances.

In this regard, some people suggest that genuine psychiatry be limited to those sorts of illnesses that require hospitalization, or that have some of their roots in physiological or biochemical sources. Others argue this point by claiming that the person who comes to the psychiatrist merely for self-knowledge, support, or a measure of personal enlightenment is benefiting from the psychiatrist's medical training to the same degree as the person who is, let us say, immobilized by a psychosis, irrespective of the etiology of that psychosis. Carrying the case even further, we note those critics who claim that any form of psychotherapy is legitimately called psychiatry as long as it is practiced by a licensed (i.e., medical) psychiatrist. Yet this position is considered nonsensical by those who claim psychiatry should belong to the greater discipline of medicine by dint of its logical association with neurology. This position, actually, is maintained to the present day in the licensing examination which people must take in order to become psychiatrists. The examination demands a relatively thorough knowledge of neurology, a knowledge not normally sustained during the years of the psychiatrist's training.

This discussion may seem somewhat confusing. One might ask, has not the fundamental definition of psychiatry been agreed upon? The answer is no. Not only that, the dilemmas posed by psychiatry's position in the world of medicine on the one hand, and in the world of psychotherapy on the other—worlds which do not totally coincide—have put psychiatry in a most difficult and delicate spot. There are some who blame psychiatry for not being able to demonstrate the manner and frequency of cure achieved by other branches of medicine. Equally serious, many psychiatrists resist the totally medical model, which traditionally has been employed to define psychiatry as well as delineate the criteria by which psychiatry is assessed. Quite clearly, there is no one discipline or branch of medicine that can be irrefutably defined as pure psychiatry. Not surprisingly, then, some psychiatrists argue that it might be best to separate psychiatry from medicine altogether. Other psychiatrists counter by saying this act would lead to the end of psychiatry. Still others claim that this very disagreement says as much about psychiatry as any thesis on the subject.

In exploring the following selections, one point should be kept in mind. No matter what its definition, psychiatry (and the forms of psychotherapy that issue forth from it) has one leg in medicine and the other in all those disciplines, theories, and ideologies which influence the shape and meaning of psychotherapy generally. And while these latter influences change almost daily, it turns out that medicine, as a discipline, seems to evolve at a far slower rate, despite the speed at which technology advances. So, the psychiatrist and his or her field stand on a somewhat shaky foundation, even though psychiatry, as we suggested, is truly the parent of the art of psychotherapy. For not only do psychiatrists wrestle with issues of theory and practice; they also agonize over the future of their very profession—not an insignificant matter. The point is not for psychiatry to do whatever it can to maintain its ruling position; the point is for psychiatry to constantly rethink its self-definitions in light of the knowledge about psychotherapy that daily mounts up from the work of medical and non-medical people alike.

4

Psychotherapy and the New Psychiatry

JARL E. DYRUD

It seems appropriate from time to time to pause and reflect on our field of psychiatry. Particularly during a period of rapid growth it is incumbent upon us to draw up some sort of a map that will permit us to maintain a conceptual scheme holding together all facets of our perpetually evolving specialty. While we do construct an evolving body of fact and theory derived from a data base, psychiatry, like other medical specialties, is not a science in and of itself but a congeries of sciences and methodologies within the physician's role. We bring together scientists as well as sciences. Sometimes they speak the same language; many times they are incomprehensible to one another. It is my belief that academic psychiatrists have the particular task of achieving whatever integration of science and practice is possible and teaching it, and this is being done well in many teaching centers.

In the course of this integration, at times one or another of our areas of interest becomes active and the remainder seem to pale into insignificance; but events occurring in the physician-patient relationship give us the matrix within which these various excursions occur. There are elements of the arousal of hope or the lack of it in every such interaction, as placebo studies demonstrate. There are both patient factors and physician factors to be considered in estimating the net effectiveness of any therapeutic attempt. Psychiatrists' efforts are addressed to the problems of mental illness. When we speak of mental illness we mean the psychobiological

Reprinted by special permission of the William Alanson White Psychiatric Foundation, Inc. from *Psychiatry*, 40 (1977), 17–26. Copyright © 1977 by the William Alanson White Psychiatric Foundation, Inc.

malfunctioning of the person as a whole. This definition put forward by Adolf Meyer (1952) is a broad mandate reminiscent of Auguste Comte's ironic statement, "The subject matter of each discipline stretches literally to infinity" (Becker, 1971, p. 27).

Our "new psychiatry" is prominently psychopharmacological and behavioral in character. In addition, we have been blessed or perhaps cursed by intense exposure in the media. We have been oversold to the public, then found to be unable to deliver, and, of course, our family squabbles are prominently displayed. For these reasons it is commonly held and articulately stated that we are, in fact, overextended and in the midst of an identity crisis as a profession.

Thus, it might be salutary to remind ourselves that we are, in fact, in a subdivision of the field of medicine. We are charged with the care of those people whose miseries are not caused by an identifiable agent or circumstance belonging to another specialty. In that sense, we recognize that we care for a miscellaneous or residual population of patients. Just as we have returned pellagra psychoses and general paresis to the field of internal medicine, part of our task must be to continue to sort out and identify our unknowns in the hope of finding other specifics that can be applied. Currently, there are striking advances in biological psychiatry and new findings—whether in the possible link of dopamine receptors to schizophrenia or in acute myopathy—that cut across some of our conventional diagnostic categories. These developments may suggest some alternate strategies (Meltzer and Moline, 1970). Of equal importance are the operant approaches to essential hypertension, headache, and a host of other complaints and malfunctions that respond to intervention at a behavioral level (Budzynski, 1973). Psychotherapy research has had a very hard time of it by comparison. Yet, the study of the therapeutic matrix within which all the rest happens must remain a major aspect of every study we conduct.

To provide a vehicle for us, Jerome Frank has been single-mindedly developing what we might call an anthropological model for psychotherapy (1961). I call it anthropological because it does involve trying to map the premises, assumptions, beliefs, values, and rules on which people base their individual and social behavior. As a good anthropologist, he has concerned himself not only with the conscious model of what a therapist thinks he is doing or how he explains his behavior, but also the unconscious model, not in the Freudian sense of the unconscious, but the underlying rules and relations that define the parameters of relationships as well as the possibilities of behavioral change. To paraphrase Martin Orne, the paradox of the therapist is that unless you have some belief in a specific factor, your nonspecific factors don't work (1975). Therefore, the good therapist must split two roles in himself, the therapist-believer following his conscious model, and the researcher-critic seeing how this process relates to underlying structure. In actuality, this primary investigative mission of our specialty is congenial to few. Fortunately, the miscellaneous category of patients is so much larger than any other, that competent clinical care, the pastoral aspect of psychiatry, will always demand much of our time and effort.

My hope for the field is that we can keep our broad view while continuing to accrue knowledge, valuing the modest achievements of the past as well as the modest achievements of the present.

I stress modest because excesses of partisan advocacy have kept our field in the embarrassing position of looking more like a revolving set of sideshows than an evolving discipline. Mental hospital patients have in turn been saved by Cotton's focal infection theory, the bromides, the barbiturates, insulin, ECT, lobotomy, and now the phenothiazines. In each instance, the new method was found to obviate the necessity of the current form of psychotherapy—possibly much in the same way that the advent of antibiotics took backrubs and tightening the bottom sheet out of nursing.

Today, converging streams of research data from the biological and the behavioral fields are pouring into our journals, accompanied by the usual finding that psychotherapy is dead. It is a time of great ferment, and enthusiasm runs high, endorsed and funded by unprecedented levels of governmental support. Social psychiatry has lost much of its identity as an investigation of symptoms in an interpersonal field to a preoccupation with delivery systems for the new technology.

Unskilled people are being highly touted in the new mental health delivery systems. Highly trained people have begun to feel absurd and unwanted. Is it possible that there is a place for well-trained psychotherapeutic skills in the new psychiatry? Some years ago, B. F. Skinner proposed that an army of MA behaviorists could be trained and employed to sweep away our society's residual problems (1961). His total plan was not carried out, but steps have been taken in that direction and all over the country work is being done that, I must admit, is both interesting and valuable. Similarly, antipsychotic medication is being prescribed on a national scale of unprecedented inclusiveness. The most remote backwoods health station may have no psychiatrists, but it has chlorpromazine. Whenever you are in the middle of an era, the ruling clichés are likely to seem important new insights. We have to wait to see what percentage of the residual problems remains after this era of psychopharmacology and behaviorism has run a bit longer.

Some perceive a split between the biological/behavioral investigators and the psychotherapists. This came about in large part because the major investment of psychiatric time and effort in this country has in the past thirty years been focused on psychoanalytically oriented psychotherapy. With this preoccupation came an unprecedented flight of professional talent from hospitals to private practice, from treatment of the psychiatrically disabled to the treatment of the relatively healthy. It has been said that this was inevitable—that ours is a reactive trade, serving the customers it gets. Without making a value judgment it is fair to say that the motto of both therapists and patients in this group might be characterized as "You don't have to be sick in order to get well." As a result, the treatment of the severely ill has been left largely in the hands of the biological/behavioral therapists. I put the two together on one side for purposes of this discussion because there has been time and opportunity to develop an integration between these two sciences, known as behavioral pharmacology, that is in no way duplicated by any systematic attempt at integrating psychodynamic thinking with either of them.

I do not wish to sound too critical of our decamped colleagues—they have been addressing themselves to human misery at a different level—but the weakening of ties between them and their biological/behavioral counterparts has been damaging to the field. Ignorance thrives in isolation. Unchallenged assumptions become dogma in the absence of critical inquiry. It is true that the relatively healthy patient group is one for whom the new psychiatry has least to offer. Chemotherapy for schizophrenia, mania, or severe depression is rarely indicated for this group of patients and the anti-anxiety drugs are often irrelevant. Similarly, behavioral procedures work best with clear-cut behavioral deficits, not with existential questions of meaning. This point was elegantly illustrated by Arnold Lazarus' paper in *Psychological Reports* entitled "Where Do Behavior Therapists Take Their Troubles?" He was trying to arrange a meeting and found that the majority of the group of leading behaviorists he was trying to convene had difficulty planning a time because they were in psychoanalytic treatment. He accounted for this on the basis of their having no clear-cut behavioral deficits, but problems of meaning. Like it or not, we must acknowledge that today a large segment of our psychobiologically malfunctioning patient population is not seeking relief from pain and discomfort, not even relief from anxiety, but relief from boredom and meaninglessness.

Is there, then, a place in the new psychiatry for the study of meaning? Or more specificially, is there a place for psychoanalytic training in the education of psychiatrists in the new psychiatry? I think there is. Education is simply the general term for becoming wiser than we were. It is very clear from the October 1974 issue of *Psychiatric Annals*, focused on what residents want from their training programs, that residents still come to us for wisdom as well as the latest techniques. A residency is in important ways like being in a mental hospital. It means being kept in a place for awhile with the understanding that when you have done well enough, according to the standard of others, you will be allowed to go out into the world again, with credentials. How this time is spent is obviously critical. If our residents are to be wiser than we, then the science of man we offer them must be broad as well as deep. It must include an exposure to the best of all our sciences in order to keep open the possibility of new combinations. They must be taught a healthy skepticism as well as self-scrutiny. For people in our priestly profession, it is particularly important not only to learn the new technologies but to come to know something of things as they always are. T. S. Eliot said, "The chief use of psychology (apart from curing people, if it does) seems to me to be to restate old truths in modern jargon which people can understand; and if psychology helps people toward truth which they cannot apprehend when put in simple theological language, so much the better" (1932).

It is my view that psychoanalysts must be brought back into the mainstream of academic psychiatry. Not as carriers of a dominant ideology, but in dialogue with the biological psychiatrists and behaviorists. I shall not here review all of the old arguments centering around "Is Psychoanalysis an Art or a Science?" We have raised it, struggled with it, and become confused by it often enough. It is easy for a psychoanalyst to use psychoanalytic psychology as a way of organizing his thinking about hard research data, whether they be data of infant observation or the protocols of psychiatric interviews. It is quite another problem to use the psychoanalytic method to generate quantifiable research data. This is because the clinical method itself carries with it a subjectivity that cannot be stripped away, leaving "objective data." Nor is this subjectivity really generalizable among psychoanalysts (raters) on a cross-sectional basis. What authentic generalizability it has is between a particular patient and his particular analyst.

This question of inter-rater reliability, borrowed from the behaviorists, is turned from a defensive position to a superb counterattack by Paul Ricoeur in his book *Freud and Philosophy—An Essay on Interpretation*. He argues that the element of subjectivity in the psychoanalytic method is the heart of it, which distinguishes it from purely observational science and is more suited to the comprehension of human experience. I agree, but I am not content with leaving it entirely as a subjective mystery. The hope expressed by David Rapaport that there could be established some "canons of interpretation" (1960, p. 111) is the same hope that has kept us all students and investigators rather than simply practitioners. The mistake has been to confuse the two levels of psychoanalytic interpretation. The deep or structural concepts may well be common to the human mind. The shallow or idiosyncratic interpretations with which most psychoanalysts are involved are not science in the sense of excluding other explanations, but are, rather, heuristic devices for creating or discovering useful meanings. As Selma Fraiberg's youthful patient said to her, "It's telling fortunes backwards" (1959, p. 285).

Arthur Koestler in his book *The Ghost in the Machine* made this distinction of levels in terms of the game of chess. The fixed element is the rules of the game; the variable element is how the game is played. In that sense we must view the usual business of psychoanalysis as an explication of style no more generalizable than good literary criticism but equally valuable in setting a life as a work of art in context. No wonder that psychoanalytic thought has found such a congenial place in the humanities!

How then to conduct the dialogue? Cetainly Freud saw all of psychoanalytic theory as transitional—that is, a cluster of theories based upon observation always moving toward a science rather than fully being one. This openness has been an invitation for many attempts at synthesis between psychoanalytic and other theories of the mind. Stimulating as many of these attempts have been, they have been based on different methodologies and thus can at best provide suggestive parallels or alternative ways of looking at data.

Of these, the biological-neurological theories were perhaps Freud's favorites (even he was not immune to the problem of cross-analogizing from other disciplines). Though we have found fault with his brain model and his neural energy theories, his predictions in this area have been borne out by the demonstrations that biochemical factors are critical in some of the psychoses.

The behavioral school has attempted many parallel constructions of theory. The cumbersome one by Dollard and Miller (1950) has been followed by many more attempts over the years, including the brief suggestion of one by Howard Hunt and myself (1968). These attempts were interesting, but premature. To paraphrase Howard Hunt, in our present state of knowledge we need complementary theories to give the therapist something of a three-dimensional view of the patient's problem—revealing facets that might be missed if one metaphor were used exclusively—but only if they are used *consistently* (just as a hologram requires coherent light from two laser sources to generate a three-dimensional image) (Hunt,

1976b). Rigorous separate development may be the most reliable route to convergence of theories. The radical behaviorists of Skinner's persuasion have attempted to test the limits of the development of a theory based on purely observable events. This has been done by carefully specifying limited goals, finding ways to monitor ongoing behavior, and introducing in-course corrections. The wave of enthusiasm over this apparently simple methodology has already crested and the more sophisticated and responsible behaviorists are moving rapidly from the initial linear paradigm to the behavioral context paradigm, and even to the inclusion of organismic variables (as in William Kessen's comments on the child's version of the operant experiment) (1968). Now that the necessary early parametric studies have been done, the nouns as well as the syntax of behaviorism are being reexamined. The reification of reinforcers is giving way to a study of the reinforcement process (Morse and Kelleher). The notion of response as defined by Grayson-Stadler (an instrument maker) is being expanded similarly into a description of ongoing fluctuations in a complex field. This development suggests that the behavioral school is now capable of adding to and moving on from the phenomenological behaviorism of Merleau-Ponty.

I choose Merleau-Ponty because although his concern is with behavior as a central category, in the tradition of George Herbert Mead, he transcends it by his demonstration of the inadequacy of laboratory notions of linear cause-and-effect relationships. As John Wild writes in his introduction to Merleau-Ponty's *The Structure of Behavior*:

> Human behavior is neither a series of blind reactions to external "stimuli" nor the projection of acts which are motivated by the pure ideas of a disembodied, worldless mind. It is neither exclusively subjective nor exclusively objective, but a dialectical interchange between man and the world, which cannot be adequately expressed in traditional causal terms. It is a circular dialectic in which the independent beings of the life-field, already selected by the structure of the human body, exert a further selective operation on this body's acts. It is out of this dialectical interchange that human meanings emerge. These meanings are neither passively assimilated from an external, cosmic order that is already fixed and established, as the realists have imagined, nor constructed *de novo* by a creative mind, as the idealists have supposed.
>
> Merleau-Ponty's account of the lived body is marked by a high degree of both perceptiveness and originality. This body, as I live it from the inside, is quite different from the objective body which is observed, though each perspective is legitimate and the two overlap at certain vital points, which introduces an essential ambiguity into the whole situation of man. He is both a being among other beings in the world, and at the same time an originating source of the whole world order in which he exists.

From this quote one can see that Merleau-Ponty's phenomenological behaviorism leads back to the issues of meaning and the underlying structures of meaning. As the radical behaviorists move toward the inevitable statements about more or less enduring patterns of man's organization (they have now begun to consider such behaviors as competitiveness), they are approaching a depth-interpretive or structural point of view. There is a convergence toward dialogue. What Merleau-Ponty lacks and what they, too, need is a science of structure.

It might be well here to try to define the structural point of view. The structuralists—Piaget, Lévi-Strauss, Chomsky, and Lacan (see Piaget, 1970; Leach, 1970; Chomsky, 1967; Lacan, 1968), to name a few—have the conviction that underlying all human behavior and mental functioning (individual as well as social and cultural) are characteristic and general structures that define the possibilities and limits of man's mind. Some of them go so far as to believe that these structures are biologically innate and develop to the extent that a given culture elicits them. They further believe that the access route to the analysis of these structures is through language in its broadest sense, because they all agree that the specifically human environment is neither biological nor social but linguistic. Piaget studies cognition, Lévi-Strauss the myths of primitive societies, Chomsky the acquisition of verbal language, Lacan the analytic situation, but all are seeking to find canons of interpretation. They tend to use mathematics in a way that to me seems pseudo-precise and distracting, but the solutions offered are significant and generalize across the group.

For instance, the notion that man thinks in dichotomies and discriminates by contrast is a ubiquitous finding. That the child can conceive of a pair before he can conceive of an individual is certainly a ubiquitous finding with fascinating implications.

This notion of infrastructure, the general characteristics beneath the dream or the fantasy of the individual, was very much in Freud's mind, and early attempts at psychoanalytic social anthropology came to grief not because the notion of structures was wrong but because of confusion between the two levels of interpretation; attempts were made to universalize an explicit myth rather than to look for its transformations in disparate forms. Incest taboos, for instance, seem to be universal but exist in different cultures in a variety of disguises. Mental mechanisms such as displacement and condensation certainly play a large part in the structuralist studies of metaphor and metonymy. We might say that the *rules* of primary-process thought have a greater degree of generalizability than the content.

In our new psychiatry there is a place for psychoanalytic investigation and teaching distinct from biologizing and adopting the methodology of other groups; we should move toward the goal of finding out more about both the general and individual linguistic structures of the mind that the psychoanalytic method is uniquely designed to study. Yet, it must be clear that for training purposes the individual or idiosyncratic aspect is really more important. I think it was Oscar Wilde who commented that people who insist on going deep are really shallow because they pursue generalities—that those who pursue the shallower patterns of an individual life achieve true depth in comprehending another person. (I can't find the reference for that; if he didn't say it he should have.) If only our individual acts were reliably clothed in meaning or if they were simply operant. It would be so much easier. The psychoanalytic method does not in that sense reveal reality. It does seek to rationalize events so that we may seem more whole and consistent. We don't really know if this thinking is pre hoc, post hoc, or ad hoc. Yet this study of the attachment of fantasy-meaning to events in reality is important. We need to know it and teach it. It illuminates mystery, and not all of life's mysteries can be reduced to problems, any more than we should make mysteries out of the problems. Such a contribution is necessary but no longer sufficient for our young psychiatrists in training. What we need is the psychoanalysts' contribution to our attempts at developing a more comprehensive view, a synthesis of what we know for fairly sure about psychobiological malfunctioning and its treatment.

For those who have forgotten the investigative intent of clinical psychoanalysis and tend to see the theoretically desired outcome as proven achievement, it would be difficult to join in the venture of producing a new breed of psychotherapist for the new psychiatry. For others, it represents an opportunity not to be missed.

The new psychotherapist would stay close to the data of experience, be willing to report experiments in technique, and be broadly trained in psychoanalysis, behavioral analysis, and psychopharmacology. He would have to forge a new language. William Butler Yeats said, "I have noticed that all those who speak the thoughts of many, speak confidently, while those who speak their own are hesitating and timid, as though they spoke out of a mind and body grown sensitive to the edge of bewilderment among many impressions" (1961, p. 317). Jerome Frank has started to create that common language with words such as demoralization, hope, emotional arousal, and mastery. These are words very close to the fabric of experience.

It is easier to speak in the language of a theory than to speak about what one actually does. I say that because I have the notion that our theories are always purer than our practice, since they represent extrapolations from type situations that the individual case never quite fits. Often our theories are confined to what the therapist considers to be "the essential ingredient." In the case of Wolpe this is "systematic desensitization," in the case of psychoanalytically oriented therapists it is "interpretation," but in either case all of the devices of psychotherapy are present and in operation as well. We call them nonspecific, but I am inclined to agree with Frank that it might be more accurate to call them unspecified (1961).

If we think of patients as being distributed on a normal curve between extremes of high and low expectant trust, and if we place directive theories at the high end and evocative at the low end, we must recognize that the bulk of our patient population falls somewhere in between. In 1959, Ian Stevenson suggested this in his clinical paper, "Direct Instigation of Behavioral Changes in Psychotherapy." For instance, one procedure for treating phobia involved consideration of the patient's psychic reality while manipulating the patient's behavior in relation to reality. What was refreshing about this procedure was that it had no essential ingredient other than defining the task of therapy as the creation of a situation in which the patient learns to reduce his own anxiety. It also used graded structure in that problems were identified which could be surmounted sequentially so that both patient and doctor experienced the gratification of continuing success.

Albert Szent-Györgyi, in an article in Science (1964) commenting on the teaching of science, said that even though we have been finding a great number of new facts, teaching should actually become simpler as we begin to see meaningful integrations that cut across the different disciplines. It is as though we have gone through a period of differentiating the equations and now we can begin to assemble the integrals.

It is my view that in our field of endeavor the most exciting interface between behavior analysis and psychoanalysis is the topic of mental events, and how these mediational behaviors relate to behavioral events (Dyrud, 1971). From what has gone before it must be apparent that I see this as a mystery not yet reduced to a problem in either paradigm. Nor do I see evidence of the crucial experiment appearing from either side. If there is satisfaction with either paradigm there can only be a clash of belief systems. Actually, we have no systematic way of characterizing the relationship among language, mental events, and behavior, but it is a critical feature of our dialogue.

To the uncaptive mind the easy part of this dialogue involves a systematization of potentially common awareness rather than the reconciliation of real differences. This is not syncretism but rather making over what is covert in either system of therapy. For us psychoanalysts this means describing what one does in steps one through sixteen of the treatment process, the establishment of the hierarchy of habits which make a good patient, as well as studying the patient's style of life, his "semantics of desire" (Ricoeur, 1970). Psychoanalysts are all aware that different strategies are required at different stages of treatment in order to achieve the desired effects. One does analysis from time to time when one can. As my teacher Lewis Hill used to say, "I can analyze a person in a month, but sometimes it takes me two or three years to get him in shape for it."

For the behaviorists, on the other hand, this dialogue requires some greater recognition of the "word made flesh." That is to say, that meaningful behavior has a present reinforcement reality which may be most appropriate to work with, but in addition it has a dimension of historical signification and enacted meaning that at times may be the overriding consideration, as in the case of Howard Hunt's case report (1976a) of the school-phobic retarded child whose family was willing to consider school phobia as a problem, but totally unwilling to see the retardation.

A technique "empty of theory," such as radical behaviorism purports to be, runs the risk of bringing to bear upon the patient the therapist's unexamined fantasy life. His values, his view of the nature of man, must be simply trusted. In the first flush of enthusiasm that goes with acquiring a new technique, omnipotent fantasies are almost inevitably aroused. In fact, this unbridled optimism must have a major suggestive influence on the patient. The question of what the fallback position will be when failures are encountered must be considered.

There is precedent for an attempt to achieve a common language. Around the same time that Freud was doing his early writing about the inner life of man, Charles Peirce was laying the foundation of pragmatism and operationalism here in America. His definition of the subject as the incarnation of the predicate (Peirce, Papers) preceded George Herbert Mead's development of his concept of the act as the fundamental operational concept in psychodynamic thinking (1934). David Levy

(1962) expanded the notion of "the act" to include physiological events and mental events, thus using psychoanalysis to close the purse seine. Mind was seen as metaphor for the experiencing, remembering, behaving self that is body. This enterprise failed, or rather faded away, because it lacked the data base that an operant technology could have contributed. Now in this new intellectual climate, the era of competing methodological systems is gradually giving way to a recognition that psychotherapy research involves the study of events rather than theories.

We are now able to gain some agreement on the tasks to which different personality types must apply themselves. For instance, when we look at achieving the feeling of well-being as a criterion problem that could be defined as performing well under favorable circumstances, we recognize that different people have different problem-solving styles—i.e., operant, gestalt, trial and error—but we can generalize about their relative success or lack of it in moving toward a defined goal. We can also (and do as some behaviorists do) put greater emphasis on the acquisition of more adequate performances and the discrimination of favorable circumstances under which these performances take place. We find that hysterics who improve in treatment have, in fact, received what they need—that is, discrimination training. They simply start with too few conceptual categories for affect and experience in order to modulate their responses. Obsessionals, on the other hand, need to be catapulted into action. Schizophrenics who respond well have received unambiguous cuing that permits them to track better. Ambiguous cuing has been clearly demonstrated to increase schizophrenic confusion.

Thus, an event orientation seems essential in finding our way through the thicket of patient and therapist types to an evaluation of the soundness of a particular procedure with a particular patient. This is easier for the therapist with training in several schools of thought, who brings to his practice a wide variety of behaviors that add richness to the metaphor of whatever theoretical system with which he is identifying his work. We might feel sorry about the impoverishment of the hypothetical student trained and educated in only one discipline who encounters a patient or series of patients who do not fit his system. The reason I stress an event-oriented language is that it implies bringing together theories generated from special situations and relatively homogenous populations, to see if they can be melded into a system for comprehending the more heterogenous population found in the bell of our distribution curve.

CONCLUSION

I suggest that we move toward an event-oriented common language of treatment as a way of pooling our resources, so that our effectiveness as therapists may be advanced. At the same time, in the training of new psychiatrists we must leave out no aspect of our art or science. What we know for sure would not alone produce a competent psychiatrist. Normative training in the role is as important as ever. We must remember that the crucial experiment is almost as rare in science as it is in religion. Progress is finding a more useful paradigm. We must recognize that our theories are grids cast across the surface of life and their "laws" are the lawfulness of their own logic. Perhaps man is not as rational as behaviorists would have him, nor as irrational as the psychoanalyst would have him. In this sense our theories are all incomplete. It is essential to master at least one so that its limitations may become clear and we may then set about acquiring another. At present it appears better to have two theories to apply to an event than only one, and we as teachers of the new psychiatry must take as our task the integration of our sciences, emergent as they are, with practice as it must be taught.

At bottom the whole Weltanschauung of the moderns involves the illusion that the so-called laws of nature are explanations of natural phenomena.
In this way they stop short at the laws of nature as at something impregnable as men of former times did at God or Fate.
And both are right and wrong. The older ones are indeed clearer in the sense that they acknowledge a clear terminus, while with the new system it is supposed to look as if everything had a foundation. [Wittgenstein, 1969]

REFERENCES

Becker, E. "The Tragic Paradox of Albion Small and American Social Science," in *The Lost Science of Man*; Braziller, 1971.

Budzynski, T. H. "Biofeedback Procedures in the Clinic," *Seminars in Psychiatry* (1973) 5:537–547.

Chomsky, N. *Syntactic Structures*; The Hague: Mouton, 1967.

Dollard, J., and Miller, N. *Personality and Psychotherapy*; McGraw-Hill, 1950.

Dyrud, J. E. "Behavior Analysis, Mental Events, and Psychoanalysis," in J. Masserman (Ed.) *Science and Psychoanalysis*, Vol. 18; Grune & Stratton, 1971.

Eliot, T. S. "A Commentary," *Criterion*, April 1932.

Fraiberg, S. H. *The Magic Years*; Scribner's, 1959.

Frank, J. D. *Persuasion and Healing*; Johns Hopkins Univ. Press, 1961.

Hunt, H. and Dyrud, J. E. "Commentary on Behavior Therapy," in *Research in Psychotherapy*, Vol. 3; Amer. Psychol. Assn., 1968.

Hunt, H. "Behavioral Therapy for Adults," in D.X. Freedman and J.E. Dyrud (Eds.), *Amer. Handbook of Psychiatry*, Vol. 5; Basic Books, 1976.(a)

Hunt, H. "Behavioral Perspectives in the Treatment of Borderline Patients," Menninger Conference on Borderline Patients, March 1976, in press. (b)

Kessen, W. "The Construction and Selection of Environments," in D. C. Glass (Ed.), *Environmental Influences*; Rockefeller Univ. Press and Russell Sage Found., 1968.

Koestler, A. *The Ghost in the Machine*; Macmillan, 1968.

Lacan, J. *The Language of the Self*; Johns Hopkins Univ. Press, 1968.

Lazarus, A. A. "Where Do Behavior Therapists Take Their Troubles?," *Psychol. Reports* (1971) 28:349–350.

Leach, E. *Claude Levi-Strauss*; London: Fontana Books, 1970.

Levy, D. "The Act as a Unit," *Psychiatry* (1962) 25:295–314.

Mead, G. H. *Mind, Self and Society*; Univ. of Chicago Press, 1934.

Meltzer, H. Y., and Moline, R. "Muscle Abnormalities in Acute Psychoses," *Arch. Gen. Psychiatry* (1970) 23:481–491.

Merleau-Ponty, M. *The Structure of Behavior*; Beacon Press, 1963.

Meyer, A. "Dealing with Mental Diseases," *The Collected Papers of Adolf Meyer*, Vol. 4; Johns Hopkins Univ. Press, 1952.

Morse, W. H., and Kelleher, R. T. "Determinants of Reinforcement and Punishment," in W. K. Honig and J. E. R. Staddon (Eds.), *Operant Behavior*, Vol. 2; Appleton-Century-Crofts, in press.

Orne, M. T. "Psychotherapy in Contemporary America: Its Development and Context," In D. X. Freedman and J. E. Dyrud (Eds.), *Amer. Handbook of Psychiatry*, Vol. 5; Basic Books, 1976.

Peirce, C. The Papers of Charles Peirce; Harvard Univ. Microreproduction Service.

Piaget, J. *Structuralism*; Basic Books, 1970.

Psychiatric Annals, Vol. 4, No. 10, Oct. 1974.

Rapaport, D. "The Evidence for the System," in *The Structure of Psychoanalytic Theory*, *Psychol. Issues* (1960) Vol. 2, No. 2, Monogr. 6.

Ricoeur, P. *Freud and Philosophy*; Yale Univ., 1970.

Skinner, B. F. *Cumulative Record*; Appleton-Century-Crofts, 1961.

Stevenson, I. "Direct Investigation of Behavioral Changes in Psychotherapy," *Arch. Gen. Psychiatry* (1959) 1:99–107.

Szent-Györgyi, A. "Teaching and the Expanding Knowledge," *Science* (1964) 146:1278–1279.

Wittgenstein, L. *Notebooks 1914–1916*; London: Blackwell, 1969.

Yeats, W. B. "J. M. Synge and the Ireland of His Time," *Essays and Introductions*; Macmillan, 1961.

5

Psychiatry: Science, Meaning and Purpose

PAUL E. BEBBINGTON

The Gods did not reveal, from the beginning, all things to us; but in the course of time, through seeking we may learn, and know things better.

Xenophanes

INTRODUCTION

In this paper it is proposed to examine the nature of what the psychiatrist does in the clinical situation and how this relates to recently disseminated ideas on the appropriate activity of the scientist. This will involve consideration of the status of so-called causal explanation and psychological understanding and the relation between them. The type of description necessary to the nature of man as a purposive being will be examined. Psychoanalytic theory has been attacked for its non-scientific nature and has been defended as a psychology of meaning and as a mode of description appropriate to a teleological system. There is, therefore, both a question of the matter to which the tenets of psychoanalysis have been applied and a question of the nature of the answers it gives. An evaluation of this debate will serve to illuminate the general nature of the activity of psychiatrists, both in an empirical and in a normative sense.

Karl Popper and the Demarcation of Science

The work of Karl Popper has had an increasing influence on the thinking of psychiatrists (e.g. Lewis, 1958; Slater, 1975; Birley, 1975), as it has influenced workers in other fields (Magee, 1973). This is appropriate, as Popper's ideas on the nature of scientific activity received an admitted impetus from his work with Alfred Adler in

Reprinted by permission from *The British Journal of Psychiatry*, 130 (March 1978), 222–228.

Vienna and the difficulties he saw in regarding the hypothesizing activities of the Adlerians and Freudians in the same light as those, for instance, of Einstein (Popper, 1963). The important epistemological problem for Popper is that of the growth of knowledge, and, as he says (Popper, 1959, p 18), 'a little reflection will show that most problems connected with the growth of our knowledge must necessarily transcend any study which is confined to commonsense knowledge as opposed to scientific knowledge'. He is concerned, then, to distinguish commonsense knowledge and scientific knowledge, the problem of 'demarcation', or 'Kant's problem' as Popper calls it. In doing this, Popper was applying himself to a question of concern to the Vienna Circle in general, but his approach was radically different from the logical positivism of the other members. As he says, positivists usually interpret the problem of demarcation in a naturalistic way: 'they believe they have to discover a difference, existing in the nature of things, between empirical science on one hand and metaphysics on the other.' To do this, the philosophers of the Vienna Circle attempted to find a way in which all non-scientific statements could be shown to be meaningless. Popper avoids this difficulty: he does not deny that knowledge exists which is non-scientific but nonetheless meaningful. 'I wish to distinguish sharply between "objective science" on the one hand and "our knowledge" on the other' (Popper, 1959, p 98). He regards his demarcation as being between science and non-science and not between science and meaninglessness. This demarcation is not an empirical statement but a *conventional* one, involving a value judgement: 'I define science thus.'

Popper's demarcation arises from his consideration of the problem of the inductive gap: how many white swans must we see before we conclude 'all swans are white'; how much confirmation confirms a scientific theory. Popper regards this not as a logical conundrum but as a psychological one relating to the process of conviction. We can, however, test hypotheses in a logical way if we attempt not to confirm but to *falsify* them. If we find *one* black swan we can refute the statement 'all swans are white' using the propositions of *deductive* logic. Hence, Popper adopts refutability as the criterion of a scientific hypothesis and the objective of science is to produce low-probability statements which are subjected to all conceivable tests of refutation. 'Not for nothing do we call the laws of nature "laws". The more they prohibit the more they say' (Popper, 1959).

Popper's statements, as he says, are essentially normative. Kuhn (1971) has criticized Popper on the basis that we do in fact hold on to theories which we know fit their data imperfectly; in other words, refutation is not apparently grounds for rejection. If this is so, says Kuhn, Popper is obliged to say what *degree* of misfit is a criterion for rejection. He feels this places as much difficulty in the way of Popperian demarcation as arises for the various probabilistic verification proposals for overcoming the problem of induction. However, the writer would feel that this criticism raises a problem of the psychology of theory acceptability which would not overconcern Popper. He would still emphasize that scientific activity should seek refutation, even if we do not, for reasons of our own, follow up our findings in a perfectly logical way.

Popper himself has pointed out that psychoanalytic theory is couched in terms which are irrefutable. 'It was precisely this fact—that they always fitted, that they were always confirmed—which in the eyes of their admirers constituted the strongest argument in favour of these theories. It began to dawn on me that this apparent strength was in fact their weakness' (Popper, 1963).

This claim has been taken up by others (e.g. Medawar, 1969; Cioffi, 1970; Slater, 1975) and has been the point of departure of other authors in defence of psychoanalytic theory (Farrell, 1970a, 1970b; Rycroft, 1968). Popper (1963) himself is of the opinion that psychoanalytic theories 'describe some facts, but in the manner of myths. They contain most interesting psychological suggestions but not in testable form'. At the same time he feels such pre-scientific myths may be developed and become testable. In their present form they cannot claim to be *backed* by empirical evidence in the scientific sense—although they 'may easily be, in some genetic sense, the result of observation'. Hence, Popper most certainly does not deny some empirical content to psychoanalytic theory. Farrell (1970a), however, disagrees with the term 'myth'. 'If psychoanalytic theory were a myth, it would presumably be a closed story. But this is just what it is not.' Although we observe that Popper does not regard a myth as necessarily static, there is some cogency in Farrell's asseveration that psychoanalytic theory does progress, as for instance in the later departure of ego psychology, and that this progression bears some relation to observation. However, it is clear that this progression does not involve a formal methodology of test by the seeking of refutation. Farrell goes on, unfortunately, to make statements in justification of psychoanalytic theory which are patently unacceptable; for instance 'it is also the case that (clinical psychoanalytic material) suggests that we should use the theory to talk about it'. This is justification by conviction rather than by scientific method. Farrell also feels that there are grounds for saying that the theory is at least an approximation to the truth 'because of the fertility of its application to the humanities'.

Cioffi (1970), in a debate with Farrell (1970b) which Slater (1975) describes as 'animated' but which might better be characterized as acerbic, offers the most detailed analysis of the irrefutability of Freudian theory in terms of Freud's own writings. He states 'a pseudoscience is not constituted merely by formally defective theses but by methodologically defective procedures' and goes as far as to say 'there are a host of peculiarities of psychoanalytic theory and practice which are apparently gratuitous but which can be understood . . . as manifestations of the same impulse: the need to avoid refutation'.

Although the debate continues about demarcation, it tends to be very much a rearguard action by the proponents of psychoanalytic theory. Some, however, have offered justifications which bypass this argument. Rycroft (1968) claims that the debate is ill-founded and that the objective of psychoanalytic theory is not causal explanation but an attempt at understanding: 'the procedure (Freud) engaged in was not the scientific one of elucidating causes but the semantic one of making sense of it.' This reiterates the views of Karl Jaspers and we must now turn to examine these.

Karl Jaspers. Causality and meaning

Jaspers himself seems to have been surprised at the effect of his 1913 article (Jaspers,

1974) and of his *General Psychopathology* published in same year (Jaspers, 1963). 'All I had done was to link psychiatric reality with the traditional humanities.' However, his distinction between causal explanation and understanding was seminal.

'In the natural sciences we find causal connections *only*, but in psychology our bent for knowledge is satisfied with the comprehension of quite a different sort of connection. Psychic events "emerge" out of each other in a way which we understand. Attacked people become angry and spring to the defence, etc' (Jaspers, 1963).

For Jaspers, these meaningful connections are merely *analogous* with 'real' causal connections. Understanding is something immediate and irreducible and, he claims, not acquired inductively by experience.

Hence 'the meaningful connections of psychological events have also been called "causality from the inside" and this term has characterized the unbridgeable gulf which exists between this which can be called "causal" only as an analogy and the real causal connections, the "causality from outside"' (Jaspers, 1974). Further, 'the rules of causality are obtained inductively and culminate in theories about what lies at the root of the given reality. Particular cases are then subsumed under them. Genetically understandable connections, however, are ideal, typical connections; they are self-evident and not inductively obtained. Because we note the frequency of a meaningful connection, this does not mean the meaningful connection becomes the rule' (Jaspers, 1963).

Jaspers does not make the mistake that psychic events are not open to causal explanation. However, he implies that psychic events may only be effects and that causation has to be 'extraconscious'. Attempts to explain a concrete effect in terms of a psychic cause, as in hysteria for example, Jaspers terms 'pseudo-understanding'.

Jaspers claimed that Freud's work is a psychology of meaning and not of causal explanation 'as Freud thinks'. He criticizes the tenet of psychological determinism: 'However, it is only the postulate of unlimited causality, not the postulate of unlimited meaningfulness which is justifiable' (Jaspers, 1974).

One can see that the separation which Jaspers has effected between causality and meaning might well be received thankfully by those concerned to protect psycho-analysis from the Popperians. But we are obliged not to accept this *ex cathedra*.

Firstly, there are inconsistencies in what Jaspers himself says about the distinction. For instance, he talks of extending our understanding 'to remote connections which at first sight perhaps seem incomprehensible' (Jaspers, 1963). In this he allows the importance of hypothetical considerations in generating understanding, which belies the self-evidence of genetically understandable connections. Moreover, one could argue that self-evidence is in fact the belief we have in those commonsense models of the mind which to some degree we all possess. Further, his concept of interpretation (the imaginitive leap necessary to encompass understanding when not all relevant data are available) suggests that understanding is quantitatively related to data, which again belies self-evidence.

Secondly, the appeal to the metaphysical concept of 'ideal types' in order to justify the distinction between psychic and causal connections is not acceptable to the writer. Again, the distinction does imply a reductionist point of view which would now be regarded as old-fashioned (Jessor, 1958). This is best exemplified by Jaspers' insistence that causal links can only proceed *up* the hierarchy of concepts.

Psychoanalytic theorists would not be put off by the role of hypotheses in generating understanding. However, this is an admission which to the present writer seems to point to a different interpretation of Jaspers' dichotomy, for if hypotheses can generate understanding, why cannot all hypotheses do so? And if all hypotheses do so, are there alternatives to psychoanalytic theory in our understanding of psychic events? Once we have come this far, we are obliged to regard Jaspers' distinction in another light, for if understanding is something which attaches to theories it may be that there is no psychology of meaning separate from theories. Looked at in this way, psychological theories cease to be in a different category from other scientific theories. For, as we shall demonstrate, understanding is an aspect of meaning which attaches to all theory. Meaning contains two elements, namely import and conviction. Jaspers' *Verstehen* is an example of the latter—we have conviction of the validity of a psychic connection when we understand it empathically. The role of conviction in non-psychological theories has been elaborated by a number of writers. Hence, Einstein, in his address on Max Planck's 60th birthday (quoted in Popper, 1959), talks of 'the search for those highly universal laws from which a picture of the world can be obtained by pure deduction.' He goes on: 'there is no logical path leading to these...laws. They can only be reached by intuition and empathy.'

Popper himself (1959) has this to say in describing the importance of conviction to both logic and science: 'Yet whether statements of logic are in question or statements of empirical science, I think the answer is the same: "our knowledge, which may be described vaguely as a system of dispositions and which may be of concern to psychology, may in both cases be linked with feelings of belief or conviction: in the one case, perhaps with a feeling of being compelled to think in a certain way, in the other with that of perceptual reassurance."' Medawar claims for both myths and science the necessity of 'the property of being believable in'. It is of interest that Lewis (1949), in his address to the British Institute of Philosophy, took as his subject the psychological problem of conviction and its relation to philosophical activity.

Kuhn (1971), however, has made a concept of scientific theorizing as a language central to his explanation of scientific revolutions. He claims 'an apparently arbitrary element, compounded of personal and historical accident, is always a formative ingredient of the beliefs espoused by a given scientific community at a given time'. 'Theory must be chosen for reasons that are ultimately personal and subjective.' Some sort of mystical apperception is responsible for the decision actually reached. The choice between Kuhn's 'paradigms', then, rests not merely upon their causally interpretative qualities but upon conviction of meaningfulness. This leads to a problem of translation between paradigms: 'to translate a theory or world view into one's own language is not to make it one's own. For that one must go native, discover that one is thinking and working in, not simply translating out of, a language that was previously foreign.' Now this sounds remarkably like the process of empathic understanding as described by Jaspers. The writer is led to conclude that this process is not qualitatively different when applied to persons or to causal theories in the physical sciences. The implication is that we need not reject the language of causal theories when approaching the problem of understanding a patient. However, before we go on to talk of this possibility we must turn our attention to a further argument in support of non-scientific psychoanalytic theory.

Causality and purposive systems

A distinction between mechanism and meaning is the cardinal point of Sir Denis Hill's Ernest Jones Lecture of 1970. He uses this to separate simple mechanistic systems from the teleological character of human activity. Hill (1970) claims that models of the mind are not amenable to the type of scientific testing required by Popper because of (1) the nature of the perception involved and (2) the fact that they refer to a purposive system. It is not clear that these are in fact separate arguments, as Hill employs the word 'meaning' in three different uses without this being readily apparent.

Now the first argument is a reiteration of Jaspers and lays stress on the differentiating value of the act of identification involved in setting up models of understanding. Hence 'Psychic reality which cannot be directly perceived through the physical senses is only directly experienced in the self, but can be communicated by language and can be inferred by observation. Physical reality can only be perceived through the senses.' He adds 'we can only know "others on the inside" by an act of identification; we can only know them "on the outside" by acts of perception. The former is a method entirely absent from the physical sciences, the latter is their only method'. He says of Medawar 'he is speaking of physical science and the methods at its disposal. The scientific method . . . is dependent upon observation of what is perceptible through the senses . . . it cannot from its nature be used to disprove what is not so perceptible'. As might be expected, the writer would argue that our perception of the physical world is an interpretation relating to our meaningful models of it, that no one can perceive directly someone else's psychic reality, and that our grasp of it is based on the interaction of our sense data and our models of the mind. Hence, both the outside world and the psychic realities of others are perceived 'in the self' and through our senses.

The second line of argument uses two further separate uses of the word 'meaning'—behaviour has meaning in the sense that it is goal-directed and goal-perceptive. Hill (1970) proceeds as follows: 'the answers which scientific activity provides are always to questions as to "how things occur" and not answers to questions "why things occur". The latter are questions peculiar to human experience and are of a different order of abstraction. The first is concerned with mechanism: the second with meaning.' Now it is certain that there is a difference between a linear mechanistic system and a teleological system involving feedback. However, it is a long way from the conclusion that 'the methods of science are only applicable to questions of the first kind', and it seems hardly tenable that 'why things occur' should be a question peculiar to human experience. Hill continues, 'If this is so, psychoanalysis should admit to being a causal theory in the teleological sense rather than in the mechanistic sense, and the hypothetico-deductive model is not logically applicable, except in a very limited sense.' Unfortunately, Hill does not expand in detail what is meant by 'a very limited sense'.

The debate concerning the appropriate mode of description of teleological systems has involved others (Toulmin, 1970; Peters, 1970; Taylor, 1970; Borger, 1970; Malcolm, 1968). In sense, as Taylor (1970) points out, the abstraction of purposive descriptions from the methodology of science is as much an activity of behaviourists as it is of defenders of psychoanalysis. For they have been concerned to attempt explanations of goal-directed behaviour purely in the linear linking of events, in other words to explain purposive behaviour in terms of controlling antecedents. Taylor (1970) claims 'we can only derive the thesis of mechanism if, like most theorists of the behaviourist persuasion, we assume it beforehand . . . the *a priori* argument is shown to be bogus'. Pure behaviourists, he says, seek to explain goal-directed behaviour in terms of 'a non-teleological antecedent, that is, one which makes no mention of that property of the response which is its being appropriate, that is, required for the goal in question'. As Borger (1970) says, the distinction between teleological and non-teleological antecedents is difficult to specify.

There seems really to be some confusion between system-types and methodology. If by mechanism we are merely referring to systems which are not goal-directed, this is solely a description of a system type. We may, however, mean by mechanism a methodological decison that we should attempt to describe all natural systems in terms of causally related antecedents in a way which would eliminate the possibility of involving a description of feedback and corrective action. Now, as Borger (1970) points out, this reflects a limited view of mechanism, a view which Hill (1970) shares. A wide view of mechanism might be said to be any description which is compatible with methodological adherence to the principle of causality. Now it is perfectly possible to specify the function or 'ground plan' of a goal-directed system involving feedback in a manner so compatible, whether the system be a simple thermostat or the complex purposive behaviour of animals and humans. It would seem that Hill is confusing these two views of mechanism when he claims that scientific methodology is inappropriate to purposive systems. The present author would aver that there is nothing idiosyncratic about goal-directed systems which precludes us from attempting a causal explanation in testable terms, and that an explanation in teleological terms of, for instance, feedback and corrective action need not in principle evade refutation. Hence we conclude that Hill's (1970) contention that 'the hypothetico-deductive method is not logically applicable' to purposive human behaviour is not supportable.

Epistemology and the psychiatric formulation

It appears possible that the origin of the particular methodology of psychoanalysis and the problems arising from it derive from its concern with the individual patient. The general psychiatrist is likewise involved with the individual patient, and his knowledge and conjectures about the patient are summed up in a formulation which is the basis for therapeutic intervention. This formulation may use the language of science at different levels—at a biochemical and neurophysiological level and at a psychological level. It may involve concepts derived from psychoanalysis and from scientific psychology. It will also use commonsense concepts. These concepts together make up the language of the psychiatrist, and the formulation is an attempt at a global understanding of the patient. We will conclude this essay with a brief consideration of how this process relates to the process of scientific investigation and how the 'knowledge' of the patient relates to scientific knowledge. Hill (1970) points out the analogy of the two processes: 'Every clinician, psychoanalyst or scientist approaches a new patient or a new problem by setting up some provisional hypothesis . . . which gets progressively modified as a result of the process of interaction between the observer and the object'. Lewis (1958), however, points out, of the individual, 'Because he is unique and extremely complicated, he does not seem wholly catchable within the scientific net.' The writer would argue that the formulation is a complicated entity of statements of differing epistemological value and this is why it differs from the mere setting up of scientific hypotheses. The first element in the procedure is one of the naming of phenomena—the provision of statements like 'this is an example of . . .'. This is the equivalent of the observation of basic data, and such statements can only be *objectified* by consensus. We may not necessarily use these data except to promote our understanding, and we may then be using the language of science merely as that.

Some statements we make may take the form of 'existential statements' (Popper, 1959), e.g. 'there is a psychogenic cause for this pain'—these statements differ from hypotheses in being verifiable but not falsifiable.

Further statements are in the form of scientific hypotheses, e.g. 'this is the psychogenic cause for this pain'. Such statements are in principle refutable. In practice this may not be possible, and the statements then become an effort at understanding.

This complicated procedure of formulation is psychologically necessary to the work of the psychiatrist. It derives its practical value from the work of science but it is not purely a scientific process. When it is mistaken for such there is a danger that the knowledge so derived may be regarded as scientifically valid without critical evaluation. But although the conjecture arising from the idiographic study of the individual may lead to valid knowledge it can only do so by a collateral process of scientific investigation.

Science and psychiatry

We have argued in favour of Popper's thesis that the growth of knowledge is a function of the observation of error, and its extension that the most effective methodology of science is that which sets up hypotheses and seeks to refute them. This is a methodology which has been contested in its applicability to psychiatry. We have examined and rejected the argument that the concept of understanding necessarily encompasses knowledge which is not amenable to this scientific method. Likewise, we have not been convinced that the nature of the system of human activity necessarily prevents its application. The word 'necessarily' is of importance in these two preceding sentences: for our arguments all devolve on a methodological issue—if we can delineate that method which renders our knowledge as sure as possible, then should we not stipulate that this is the method we should use, whatever practical difficuties may hinder us? There are, of course, other methodologies—the methodology of history is of critical appraisal of mutual and internal consistency of sources (Popper, 1963)—and some have advocated these (e.g. Farrell, 1970a). But where there are questions of the appropriate methodology, we should take the best.

It seems likely that the application of the principle of refutability to psychoanalysis would involve major change in the form of the theory. Local rather than global propositions would be tested, and it might seem appropriate to jettison whole 'metapsychological propositions' (Rapaport and Gill, 1959), as indeed Bowlby (1969) has done with libido theory. Although, as Slater (1975) emphasizes, this represents an enormous task, the author would feel that if the insights afforded by the conjectures of psychoanalysis are to be of full value they must be subject to test.

REFERENCES

Birley, J. L. T. (1975) The history of psychiatry as the history of an art. *British Journal of Psychiatry*, **127**, 393–400.
Borger, R. (1970) The explanation of purposive behaviour: comment. In *Explanation in the Behavioural Sciences* (eds R. Borger and F. Cioffi). Cambridge University Press.
Bowlby, John (1969) *Attachment and Loss. Vol I. Attachment*. London: Hogarth.
Cioffi, F. (1970) Freud and the idea of a pseudoscience. In *Explanation in the Behavioural Sciences* (eds R. Borger and F. Cioffi). Cambridge University Press.
Farrell, B. A. (1970a) Psychoanalytic theory. In *Freud and Psychology* (eds S. G. M. Lee and M. Herbert). Harmondsworth, Middlesex: Penguin Books.
_____ (1970b) Psychoanalysis: the method. In *Explanation in the Behavioural Sciences* (eds R. Borger and F. Cioffi). Cambridge University Press.
Hill, D. (1970) On the contribution of psychoanalysis to psychiatry: mechanism and meaning. *British Journal of Psychiatry*, **117**, 609–15.
Jaspers, K. (1963) *General Psychopathology*. Translated from the German 7th edition by Hoenig, J. and Hamilton, M. A. Manchester University Press.
_____ (1974) 'Causal and meaningful' connections between life history and psychosis. In *Themes and Variations in European Psychiatry* (eds S. R. Hirsch and M. Shepherd). Bristol: John Wright & Sons.
Jessor, R. (1958) The problem of reductionism in psychology. *Psychological Review*, **65**, 170–8.
Kuhn, T. S. (1971) *The Structure of Scientific Revolutions*. 2nd Edition. University of Chicago Press.
Lewis, A. J. (1949) Philosophy and psychiatry. *Philosophy*, **24**, 99–117.
_____ (1958) Between guesswork and certainty in psychiatry. *Lancet i*, 171–5 and 227–30.
Magee, B. (1973) *Popper*. London: Fontana, William Collins & Co.
Malcolm, M. (1968) The conceivability of mechanism. *Philosophical Review*, **77**, 45–72.
Medawar, P. B. (1969) Science and literature. *Encounter*, **32**, 15–23.
Peters, R. S. (1970) Reasons and causes: comment. In *Explanation in the Behavioural Sciences* (eds R. Borger and F. Cioffi). Cambridge University Press.
Popper, K. R. (1959) *The Logic of Scientific Discovery*. London: Hutchinson & Co.
_____ (1963) *Conjectures and Refutations*. London: Routledge and Kegan Paul.
Rapaport, D. & Gill, M. M. (1959) The points of view and assumptions of metapsychology. *International Journal of Psychoanalysis*, **40**, 153–62.
Rycroft, C. (1968) Causes and meaning. In *Psychoanalysis Observed* (ed. C. Rycroft). Harmondsworth, Middlesex: Penguin Books.
Slater, E. T. O. (1975) The psychiatrist in search of a science: III—the depth psychologies. *British Journal of Psychiatry*, **126**, 205–24.
Taylor, C. (1970) The explanation of purposive behaviour. In *Explanation in the Behavioural Sciences* (eds R. Borger and F. Cioffi). Cambridge University Press.
Toulmin, S. (1970) Reasons and causes. In *Explanation in the Behavioural Sciences* (eds Borger and F. Cioffi). Cambridge University Press.

6

Psychiatry in Crisis

JAMES S. EATON, JR.,
AND LEONARD S. GOLDSTEIN

Psychiatry today faces sociopolitical, economic, and philosophical pressures that threaten its existence as a valued medical specialty. Recent legislation that decreases the numbers of foreign medical graduates eligible to practice in the United States, increases the numbers of community mental health centers and types of services they offer, and limits federal support of psychiatric education will affect the future of psychiatry as a profession and discipline. Forthcoming legislation and federal health policies will be related to the ability of the profession to demonstrate its unique role in the provision of mental health and health services. The authors offer suggestions for the education of the American public regarding the important role of psychiatry in America's health and mental health care system.

A crisis for psychiatry is in the making. Within recent months there have been a number of events of far-reaching significance that demand the immediate attention of all who are concerned about the future of health and mental health services in this country.

We wish to discuss this crisis, knowing full well that many have become weary of hearing about crises within psychiatry that are based on such concerns as lack of agreement among psychiatrists about philosophic directions of the profession, disagreement about treatment modes, etc. Our present concern is that psychiatry—as a profession and as a discipline—is being buffeted by a number of external ill winds that threaten its continued existence as a valued specialty of American medicine.

Reprinted by permission from *American Journal of Psychiatry*, 134 (1977), 642-645. Copyright © 1977 by the American Psychiatric Association.

Psychiatry today is at the convergence of many sociopolitical, economic, and philosophic dynamics. As a result it is being pressed from all sides. Ironically, psychiatry is faced with defending its legitimacy as a vital part of the mental health and health care team precisely at the time when breakthroughs are occurring in neurobiologic, psychopharmacologic, behavioral, and psychosocial research. Discoveries about the prevention and treatment of severe mental illness require the reasoned application of new knowledge and skills by well-trained physicians who have special expertise in the psychological and behavioral sciences—in short, by psychiatrists. What sort of pressures and threats exist? Can we define the conflicting pressures that psychiatry now faces?

INCREASED NEED FOR PSYCHIATRY

There are definite indications of a continuing decrease in the number of psychiatrists compared with a rapidly increasing need for psychiatrists. There are a number of complex interrelated reasons for this phenomenon:

The Health Professions Educational Assistance Act of 1976 (Public Law 94-484) will have a major effect on the supply/demand dynamic of psychiatrists. This legislation removes foreign medical graduates (FMGs) from the category of preferential immigrants, institutes controls on student visas, and requires all FMGs to pass National Board of Medical Examiners Examinations Parts I and II and competency exams in the English language before they enter the United States for further professional training or employment. Following training, these people must return to their homelands unless they possess a more permanent visa.

Data from the American Psychiatric Association (1) for the academic year 1975–1976 show that FMGs comprised 39% of all psychiatric residents, a 30% increase over a 3-year period from the 1972–1973 figure of 29%. Thus we are talking about the sudden reversal of a rapidly growing trend.

More significant, perhaps, is that several studies (1, 2) show an absolute decrease in the number of American graduates in psychiatric residencies (from 3,300 in 1972–1973 to 2,900 in 1975–1976—a drop of over 12%). It should be noted that the crunch will be especially felt in state and county mental hospitals, where in 1975 over 54% of full-time-equivalent (FTE) staff psychiatrists and over 60% of psychiatric residents were FMGs (3).

As we increase the sensitivity of primary care physicians to psychosocial problems and psychiatric illness among their patients, there will undoubtedly be a greater need for psychiatric consultation and supervision of such practitioners, as well as an increase in the numbers, sophistication, and difficulty of psychiatric referrals. There is much unrecognized and untreated mental illness in this country today (4), and primary care physicians will begin to diagnose and treat these illnesses much more often (5). This trend will be accentuated by Public Law 94-484, which stimulates and supports the development and training of primary care physicians and requires psychiatric input to the primary care training programs.

The growing number of "right to treatment" suits creates additional pressure for increasing the number of psychiatrists in the mental health service delivery system;

most judgments have mandated a greater psychiatrist-to-patient ratio in state hospitals. Individual treatment plans, more day-to-day contact with all professional hospital staff members, and more frequent review of admitting diagnoses and treatment plans for patients are being called for.

Recent community mental health center legislation (Public Law 94-63) has had and will continue to have a major impact on the entire issue. This legislation requires an increase in the types of services offered by community mental health centers and in the number of centers throughout the country. This expansion is significant. The NIMH 5-year plan (6) on the development of CMHCs estimates 860 new centers by 1981, and the Mental Health Association is advocating 100 new centers per year over the next 5 years.

Clearly implied in this law is the expectation that once the 8 years of community mental health center funding runs out the centers will be self-sufficient. Such self-sufficiency will be based, to a large degree, on the linkages established with other agencies, especially in health, that have monies for the provision of mental health services.

Based on this information there will be a greatly increased need for quality professional staff in these centers, particularly psychiatrists, who among all mental health personnel are better able to relate to their medical colleagues.

These data are even more alarming when one considers the present direction of staffing patterns in community mental health centers. The mean number of psychiatrists per CMHC steadily declined from 1970 to 1975 (7). In 1975 only 4.6% of the staff in community mental health centers were psychiatrists, compared with 9% psychologists, 12.9% social workers, 9.4% registered nurses, and 37% other mental health services workers. If one considers data on the average numbers of FTEs among professional staff, a 37% decrease in the number of psychiatric FTEs (from 6.8 to 4.3) per CMHC is evident over the same 5-year period compared with significant increases in FTE psychologists and social workers and a minor increase of FTEs among other mental health service workers, excluding nurses. For nurses, the data reflect a slight drop (table 1).

Obviously, these data should stimulate studies to determine why there has been such a significant drop in the number of psychiatrists on mental health center staffs. Such a study is greatly needed at this time and would do much toward pinpointing the problems and helping to develop solutions that would lead to more effective and balanced mental health services provided by the community mental health centers.

VALUE OF PSYCHIATRY

As persuasive as these data are in terms of the need for greater numbers of psychiatrists, there are strong forces at play that would question the value of psychiatry and that would argue against the unique role of the psychiatrist in bridging the gap between the biologic and psychosocial determinants of behavior in both health and illness.

The Health Professions Educational Assistance Act of 1976 targets the primary care specialties for particular concern. Although the act authorizes some program assistance in the areas of medical humanism, human behavior, and psychiatric aspects of medical and dental practice (3 out of 21 targeted special areas), clearly the thrust of this legislation will only serve to decrease the federal support of psychiatric education compared with the support of education in other health disciplines.

A second factor is the budgetary allocation for the support of clinical mental health training under previous mental health training authorities. The amount of money available for psychiatric training has decreased drastically from over $41 million expended in fiscal year 1969 to only $25 million expended in 1976—an absolute drop of $16 million or 40% (over 65% if inflation is considered) (8).

While psychiatry has been receiving about 37% of all NIMH mental health clinical training monies, there are strong forces at play that would cut this apportionment severely in favor of greater funding for paraprofessional training programs, state manpower planning activities, etc.

Any relative decrease in the fiscal year 1978 allocations to the NIMH Psychiatry Education Branch at the same time that an absolute decrease in mental health clinical training support continues would have the effect of cutting presently supported psychiatry residency, child psychiatry, medical student education, and primary care mental health physician training programs 30% from the 1977 level. The fact that this is a real possibility reflects a lack of awareness by the general public about the value of psychiatry.

In August 1975 NIMH developed a Services Manpower Task Force that was charged by the Director of NIMH with developing a rational mental health training and manpower development plan for the future—a plan that would be more responsive to the mental health service needs of the country.

This effort stimulated much activity. A number of work groups composed of NIMH staff and consultants met; they were also attended by representatives of outside

TABLE 1
Staffing Patterns in Federally Funded CMHCs in the United States from 1970 to 1975

	Average Number of Full-Time Equivalent Staff per CMHC					
Year	Psychiatrists	Psychologists*	Social Workers**	Registered Nurses***	Other Professionals	Mental Health Workers
1970	6.8	4.9	9.7	9.7	8.9	23.5
1971	5.7	4.8	9.3	9.9	11.1	22.0
1972	5.4	6.1	10.3	9.2	8.8	23.2
1973	4.9	6.5	10.7	8.5	9.9	22.5
1974	4.6	7.5	11.0	8.7	11.4	22.4
1975	4.3	8.5	12.2	8.9	13.5	22.0

*Psychologists counted included those with B.S., M.A., and Ph.D. degrees.
**Social workers counted included those with B.A., M.A., and M.S.W. degrees.
***Registered nurses counted included those with A.A. through Master's degrees.

professional organizations and consumer groups. These work groups reported to the Director of NIMH in December 1976; a few of them made recommendations that would have resulted in decreased federal support of psychiatry education, not recognizing the unique role of psychiatry in the delivery of mental health services. It is appropriate that our colleagues in mental health nursing, psychology, and social work, as well as mental health paraprofessionals, have better training for an expanded role in mental health care and delivery—largely as consultants to primary health care personnel. However, it seems to us that the uniquely important role of the psychiatric physician is frequently overlooked. It will be especially interesting to see what receptivity, or lack thereof, the Carter administration will have to this effort.

Another adverse effect on psychiatry and all other postgraduate training among health professionals comes from what we call "functional egalitarianism." This is the notion that everyone can do almost everything—all it takes is a warm heart and an extended hand. This role-blurring attitude has significant implications for health professionals who have acquired unique skills, knowledge, and attitudes over long, arduous years of education and experience. It is important to remember that differentiation must occur before true collaboration can take place. Of course, psychiatry does not suffer alone these "antielitist" attacks.

Whether psychiatry is seen as having a unique role in the provision of mental health and health services and whether it, then, is perceived as a manpower shortage area will affect all forthcoming health legislation and federal health policies. Thus it inevitably will affect all psychiatric educators and practitioners.

WHAT NEEDS TO BE DONE?

Too many of the developing policies that we mention are being based on dataless assumptions and antiprofessional bias. Hard, honest, objective data must be gathered.

The profession of psychiatry must take the lead in developing studies that have specific goals:

1. Investigations of the reasons for the decreasing number of American medical graduates and American osteopathic graduates entering psychiatry.

2. Assessment of the effect of the projected decrease in foreign medical graduates providing service to the American health and mental health care system.

3. Assessment of the present and anticipated effect of decreased training monies for psychiatric education.

4. Analysis of the impact of the present and future policies of state and federal health and mental health agencies on psychiatric education. The extent to which these public agencies are willing to support quality educational programs (with eventual payoff in improved future services) in the face of severe and immediate service needs must be determined.

We must, of course, be prepared to demonstrate this difference, worth, and uniqueness in a variety of service delivery, research, and educational settings; this is where quality training programs make the difference.

THE RELEVANCE OF QUALITY PSYCHIATRIC EDUCATION

In the last few years there has been a great renewal of interest in upgrading and revitalizing psychiatric educational programs throughout the United States. In some ways, the Psychiatry Education Branch at NIMH has helped to stimulate this interest (9).

Within the past 10 years there has been a growing movement toward developing a science of medical education. Much is being done to determine those variables which influence the students' learning processes, and more rational methods for developing and revising curricula have resulted. Setting explicit goals and objectives and devising certain curricular strategies aimed at developing knowledge, skills, and attitudes are now generally accepted as the best ways to develop curricula for wide varieties of medical education programs. If this is done, training program directors can more easily evaluate the results of their programs and can use the evaluation results to revise future programs.

As psychiatry has accommodated wide swings in philosophic direction over the past 15 years, it has become clear that psychiatric educational programs would suffer unless they achieved a reasonable balance in curricular content, patient populations, and educational settings. This balance, of course, should not be educational dilettantism but rather responsible pluralism that allows for accents of strength in educational programs.

Pressure for public accountability in psychiatric education is another reason for more manifest interest in this area. Considering the large amount of public money that goes into psychiatric education, one can easily understand why more stringent attention is being given to the quality of this federal support effort.

The pressure for certification and recertification of psychiatrists naturally places added pressure on training programs to turn out good "products." The psychiatric residency graduate should have the competence to deal with a wide range of clinical problems in a variety of settings. Further, the graduate should be capable of continuing self-education and comfortable with an attitude geared to life-long learning.

Significant research breakthroughs have pushed basic sciences to the clinical bedside and encouraged educators to develop curricula showing the interrelationship of basic and clinical sciences. New knowledge about the mechanisms of action of psychopharmacologic agents, discoveries dealing with neurotransmitters at the cellular and subcellular levels, and our greater appreciation of the individual variability of patient responses to pharmacologic interventions are examples of the relevance of basic science to immediate clinical practice. Many other examples could be cited.

Finally, psychiatrists and behavioral scientists have been more actively involved in primary care educational programs, helping the practitioner to understand and deal with attitudes of their patients concerning such potentially self-destructive behaviors as smoking, alcohol consumption, accident-prone driving, etc. In essence a patient's lifestyle and such issues as patient compliance have become topics of increased interest in terms of psychiatric education. Of course these are ripe areas of research activity for psychiatrists who, as behavioral science physicians, can actively involve themselves at the clinical bedside.

There is vigor and vitality in psychiatric education today. Most of those involved in psychiatric education are deeply committed to their work, i.e., improving the quality of educational programs for all physicians. This commitment will do much to assure that the products of their education programs will be broadly trained and handsomely experienced by the end of their formal training and that these psychiatrists and other physicians will go on to pursue life-long learning experiences as a part of their professional responsibilities.

It is our opinion that well-trained psychiatrists will be able to demonstrate their value in the mental health and health fields. Failure to do this might well lead to a dismantling of much of the present psychiatric educational system and a costly loss of quality psychiatric services in the future. We must explain a little better than we have in the past what we are about and what our capabilities—and limitations—are. That is where the job for every one of us lies, the education of the American public.

REFERENCES

1. Gurel L: APA Resident Census Data. Proceedings of American Association of Directors of Psychiatry Residency Training, 1976, Hartford, AADPRT, 1976.
2. Gurel L: A Survey of Academic Resources in Psychiatry Residency Training. Washington, DC, American Psychiatric Association, 1973.
3. Jenkins J, Witkin M: Foreign medical graduates employed in state and county mental hospitals. National Institute of Mental Health Statistical Note 131. Rockville, Md, NIMH, 1976.
4. Kramer M: Some perspectives on the role of biostatistics and epidemiology in the prevention and control of mental disorders. Milbank Memorial Fund Quarterly, Summer 1975, pp 293-296
5. Goldberg R, Haas M, Eaton J, et al: Psychiatry and the primary care physician. JAMA 236:944-945, 1976.
6. A Report to the US Congress on a Five-Year Plan for the Development of Community Mental Health Centers Under the Community Mental Health Centers Amendments of 1975, Title III, of Public Law 94-63. Rockville, Md, National Institute of Mental Health, 1976.
7. Provisional Data on Federally Funded Community Mental Health Centers 1974-1975. Rockville, Md, National Institute of Mental Health, Division of Biometry and Epidemiology, Survey and Reports Branch, 1976.
8. Data on Training Grants Awarded. Rockville, Md, National Institute of Mental Health, Division of Manpower and Training, 1976.
9. Eaton J, Daniels R, Pardes H: Psychiatric education: state of the art, 1976. Am J Psychiatry, March Supplement, 1977, pp 2-6.

Part Three

Traditional Forms of Psychotherapy

In the previous section we gave full attention to the role of psychiatry in the historical emergence and present state of the art of psychotherapy. In this and the following section we examine in more detail the theory and practice of psychotherapy in some of its rich variety. Unfortunately, space does not permit us to do justice to the truly extraordinary range of techniques and styles, all of them, seemingly, underwritten by logical and sensible theory. We will, however, present several forms of psychotherapy, which we have divided into the more traditional on one hand, and contemporary on the other, although this distinction cannot be a perfectly precise one.

As with many aspects of our culture, we tend to look at these different forms of psychotherapy in terms of a rather foreshortened time frame. We speak of an approach to psychotherapy, for example, as being traditional. But on closer inspection, traditional turns out to encompass a period of less than fifty, or even thirty, years. So whereas we believe we are going back into history, we discover that, in fact, our history is much shorter than we once imagined. Thus, when we speak here of so-called traditional forms of psychotherapy, we mean only those forms that seem to have been around a bit longer than others, and in addition have influenced the so-called contemporary forms. Said simply, there are forms of psychotherapy that seem relatively new, or at least the issues that they address are relatively new. Other forms, in contrast, derive from more traditional theories and experiments in psychiatry and psychology. Thus, one may well consider one's work to be highly innovative and ingenious, but history may show it to be a slight transformation of earlier work, if not outrightly derivative.

The four traditional approaches are represented here by psychotherapists' concerns with the unconscious, drugs or drug treatment, and the effect on the patient or groups generally, and family groups in particular. More specifically, the following three selections represent ways in which people have begun to address the problem of how best to treat an ill person. But note, if the way to treat the patient is with drugs, or in a group, or with his or her family present, or by himself or herself in a slightly suggestive setting where all sorts of material from the unconscious may be generated, then not so indirectly each of these various treatment strategies has been derived from uniquely different conceptions of the personality and the factors that give rise to mental stress or illness. Or, stated in overly extreme terms, even when two people agree on the basis of a person's problem, they may disagree on the method of locating and ultimately dealing with (treating) that problem.

If one examines the following selections carefully, some rather fascinating issues begin to take shape. For example, if the appropriate form of treatment is seen as the prescription of drugs, then is the patient thereby being denied the right to self-knowledge or enlightenment? On the other hand, drugs may be seen not only to relieve stress, but in addition to make it possible for the patient to engage in so-called learning or educational forms of psychotherapy. Perhaps these two seemingly discrepant types of therapy might be used in conjunction more often than they presently are; perhaps, too, one might wish to take issue with the enormous amount of drug dispensing that passes as a legitimate form of psychotherapy. That is one issue.

Another issue is the matter of believing that psychological problems are formed, as it were, in the mind by dint of what a person has taken in, absorbed, internalized from the outside. The problem for the psychotherapist is to help the person understand how he or she has experienced these external stimuli and rearranged or recontextualized them psychically. While some would agree with this basic premise, others might insist that the material of the mind, if we may call it that, is internalized not precisely from external stimuli, but from that partly external, partly internal process known as the bond between people, the relationship. Thus, the only way to know how people respond to or deal with their social worlds, albeit in their most private and idiosyncratic ways, is to observe them in the presence of a group. The method of psychotherapy that would follow from such a perspective would then offer new understanding of mental processes, as well as provide new modes of offering psychotherapeutic treatment.

A third position would be to argue that essentially the personality is formed in the context, let us say, of the individual's family. Accordingly, a person having problems with his or her present life must explore these problems in the presence of the family. Once again, note well the important assumption being made; namely that contemporary events are being experienced by the person, irrespective of age, partly as a function of the person's role as a child in his or her family. Clearly, it is quite possible for a family therapist to be very committed to psychoanalytic theory but believe that the classical psychoanalytic framework, which we also examine in this section, is utterly inappropriate for tapping this psychological material in the patient.

The same could be said for so-called group therapists. While holding to various psychological theories, they nonetheless may find variations of the group psychotherapeutic process especially congenial.

In contemporary terms, all of these issues may seem relatively tame, even outdated. But one is advised to recall that bitter debates raged not so long ago over just these issues, and in some quarters, the questions have not been settled in the slightest. The traditional forms of psychotherapy are employed, therefore, with practitioners often feeling a trifle unsettled, if not uneasy, about the style and approach they find both congenial and efficacious.

7

Family Therapy: Clinical Hodgepodge or Clinical Science?

GERALD H. ZUK

A summary of my viewpoint in family therapy is given which supplies basic principles of what I believe is a comprehensive theory and technique. Critics are saying today, with some justification, that family therapy is a hodgepodge of part-theories and part-techniques; that it is more an art form than clinical science. Therefore, those that claim an integrated theory and technique have an obligation to set it out in simple, straightforward terms which invite rigorous evaluation. Summaries aid such a goal when they reduce claims to basic principles.

I propose to summarize my position in the field of family therapy, a position which I believe comprises a comprehensive theory and technique. My summary will be a statement of basic principles, assumptions, propositions, and inferences. It is, somewhat paradoxically, often difficult in a lengthy clinical essay, monograph, or book to discern the basic elements that underlie a theory and technique. Such material may contain inconsistent or contradictory claims which, because of the method of exposition, are not apparent. For example, there is the claim in recent years of contributors to family therapy who—obviously deeply imbued with psychoanalytic notions—still insist they are really systems-oriented workers. This has resulted in a corruption of the term systems-oriented to the point at which it is more or less meaningless—or even misleading.

Reprinted by permission from *Journal of Marriage and Family Counseling*, 2 (October 1976), 299–303.

I would like to summarize the principles, et cetera, that appear to me to reflect more or less accurately my viewpoint in family therapy, thus offering the reader an opportunity to assess the consistencies and inconsistencies therein, omissions (or erroneous commissions), validity of claims, and the capacity of the position to generate meaningful hypotheses. I hope in so doing to encourage other claimants to duplicate my effort. In my judgment this would be a constructive step in the process of comparing the values espoused by the various claimants. By boiling down claims and putting them in a summary form, it should be easier to make constructive comparisons, and might help discourage a major criticism of family therapy: namely, that it consists of a hodgepodge of techniques and part-theories espoused by a variety of "schools" whose ardent followers are sometimes given to excess because they either ignore or disregard suggestions that they subject claims to rigorous test. Due to the presence of such advocates the field has become perhaps unduly politicized.

Recently, in major psychiatric journals such prominent spokesmen for psychiatry as Brown (1976) and Marmor (1975) stated that in psychotherapy it is the wisdom and experience of the therapist that really count, not theory or technique. Brown in particular says that while "There has been an increment of knowledge in the area of marital and family therapy[,] ...[t]he critical variable today is the same as it was 20 years ago—the maturity and wisdom of the helping person (p. 493)." In a recent article in a newspaper distributed to most U.S. psychologists, Keebler (1976), a journalist, does much to convey the impression of family therapy as a hodgepodge done by well-meaning but freewheeling therapists. The main message to the uninitiated or beginner by Keebler is caveat emptor.

There is more than a small measure of truth in what the critics are saying. Glick and Kessler (1975) and Olson (1975) have recited the methodological gaps and conceptual weaknesses in family therapy research. There continues to be an over-reliance on the successful case to support a particular technique or theory. These deficiencies have indeed tended to the development of what may be more properly called part-techniques and part-theories. Although in many respects a useful book and one that accurately reflects a rich diversity of viewpoints, one cannot help but come away from reading a book like *The Book of Family Therapy*, by Ferber, Mendelsohn, and Napier without agreeing with the critics.

As one who has been engaged over the past 15 years in the rather frustrating business of trying to develop a comprehensive theory of family therapy (Zuk, 1972) and a method of teaching it (Zuk, 1975) that does not require the student to emulate my personal style or idiosyncrasies, I am deeply concerned by efforts to picture the field as simply an art form. Without denying the importance of artistry, I believe there is an obligation to subject the various concepts and techniques that have emerged in the field to increasingly rigorous research, and that those found inadequate, deficient, or ineffective, should be discarded. During the past few years I have—although not without some trepidation—had my viewpoint subject to such a rigorous test by two workers, Garrigan and Bambrick (1975, 1976), in what I believe is the most carefully controlled series of studies available in the field. Reports of successful cases have been useful, even in instances where the evaluation of success has been done by the therapist himself. But what is especially needed in the field today is precisely the kind and quality of research undertaken by Garrigan and Bambrick. Using rigorous experimental design, adequate controls, and valid and reliable measures, they were able to train in a brief time relatively unsophisticated graduate students in counseling in my technique and theory of family therapy. These "therapists" then conducted a time-limited series of interviews with families having children at a school for emotionally disturbed. In replicated studies, groups of emotionally disturbed children showed improved behavior in the classroom and at home; and parents and children showed better attitudes toward each other. The "therapists" did not become fully experienced family therapists, but they were able to absorb some basics of a particular method in a relatively brief time and utilize what they learned to the benefit of their patient-families.

I believe studies such as those of Garrigan and Bambrick are absolutely essential to the progress of the field at this time. The ardent advocacy by members of "schools" has reached a point of diminished or zero returns, and credibility must now be established by hard-nosed evaluation.

What follows now is a summary of my viewpoint which contains what I believe are the essential elements. I offer it to serve as a stimulus for others to do the same in order that critical comparisons may be made without the complexities or diversions or distractions that lengthy essays, monographs, or book material often interpose between reader and author. I hope also along with other such summaries that it may especially stimulate researchers to test assumptions that are held to be basic or fundamental by their authors. Only in this way can the validity of claims made by the various "schools" be fairly and properly determined on a scientific rather than purely adversary basis.

I. Some General Propositions

A) The family is a bundle of values derived in large measure from the institutions in which it claims membership, such as church, civic associations and fraternal orders, labor unions, and so on. Its ethnic, racial, religious, and neighborhood affiliations are important considerations in defining its "identity" and therefore the therapist will take pains to discover them and generally support them.

B) The therapist is interested in family history, but focuses on current family functioning and activities. His style of relating to the family may be bold and confrontational, or reserved and non-directive, depending on his evaluation of the status of the family, e.g., its background, its expectations about therapy, how many interviews have been held, the nature of pathogenic relating that exists, and the progress that has been made.

C) The therapist is interested in all conflicts experienced by the family, but focuses on three: 1) that between husband and wife; 2) that between parents and children; 3) that between the nuclear family and other larger social combinations, such as the neighborhood.

D) The therapist employs all established therapeutic techniques or devices to effect useful change, but emphasizes the special set of leverages available to him because he is working with a unique group, namely, the family. In the next section(s) that set will be defined.

II. Role Functions of the Therapist

A) The Go-Between. The therapist exerts leverage as a go-between by facilitating communications among family members, by negotiating conflicts, and by limit setting.

B) Side-Taker. The therapist exerts leverage as a side-taker by siding with some members against others in a dispute, or with or against the family as a whole in a dispute with an outside source, such as the neighborhood.

C) Celebrant. The therapist exerts leverage as a celebrant by offering or being asked to officiate at an event deemed important by the family, such as a runaway or divorce or job loss.

III. Values Expressed by Therapist and Families

A) Neither the therapist nor family is value-free. In interviews they express many values which may be categorized as follows: 1) "continuity" values; or 2) "discontinuity" values. "Continuity" values espouse the goodness of compassion, justice, equality, and relatedness, e.g., between the generations or neighbors. "Discontinuity" values espouse the goodness of systems of controls, of rational approaches to problems, of law and legal codes, of orderly procedures, and discipline. In conflict between husband and wife, wives usually espouse the "continuity" values. In conflict between parents and children, children usually espouse the "continuity" values. In conflict between the nuclear family and neighborhood, the nuclear family usually espouses the "continuity" values. Thus values are not randomly communicated in these conflicts, by and large, and the therapist, depending on his evaluation, may side with or against "continuity" or "discontinuity" values as expressed in family conflict.

IV. Pathogenic Relating in Families

A) Pathogenic relating refers to those inflammatory, malevolent processes the therapist directly observes in family interviews, such as silencing of members by others, open or covert threats, scapegoating of other kinds, or other systematic efforts to control or manipulate members' behavior that in the judgment of the therapist are destructive to the functioning of a member or members.

B) The general goal of the therapist is to reduce pathogenic relating, or eliminate it, using those role functions described in Section II, while expressing differentially those values described in Section III. Pathogenic relating tends to erupt after an impasse in competing values, thus the therapist must also address the underlying value conflicts.

V. Some Types and Practical Goals of Family Therapy

A) There are four types of contracts families make with therapists: 1) for the purpose of crisis-resolution, lasting one to six interviews; 2) for the purpose of short-term therapy, lasting 10-15 interviews; 3) for the purpose of middle-range therapy, lasting 25-30 interviews; 4) for the purpose of long-term therapy, lasting 40 or more interviews.

The goal of each is somewhat different—from tension-reduction in (1) to increased family solidarity but with better acceptance of individual liberties in 4).

B) Whereas the effort of the therapist is to evaluate and reduce or eliminate pathogenic relating in the family, his practical goals are those described above—tension-reduction, symptom-reduction, improved family cooperation, and so on. These changes are measured on an individual, not family level for two main reasons: 1) because *families* will evaluate the success of therapy in terms of its effect on individual members; and 2) because valid, reliable measures of family change are still nonexistent.

VI. The Phases of Family Therapy

A) The engagement period, lasting roughly the first four or five interviews, is the first phase of family therapy because it is the first critical issue raised between therapist and family. The engagement is actually the prototype of all critical issues, and each subsequent issue as it arises may be considered a phase of therapy.

B) Termination is the final critical issue in therapy which, like the engagement, contains the potential for significant positive therapeutic movement. It occurs when therapist or family, jointly or unilaterally, decides that a satisfactory goal has been achieved, or that such a goal is unattainable under present circumstances.

C) *Since the majority of families limit the time the therapist has to work to six months or less,* it is of little or no value to the therapist to distinguish between critical issues as to which are "deeper" and which are "superficial."

VII. Limitations and Contraindications

A) There are numerous limitations in family therapy, as in other psychotherapies, starting with simple lack of motivation to appear for interviews, which often stems from lack of readiness to undertake the stress of the program. Certain types of presenting problems are not favorable prospects, e.g., families with an alcoholic member or chronic drug abuser. Single-parent families with very young children are often not favorable because it often turns into an individual therapy of the parent in the presence of the young children.

B) While there are numerous practical limitations, there is only one principle of contraindication which is evoked in those relatively few instances where the therapist is trapped into serving as an agent of a referral source for the purpose of carrying out a disciplinary action, such as occurs once in a while in a court or school referral. In such instances to undertake a course of therapy is to produce more harm than good.

REFERENCES

Brown, B. S. The life of psychiatry. *American Journal of Psychiatry*, 1976, *133*, 489–495.

Garrigan, J. J., & Bambrick, A. F. Short-term family therapy with disturbed children. *Journal of Marriage and Family Counseling*, 1975, *1*, 381–388.

Garrigan, J. J., & Bambrick, A. F. Family therapy for disturbed children: Some experimental results in special education. *Journal of Marriage and Family Counseling*, in press.

Glick, I., & Kessler, D. *Marriage and family therapy*. New York: Grune & Stratton, 1975.

Keebler, N. Family therapy: A profusion of methods and meanings. *APA Monitor*, 1976, *4*, 4–5.

Marmor, J. The nature of the psychotherapeutic process revisited. *Canadian Psychiatric Association Journal*, 1975, *20*, 557–565.

Olson, D. H. Marital and family therapy: A critical overview. In A. S. Gurman, & D. G. Rice (Eds.), *Couples in conflict*. New York: Behavioral Publications, 1972.

Zuk, G. H. *Family therapy: A triadic-based approach*. New York: Behavioral Publications, 1972.

Zuk, G. H. *Process and practice in family therapy*. Haverford, PA: Psychiatry & Behavior Science Books, 1975.

8

Psychotherapy and Pharmacotherapy: Conceptual Issues

JOHN P. DOCHERTY, STEPHEN R. MARDER,
DANIEL P. VAN KAMMEN, AND SAMUEL G. SIRIS

Of the many difficulties in maintaining an integration of psychotherapeutic and pharmacotherapeutic treatment, one of the most important is "the problem of bimodal relatedness," that is, the distinction between relating to the pateint as a diseased organ or object of study and as a disturbed person. The authors identify the forces that act to inappropriately emphaisze one mode or the other and discuss major difficulties that arise because of failure to maintain a bimodal relatedness. In a setting of combined therapy, maintaining and safeguarding the optimal relationship of collaborative subject-subject relatedness can prevent the emergence of problems destructive to effective psychiatric treatment and research.

A clear rationale for the co-utilization of psychotherapy and pharmacotherapy is of fundamental importance in contemporary psychiatry. Yet psychiatry currently lacks an integrated theory that combines psychodynamic insights and recent discoveries concerning the pharmacological action of drugs. We suggest that this deficit is due not only to a lack of adequate research data but also to the strong conceptual antagonisms inherent in developing a comprehensive psychobiological view of psychiatric patients. The recent report by the Group for the Advancement of Psychiatry on pharmacotherapy and psychotherapy (1) pointed out that although it is not difficult to understand why psychogenic illness could be treated somatically—nor, reciprocally, why somatic illness could benefit from psychological intervention—the

Reprinted by permission from *American Journal of Psychiatry,* 134 (1977), 529–533. Copyright © 1977 by the American Psychiatric Association.

tendency to polarize these treatments is strong and persistent. At this juncture it would seem that progress may be made most effectively by determining the *sources* of the conceptual difficulties and antagonisms in this area.

In our clinical psychopharmacological research with acute schizophrenic patients, we have identified several specific difficulties in maintaining an integration of psychotherapeutic and pharmacotherapeutic treatment. One of the most important we have called "the problem of bimodal relatedness." This refers to the complex form of relatedness that the psychiatrist must establish with the patient. It involves a distinction between relating to the patient as a diseased organ or object of study (subject-object mode) or as a disturbed person (subject-subject mode). Our experience has demonstrated that, although it may be extremely stressful for psychiatrists to maintain an appropriate balance and integration of both modes, a smooth psychobiological integration is possible.

In this paper we will begin by identifying the forces in a setting of combined therapy that act to inappropriately emphasize one mode or the other. We will then demonstrate how an appreciation of these forces led to practical policy decisions that have improved therapist-patient interactions on our research unit.

FORCES PROMOTING SUBJECT-OBJECT OR SUBJECT-SUBJECT RELATEDNESS

First we will examine the forces that promote subject-object relatedness at the expense of subject-subject relatedness.

Forces Encouraging a Subject-Object Relationship

Focus on the physiochemical system. When we as subjects (clincial investigators) regard a neuron, for example, we properly regard it as an object and, in our subsequent attempts to know it further, *act on* it and manipulate it. This clearly implies a form of relatedness that has been generally designated as subject-object relatedness and is analogous to Buber's "I-It" relationship (2). Thus interest in the biological disturbances associated with a mental illness such as schizophrenia elicits a subject-object relationship. In general medicine a recognition of this form of relatedness is expressed in the complaints of patients who have felt themselves regarded by their physician as solely "a case of hepatitis" or "a case of pneumonia" and is probably also expressed in physicians' complaints about the lack of patient "compliance" in taking medication the way the doctor "ordered."

The prevailing model of science. In terms of the impact of research, the classic model of science that has dominated modern research thinking further reinforces this tendency to establish a subject-object relationship. This model is derived from the physical sciences and is, as Whitehead (3) noted, fundamentally based on the great bifurcation of nature: "a dichotomizing of the world into subject and object, the knower and the known."

Forces Encouraging a Subject-Subject Relationship

Distinctive emergent property of the personality system. An examination of figure 1 reveals organizational features that promote a recognition of the patient as an independent other with an autonomous subjectivity. This recognition evokes a mode of relatedness with that person which can be designated a subject-subject relationship and which Buber has termed an "I-Thou" relationship (2).

The following specific features are of relevance here: the systems depicted in figure 1 are hierarchically ordered (a system is constrained by, and reciprocally is controlling of, the immediately adjacent system), and each intact system possesses the property of maintaining and restoring its equilibrium under the impact of stress.

These features encourage a subject-subject relationship. Disturbances in the personality system impinge directly on the social system. A social system has persons as its major components, and a disturbance at the level of the *person* imposes a direct stress at the level of the social system. Thus, for example, it is a mistake to say that mental illness is the same as any other illness, even though this may be recognized as a well-intentioned effort to alleviate destructive and prejudicial attitudes toward the mentally ill. Persisting personal disequilibrium requires reequilibrium at the level of the social system. Persisting personal disequilibrium is very different from the types of physical disturbances we refer to as "medical" illnesses. For example, a broken arm may necessitate a shift in the personality system. However, an equilibrium may be attained at the personality system level so that the person, although changed, is not disturbed as a person and remains congruent with the social system.

The above considerations highlight an important difference between the relatedness of persons toward one another and their relationship toward physio-chemical aspects of themselves or others, and they bring into focus the presence of a distinctive emergent property at the level of the personality system. This emergent property is the subjectivity of the other; that is, the other is not only an object-to-be-known but a knower in his own right or, as Cassirer (4), Edelson (5), and Langer (6) have written, "a maker of symbols." The recognition of this subjective consciousness is thus brought vividly to mind by the manifest disturbance in that subjectivity, and it encourages a subject-subject relationship.

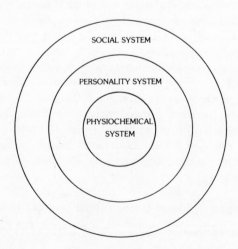

INCOMPATIBILITIES OF THE SUBJECT-OBJECT AND SUBJECT-SUBJECT MODES

There are several incompatibilities between the subject-object and subject-subject modes of relatedness (see appendix 1). Numerous difficulties for a psychotherapeutic and pharmacotherapeutic approach derive from the incompatibilities of these two forms of relatedness and the inappropriate substitution of one for the other. The simultaneous maintenance of these two forms of relatedness imposes a difficult strain and elicits a predictable desire to simplify matters. Since for both research purposes and somatic treatment the subject-object relationship cannot be abandoned, the simplification is usually in the form of attenuation of the subject-subject relationship. The deleterious effects of this in general medicine—primarily discussed under the rubric of the quality of the doctor-patient relationship—are brought to our attention from many quarters and need not be reviewed here. In the area of psychiatry, however, we encounter some special problems.

PROBLEMS RESULTING FROM FAILURE TO MAINTAIN BIMODAL RELATEDNESS

Antitherapeutic Impact on the Patient

In our setting, where our work is with schizophrenic patients who live in dread of the loss of their subjectivity and of their sense of self, it hardly needs to be said that a relationship which assumes the absence of that subjectivity is antitherapeutic and corroborates the patient's worst fears. On a lesser level, for any psychiatric patient who questions his or her worth as a human being, the denial of that which is distinctively human about him or her tends to be experienced as confirmation of that worthlessness.

Effect on Psychotherapy

The simplification in favor of the subject-object relationship renders far more difficult the maintenance of good psychotherapy. In good psychotherapy a tenuous and delicate balance is achieved. For example, use of the psychoanalytic method provides a way for bracketing the subjectivity of the patient, so that subjectivity itself can become the object of scrutiny and understanding (7, 8). Thus, the therapeutic relationship bears within itself this very same tension: to reduce the subject to a nonconscious object (to withdraw, remain aloof) or to overidentify with the patient (to transform the relationship into a solely subject-subject one, characterized at the extreme in the excesses of the "touchy-feely movement"). The previously mentioned forces that emphasize the patient as object would tend to drive this delicately balanced psychotherapeutic relationship into such an inappropriate subject-subject relationship. This tendency is reflected in such events as nurses on research units declaring that their role is that of "patient advocate."

Thus this real stress on the integrity of the psychotherapeutic relationship is a major source of the tension between psychotherapy and pharmacotherapy and, indeed, between psychotherapy and clinical research.

False Identification of the Personality System with the Physiochemical System

The third problem resulting from a failure to appreciate and maintain bimodal relatedness manifests itself in two interesting ways: confounded evaluation of the effects of psychoactive drugs and the arousal of primitive intrapsychic anxiety. The problem of evaluating drug effects is essentially this: viewing the patient or research subject solely as an object facilitates an inappropriate collapse of our differentiated systems of knowledge, such that drug effects tend to be linked *directly* with changes in the subjectivity of the patient. Currently, a prevalent way of conceptualizing the psychological and biological integration does, in fact, consist of falsely identifying the physiochemical system and the personality system—for example, assuming that the subjectively experienced symbolic world of depression is equivalent to the physiochemical state altered by "antidepressant" drugs.

Both Sarwer-Foner (9) and Irwin (10) have pointed out that a careful distinction must be made so that drugs are viewed as acting directly at the level of the physiochemical system and only indirectly at the level of the personality system. As Irwin has stated, "Drugs do not affect behavior directly. As chemicals they can only interact with other chemicals.... Drugs, thus, successively affect the various levels of integration from the simplest to the most complex—from the chemical to the psychosocial sphere" (10, p. 151). He has also noted the difficulties in the evaluation of drug action and appropriate drug use that result from a failure to appreciate and use this distinction.

Further, the false identification of the personality system with the physiochemical system elicits the second difficulty mentioned above—the arousal of primitive intrapsychic anxiety. This results from the threat of dissolution of self with the loss of ego boundaries and self-other differentiation that follows the identification of self with organic matter. This dynamic is especially clear in schizophrenic patients who refuse to consider a somatic component to their illness and express the fear that if this were true, they would no longer exist. It is also apparent in some researchers who regard and treat patients as a presymbiotic extension of the self and who defend against this by heightening the subject-object relationship with the research subject. In a more subtle way this dynamic is also apparent in the expressed concerns of some psychotherapists that drugs, regardless of their physiochemical action, rob the patient of his or her autonomy.

Quality of the Research

Failure to maintain bimodal relatedness affects the quality of research. What brings patients for psychiatric treatment is disturbance at the level of their subjectivity. However, establishing only a subject-object relatedness to these patients entails the inevitable warp, distortion, and strain of the procrustean bed. In terms of research, it reduces us to working only with behavioral data and thus severely compromises the research. For example, one of our patients recently remarked, "No matter how we may look to you, or what value you attach to it, only we know how we feel and how the drug is affecting us inside." That state is, after all, a focal concern of our work.

Ethics

Finally, ignoring bimodal relatedness causes issues of ethics to be raised in an antagonistic way. This occurs because the essential ethic of human relationships requires that the type of relatedness established must not be discordant with the values, mores, and welfare of the larger societal system in which it is embedded. When we emphasize the subject-object relationship to the relative exclusion of subject-subject relatedness, however, we clearly transgress present societal values and thus act unethically in a very basic sense.

RECOMMENDATIONS FOR STABILIZING BIMODAL RELATEDNESS

Based on an understanding of the problems described above, the question now becomes, What can be done to foster the integrity of research and practice with combined psychotherapy and pharmacotherapy? From our analysis thus far, it clearly entails seeing that a balanced bimodal relatedness is maintained. This primarily means safeguarding the presence of an appropriate subject-subject relatedness.

This leads to two further questions: 1) What is the optimal form of subject-subject relatedness for psychological-biological research and practice? 2) What steps can be taken to maintain and promote that relationship?

Possible answers to the first question may be found by examining the discussion that has taken place around the issue of informed consent, which seems to be rooted in the same core problem of bimodal relatedness. Basically, four categories of subject-subject relationship have been proposed to maintain an ethical system of informed consent. These may be rank-ordered from least satisfactory to optimal. Any system should provide for the presence of all four. However, the less satisfactory forms should be fail-safe devices that only come into play when the more satisfactory forms fail to function. The four categories are as follows:

1. *Adversary relationship.* This is the most time-consuming, rigid, and minimal form of human relatedness. The assumption here is that there is an intent to exploit, against which vigorous remedy must be sought. This form of relatedness is mediated through the agency of an adjudicatory system of courts and lawyers.

2. *Bureaucratically regulated relationship.* Here, a set of guidelines is issued that is binding on both parties and that fairly rigidly defines from without the nature of the relationship. This form of relatedness is mediated through the agency of an administrative or executive body that issues and implements binding directives.

3. *Advocacy relationship.* This type of relationship is somewhat more flexible. However, it entails an assumption of impaired ability to relate on the part of one of the subjects. It has the drawback of decreasing the intimacy and immediacy between the two concerned subjects. It is mediated by aligning one of the subjects with a presumably more competent third party.

4. *Collaborative relationship.* This would seem to be the optimal form of subject-subject relatedness. It is the most flexible, responsive, and mutually satisfying. It is also clearly the one that would be most helpful in maintaining the balance of the psychotherapeutic situation and would keep the patient available for full participation in the research. If truly established, it is the one, from the patient's viewpoint, that

allows the greatest comfort and security. It is a well-established phenomenon, for example, that when physicians become ill they regularly tend to seek treatment from friends rather than from renowned experts.

We might now ask what form this collaborative relationship takes in the physician-patient and researcher-subject dyad. This question has had the benefit of a penetrating analysis by Parsons (11), whose work also points toward an answer to the question we posed earlier about the steps to be taken to promote the optimal subject-subject relationship. Briefly, Parsons pointed out that for both physician-patient and investigator-subject the relationships are fiduciary ones with the asymmetry introduced because of the "competency gap" existing between the two parties. Most importantly, he pointed out that the functional basis for maintaining this relationship is trust. It is thus toward the enhancement of trust that we should direct our energies if we wish to sustain this form of subject-subject relatedness.

However, there are severe strains on this trust in the setting of psychiatric research and practice that need to be taken into account. They are as follows:

1. Great gaps in knowledge exist between physician and patient, and the greater the distance, the more trust is required.

2. In a research setting even more strain is added. Feedback is delayed for a long time. The results of the procedures that the patients are asked to undergo are rarely immediately available.

3. The double-blind research strategy demands extreme trust on the part of the patient. If a complaint is made about the effect the patient ascribes to a drug, he is given no information to judge whether or not the physician actually attended to him. On a ward such as ours where schizophrenic patients live with the fear of an ultimate paranoid transformation—that their lives and their minds are being controlled by others—this issue can reach crisis proportions.

What, then, can we do to ensure the maintenance of this trust, thereby supporting the subject-subject relationship and the joint conduct of psychotherapy and pharmocotherapy?

1. We can close the gaps in knowledge with relevant information. Several approaches are important here. Patient and staff education should be a continuing, stable part of the ward structure. Assiduous efforts should be made to answer all patients' questions as clearly and promptly as possible. As suggested by Carpenter and Langsner (12), all other staff, especially nursing staff, should assume a more active role in the education of the patients. There are two reasons for this: the cost factor, which currently limits the practice of informing the patient, is reduced, and the focus for trust is distributed, which decreases the intensity and consequent ambivalence of the subject-subject relationship that we are interested in maintaining. The final approach that can be used to close the gaps in knowledge is to provide a clear and visible means for conveying questions of concern that impinge on the issue of trust and to make a clear and visible response. This may be accomplished by scheduling a weekly research meeting during which all staff, patients, and collaborating investigators openly examine all issues relating to the research and its interface with clinical care (13). In addition, on the ward a special book may be kept in the nursing

station in which questions can be recorded daily and answers similarly recorded. Finally, the physician in charge of double-blind medications should be readily available to see all patients whenever a question arises; this may be reasonably accomplished by establishing a regularly scheduled time for this task.

2. Research results should be presented to the community on a continuing basis. The clinical implications of research that are particularly interesting to patients should be emphasized.

3. When each patient's protocol is completed, a full and detailed report should be made to the community on the results of the double-blind studies. Those questions of trust which arose through the course of this study should be particularly addressed.

The use of these principles may be demonstrated by the following clinical example from our unit.

Case 1. A 27-year-old woman with a diagnosis of schizo-affective schizophrenia, depressed type, reluctantly cooperated during the first 5 months of our clinical research program. She claimed that she was glad that at least some part of her seemed valuable to someone—in this case, at least the research staff valued her as a researchable object. During the last 6 weeks of her hospitalization, she surprised everyone by announcing that she refused to participate in the baseline and probenecid lumbar punctures that had been scheduled. Further discussion revealed that the original reasons for participation no longer seemed to justify her having to suffer the post-lumbar puncture headache that she had had several months before. We were able to diagnose the problem as one in which our previous subject-object mode of relatedness vis-à-vis the issue of research participation was antitherapeutic and actually destructive to the research. In order to establish a collaborative relationship, we gave the patient a detailed explanation of the research strategy of the unit and the vital part that CSF amine metabolite studies played. She acknowledged that this explanation was what she had acutally hoped for. After her eventual participation, she stated that this interaction was a landmark in her hospitalization and that it had significantly improved her self-esteem.

In this particular example, a drift away from a collaborative subject-subject relationship to a subject-object relationship was diagnosed and corrected.

Finally, all of these specifics must rest in a setting where the daily activity conveys to the patient the staff's concern for his or her health and well-being. Reciprocally, the staff should accord the patient the dignity of expecting responsible concern for their joint enterprise.

REFERENCES

1. Group for the Advancement of Psychiatry: Pharmacotherapy and Psychotherapy: Paradoxes, Problems and Progress. Report 93. New York, GAP, 1975
2. Buber M: I and Thou. New York, Charles Scribner's Sons, 1958
3. Whitehead AN: Science and the Modern World. New York, Macmillan Co. 1925
4. Cassirer E: An Essay on Man. New Haven, Yale University Press, 1944
5. Edelson M: The Idea of a Mental Illness. New Haven, Yale University Press, 1971
6. Langer SK: Philosophy in a New Key: A Study in the Symbolism of Reason, Rite and Art. New York, New American Library, 1942
7. Klauber J: The psychoanalyst as a person. Br J Med Psychol 41:315-322, 1968
8. Olinick S: On empathy and regression in service of the other. Br J Med Psychol 42:41-50, 1969
9. Sarwer-Foner GJ: The role of neuroleptic medication in psychotherapeutic interaction. Compr Psychiatry 1:291-300, 1960
10. Irwin S: Framework for the selection and use of psychoactive drugs, in Neuro-Psycho-Pharmacology: Proceedings of the Fifth International Congress of the Collegium Internationale Neuropsychopharmacologium. Edited by Brill HF. New York, Excerpta Medica Foundation, 1967, pp 150-156
11. Parsons T: Research with human subjects and the "professional complex." Daedalus 98:325-360, 1969
12. Carpenter WT Jr, Langsner CA: The nurse's role in informed consent. Nursing Times 71:1049-1051, 1975
13. Carpenter WT Jr: A new setting for informed consent. Lancet 1:500-501, 1974.

APPENDIX 1
Incompatibilities Between the Subject-Object and Subject-Subject Modes of Relatedness

SUBJECT OBJECT MODE

1. Act on
2. For gratification of subject
3. Take from
4. Decide for
5. Observe
6. More intellectual
7. Dominate
8. Coerce

SUBJECT-SUBJECT MODE

1. Act with
2. For mutual gratification
3. Share with
4. Negotiate with
5. Experience with
6. More affective
7. Cooperate
8. Convince

9

Problems in Integrating Traditional Group Therapies with New Group Forms

MORTON A. LIEBERMAN

Periodically the field of group psychotherapy enters into a cataclysmic state during which it responds as if it experiences itself facing an alien horde. We have, during the last four or five years, shown every sign of such response to that large body of change endeavors conducted in groups labeled the "new therapies." Some perspective can be gained on our current cataclysm if we step back for a moment and examine our responses in the Fifties and early Sixties to what we then called "group dynamics." One can discern a clear developmental sequence in response to that alien horde. At first the very existence of the group dynamicists was ignored; we acted as if their activities had little to do with our field and as though they would go away if we did not acknowledge them. As we know all too well, denial is a costly and relatively inefficient mechanism. The next stage was attack. Aggression offers a much more variegated form of response and can manifest itself in a variety of garb; ridicule, for example, or accusing the others of mysticism ("How can you 'treat' a group?"). A headier weapon was challenging the therapeutic significance of the alien's work ("It's only symptom relief, not real change.").

When the threat became more acute, larger canon, if I may be forgiven the pun, were rolled out. We questioned the invaders' product; rather than helping people, we

Reprinted by permission from *International Journal of Group Psychotherapy*, XXVII (January 1977), 19–32.

suggested, they may be harming them. To add injury to insult, we attempted to make these aliens non-persons by maintaining that, lacking experience or training comparable to our own, they must be less than professional or competent. These defenses gained time but ultimately failed. Our cohesiveness was breached and we found some of the aliens within our own house. At this point, we turned to the ultimate defense, incorporation, and its last stage, absorption. For some of us, it has been total ingestion, so that the alien is no longer an alien and the boundaries between what we do and think and what they do and think have ceased to exist. Our stomachs may ache, but we have a sense of victory in that we no longer see a threatening horde on the horizon. Others of us have practiced selective ingestion, assimilating portions of the alien found palatable. Still others of us have chosen to modify the alien so that he is not an alien any longer, or to modify ourselves so that "we" and "they" are no longer an appropriate way to view the world.

Apparently, we have completed the process with regard to the group dynamicists since, aside from an occasional murmur by those in our field who are prone to repetition compulsion, little is said currently vis-à-vis that now ancient and tamed alien horde. However, in examining group therapists' response to the "newer therapies," many of the current reactions to Encounter, behavioral therapies, T.A., Gestalt, and so on match the variety of reactions seen in yesterday's response to "group dynamics."

In an effort to pinpoint our current location in the process of accommodation to the "newer therapies," this paper is directed toward examining the nature and shape of the new aliens in order to distinguish what makes them different from us. Much of my attention will be devoted to group-based mental health activities that may appear to lie outside the boundaries of group psychotherapy.

Distinctions between group psychotherapies and other types of groups for healing are increasingly difficult to make. We have been accustomed to think of such distinctions in terms of differences in clientele, an assumption that, as I hope to demonstrate, is unwarranted. Sometimes such distinctions are made on the grounds that group therapy is the province of the professionals, whereas the wide variety of other types of healing groups are commonly led by laymen. Increasingly this distinction becomes hard to maintain. One can find well-credentialed professionals practicing the range from traditional to unconventional forms of group healing efforts. Among those leading today's people-changing groups outside of traditional settings are professionals who have been prepared by long years of training in prestigious institutions, as well as individuals whose sole preparation has consisted of a two-week institute, or, for that matter, no more than a purely personal judgment that they have something to give. The boundary lines between the more traditional healing groups and their modern counterparts are further blurred by the increasing variation in institutional settings where group healing activities take place. While many healing groups are still to be found in traditional help-giving settings, more and more frequently such activities are conducted in growth centers, a new institution specifically formed for conducting people-changing groups.

For good or ill, innovations in recent years have largely emanated, not from traditional mental health professionals, but from the newer forms of group activity. The new group forms are having increased impact on the practice of group psychotherapy, a fact of life which further obscures the distinctions between professionally dominated forms and the newer, more nonprofessional forms. Not to be dismissed is the possibility that the newer forms of group healing provide service for more clients who are seeking relief from psychological stress than do the traditional forms.

Discussions about integrating old and new therapies usually focus on dynamic theories of group psychotherapy in contrast to the variety of practices variously labeled Transactional Analysis, Gestalt, Encounter, and so forth. Yet, scanning the field of group-based activities whose central task is the behavioral alteration of individuals and the relief of psychological misery would suggest that the range of such activities extends far beyond those mentioned. Let me briefly examine four major types of group-based change currently practiced in our society. At one end of a continuum are those activities that formally fall within the purview of societally sanctioned, professionally led groups: group psychotherapy. Group therapy has as its avowed public goal the production of mental health, its activities operate explicitly within a medical framework, and it sees as its relevant population those who define themselves as patients experiencing psychological misery. Its emphasis on malfunctioning, defined in terms of "sick behavior" by which prospective participants bring themselves into the formally defined system, implies that some individuals within society are legitimized as appropriate clientele and others are seen as inappropriate.

At the opposite end of the continuum are a variety of self-help movements— Alcoholics Anonymous, Synanon, Recovery, Inc., and so forth. Although by intention these groups are not professionally led, as lay movements they share some notions of appropriate clientele with group psychotherapy. The definition of appropriateness is usually much narrower than in group psychotherapy, but there are clear-cut inclusion-exclusion principles. One must be an alcoholic, an abuser of drugs, a child-abuser, a parent of a child who has a particular disease, etc. These types of self-help groups are limited to individuals who have a common symptom, problem, or life predicament.

A third set of healing groups falls under the rubric of the Human Potential movement and includes such variously labeled activities as sensitivity training, encounter groups, and so on. Although there are many instances of nonprofessional leadership, these activities usually do involve professionals, whether legitimized by traditional disciplines or by newer types of training institutions. A major distinction between the previously mentioned activities and encounter or growth groups is that the latter view themselves as having universal applicability. Unlike group therapy, which emphasizes patienthood, or self-help programs, which emphasize a common problem, the Human Potential movement emphasizes the relevance of its activities to all who want to change, grow, and develop.

Finally, we come to consciousness-raising groups, which share with self-help groups a commitment to peer control but have much broader criteria for inclusion. Although, unlike the Human Potential movement, they do not admit everyone, consciousness-raising groups are formed on the basis of very general demographic similarities: sex, race, ethnicity, age, or sexual behavior. The tie that binds is not an aberrant personal behavior but a social characteristic of a large subgroup of people, which permits wide latitude regarding personal peculiarities.

These explanations describe how these institutions classify themselves and their clients, but do they reflect clients' expectations? Are these rather abstract distinctions in any way relevant to the dimensions by which a client chooses among therapy groups, consciousness-raising groups, self-help groups, or the many group activities within the Human Potential movement? What follows is a summary of findings[1] gathered from participants who enter sensitivity training, various types of human potential groups, psychotherapeutic settings, and women's consciousness-raising groups.

These studies provide survey information on the users of these new activities: Why do they come? What do they expect? How, if at all, do they differ from the users of traditional psychotherapy? Specifically, do the goals and the expectations of participants entering traditional mental health institutions differ from the goals and expectations of participants entering activities in the Human Potential movement or women's consciousness-raising groups?

Self-administered questionaries were sent to 656 prospective participants at five growth centers (426 returned the Q), 125 NTL participants (108 returned the Q), and a nationwide sample of 1700 participants in women's CR groups (the first 200 respondents were used in the analysis). A contrast sample to the Human Potential participants was generated from similar questionnaires given to 150 applicants to five private psychiatric clinics (89 returned the Q). The questionnaires were completed prior to participation.

A broad range of questions about motivations, perceptions, and attitudes were asked. Two measures of psychological disturbance were included which, in previous studies, differentiated psychiatric patients from nonpatients: life stress (Paykel et al., 1971) and (self-reported) psychiatric symptoms (Frank et al., 1957). The samples were also examined for their help-seeking characteristics defined as endorsing such goals as: to deal with current life problems, to bring about change in self, to resolve long-term life problems, to obtain relief from things I do or feel that are troubling me, to obtain help, to work on personal problems. A national probability sample (Uhlenhuth et al., 1972) provided normative data on stress and symptoms for contrast with the clinic, growth center, and women's CR samples.

Table I shows the stress scores, the symptom scores, and the help-seeking motivation in contrast to goals reflecting self-improvement, professional development, social or recreational interests. Table I also shows the percentage of people within each of these systems who were currently or had previously been in psychotherapy.

[1]The survey on growth centers was conducted by Dr. J. Gardner and myself ("Institutional Alternatives to Psychotherapy: A Study of Growth Center Users," *Archives of General Psychiatry*, 1975); the study on women's consciousness-raising groups was conducted by Dr. D. Kravetz of the University of Wisconsin and myself.

An examination of this table reveals that, although the degree to which the various systems attract participants exhibiting high levels of distress (life stress and symptomatology) and avowed help-seeking motivation differs, participants in all systems were considerably higher than a normative population on stress and symptoms. Another way to portray the same set of data is to indicate the number of individuals entering such systems with direct psychotherapeutic or help-seeking goals; for the psychotherapy patients, of course, the number reaches almost 100 percent (98%); for the growth center participants, 70 percent; for the NTL sample, 54 percent; and for the women in consciousness-raising groups, 65 percent. Thus, the patientlike characteristics of these samples emerged strongly on all the variables. They resembled a clinic population much more than they did a normal population.

The Human Potential movement's appeal is not primarily for hedonistic, playful seekers after joy. Rather, participant goals are instrumental and focus primarily around issues of obtaining help with personal problems. Those who enter women's CR groups are not primarily engaged in a political act. For one half to three-quarters of the sample, their stated reasons for attending were related to relieving their psychological misery. No matter whether we examine psychotherapeutic, Human Potential, or women's groups, it is the same group of clients with the same needs who are entering all three. Thus, despite the relatively large differences in institutional character, in methods, and in the theoretical orientations underlying them (which is the usual issue when integration is discussed), the fact is that integration has already taken place on a client level. It is not that people neatly select out, on the basis of specific needs, which of these systems to enter. They enter, usually serially but for many simultaneously, two or more of these systems.

Is the notion of integration of the kind we are discussing perhaps an outmoded idea unless we also examine the influence of our clients on the practice of therapy and of leadership? Certainly the fact that clients have experienced other systems must influence the practice of any one system. To each they bring experience and expectations based upon the other, and probably exert considerable influence

TABLE 1
Mean Stress, Symptom, Help-Seeking Scores* of Clients in Various Experiential Groups

Experiential Groups	Stress		Symptoms		Help-Seeking		Previous or Current Psychotherapy
	X	S.D.	X	S.D.	X	S.D.	
Normative Population (Oakland Study) (N = 700)	5.6	(5.6)	9.8	(9.5)	---		---
Growth Center (N = 426)	7.8	(6.1)	23.3	(12.7)	12.1	(4.7)	81%
NTL (N = 108)	7.6	(4.2)	19.0	(12.8)	13.8	(4.6)	54%
Women's CR (N = 200)	8.3	(7.1)	22.6	(14.9)	14.9	(4.7)	56%
Clinic (N = 89)	10.9	(7.3)	36.8	(14.9)	7.6	(2.1)	---

*Stress 0-100; Help-Seeking 6-24; (6-high, 24-low)

on what we, as therapists, do. For example, the probable increase in therapist transparency among most practitioners is more likely a product of patient expectation than of any radical shifts in theroretical perspective. The traditional "blank screen" demeanor is just not possible any more with most clients. This has nothing to do, I think, with a major discovery or realignment but with responding to the demands, needs, and expectations of the clients themselves.

This is not to imply that there are no distinctions among these systems. For example, expectations of how change takes place are distinct. A list of eleven experiences commonly associated with change was shown to all respondents prior to participation. They were asked to indicate how important they thought each experience would be in achieving the goals they brought to NTL, growth center, clinic, or CR group. The list included experimentation, learning positive qualities, seeing undesirable things about self, obtaining insight, being confronted and challenged, feeling excitement and joy, being supported, getting advice, revelation, experiencing negative feelings, and becoming anxious or depressed. Rank order correlations among the four settings revealed that NTL and the growth center participants had similar process expectations ($r = .8$); clinic participants correlated $-.2$ with all other

TABLE 2.
Process Expectations

Encounter Study	Ranks Based on Group Means			
Item	Clinic Patients	Growth Centers	NTL T-Groups	Women's CR Groups
1. Experiment with new behavior.	10	3	6	5
2. Learn positive qualities.	7	5	5	2
3. See undesirable things about self.	2	4	3	7
4. Get insight from understanding of past.	1	9	10	3
5. Be confronted and challenged.	5	2	1	10
6. Experience excitement and joy.	11	1	2	4
7. Be supported and valued.	9	6	4	1
8. Reveal secrets.	6	10	11	6
9. Receive advice.	8	11	9	9
10. Experience negative feelings.	4	8	8	8
11. Become anxious or depressed.	5	7	7	11

settings; consciousness-raising groups had little similarity with any of the settings. Thus, at least three of the institutions—consciousness-raising groups, clinics, and growth centers/NTL—were seen by prospective participants as possessing a distinct type of change experience.

Table 2 shows the "process" expectations toward these four institutions. Participants entering NTL emphasize confrontation, joy, discovery of undesirable things about self; those entering growth centers also emphasize confrontation and joy but place more emphasis on experimentation. By and large, traditional change-induction methods, revelation, advice, and insight, are eschewed, as well as the painful aspects of change-induction itself. In contrast, clinic patients expect the painful aspects of change to form the core experience and see little joy or pleasure in the process. Women in consciousness-raising groups emphasize the supporting qualities of the experience and clearly do not perceive the system as being one in which aggressiveness or pain is involved.

Thus, our findings highlight the fact that the clientele are going to the "old" and "new" with similar needs but with variations in how they think such needs will be met.

STRUCTURAL AND TECHNICAL DIFFERENCE AMONG GROUPS

If both the goals and the client systems overlap among the various settings that use group methods for healing, what are some of the important distinctions among them? Perhaps the most important technological change characterizing the newer forms is reflected in techniques for lessening the psychological distance between leader and participant. A variety of methods serve this function; the transparency of the therapist (personal revelations and so forth), the use of informal settings, the emphasis on assuming the stance of participant, the emphasis that characterizes some of the new forms on diminishing the importance of the expertise of the leader and defining him more nearly as a peer, and, finally, the use of physical contact (touching); all are devices which seem to be calculated to reduce the psychological distance between the changer and the changing.

Few guidelines exist by which to assess the importance of such differences from the traditional patient-therapist relationship. Perhaps all that can be said with certainty is that such changes reflect current social mores, which have increasingly moved away from emphasis on the priestly status of healing professionals and other experts. The new forms, having developed more recently, can be said to be more sensitive than the old to current cultural expectations.

A second major distinction between therapy and encounter groups, on the one hand, and most self-help and consciousness-raising groups, on the other, relates to their conception of the function of the group as a mechanism for personal change. Both psychotherapy and encounter groups of almost all theoretical persuasions share, as a fundamental assumption, a view of the group as a *social microcosm*. It is this aspect of the group, that is, its reflection of the interpersonal issues that confront individuals in the larger society, that is most highly prized as the group property which induces individual change. Varying types of encounter and psychotherapeutic schools of thought differ, of course, about which transactions are most important: those between patient and therapist or those among patients. They also differ regarding which emotional states are most conducive to positive change. But underneath all the activities that fall into these two types lies the assumption that cure or change is based on the exploration and reworking of relationships in the group.

Self-help groups and consciousness-raising groups have a rather different view as to the issue of the group as a microcosm. The interaction among members appears to be somewhat de-emphasized as a vehicle for change. The group is a supportive environment for developing new behavior not within the group primarily but outside of it. The group becomes a vehicle for cognitive restructuring, but analysis of the transactions among members is not the basic tool of change.

Another characteristic that contrasts these four systems is the degree to which they stress differentiation versus nondifferentiation among their members. Belonging to the class of "being neurotic" or having psychological difficulty or being a patient is a vague and relatively unbound identification compared to being a member of a minority group, for example, a woman in a consciousness-raising group. Being interested in growth and development is an indistinct and obviously more vague basis for forming an identity with a communal effort than being an alcoholic or a child-abuser. It is easier for consciousness-raising groups and self-help groups to stress identity with a common core problem than it is for psychotherapy and encounter groups. Although it is typical for a psychotherapeutic group to go through a period in which similarities are stressed, this is usually an early developmental phase and represents an attempt of the group to achieve some form of cohesiveness. It is not the *raison d'être* of the group, as it may be for a consciousness-raising or self-help group. In fact, there is some evidence (Lieberman et al., 1975) that individuals in encounter groups who remain committed to a sense of similarity are less likely to be changed positively by such an experience. However, the potency of both self-help and consciousness-raising groups appears to stem from their continued insistence on the possession of a common problem, and members believe that they are deriving support from their identification with a common core issue.

An important distinction among the various systems of group-based healing rests in their attribution system: the cognitive and conative structure explicitly and implicitly communicated regarding the source of human misery and how one resolves it. An obvious example would be the degree to which the systems emphasize internal versus external sources of the problem. Most familiar are the psychotherapeutic systems that attribute the source of psychological difficulty to the personal past. This is in contrast to the women's consciousness-raising movement, which emphasizes an external locus of the problem: an impersonal, sexist society. In our attempt to understand what processes may be psychotherapeutic, I beleive we have paid too little attention to the effect of varying attribution systems on change. One of the intriguing impressions from our study of encounter groups (Lieberman et al., 1973) was that, in comparing a wide variety of theories of change as expressed in leader orientation, it did not seem to make much difference which theory was "taught" as long as some cognitive structure was taken away from the group to explain one's problems and how to resolve them. Whether this observation would fit the larger differences in attribution systems one can assume between, for example, a psychotherapeutic group and a women's consciousness-raising group is a major unknown.

DISCUSSION AND SUMMARY

To summarize, the central issue is *the integration of the old and new forms.* (I have tried to be inclusive in defining the new forms since individuals with psychological misery currently seek help in a large variety of systems.) Certainly in some ways our clients and patients have taken the major steps toward integration for us. They bring similar needs and goals into a wide variety of group settings and seem to make few important distinctions between them. The number of individuals in our survey who participated in psychotherapy as well as growth centers and women's CR groups is considerable. Could it be, in fact, that all of us are dealing with a relatively permanent client system of some x million people who are perpetual seekers after help and who rotate through these various systems?

If, from the clients' point of view, integration of old and new forms has largely been accomplished, is integration possible among the purveyors? While the distance between the various systems, in my opinion, lies less in the practice than it does in perspectives and values among purveyors, the issue of integration usually focuses on the problem of integrating theories. If integration of theories starts at the level of the assumptive set about what it is that ails man, then I believe it is well-nigh impossible to bridge the large chasm between the various points of view. They are not reconcilable, for they begin with a distinct set of assumptions of how it is that individuals develop the psychological misery that needs help. Nor do I think that one can bridge the gaps between the various perspectives on what is central to change induction. What people need to change, grow, develop, mature is something intrinsically bound to how theorists define what is wrong with individuals, so that intellectually leaping these gaps is almost impossible. For example, self-help groups do not view the group as a social microcosm for exploiting the here-and-now, while this group characteristic is at the very heart of most therapeutic and encounter group procedures.

If, by integration, we mean technical integration, certainly this occurs, but I see this not as integration in any real sense of the word. Rather, it is an amalgamation of unrelated pieces, a product of therapeutic despair that causes us to seek constantly after new devices, perspectives, ways of helping people. The constant repetition within the American Group Psychotherapy Association of the same workshops would attest to this; perhaps mental health professionals are the greatest help-seekers of them all, and we attempt to cope with the difficult task of helping our fellow-men by constantly searching out new devices. In my opinion, the only route to meaningful integration lies in the systematic exploration of help-giving systems to determine what are really the active ingredients of change and for whom. I think the most reasonable hope for breakthrough in our field will come when we are able to specify particular settings, techniques, or ways of applying our skills to particular sets of people and their needs.

REFERENCES

Frank, J. D. et al. (1957), Why Patients Leave Psychotherapy. *Arch. Neur. & Psychiat.*, 77:282–299.

Lieberman, M.A., Yalom, I.D., and Miles, M.B. (1973), *Encounter Groups: First Facts*. New York: Basic Books.

Paykel, E.S. et al. (1971), Scaling of Life Events. *Arch. Gen. Psychiat.*, 25:340–347.

Uhlenhuth, E. H. et al. (1972), The Demography of Life Stress. Presented at meetings of the American College of Neuro-psychopharmacology, San Juan, Puerto Rico, December, 1972.

Part Four

Modern Forms of Psychotherapy

To say the least, there has been no stagnation in the forms of psychotherapy over the past few decades. Indeed, every day seems to bring forth the announcement and justification, if not celebration, of still another school of psychotherapy. For some people, the ever-expanding directory of psychotherapies is cause for celebration. For other people, however, it is a matter of dire seriousness and concern. If one cannot accurately catalogue the various contemporary forms and theories of psychotherapy, how then can one work out the appropriate credentials for those advancing the new forms?

But that's just the point, the new cadres of psychotherapy would argue. The basis of traditional credentials has been a serious, and not always creative, influence on the shape of psychotherapy in the first place. Indeed, much of contemporary psychotherapy reflects a very definite dissatisfaction with the traditional therapies and therapist. Hence not only are the traditional theories and techniques under attack, but with them, training institutions and governing boards are being publicly challenged. Yet we would leave the reader with an unfair perspective if we dropped the matter at this point. For, to be fair, while certain forms of contemporary psychotherapy have been developed in response or reaction to tradition, many contemporary forms have been derived from the traditional forms, updated as it were. Still other forms of psychotherapy have emerged out of contemporary social issues and philosophies, with very little consideration given to the past. This last point, actually, is the basis for the following selections and thereby deserves some elaboration.

To be sure, there are a great many aspects to the evolution of psychotherapy over the last seventy years. While historians of the subject make it only too clear that social and historical factors influenced the practice of psychotherapy and the form of engagement called for in the psychotherapeutic process, it is also evident that many contemporary forms of psychotherapy have evolved directly in response to social and historical conditions. That is, many therapists openly argued for the political nature of psychotherapy. What went on, they said, in the therapeutic relationship not only reflected some of society's greatest problems; the problems, in a sense, were perpetuated and legitimized in psychotherapy. Put a little differently, the new critics of psychotherapy alleged that society was in great measure the source of a person's problems, and hence a form of psychotherapy that did not take this incontrovertible fact into account was utterly misled, and possibly dangerous too. An example of this conflict can be seen in the role of sexuality. At the turn of the century a highly repressed, Victorian culture's attitudes toward sexuality clearly influenced the sort of problems one brought into psychotherapy, as well as the approach to those problems taken by the psychotherapist. Nowadays, as social values shift and acquire their more up-to-date forms, we notice stark differences in the sorts of so-called sexual problems brought into treatment by patients, as well as corresponding changes in the approaches to these problems by therapists. The contemporary psychotherapist, however, would say both of these examples are lacking in one basic insight—namely, society's conception of sexuality and the distinctions made between the so-called masculine and feminine are at the root of the problems of psychotherapy, not just the problems brought to therapists by their patients. In fact—and this is an important point—we may be doing people an unforgivable injustice merely by labeling them patients. Perhaps it would be best to call them victims, or short of this, clients.

The point is hardly a subtle one. Many of the so-called contemporary forms of psychotherapy have been established in order to take a stand not only against the stressful aspects of culture and society, but with the assumption that it makes sense to hunt for the source of an individual's problems in our institutions and in the life styles promoted by these institutions. And something else: Many contemporary approaches to psychotherapy are not as concerned with the etiology of a problem or stress as they are with relieving the tension. That is, whereas some of the traditional therapies were aimed at self-understanding, or indeed conceived of the therapeutic process as a valuable research tool, some of the more contemporary psychotherapies address themselves pure and simple to the alleviation of the problem. But, some might well argue, how can a problem be solved when its source is unknown, and the very reason for its presence is not understood? The question is a significant one, and some of the selections throughout this book are addressed to just this point. For now, let us merely suggest that some of the contemporary forms of psychotherapy believe strongly that while the (historical) source of a person's problem is not all that significant vis-à-vis the treatment aspect of psychotherapy, changing aspects of the person's present life style are essential to the treatment process. And so these therapies are designed to approach the client's problems head-on by instituting both personal and, when possible, social change. The results usually are shorter treatment programs and claims by psychotherapists and clients alike of definite progress and noticeable improvement. Adjustment, then, is no longer the key concept that it seemed to be in the traditional psychotherapies. Change has become the relevant word, in an era when the concept of relevance itself has become quintessential.

10

New Approaches in Counselling: Healthy Diversity or Anti-Therapeutic?

C.H. PATTERSON

Concern is expressed about the proliferation of new or 'innovative' approaches in counselling or psychotherapy. Most of these approaches appear to be regressive in that they ignore what we have learned about the importance of certain conditions for the therapeutic relationship. They place the counsellor or therapist in the position of a charismatic expert controlling and directing the lives of his clients. The potential dangers of these methods are noted. Yet there seems to be no good way to protect clients either from well-intentioned but misguided professionals or from the untrained non-professional. If professionals are not successful in policing the field, injured consumers and an aroused public may succeed in imposing unnecessarily rigid restrictions on all practice of counselling and psychotherapy.

'The field of psychotherapy is in a mess'. So said Rogers (1961). Around the same time another author wrote:

'The present situation in psychotherapy is not unlike that of a man who mounted his horse and rode off in all directions. The theoretical orientation of therapists is based on widely divergent hypotheses, theories and ideologies. . . . Individual practitioners of any art are expected to vary, but some well-organised schools of therapy also seem to be working at cross-purposes with other equally well-organised schools' (Ungersma, 1961).

Reprinted by permission from *British Journal of Guidance and Counselling*, 5 (January 1977), 19–25.

At that time I did not share the pessimism represented by these quotations. I was engaged in writing a review of the major schools of counselling or psychotherapy (Patterson, 1966). The final chapter of this book was entitled 'Divergences and Convergences in Counselling or Psychotherapy'. I was convinced that there were some basic common elements in all the major schools or approaches, namely the three therapist-offered conditions proposed by Rogers (1957) as the necessary and sufficient therapist conditions for therapeutic personality change: empathic understanding, unconditional positive regard or respect, and congruence or therapeutic genuineness. In addition to the recognition that these conditions are implicit if not explicit in all the major theories, there was accumulating evidence that where these conditions are present in counselling or psychotherapy at high levels (regardless of the school or theory espoused by the therapist) positive outcomes occur as measured by a wide variety of criteria or instruments, and that where these conditions are not present to a minimal degree, positive outcomes are not present and indeed there is often deterioration in clients (see e.g. Truax and Carkhuff, 1967; Rogers *et al.*, 1967; Carkhuff, 1969; Truax and Mitchell, 1971).

Thus there seemed to be developing a convergence upon the recognition and acceptance of these conditions as basic to all effective counselling or psychotherapy. To be sure, the behaviourists appeared to ignore them, insisting that change occurred only as a result of the application of behaviouristic techniques. But the importance of the relationship has now been recognised and demonstrated even in behaviour therapy. Thus I was led to write (during my year in England) that 'the days of "schools" in counselling or psychotherapy are drawing to a close' (Patterson, 1974).

I have now become convinced that I was premature in making this statement. In the last few years we have witnessed an increasing trend towards divergence. Anything goes now in psychotherapy. The field *is* in a mess. Rogers, in making his 1961 statement, added that he felt the confusion was a healthy climate for new ideas, theories, methods and concepts. Certainly new ideas and techniques are being promulgated. Every few months we have a new technique or approach being advocated in books and journal articles. But what is discouraging—and disturbing—is the lack of, or the inadequacy of, theory and concepts supporting the new methods or techniques; the ignoring, or ignorance of, the research supporting what have come to be known as the core conditions; the evangelistic fervour with which many of the approaches are advocated; the lack of concern for any evidence of their effectiveness except possibly testimonials; the failure to recognise that what is called counselling or psychotherapy can be for better or worse—that people can be hurt as well as helped; and finally, the eagerness with which the approaches are commercialised. Many of the originators of new approaches are not satisfied with publishing books and articles, and then waiting for their ideas to be subjected to critical scrutiny, evaluation and research before eventually being accepted or rejected, or modified and revised and finally incorporated in the teaching and training programmes of universities. Instead, many of these methods are being promoted by advertising and workshops and short-term training courses, or are the basis for institutes or organisations which issue diplomas and certificates, all resembling the development of a cult (e.g. scientology, EST,[1] transactional analysis (TA), primal scream therapy, and even Gestalt therapy).

It is argued that such means of promulgating new and innovative ideas are necessary because of the resistance of organised education to new ideas. But many universities in the USA are scrambling to get in on the new movements. It is disturbing that so many academics, who presumably have been trained in research and in insistence on evidence for effectiveness, are accepting and teaching methods which are unsupported by such evidence. Even they seem to have little if any concern about the possibility of harm or damage to those subjected to these untested methods.

The use for freedom to do anything is often argued on the basis of the desirability of experimentation. This is the position taken by Corsini (1970), referring to the group movement:

'I think that the best thing right now is *hands off*. It's probably best not to try any policing. We just don't know enough . . . I think we must all trust one another, even the people we know are fools and have no business trying to do group therapy or sensitivity training or encounter work. I don't think that anyone can know what is right and what is wrong. A couple of years ago if a psychologist had done what some people are now doing, he would have been arrested. We are in a mad period of uncontrolled growth, development and experimentation and I think this is good. After a while the excesses will become evident, the dross will be cleaned off, and we may get some greater understanding.'

There seems, however, to be a confusion here between experimentation and experiment. In an experiment there is a planned evaluation of the results or effects of the treatment. But those who are practising most of these new methods are not conducting experiments. They are not collecting systematic data on outcomes and relating outcomes to treatments. Further, in research on human beings there are standards for the protection of subjects. Yet there is little if any concern for the protection of subjects, or clients, who are subjected to the new methods or techniques. Standards accepted for research are not applied to experimentation in the counselling field.

Indeed, some reject any ethical concern and leave it up to the law:

'The law sets limits on the behaviours that one individual may show towards another, and these limits will surely apply within a group if its members call for aid. If they do not seek the protection of the law, then can we, as psychologists, set limits when the individual does not? Can we deny to any psychologist—or to anyone else—the right to lead a group based on his own responsibility, any group whatsoever, with whatever goals? Can we set *ethical* limits on whether a

---

[1]Not electro-shock therapy, but (Werner) Erhard Seminars Training. For a description of the admittedly rip-off nature of the 'training' see *Time*, 7 June 1976, pp. 53–54.

trainer should be able to assault a group member, or to strip her, if in the situation, he thinks it appropriate, and she elected to accept it? Can he not do whatever the situation demands as he sees it, recognising that the law is concerned only if charges are pressed?' (Verplanck, 1976).

Well, in the USA charges are being pressed. Malpractice suits are increasing. Many of them involve sexual exploitation of female clients by male therapists. Such behaviour is no longer to be covered by insurance. And the Ethics Committee of the American Psychological Association has proposed adding the statement 'Sexual intimacies with clients are unethical' to the APA Code of Ethics. But there are other harmful behaviours that are not specified in the Code. Indeed, all such possible behaviours could not be specifically included even if agreed upon, for it is difficult to specify every damaging practice before its occurrence. It thus becomes a matter of determining whether a specific behaviour is unethical according to a general principle stated in the Code.

Some behaviours would seem to be indefensible in ethical terms. A psychologist in California has been sued by a patient who was subjected to 'rage reduction therapy', a technique to break down a patient's resistance by subjecting him/her to prolonged tactile stimulation while immobilised, thus inducing the expression of 'repressed' anger or rage. The patient had been strapped down and subjected to 'tickle torture' for 12 hours. In another suit, a woman claimed head injuries as a result of being struck by the therapist in group therapy. A group of therapists was also sued for damages for dislocated vertebrae sustained when the patient was held horizontally at shoulder height and then dropped (APA, 1976)

It is however difficult to control such behaviours, either through ethical codes or simply through the threat of possible lawsuits. Persons who are not members of a professional association are not influenced by ethical codes. One would think that common sense, as well as professional judgement, would deter such extreme treatment methods. Apparently this is not the case. For every situation which comes to light through charges of unethical conduct or lawsuits, there must be dozens, even hundreds, which are unknown either because the damage or injury was slight, or because the patients—or victims—are unaware of the psychological damage that has been done. Such lack of awareness may arise from trust and confidence in the therapist, and indeed the research of Lieberman et al. (1973) on encounter groups suggests that it is the charismatic therapist who does the most harm.

Such charismatic therapists or group leaders, who are apt to be poorly-qualified and motivated more by money and ego satisfaction than a desire to help people, are likely to draw people who are seeking a 'turn-on' experience (euphemistically called a 'growth' experience). These people, while apparently normal, can be psychologically vulnerable, though many become hardened group addicts. Some, as well as some leaders, use the groups for sexual exploitation. Certainly many such groups are not therapeutic; but by not making any claim that they are, leaders can avoid meeting any standards of professional education or experience.

In my view most of the proliferating new approaches, even those developed by people with professional training and experience, represent a regression rather than an advance. They are not a continuation or progression of the development of the 1960s, but actually are a return to earlier methods and techniques. The convergence of the 1960s was toward the development of a relationship in which the counsellor or therapist respects the client as a person with the potential for growing and developing, capable of working through his problems, making his own decisions, taking responsibility for himself, and developing a desirable autonomy and independence. The counsellor or therapist is necessary and important, but as a facilitator who provides an atmosphere or relationship conducive to growth, rather than as a director. He is an expert not in providing answers and solutions (no-one can really do this for another's life), but in providing the conditions which allow the client to discover his own answers and solutions. The relationship approaches that of equals: it is more horizontal than vertical.

When, however, one looks at the characteristics of the new approaches, they appear to have one thing in common: they involve the counsellor or therapist as an expert, actively engaged in techniques of a directive, controlling type, resulting in a vertical relationship with the client. This constitutes a reversion to earlier more authoritarian approaches. To the extent that they are successful it is mainly through the immediate but usually temporary placebo effect, which is maximised by suggestion and the counsellor's authority and prestige.

It appears, then, that these new approaches represent a change in attitude toward the client. And they are likely to appeal to counsellors, or potential counsellors, who lack respect for or confidence in the client. A group of students and counsellors may thus be attracted to the field who, by adopting these methods, will change the practice of counselling or psychotherapy for years to come. It may be argued that if the methods are ineffective this will eventually become evident, and that the effectiveness of the core conditions will be rediscovered. It may also be argued that experience will reveal the limits of the methods, so that (as some research has indicated) practitioners will move with experience toward the more egalitarian relationship methods. But we will have lost considerable time going up a blind alley and, even more important, have failed to help, or even have hurt, many clients who could have been helped.

The characteristics of the new approaches, which are shared by the recently fast-developing behaviour therapies, suggest that two major distinct if not incompatible approaches are emerging. One might be designated the technological approach, represented most clearly and systematically by behaviour therapies. This involves the application of techniques by an expert, on the basis of identifying a specific or discrete problem and selecting the appropriate specific technique for its solution. Therapy becomes a matter of technological operations; the therapist is a technician rather than a person. The newer approaches are not as systematic as behaviour modification, but they fit this general model, with the focus upon the technical operations or activities of the counsellor or therapist rather than upon the client-therapist relationship.

The second model might be called the existentialist approach. It is unstructured, and has been described as the technique of no technique. The operations of the therapist are not prescribed, but are based upon feelings or intuition. The emphasis is upon the experiencing of the client and the therapist. While it is a real, genuine, spontaneous personal encounter, it has elements of vagueness and mysteriousness which turn many away.

A third model seems, however, to be possible, representing an approach developing from client-centred therapy. It might be called the relationship model. It is relatively unstructured, involving a real, spontaneous personal encounter. It is unplanned in its details and in terms of specific objectives, but recognises a broad, ultimate aim which might be designated as the development of a more self-actualising person, with specific behaviour changes developing along with, or as by-products of, self-actualisation. The relationship is not entirely unstructured: the therapist's behaviour—his techniques, if you will—involves the implementation of the conditions of a therapeutic relationship. The client defines his own problems, and through self-exploration works through their resolution, becoming in the process a more independent, responsible, competent, confident, autonomous—in short, a more self-actualising—person. This approach is not so vague, intuitive and diffuse as the existentialist approach. It recognises and defines the conditions of a therapeutic relationship and the ways in which they can be implemented. It is not, as many believe, a non-specific treatment: it provides the specific conditions for the development of self-actualising persons.

The behaviouristic and the relationship models are not necessarily incompatible. They deal with different levels of behaviour and different psychological variables. Behaviour modification is concerned with specific overt behaviours, while relationship therapy is concerned not only with behaviour in a broader sense, but with perceptions, feelings, attitudes and beliefs. Relationship factors are present in behaviour modification and are necessary for its highest effectiveness. Conversely, behaviouristic elements—e.g., reinforcement—are present in relationship therapy, which can be described in part at least in behaviouristic terminology. Both approaches are concerned about effects and outcomes, and both are involved in research to investigate results.

It is the newer approaches which are of concern because their advocates do not seem to be interested in research or in long-term outcomes. They seem to be oblivious to the fact that psychological intervention can be for better or for worse. They ignore the medical principle of minimal intervention or conservative management, which recognises that the greater the intervention the greater the danger of harm or damage—a principle which seems clearly applicable in the psychological realm.

The new is not always better. It must be subjected to research and evaluation, with protection for those who are experimented upon, who are not to be exploited for profit and prestige. It is unfortunate that there is not some effective way to protect clients from unproved methods of treatment, as (at least to some extent) patients are protected from unproven drugs in the USA. Ralph Nader has recently turned his attention to the practice of counselling or psychotherapy, and may well focus his efforts to policing the field if exposure of abuses continues. If the excesses now being practised continue to proliferate, and malpractice suits increase, an enraged American public and Congress may well impose controls and restrictions which may go to an undesirable extreme. The same could happen in other countries, including Britain. It is unfortunate that so many educated or professional people uncritically accept what is new under the pressure of being innovative and current, and the allure of fame and fortune, and are so unconcerned about the possible harm to a gullible public.

REFERENCES

American Psychological Association: 'Confusion Reigns in APA Malpractice Plan'. *APA Monitor*, Volume 7 No.3, 1976, p.11.

Carkhuff, R.R.: *Helping and Human Relations*. Volumes I and II. New York: Holt, Rinehart and Winston, 1969.

Corsini, R.J.: 'Issues in Encounter Groups: Comments on Coulson's Article'. *The Counseling Psychologist*, Volume 2 No.2, 1970, pp. 28-34.

Lieberman, M.A., Yalom, I.D., and Miles, M.B.: *Encounter Groups: First Facts*. New York: Basic Books, 1973.

Patterson, C.H.: *Theories of Counseling and Psychotherapy*. New York: Harper & Row, 1966.

Patterson, C.H.: *Relationship Counseling and Psychotherapy*. New York: Harper & Row, 1974.

Rogers, C.R.: 'The Necessary and Sufficient Conditions of Therapeutic Personality Change'. *Journal of Consulting Psychology*, Volume 21, 1957, pp. 95-103.

Rogers, C.R.: 'Divergent Trends'. In May, R. (ed.): *Existential Psychology*. New York: Random House, 1961.

Rogers, C.R., Gendlin, E.T., Kiesler, D.J., and Truax, C.B.: *The Therapeutic Relationship and its Impact: a Study of Psychotherapy with Schizophrenics*. Madison, Wisconsin: University of Wisconsin Press, 1967.

Truax, C.B., and Carkhuff, R.R.: *Toward Effective Counseling and Psychotherapy*. Chicago: Aldine, 1967.

Truax, C.B., and Mitchell, K.M.: 'Research on Certain Therapist Interpersonal Skills in Relation to Process and Outcome'. In Bergin, A.E., and Garfield, S.L. (eds.): *Handbook of Psychotherapy and Behavior Change*, pp. 229-344. New York: Wiley, 1971.

Ungersma, A.J.: *Search for Meaning*. Philadelphia: Westminster Press, 1961.

Verplanck, W.J.: 'Trainers, Trainees and Ethics'. *The Counseling Psychologist*, Volume 2 No. 2, 1976, pp. 71-75.

11

Non-Sexist "Marital" Therapy

DAVID G. RICE AND JOY K. RICE

Certain factors limit marital therapists in dealing with individuals conflicted over and disenchanted about "traditional" marriage: 1) the therapist's gender, 2) the presence of sex-role stereotyped behaviors and expectations, and 3) the therapist's own marital experience. Specific helpful experiences (working with a co-therapist of the opposite sex, examining attitudes and biases toward divorce) and therapeutic techniques (working out a schedule for sharing household tasks and childcare, restructuring the marital contract, and dealing with open companionship) are discussed. The general therapeutic goal is working toward an equal sharing of overt power, with social, economic, and political considerations and intrapsychic forces given comparable consideration.

We are in an era of exploring and discovering new "marital"[1] life styles. Many couples have become disenchanted with "traditional" marriage (also known as "instrumental" or "utilitarian" marriage), and are seeking alternative ways of forming and maintaining committed interpersonal relationships (Bernard, 1973; Bird, 1969; Howe, 1972). For the purposes of this paper, "traditional" marriage is operationally defined as that in which the husband bears major responsibility for the economic maintenance of the family unit and the wife major responsibility for the domestic and childcare maintenance. Each may contribute to the other's "area" (e.g., the wife may work and the husband may help with household chores) but the major responsibility is held by

---

[1]Throughout this paper the terms "marital" and "couples" will be used in reference to individuals in an interpersonal relationship characterized by a commitment to one another. Although this will usually mean they are legally married, the issues raised and solutions proposed apply equally well to any two (or more) people in this type of relationship.

Reprinted by permission from *Journal of Marriage and Family Counseling,* 3 (January 1977), 3-10.

one spouse and the roles remain fixed as ascribed above. "Traditional" marriage by this definition is contrasted with "egalitarian" marriage in which economic, domestic, and childcare responsibilities especially are shared and the role ascriptions in this regard remain flexible and "open." Contributions to maintaining the family unit are thus based on personal preference and individual capabilities rather than dictated by social and gender role conditioning.

The process of changing a "traditional" marital relationship is often stressful and the individuals involved may seek professional help. Given the much greater ratio of male to female therapists in our society, the strong odds are that the couple will seek out or be referred to a male therapist (Chesler, 1971). In our experience, unless a male therapist has been in a nontraditional relationship with a woman, or has *had* to restructure his own marriage, his values and biases are likely to be those of "traditional" marriage. Indeed, given the social status and power of the husband's position in the traditional marital relationship (Bernard, 1971; Firestone, 1971) and given human nature, there is usually little impetus for a male therapist to change his interpersonal relationship patterns unless personal experience has motivated him to do so. If the couple is referred to a female therapist, one might expect that they would be less likely to encounter "traditional" marital values and biases. However, a woman therapist herself must have experienced the need to restructure her own relationships on an equalitarian basis and to face the issues and limitations involved in "traditional" marital patterning. If not, the patient couple may feel quickly some dissonance and value conflict with a therapist of either gender (Fabrikant, 1974).

Not only is the therapist likely to have a "traditional" type of marriage but, in addition, the bulk of his/her professional experience probably has been weighted toward treating couples or families with this type of interpersonal relationship pattern. Despite the therapist's proclamation of openness and "neutrality" of judgment, an increasing number of patients are likely to perceive a disparity in experience and values early in therapy, and soon feel that the therapist has little to offer in solving their problems, short of helping them to "get back into" a traditional-type relationship. Their contact with psychotherapy seems destined to result in disappointment and frustration (Krakauer, 1972). The problem in this situation rests as much with the therapist as with the clients. To deal successfully with such individuals, a good deal of therapeutic flexibility and true openness to changing one's values is required by the professional. Many couples who seek marital therapy will still want help with a dysfunctional, but "traditional" relationship. The therapist-patient value dissonance referred to above will be less likely to occur in such cases. But an increasing number of couples are seeking to evaluate and potentially restructure their marital relationship in light of such considerations as economic pressures, the greater societal acceptance of divorce, and the popularity of "open marriage" (O'Neill & O'Neill, 1972). This paper will raise issues and provide certain guidelines to help therapists deal with couples who are in conflict over changing "marital" life styles and values.

Partly in response to the Women's Liberation Movement, "traditional" marriage has also been affected sharply by women and men who feel an affinity with new feminist issues and values. For example, a higher proportion of women are choosing to remain single, the birth rate is dropping, more women are entering and remaining in the labor force, and the divorce rate continues to increase (Carnegie Commission, 1973). Laws (1971) has thoroughly delineated how the field of marital counseling, and particularly the standards of marital adjustment, have been strongly weighted toward maintaining "traditional" marriage. Yet, individuals in nontraditional, "egalitarian" marriages report greater felt marital satisfaction (Bailyn, 1970).

In summary, the main factors likely to limit therapist effectiveness in dealing with individuals who are conflicted and disenchanted about traditional marriage are; 1) the gender and sex role conditioning of the therapist, 2) the effect of socially reinforced sexrole stereotypes, which have offered the women less access to sources of sustained self-esteem and enhanced personal growth, and 3) the therapist's own marital situation and/or experience, which may be "traditional" in nature and limiting in flexibility and receptiveness to alternative models. Once the therapist is aware of these difficulties, however, certain experiences can be used to maximize effectiveness in working with individuals in conflicted marital relationships. We will discuss three general types of such experiences: working with a co-therapist of the opposite sex, gaining an openness to alternative life styles, and some specific therapeutic marital tasks and procedures.

THERAPEUTIC IMPLICATIONS

Working With a Co-therapist of the Opposite Sex

A useful, and perhaps most easily arranged, experience for a therapist is to work with co-therapists of the opposite sex. This can be a powerful learning situation for the therapist and an effective interpersonal modeling experience for the patients. It is critical, however, that the co-therapist relationship not model simply the traditional pattern of male-female relating (Rice & Rice, 1975). The therapists should have comparable professional status, and regard one another as peers. They should both be experienced therapists, or at least relatively similar in their degree of experience. The office used for therapy should ideally be a "neutral" one, and both therapists should begin working with the couple as early in therapy as possible, before "individual" relationships are formed. In addition, the co-therapists need to be careful that they do not overtly or covertly "assign" to one another specific gender-related therapeutic "tasks." Too often, there is an implicit message for the female therapist to "take care of feelings" and for the male therapist to "provide the interpretations." In this case, the co-therapists are modeling the traditional type of male-instrumental, female-expressive relationship pattern that the couple is attempting to change. The result could be simply to reinforce the status quo, and lead the patients to become disillusioned with their therapists.

Despite these possible difficulties, the experience of working with a statusful and competent co-therapist of the opposite sex can be a powerful force in helping therapists to increase their sensitivity to conflictual male-female relationship patterns. This occurs in part via the opportunity to perceive the feelings of each marital partner from the perspective of another person who, hopefully, has dealt with conflicts surrounding socially stereotyped sex-role conditioned behaviors. Paradoxically, those therapists most sensitive to role-stereotyped behaviors may be the ones most likely to work with co-therapists of the opposite gender. They may need this experience as a stimulus for change *less* than those therapists not likely to choose to work within this format.

Gaining an Openness to Alternative Marital Life Styles

This is attained most directly by the therapist changing his or her own marital relationship. If one is successful at this task, the rewards of enhanced self-esteem and felt competence by one's mate or partner can be powerful and satisfying. The first step in this process (and perhaps the first therapeutic task with a couple) is the working toward a sharing of overt power in the relationship.

Before therapists can be open to non-traditional "marital" life styles, they need to examine especially their attitudes and/or biases toward divorce. Despite the proclamation of "neutrality," marital therapists frequently have seen themselves as directed more toward maintaining marital relationships than helping to dissolve them (Fisher, 1973). In a growing number of cases (as witnessed by the increasing divorce rate), the amount of change required by the partners in order to restructure their relationship may be too great. Or, more likely, one of the individuals more than the other may retain the wish for a "traditional" marriage. In this case, he or she will probably feel more satisfied by an involvement with or marriage to someone who shares similar values. The therapist needs to be prepared for the possibility that many of the couples in the marital situations referred to in this paper will "choose" to terminate their marriage. Such individuals can be helped effectively to achieve such a resolution (Toomim, 1972) if the therapist is open to the idea that divorce or separation does not necessarily represent a therapeutic "failure."

Specific Therapeutic Techniques

Certain tasks and procedures can be effective in helping couples to restructure their marital relationship patterns. The general goal with such techniques is a more equalized sharing of overt power in the relationship. We operate from the hypothesis that a sharing of overt and socially recognized power leads to enhanced self-esteem and promotes personal growth for both individuals. Viewing the task of marital therapy along these lines does not imply that intrapsychic forces and behaviors are not important. Indeed, they may provide among other things useful insight into resistances for changing behavior and sensitize the therapist to cross-generational conflicts and repetitive patterns. However, it is the position of this paper that social, economic, and political determinants should be given equal weight with intrapsychic considerations in approaching the treatment of marital dysfunction. Specific techniques we have found helpful are:

a) Actively working out with the couple a *division of labor* schedule that delineates the equal sharing of household duties, including child care. Traditionally marital partners have resisted sharing many of these low social status value tasks. If such duties can be shared, it may free both partners to pursue activities, particularly education and gainful employment, that potentially can offer greater social and personal fulfillment.

b) Exploring and spelling out in as careful detail as possible the *marital contract* (Sager, et al., 1971), especially the explicit and implicit sex role expectations and behaviors. It is important that both partners have a direct and active say in this. Spelling out the *current* marital contract is useful particularly in helping couples to see how they have changed in their values and expectations over time. It is likely that their initial relationship contract (usually loosely formulated at the time of marriage or formal spoken commitment) is based on traditional sex-role stereotyped notions and needs extensive revision. Most individuals find this difficult to do on their own, as each naturally wants things to be more or less "my way" or they have difficulty in facing up to the personal and relationship changes that have occurred. Having a therapist ("*referee*") present can be very helpful under these circumstances.

Many of the couples we have seen in therapy over the past several years report far less sex role stereotyping in their relationship prior to "tying the knot." For example, they may have lived together, with the man doing the cooking while his partner furthered her education. In such relationships, sex typically was easy and plentiful, and other close friends and interests were not just limited, but encouraged. Usually the change in patterning occurred when the marriage "vows" were taken, but often it was the arrival of a first child that precipitated a real change in power and relationship status between the partners (Laws, 1971). Hoffman (1960) has shown how a woman's power decreases with each child born. This relates to the fact that child care in our society is not only delegated to women, but has low social and economic value. If the woman quits her job to stay home with the child for more than a brief interval, given societal values, the marital relationship is almost certainly destined for a change in the power equilibrium. The build-up of resentment over these relationship changes can often lead to a breakdown in affectional and sexual gratification as well.

At this point, the issue becomes one of how to deal with the power disparity in the marital relationship related to basically economic inequity? Advising the woman to return to work can sometimes be helpful, particularly if she can obtain a job commensurate with her talents and earning power. However, the lack of equal opportunities in higher education, work, pay, and advancement for women (Carnegie Commission, 1973; Epstein, 1971) place some limitations on this as a solution to marital discord. Another prerequisite for resolving the power disparity would be a quality, fully funded national day care system; at present, the United States is the only advanced Western nation in the world that lacks such a system (Horton, 1971).

Many women, however, question why they should have to take a full or even a part-time job to achieve a more equalitarian partnership. Why should women feel compelled to "buy" an achievement model, given the stress it has brought men (Miller, 1972). Ideally, each sex should have a choice of working or "staying at home." Yet, unless the marriage is relatively new and the partners relatively young, it is extremely difficult in our experience for couples "locked into" a traditional marital model to try to successfully implement a "shared role relationship" (Baber, 1953)." The basic issue once again is an economic one. If both individuals work part-time, they are likely to experience some reduction in income, due to their differential earning power. And if they both cut down from full time to part-time jobs, they will be making a considerable financial sacrifice, since society is only beginning to recognize the viability of part-time work, and it is typically not as highly rewarded, e.g., with comparable fringe benefits (Schwartz, 1973). These economic, political, and social issues need to be explored with a couple so they become fully aware of the ramifications, costs, and benefits of restructuring their relationship. Many therapists traditionally have explained sex role conflict and marital problems only in terms of intrapsychic etiology, without credence to the enormous societal barriers working against a real vital partnership in marriage. Therapists can often explore fruitfully these realistic social barriers as well as the "psychodynamics" of the relationship by offering personal examples and possible solutions which are relevant to the couple's current dilemma.

c) Arranging a *structured separation* experience with counseling (Toomim, 1972). Although a temporary separation may seem like a drastic step in solving marital problems, it often is a helpful growth experience that may reunite a couple rather than further dissolve their relationship. This is an effective technique particularly when individuals are locked into a mutually dependent and growth-stultifying relationship. Even a weekend away from one another can begin to "unlock" the unproductive ways in which they have become bonded and can permit each partner to experiment with new behaviors and ways of relating. A burst of felt independence can be important in helping individuals to feel ultimately that they genuinely "choose" to be with one another.

d) Reinforcing an *open companionship* model for both spouses (O'Neill & O'Neill, 1972). It is important to the fulfillment of many married individuals that they feel the freedom to form relationships with other people. These can vary in degree of intimacy depending upon the *agreed upon* preferences of the couple. Achieving open companionship is important in freeing the partners from the popular myth that in a "good marriage" each must satisfy *all* the needs of the other. As soon as this notion is recognized as realistically impossible, the individuals may be freed up to experience and grow through other relationships. In their discussion of "Open Marriage," the O'Neills' do not deal with therapeutic methods of helping a couple to achieve open companionship. We believe the therapist can play a key role in this process, by making sure issues are faced, feelings are expressed openly and directly, and the "ground rules" agreed upon before the individuals begin what has been traditionally a secretive, exploitive, and often destructive process of forming outside relationships.

These relationships may or may not include sexual intimacy. Given religious and social constraints on extramarital sexual behavior and the wish to maintain a "romantic love" notion of marriage (which includes jealousy, possessiveness, and sexual exclusivity), most couples in our experience opt for open companionship, but sexual fidelity. Interestingly, this choice may occur following a period of extramarital sexual experience (see Rogers, 1972).

A case study will illustrate these therapeutic techniques:

Jean and Larry M. (pseudonyms), a couple in their late 20's, entered marital therapy with the complaint that "we are fighting all the time." They had been married for five years; Larry was completing his graduate education and Jean was employed in a government service position. The couple had a four-year-old daughter. The marriage began with the perception on the wife's part that she was "lucky" to find someone "strong and competent" who would take care of and provide security for her. However, she explained, over time she became increasingly aware that Larry had not individuated from his own family and often placed their wishes above her own. This led to a good deal of disillusionment and open conflict. The pattern became one of mutual withdrawal and retreat to other activities followed by accusations of disinterest and a subsequent nonproductive confrontation, with each blaming the other. Jean especially complained about their lack of meaningful time together.

Early therapeutic exploration focused on the power dynamics in the relationship: Jean felt in a "onedown" position by virtue of her initial "set" in the marriage and her constant pleas for attention and time together. Their sexual relationship was affected in a power "trade-off" with Jean willing to "give" sexually only as little as she received from Larry in the other aspects of their relationship. Larry felt uncomfortable with the fact that Jean was making the major economic contribution and reacted to this by overemphasizing the "importance" of his studies and ignoring her requests to share in the household tasks and child care. He spent his time in usually nonproductive studying, being conflicted frequently over whether he should attend to his wife or his "books."

Exploration of the implicit marital contract was accompanied by the use of all of the previously mentioned therapeutic techniques in an attempt to replace the above patterns of relating with more mutually satisfying behaviors: To ameliorate the initial complaint and to structure immediate behavioral change, the therapist worked out with the couple a specific time schedule that: 1) included a weekly division of labor contract, which could be modified with changes in commitments, interests, and/or increased trust, and 2) provided specific weekly free time together to relate as they wished. The fact of knowing when they would be getting together helped each partner to use his/her time more productively. Implicit assumptions about spouse responsibilities in both domestic and economic spheres was carefully explored and old assumptions challenged. It was also agreed that each spouse would deal with separation and individuation issues with his/her own parents on a separate basis. This helped to avoid the use of parental pressures and expectations as a way of manipulating one another into the untenable position of being forced to choose between spouse and parent.

The individuation issue was similarly faced in the question of time for outside friends and interests. Jean's original requests for increased intimacy were seen on another level to reflect her own achievement fears and the expected rejection from Larry attendant to her success. In effect, she was "paralyzed" in her professional endeavors by unconsciously contracting to wait for him to also achieve by finishing school and eventually "surpassing" her. Her anger, however, was not directed towards this felt inhibition but overtly manifested toward Larry by way of his lack of time with her.

Once these dynamics were explored and Jean made aware of her tradeoff and the real source of her anger, some of the pressure for companionship was relieved. Larry already had a significant circle of friends and interests outside work. In time, Jean developed a satisfying relationship with a colleague and joined a women's group as well. The latter in particular was instrumental in aiding her to seek out other sources of interpersonal gratification and supported her wishes for an equitable division of work within the family.

In therapy, it was also suggested that Jean keep a certain mutually agreed upon portion of her earnings as money she could spend on herself and not need to account for to her husband. This helped to give her some economic leverage and reinforcement for her work efforts and served as a step in the direction of redistributing more equitably the overt power in the relationship.

Faced with the prospect of abandoning his pattern of withdrawal and retreat into the passive-aggressive "child" position, Larry at first refused to recognize his wife's efforts towards honest confrontation of her anger and her admission of manipulating sex and intimacy to achieve a power tradeoff. At this point, the therapist met his negativism not with reassurance and suggestions to trust and believe in his wife (approaches destined to be used as further means of resistance) but with a reinforcement of his separation wishes, noting that perhaps the time was now appropriate for a structured separation. Hopefully, such a separation would permit both partners the time, distance, and perspective necessary to realistically assess their motivation for change and their behavior with or without their spouse. When confronted with the actual possibility of separation, Larry gradually abandoned his position of regression, agreeing to "experiment" with a week alone with his daughter while his wife attended a workshop and lived with a former female classmate. This experience, while short-term and hardly a model separation, was extremely valuable in permitting each of them to face their needs for both independence and intimacy. Larry also benefited from the new experience of caring solely for his daughter.

The above maneuvers helped improve both partners' self-esteem and measurably reduced the nature and degree of marital conflict. Their sexual relationship improved. A feeling of mutual respect was slowly established as each spouse came to realize the other could "hold his/her own" in the relationship. The original marital contract (i.e., the "strong" spouse providing support for the "weak" spouse and obtaining narcissistic gratification in return) was replaced with one which involved mutual support and appreciation of each others' special capabilities and basic competence.

In summary, we have presented several techniques that a therapist can use to help individuals in restructuring traditional marital patterning. These include: a) working out a schedule for sharing household and child care responsibilities; b) elaborating and revising the marital "contract;" c) trying out separation experiences; and d) exploring open companionship. We feel this type of therapy can free men and women from sex role stereotyped patterns of relatedness and help them to form interpersonal bonds that offer possibilities for enhanced personal and conjoint growth.

REFERENCES

Baber, R.E. *Marriage and the family*, (2nd ed.). New York: McGraw-Hill, 1953, 10.

Bailyn, L. Career and family orientations of husbands and wives in relation to marital happiness. *Human Relations*, 1970, *23*, 97–113.

Bernard, J. *The future of marriage*. New York: World Publishing Co., 1973.

Bird, C. *Born female*. New York: Simon & Shuster, 1969.

The Carnegie Commission on Higher Education. *Opportunities for women in higher education*. New York: McGraw-Hill, 1973.

Chesler, P. Men drive women crazy. *Psychology Today*, 1971, *5*, 18–27.

Epstein, C.F. *Woman's Place: Options and limits in professional careers*. Berkeley, CA: University of California Press, 1971.

Fabrikant, B. The Psychotherapist and the female patient: Perceptions, misperceptions, and change. In V. Franks, & V. Burtle, (Eds.), *Women in therapy*. New York: Brunner-Mazel, 1974, pp. 83–110.

Firestone, S. *The dialectic of sex*. New York: Bantam Books, 1971.

Fisher, E.O. A guide to divorce counseling. *Family Coordinator*, 1973, *22*, 55–61.

Hoffman, L. Effects of the employment of mothers on parental power relations and the division of household tasks. *Marriage and Family Living*, 1960, 22, 27–35.

Horton, M. Liberated women: Children? *Clinical Child Psychology Newsletter*, 1971, *10*, 710.

Howe, L.K. *The future of the family*. New York: Simon & Shuster, 1972.

Krakauer, A. A good therapist is hard to find. *Ms.*, 1972, *1*, 33–35.

Laws, J.L. A feminist review of the marital adjustment literature: The rape of the Locke. *Journal of Marriage and the Family*, 1971, *33*, 483–516.

Miller, S.M. Confusions of a middleclass husband. In. L.K. Howe, (Ed.), *The Future of the Family*. New York: Simon & Shuster, 1972, 95–108.

O'Neill, N. & O'Neill, G. *Open Marriage*. New York: Avon, 1972.

Rice, J. K. & Rice, D. G. Status and sex role issues in co-therapy. In A. S. Gurman & D. G. Rice, (Eds.), *Couples in conflict: New directions in marital therapy*. New York: Aronson, 1975, 145–150.

Rogers, C. *Becoming partners*. New York: Delta, 1972. Fifteen years of a radically changing marriage, pp. 161–198.

Sager, C., Kaplan, H. S., Gundlack, R. H., Kremer, M., Lerz, R., & Royce, J. R. The marriage contract. *Family Process*, 1971, *10*, 311–326.

Schwartz, F.N. Women and employers: Their related needs and attitudes. In R. B. Kundsin, (Ed.), Successful women in the sciences: An analysis of determinants. *Annals of the New York Academy of Sciences*. 1973. *208*, 161–165.

Toomim, M. K. Structured separation with counseling: A therapeutic approach for couples in conflict. *Family Process*, 1972, *11*, 229–310.

12

Concurrent Sex Therapy and Psychoanalytic Psychotherapy by Separate Therapists: Effectiveness and Implications

ALEXANDER LEVAY, JOSEF WEISSBERG, AND ALVIN BLAUSTEIN

Since the publication of Masters and Johnson's Human Sexual Inadequacy in 1970, sex therapy has become an established, though controversial, new approach to the treatment of sexual disorders. Masters and Johnson adopted the position that any other form of psychotherapy should be avoided or suspended during the two- or three-week period of sex therapy. Helen Kaplan, in considering sex therapy to be a type of psychotherapy, has stressed that the skillful trained psychotherapist uses his awareness of the psychodynamics and unconscious conflicts of the couple in modifying and tailoring the sex therapy program to their individual needs. In the present study, sex therapy, utilizing a second therapist, was introduced into an ongoing psychoanalytic psychotherapy.

LITERATURE REVIEW

There are specific references in the literature to similar therapeutic approaches, although many related issues have been dealt with by various authors:

Flescher's (1968, 1958) "Dual Therapy" technique involves the treatment of one patient by a male and female therapist on alternate days. He states that many transference and countertransference problems are elucidated and resolved more easily by this technique.

Reprinted by permission of the William Alanson White Psychiatric Foundation, Inc. from *Psychiatry*, 39 (1976), 355–363. Copyright © 1976 by the William Alanson White Psychiatric Foundation, Inc.

Woody reports two cases of integrated aversion therapy and supportive psychotherapy by separate therapists in an inpatient setting. The patients suffered from specific perversions (transvestitism and fetishism) and were reported as benefiting from the dual approach. Kaplan reports on the sequential and alternating use of sex therapy and psychoanalytic psychotherapy by the same therapist. There are, in addition, several clinical and theoretical reports (Birk and Brinkley-Birk; Gullick and Blanchard) on the combined use of behavioral and psychoanalytic psychotherapeutic techniques by the same therapist. The literature reveals a paucity of discussions, even on an experimental basis, of concomitant treatment of one patient by two therapists.

METHODOLOGY

In the context of a psychoanalytic research study group, a couple with sexual problems was selected, one of whom—the wife—was already involved in psychoanalytic psychotherapy. The couple was referred to a sex therapist, a psychoanalyst who had received formal training at the Reproductive Biology Research Foundation in St. Louis. The couple was informed of the existence of the study and apprised of its purposes. Their permission was secured to tape record all sex therapy and psychotherapy sessions for the duration of the study, and to allow both therapists and all study group members to listen to the tapes. Sex therapy sessions were scheduled weekly for four months. The psychotherapy with the wife was continued on a twice-weekly basis. The study group met monthly and heard representative segments of both therapies from the previous month. Six months after the termination of sex therapy, the couple was interviewed by a third research group member for an in-depth evaluation of their treatment experience and the results, including the effect of the study.

THE SEX THERAPY

Sex therapy is a structured, step-by-step educational experience in functional sexual behavior for a couple. The couple, rather than the dysfunctional individual, is the patient. Both members of the couple are treated as equal partners in the problem, even if one of them does not suffer from an explicit dysfunction. The treatment goal is the establishment of functional sexual behavior based on mutual pleasure, rather than a specific resolution of the individual dysfunction itself. Treatment goals are individually tailored at the onset of therapy to be consistent with the couple's expectations, backgrounds, and realistic limiting factors. Once these goals have been set and mutually agreed upon, the couple is expected to abide by the treatment rules and expectations for the duration of the treatment, even if some of these may not meet with their preferences or be consistent with their previous therapeutic experience. Patients' treatment behavior is evaluated throughout the treatment and corrected whenever necessary. The focal point of the treatment is the assignment of specific tasks for the bedroom in graded sequence. These represent essential component parts of functional sexual behavior. By reviewing with the couple how each of these exercises was performed and experienced, the therapist is enabled to correct "mistakes," such as undue emphasis on performance and goal orientation. Among frequently encountered "mistakes" are exaggerated emphasis on the partner's satisfaction at the expense of one's own pleasure, and preoccupation with achieving erection, ejaculatory control, and orgasms. Stress is laid on the here and now, and on the conscious individual experience as well as on the interpersonal interaction. No attempt is made to avoid expressing value judgments regarding functional behavior. New assignments are not made until previous ones are performed comfortably and with pleasure. Special techniques are employed at appropriate times, such as the squeeze method for ejaculatory control and the use of vaginal dilators in the treatment of vaginismus. Throughout the therapy much information is provided on sexual anatomy, physiology, and psychology. The therapist actively encourages open, honest, nonjudgmental communication. The therapist plays an active and supportive role throughout. During the course of treatment all sexual activity is limited to that prescribed by the therapist.

The original Masters and Johnson method called for a two-week daily treatment regimen. For a number of practical as well as therapeutic reasons, this has been modified in many clinics to a once-a-week therapy in which the two-week program is spread out over a three- to four-month period. Masters and Johnson feel that all couples must be treated by male-female cotherapy teams. This, too, is handled by many as an option, essential only in a minority of cases.

Couples have a screening interview, as much to establish their suitability for this type of treatment as to help them gain a realistic view of their problem, the therapy, and the therapist. Some of the more frequently encountered contraindications are lack of motivation, especially to work out the sexual problem for oneself; marital problems precluding cooperation between partners; ongoing extramarital relationships; inability of one or both partners to cooperate with the therapist; major life crises; and psychotic or prepsychotic states. Next, in separate sessions, a complete history is elicited as indirectly as possible. The sexual history emphasizes not only dysfunction, but also positive and pleasurable aspects. Discretion regarding the past is granted each spouse but no secrecy is promised for new events which may develop during the course of treatment. This is designed to prevent entrapment of the therapist in which he is defaulting on one patient by guarding the secrets of the other.

Physical examinations and laboratory studies follow. There are considerable advantages in having the physical examinations performed by the sex therapist. These are: seeing the bodies and the genitals as they are, rather than as they are described; observing patients' reactions to their own bodies, and to the doctor's examining them; learning each individual's autonomic response patterns to the stress of the examination; and discovering new clues to historical data. Patients are very reassured by the doctor's having examined parts of their bodies about which they are concerned. The physical examination augments basic trust and cements the therapeutic alliance.

A formal presentation is then made to the couple, summarizing the therapist's findings and recommendations; the probable origins of the difficulty and the contribution of each partner, the assessment of assets and liabilities, the outline of the projected course of treatment, provision of sexual and clinical information, and demonstration of principles of communication.

The first of two sensate-focus exercises is then described. The couple is instructed to undress in their bedroom with some light on. One is assigned to initiate playing with the partner's body *the way he or she always wanted to*. An attitude of playful exploration is encouraged. Genitals and breasts are off limits. The partner who is being played with is only to experience sensations and to protect the other from causing discomfort, since this is not his or her intention. After fifteen or twenty minutes the couple is to exchange roles and repeat the procedure. If at the end of this experience either feels sexually aroused, he or she is encouraged to masturbate in the presence of the partner. The second sensate-focus exercise includes playing with the genitals of the partner following the same format. The couple is also instructed to examine each other's genitals. During this phase partners indicate to each other how they prefer to be touched, so that this can be included in the repertory of the other. Oro-genital contact is encouraged as an option. The emphasis is placed on moment-to-moment pleasurable sensation rather than on goal-oriented achievement. The rate of progression of assignments is carefully tailored for each couple.

Mutual genital caressing follows. Intercourse is then added, usually in the female-astride position. Intercourse is usually delayed until both partners can participate in mutual touching or oro-genital contact with full sexual responsiveness and orgasm. The couple is then instructed in various other suitable intercourse positions and therapy is tapered off. Couples may require special assistance in integrating their newfound gains into their everyday lives once therapy has been completed.

CASE HISTORY

The 40-year-old wife had been seen by her current analytic therapist twice weekly for two two-year periods, separated by a four-year interval during which she was seen about a dozen times. She had seen several therapists previously. Her presenting complaints were inability to get along with her husband and to enjoy sex. The couple had three teen-aged children, and the wife had had a tubal ligation following an abortion ten years earlier.

The wife had been born in France, her parents having emigrated from Hungary some years earlier. She had one brother twenty years her senior, who had already left home at the time of her birth. She was raised by governesses and saw little of her parents until moving to this country at age 8. Her mother was distant, demanding, and contentious, while her father was alternatively doting and sulking, depending on whether or not her behavior satisfied him. Sex was never mentioned explicitly. Still, at age 17, it came as no surprise to her when her father disapproved violently of her talking to boys. At age 20, while in college, she began seriously seeing the man who became her husband, whom she had known for many years. During the courtship she was sexually aggressive but her fiancé insisted on deferring sexual intercourse until after the wedding. The honeymoon was disappointing. She had never experienced orgasm during intercourse, and until recently, only rarely during manual or lingual manipulation of her clitoris by her husband. Masturbation was possible only by thigh squeezing. Attempts at manual masturbation produced severe anxiety and were always abandoned prior to orgasm.

The husband is a highly obsessive but sincerely committed professional, who developed ulcerative colitis at age 5 and had an ileostomy performed at age 16. At the time of his marriage, at age 22, he suffered a serious exacerbation of his ulcerative colitis, which lasted for two years. Symptoms abated after a laparotomy with lysis of adhesions. Re-anastomosis at that time proved impossible. During the acute phase of his illness he visited a psychiatric clinic once weekly for a year. He has dealt with his ileostomy chiefly with denial. Very few people know that he has an ileostomy, and he leads an impressively active life. The patient denied any strong feelings concerning his ileostomy, although occasionally she dreamt of his expressing rage by spewing feces through the stoma. His disease had been well controlled for many years.

Their relationship was characterized by her slavish obedience and consequent resentment. The two of them conspired to elevate the husband to a position of moral perfection. Thus, they agreed that he served his clients more conscientiously than any other lawyer in the city. Of course, this necessitated long working hours. When he came home late, the wife was caught in a dilemma. He would righteously defend the demands of his work and she would be unable to express her desire for his presence or her resentment at being deprived of it. When she did complain, she received a rather elaborate lecture on ethical and moral values, which left her more angry and depressed. Her rage found expression in increasingly frequent, tantrumlike outbursts. His parents, who lived in Arizona, would visit during July and August. She would submit meekly to their demands, but her mounting rage would lead ultimately to an outburst, often involving physical threats to them, and would then subside with unbearable guilt and depression.

Her chronic rage and self-deprecation further interfered with her sexual enjoyment. She viewed orgasm as an achievement and every unfulfilling sexual experience as a failure. Although she enjoyed nongenital contact with her husband, she came to regard every overture on his part as leading to a confirmation of her lack of femininity. She was torn between her desire to avert such overtures and her wish to gratify her husband's legitimate and justifiable needs. She felt trapped in a cycle of rage and guilt.

Treatment was directed toward examining the roots of her defective self-esteem and her sexual inhibition. After two years she felt considerably more comfortable; and, although the explosive battles with her husband continued, they were shorter, less violent, separated by longer intervals, and followed by considerably less guilt and self-denigration. She had begun to perceive his role in perpetuating the situation and was relieved at not having to be the sole bearer of the burden of their difficulties. She stated her desire to stop treatment and in the ensuing four years was seen only infrequently, usually after a particularly violent blow-up.

Four years later she reentered treatment, feeling she wanted to do something definitive to better her relationship with her husband; wanting to improve her sexual adaptation, which she had always been reluctant to discuss explicitly; and feeling she should do something about developing a career for herself now that her children were growing up. It became apparent that it would be necessary to involve her husband in any therapeutic approach. Since he refused to enter individual therapy, it was arranged that he accompany his wife once weekly. After an initial period of suspicious defensiveness, he responded gratifyingly, and together the couple was able to work through some of their destructive response patterns. Predictably enough, the wife derived further fuel for self-denigration from his improvement; her husband had changed radically in just a few months, whereas she had taken many years to make comparable progress. After a year, it was suggested that the husband discontinue regular visits and relinquish this therapy time to his wife, for work on her remaining difficulties. The husband himself was struck by the reluctance with which he retired from the conjoint sessions. He precipitated a few flare-ups in order to be seen again, and the relationship for the next year was remarkably smooth.

The wife's self-esteem had become more intact, and she began making plans to obtain training for a career. She felt that her therapeutic goals had all been achieved, save for sexual improvement. Although she talked much more freely about sex, there was little change in her attitude and response. At this point, one year following the end of the conjoint therapy, the suggestion was made that she and her husband enter sex therapy, while she remain in individual therapy.

Course of Concurrent Therapy

Following her individual visit with the sex therapist, the wife was quite pleased and regarded the project optimistically. During the second session, however, when she was seen with her husband, she felt that the therapist sided with him against her, and became angry. Although the analytic therapist was prepared for some competitive resentment when a colleague intruded on his therapeutic territory, even though he did so at his invitation, he was surprised by the intensity of his indignation when his patient reported that the sex therapist had been praising the virtues of her husband and wondering at her failure to respond to him. She reported that the sex therapist had suggested that she and her husband listen to the analytic tapes together. She felt that this would feed into her husband's need to control her and would kill the only vestige of privacy she had—that is, in her analytic therapy. At this point the two therapists met. It became apparent that the wife had been guilty of some distortion. For example, the sex therapist had suggested that the couple might replay tapes of their joint sessions, not those of her individual sessions. It was clear that she was unconsciously attempting to provoke a battle between the two therapists in much the same way as she had frequently divided her parents. When this was interpreted to her, she was able to begin to deal directly with the frightening prospect that she might in the near future become capable of and have to bear the responsibility for adult sexual responses.

After the meeting of the two therapists, the analytic therapist was able to deal with the wife's objections to the sex therapist in terms of her fear of the sexual activity she expected him to encourage. Her first response was to suffer an attack of acute anxiety while the sex therapist was describing the procedure for the initial sensate-focus exercise. She also felt quite guilty about the deprivation suffered by her husband due to the proscription of genital sex.

Though she continued consciously to be furious with the sex therapist and to be terrified of the exercises, she dreamt of the analytic therapist as a reliable but not very skillful driver of an old automobile, and at the same time dreamt that the sex therapist and his many assistants were actively and heroically keeping her house from falling apart.

After the next group meeting, the sex therapist gave the wife the tapes of his session, and she requested and was given the tapes of the analytic therapist. He was amazed at the next session to learn that she and her husband had listened to them together. She described this as a worthwhile experience, since her husband had responded sympathetically to the depression and angry frustration which had been so prominently expressed in them. She asked the analytic therapist to continue giving her his tapes, and he consented for the duration of the concurrent therapy.

During the second month of dual therapy, the patient attempted to masturbate digitally. Although it was necessary for her to keep her ankles crossed to avert anxiety, she was able for the first time to produce an orgasm in this way. She then fell asleep and dreamt of suffering paralysis of all limbs and dying. Her associations to this dream were to an episode at age 20, when she had a bitter quarrel with her mother about whether she would accompany her parents on an extended trip or stay home with her fiancé. Shortly after, her mother became weak and faint and a physician was called. In retrospect, she felt that these represented the first symptoms of the brain tumor which proved fatal to the mother. The analytic therapist was then told that the exercises had become much easier and more pleasurable, but the sex therapist consistently received a less optimistic picture.

The wife seemed to tolerate poorly what she and her husband regarded as good performance and once again became quite anxious about experiencing sexual pleasure, which she would avoid by retreating into obsessive thoughts. Her fury at the sex therapist was exacerbated, particularly when he responded to increased tension by suggesting that she take a week off from the exercises. The husband's support, while overtly consistent, was tempered by his repeated complaints at being deprived of intercourse, which fed the wife's guilt.

Some early associations were produced when the split in the transference, exemplified by her presenting herself as fragile to the sex therapist while describing significant improvement to the analytic therapist, was pointed out: She had been allergic to cow's milk in infancy and had required hypodermoclysis for nutrition, followed by feeding by a series of wet nurses. In relating this, she felt that these women were uninterested in her, had children of their own, and nursed her only for money. Thus, in her mind, early pleasurable experiences had been accompanied by communications concerning her unworthiness.

At this point in the therapy, she took a short vacation with her husband. During the few days they were away, she was more freely and responsively interested in sex than she ever had been. Her husband, however, much to her amazement, was unable to achieve a full erection. He was reluctant to acknowledge the significance of his flagging potency in the presence of his wife's new sexual responsiveness. He reported a dream to the sex therapist in which he was chased by knife- and gun-wielding Japanese warriors, an image he traced to looking at Japanese erotic art.

For the remainder of the conjoint therapy, the wife followed strides forward with regression and recrudescence of her inhibitory symptoms. During these periods her attitude toward the sex therapist was characterized by extreme contentiousness, which was interpreted as defensive. Her rage to some extent seemed to represent a displacement of her disappointment in her husband's unwillingness to deal with his contribution to the dysfunction.

When the sex therapist proposed ending his role in the treatment, the wife found all sorts of objections to him to justify her rage at his abandonment. Her vilification of him contrasted strikingly with her portrayal of him in her dreams, where he always emerged as sophisticated, skillful and omniscient, often in contrast to the analytic therapist, who was seen as rather pedestrian and plodding.

Joint therapy was ended after four months. In the months following, the wife's conscious attitude to the sex therapist more closely approximated that implied in her dreams. Her gains appeared to be maintained and she spoke of him from time to time with fondness and great regard. Analytic therapy was terminated eight months after the end of joint therapy.

Evaluation of the Results of Treatment

Evaluation interviews with the husband and wife were conducted six months following the end of sex therapy. The wife was orgastic by manual manipulation by the husband and in masturbation. Fear of excitement was no longer present. She consciously enjoyed intercourse and the frequency had increased markedly. There was much less emphasis on the importance of orgasm for self-esteem. She felt less fearful of her husband's reactions and criticism. The couple more openly shared their fantasies. The husband's potency disturbance disappeared. Though attributing most of her progress to her psychotherapy, and in spite of tensions connected with the sex therapy, she found the joint experience beneficial and did not think she could have achieved as much as she did without the sex therapy. Apparently there had been no important disruption in her relationship to her analytic therapist. Even her knowledge that the tapes of her sessions were being shared with an unseen group of psychiatrists did not produce discernible negative effects. The couple was later seen in a one-year follow-up visit by the sex therapist. He found that the gains they had made had been maintained. They seemed comparatively free from tension and happy in a work relationship they had established since she had taken a position in his law firm. The frequency of sexual relations had increased to three times a week. Sex had become a pleasurable and well-integrated part of their life together, rather than a source of conflict and recrimination. The wife reported experiencing orgasm in intercourse regularly, though requiring manual stimulation by her husband.

CONCLUSIONS

Our experience supports the notion that sex therapy and psychoanalytic psychotherapy can be conducted concurrently by two different therapists with greater benefit to the patients than by either therapy alone. There must be good communication between the two therapists and care must be taken early to explain to the patients the divergent methodologies involved. The study itself was helpful to both therapists in their work and did not have any discernible negative effects on the patients.

Most analysts do not have a working knowledge of sex therapy. They may perceive a given therapeutic maneuver as an error in judgment or as a countertransference reaction by the sex therapist. Thus, when in the early phases of treatment, the sex therapist pointed out to the wife that she seemingly had an eager and cooperative sexual partner in her husband, the patient and the analytic therapist reacted as if the sex therapist were taking sides with the husband rather than focusing on the status of the relationship. It was helpful to the analytic therapist to learn that in sex therapy one proceeds by identifying things as they are in the here-and-now.

Another important area of communication between the therapists concerned patient behavior in treatment. The wife dramatically split the transference, reacting to the sex therapist with much hostility and contentiousness, and denying all progress. The sex therapist's morale was maintained by the more optimistic communications reported by the analytic therapist. The sex therapist was also greatly helped by the analytic data that were reported to him by the analytic therapist. For example, he had been completely unaware of the anxiety attack that the wife experienced during the first sensate-focus instruction and her associations to it. These data enabled him to deal more effectively with her resistance, which represented her view of him and her husband as insufficiently caring figures. Another example involved the dream following the first orgastic response to digital stimulation, which clearly equated sexual responsiveness with murderous aggressive impulses toward her mother.

The analytic therapy benefited as well. As might be expected, a flood of dreams and striking associations came forth as her sexual inhibitions were challenged in the sex therapy, which provided fuel for the therapeutic work. The husband's role in perpetuating the couple's symptoms was more clearly delineated.

Our experience suggests a challenge to the well-entrenched idea among psychoanalytically oriented psychotherapists that treatment of a patient by more than one therapist at the same time is ineffective or even damaging. It is claimed that the transference will be diluted and that countertransference reactions will be directed toward the other therapist. In our case the transference was split in a dramatic way: the sex therapist represented the hostile, depriving mother, while the analytic therapist was endowed with the qualities of the loving, tolerant, but sexually repressive father. These representations developed despite our feeling that the analytic therapist was more similar personally to the mother, and the sex therapist seemed to resemble the father. The nature of the two transferences, as might be predicted, reflected the patient's intrapsychic needs and the different behavior required of the two therapists. Forces promoting countertransference deflection, such as rivalry between the therapists, were minimized by the meticulous maintenance of open communications.

Dual therapy might have wider application. For example, in cases with severely conflicted partners in whom sexual inhibition is greatly overdetermined, it may be impossible for one therapist to deal with both the sex therapy instruction and encouragement, and a dispassionate examination of the intrapsychic determinants. The rather extreme resistance offered to sex therapy by our patient, we feel, would have forced her to discontinue had she not been able to resolve some of her conflicts in her analytic therapy. Also, had it not been for the specific assignment of sexual tasks in the sex therapy, her unconscious conflicts and resistances to adult sexual functioning could not have been demonstrated to her and worked through. Possibly other types of behavioral therapy could successfully be combined with psychoanalytic therapy, in which the behavioral therapy would serve as a structured and therapeutically controlled stimulus to the mobilization of repressed conflict, affect, and historical material.

Masters and Johnson, Flescher, and others have written of the value of various combinations of male and female therapists in resolving conflicts which could not adequately have been dealt with by a male or female therapist alone. The basis for this idea has been that the gender of the therapist is an essential determinant of the nature of the transference neurosis. Our experience in this case, however, indicates that in concomitant treatment with two therapists of the same gender, a maternal-paternal transference split did in fact occur.

Most theories of psychotherapy lean heavily on the use of transference phenomena. We feel that our experience, in which the unique feature of the transference was that the observer and target therapists were both participants, provided an opportunity to observe objectively the emergence and evolution of transference reactions. Further application of this method might provide data extending our understanding of the nature of the psychotherapeutic process, as well as furnishing a more effective modality for treatment of sexual disorders refractory to conventional methods.

REFERENCES

Birk, L., and Brinkley-Birk, A. W. "Psychoanalysis and Behavior Therapy," *Amer. J. Psychiatry* (1974) 131:499–510.
Flescher, J. "The 'Dual Method' in Analytic Psychotherapy," in A. Esman (Ed.), *New Frontiers in Child Guidance*; Int. Univ. Press, 1958.
Flescher, J. "Dual Analysis," *Current Psychiatric Therapies* (1968) 8:38–46.
Gullick, E., and Blanchard, E. "The Use of Psychotherapy and Behavior Therapy in the Treatment of an Obsessional Disorder: An Experimental Case Study," *J. Nervous and Mental Dis.* (1973) 156:427–431.
Kaplan, H. S. *The New Sex Therapy*; Brunner/Mazel, 1974.
Masters, W., and Johnson, V. *Human Sexual Inadequacy*; Little, Brown, 1970.
Woody, R. "Integrated Aversion Therapy and Psychotherapy: Two Sexual Deviation Case Studies," *J. Sex. Res.* (1973) 9:313–324.

13

What is Multimodal Therapy? A Brief Overview

ARNOLD A. LAZARUS

Singularity of thought is a great impediment to learning and progress. There is a desire to find one right, precise, and perfect solution to human problems. People often ask the following questions: "What is the cause of anxiety?" "What is the reason for our high crime rate?" "What is the cure for insomnia?" "What is the result of corporal punishment?" Singular questions result in singular, or unimodal, answers. There is no single cause of anxiety, or crime, or insomnia. Human processes are multileveled and multilayered. Let us always ask plural questions: "What are the causes of anxiety?" "What are the reasons for our high crime rate?" The search for a cure for almost anything is likely to yield frustration and disappointment. We need to search for cures (plural), to look for the results of our interventions, and to study the effects of our numerous efforts.

Unimodal practitioners tend to embrace a particular method, or school, or theory with fervor and zeal. There are those who push relaxation as a virtual panacea. Others believe that meditation can save the world. In some circles, social assertiveness is considered the be-all of interpersonal effectiveness. There are many who support primal therapy as the one and only treatment for neurotic disorders. To some, the achievement of insight is the sole therapeutic objective. Drug treatment represents the only way to go for certain biologically oriented individuals. The list is almost endless.

Yet, everyone tends to agree that it is important to avoid fitting the patient to the

Reprinted by permission *Elementary School Guidance and Counseling*, 13 (1978), 6–11.
Copyright © 1978 by the American Personnel and Guidance Association.

treatment. How best to fit the treatment to the patient is one of the most critical issues if positive outcomes are to be achieved. Again, the need for pluralism cannot be overstated. Unimodalists offer their own specialty whether or not the consumer really needs it. In the fields of counseling and psychotherapy, it was shown many years ago by the famous psychiatrist Adolph Meyer that every problem has biological, psychological, and sociological implications. Meyer was probably the forerunner of many present-day multifaceted approaches to counseling and therapy.

Apart from those who still adhere rigidly to specific schools or theories, most practitioners are inclined to be eclectic. But while the eclectic therapist probably has more to offer than the narrow school adherent, the problem with most eclectics is that they embrace such diverse theories and methods that they lack a systematic structure for their array of interventions. The fact that almost anything can help some of the people some of the time, causes counselors and therapists to engage in superstitious behavior. They apply "method x" and find that the client derives impressive benefits. Thereafter, they assume that "method x" caused the positive outcome. The confusion between causation and correlation retards progress and generates endless circular arguments. Before we can make cause-and-effect connections, careful and repeated observations are essential. And this brings us to the evolution of the multimodal orientation.

THE ESSENCE OF THE MULTIMODAL APPROACH

The emphasis on pluralistic thinking underscores the fact that there is no single or best approach to treating phobias, or anxiety, or obesity, or drug addiction, or delinquency, or any other problem. One of the first things we learn in psychology is that we are all unique, yet many systems of therapy imply that we all come from identical molds. The multimodal approach is predicated on the assumption that counseling and therapy need to be tailored to the individual needs of each person and situation. Nevertheless, there are basic guiding principles to ensure that we ask crucial assessment questions and emerge with a complete profile of problem areas that need specific attention. In general, treatment can only be as good as the diagnosis that precedes or accompanies it.

Careful and systematic follow-up studies led to the conclusion that relapse occurs far more frequently than most practitioners realize (or admit!). Upon investigating the reasons for relapses across a variety of cases, it became clear that most people failed to acquire a sufficiently broad range of coping skills to permit them to deal effectively with life's demands. For instance, after undergoing years of psychoanalysis, people would often emerge with many insights, but devoid of various adaptive behaviors such as social assertiveness, sexual proficiency, relaxation-meditation techniques, and other tension-reducing skills. People often need coaching, training, modeling, and overt rehearsal, all of which are conspicuously absent in traditional systems of psychotherapy. If therapy is incomplete, relapse is likely to occur within a few months to a couple of years afterwards. What do we mean by complete therapy?

Because we are biological beings who move, feel, sense, imagine, think, and relate to one another, each of these dimensions requires our attention when problems emerge. We are referring to seven modes: behavior, affect, sensation, imagery, cognition, interpersonal relationships, and our basic biological makeup. In music, the scale is made up of seven notes—ABCDEFG. The seven notes (with some sharps or flats) can produce every tune from Chopsticks to a classical piano concerto. The multimodal view is that personality is made up of behavior, affect, sensation, imagery, cognition, interpersonal responses, and biological substrate. If we take the first letters from each of these functions, we have BASIC IB. While the biological modality comprises everything from nutrition, exercise, and general physical health to organic pathology, the most frequent aspect in therapy is the use of medication or drugs. A more catchy acronym is derived if we subsume the biological mode under drugs. We then have BASIC ID to convey the seven separate but related dimensions of personality. (But let us remember that "D" denotes much more than drugs.)

Multimodal therapy is the thorough assessment (and where indicated) the systematic correction of problems across the BASIC ID. Here is a brief summary of the "ingredients" within each modality.

Behavior:

This refers mainly to overt responses, to acts, habits, gestures, reactions, etc., that are observable and measurable. A basic question to be answered is: "What responses need to be increased, and what needs to be decreased?" Clients are often asked what they would like to start doing and stop doing.

Affect:

This refers to emotions, moods, and intense feelings. By ascertaining what makes a person feel sad, or mad, or glad, or scared, one is dwelling on central issues. To further inquire how the person behaves during any intense emotional event, yields clues about specific ways of obtaining control over unwanted emotions.

Sensation:

Touching, tasting, smelling, seeing, and hearing are our five basic senses. But this modality is also concerned with other sensations such as the "butterflies in the stomach" often felt during anxiety, or the lightheadedness and dizziness that accompanies hyperventilation, or the pleasant surge of energy when one is extremely happy. The sensory mode provides direct clues to peoples' specific pleasures and displeasures in life. One of the goals of successful counseling is to enable clients to decrease negative sensations (e.g., tension, pain, discomfort) and to increase positive sensations (e.g., relaxation, sensual pleasure, esthetic delights).

Imagery:

The attainment of a realistic and positive self-image is probably one of the main keys to mental health. I believe that a person cannot perform in reality that which he or she is incapable of picturing in imagery. Let's say that we are teaching a child to ride a bicycle. My hypothesis is that before the child masters the art, he or she will first have to be able to picture himself or herself successfully balancing and riding the bicycle in imagination. Imagery is one of the most creative and effective ways of gaining access to all the other modalities. The reader may want to refer to a self-help book called *In the Mind's Eye* in which I have described more than 20 different imagery techniques (Lazarus 1978).

Cognition:

One's values, beliefs, attitudes, decision-making processes, problem-solving skills, opinions, and reasoning powers all fall under cognition. In a multimodal approach, the counselor is interested in specific cognitions and their influence upon behaviors, affective processes, sensory input, and so forth. At the very least, it is necessary to change one's faulty thinking and one's unadaptive behaviors if meaningful changes are to accrue (Lazarus & Fay 1977).

Interpersonal relationships:

How do you interact with significant others? What do you expect from other people? What do other people want from you? These are the basic interpersonal questions we need to be able to answer when assessing a client. Because many emotional difficulties are maintained by specific people in the client's environment, this modality often provides clues to unraveling otherwise insoluble problems. In counseling or therapy, this usually calls for family conferences so one may assess basic communication patterns that foster ongoing problems.

Drugs:

It will be recalled that in the "D" modality, we are concerned with the general physical well-being of the client. Obvious medical difficulties are dealt with by the referring or family physician, but the counselor needs to be on the alert for less obvious factors. Diet, exercise, sleep habits, cleanliness and general hygiene all fall under this category. It is important to know when to call upon the services of physicians—for example, when to recommend a neurological consultation, an endocrinological investigation, or a psychiatric evaluation.

THE MODALITY PROFILE

By assessing the BASIC ID, one emerges with a problem-oriented personality profile of each case. Thus, after testing a 10-year-old school phobic child, he and his parents were interviewed and the following profile emerged.

Behavior:

He cries in the mornings before school. Says he feels ill.

Affect:

He appears frightened and anxious.

Sensation:

He complains of stomach pains and headaches.

Imagery:

Projective tests reveal recurring themes about his mother's death.

Cognition:

IQ tests reveal a high level of intelligence. Quality of schoolwork has been excellent.

Interpersonal:

There is some friction at home with a younger sibling. The parents both seem to be overachievers. The child is rather shy.

Drugs:

The problems started soon after the mother underwent minor surgery. The child is healthy.

The Modality Profile enables one to appreciate the interactive influence of each area, and one is thereby able to intervene efficiently and effectively. For example, in the present case it seems clear that we are dealing mainly with problems of separation anxiety. As these problems were precipitated by the mother's surgery, the counselor will want to know exactly how the child was prepared for this event. Exactly what was he told? Here we have a bright, somewhat introverted, and highly sensitive child in the midst of a situational crisis. How is this best handled multimodally? (See Table 1.)

Behavior:

Advise the parents to adopt a reassuring but firm stand on school mornings. Inform him that he will feel fine once he is at his desk doing his schoolwork.

Affect:

Acknowledge that he is feeling anxious but again assure him that these negative feelings will soon pass.

Sensation:

Tempt him with some of his favorite foods (even ice cream for breakfast). Explain to him that by having even a light snack, he will feel better. (It is a physiological fact that eating usually inhibits anxiety.)

Imagery:

The counselor and the parents can make up stories that his mother is quite healthy. The aim here is to give him mental pictures of a basic safety theme while he and his

TABLE 1
School Phobic Child

Mode	Problem	Intervention
Behavior	Cries Feels ill	Parent consultation Child counseling
Affect	Anxious	Support, relaxation
Sensation	Stomach pains	Nutrition advice
Imagery	Mother's death feared	Storytelling
Cognition	Schoolwork excellent Overconcern regarding mother's whereabouts	Positive rewards in school Catalogue mother's activities
Interpersonal	Sibling friction Shyness	Family counseling Communication training
Drugs	Overanxious	Minor tranquilizer

mother are apart. (The reader may wish to read the chapter on "emotive imagery," which deals with children's phobias in Lazarus 1978.)

Cognition:

Explain to the child that while he is at school, his mother will be doing predictable things. It is important for the mother to list her activities so the child is able to verbalize something such as, "It is now 11 A.M. My mother is probably showing someone a house (she was in real estate) after which she will do some shopping and bring me home some of my favorite pies."

Interpersonal:

Some sessions with the entire family seem indicated. This will probably help to establish better communication patterns between the siblings, between the parents, and within the various parent-child dyads.

Drugs:

If the child remains unduly anxious, a minor tranquilizer might be prescribed by the family physician on a temporary basis.

In a relatively straightforward case such as the foregoing, most counselors would probably follow a similar series of strategies. Note, however, how the multimodal orientation systematically calls for interventions of diverse kinds. The question as to whether family therapy or individual therapy is indicated is not asked. Rather, it is a matter of when a given modality is invoked. The result of multimodal therapy is not merely a symptomatic change. Certainly the child was soon back at school and his anxieties had abated. But a close family union, a good atmosphere in the home, a loving climate was established, and a great degree of general sympathy and understanding is now present.

SUMMARY

In more complex cases, the construction of a BASIC ID profile provides an even clearer "assessment map" that permits systematic and comprehensive coverage of each problem area. Our follow-ups indicate that we are thereby achieving rapid and durable results (Lazarus 1976).

REFERENCES

Lazarus, A.A. *In the mind's eye.* New York: Rawson, 1978.
Lazarus, A.A. *Multimodal behavior therapy.* New York: Springer, 1976.
Lazarus, A.A., & Fay, A. *I can if I want to.* New York: Warner, 1977.

Part Five

Child Psychotherapy

Because of its special nature, we have devoted an entire section to some of the main aspects of child psychotherapy. Any general debate about psychotherapy has implications for child psychotherapy. True enough. But child psychotherapy, in addition, wrestles with its own characteristic problems, some of which are elucidated or at least hinted at in the following selections.

Someone once remarked that the definition of a child psychotherapist is someone who once practiced child psychotherapy. The remark implies something that statistics bear out—namely, a relatively large number of men and women begin their careers as child therapists or analysts, but in time give this up and choose instead to see older patients. In some cases these therapists move on to treating adolescents; but again, statistics reveal that many psychotherapists end up treating adults, despite the fact that the greater amount of their training was aimed at working with children.

We pause at this issue because the reader should not be left with any inaccurate impressions. We are not suggesting that psychotherapists who somehow turn away from children are in any way to be chastised or criticized. On the contrary. It may well be, as the selections reveal, that this move reflects the variety of very significant issues surrounding the practice of child psychotherapy. To begin with, there are those people who feel child psychotherapy, except in the most extreme cases of severe mental illness, is a precarious two-edged sword. To be sure, a particular child may need the services of a psychotherapist, but will the psychotherapy process itself contribute to the child's belief that he or she is mentally ill? Said differently, if one assumes that a child has psychological problems essentially because of environmental factors, which typically means stress in the family setting, then will not psychotherapy only add to the child's burdens and enhance his or her sense of being somehow victimized? Thinking along just these lines, certain child psychotherapists have said that one should reserve therapy for only the most serious cases and do everything possible to keep other children out of psychotherapists' offices. In other words, all the therapy in the world will have only the most minimal effect until the so-called stressful aspects of the environment are "treated." In a less extreme mood, other psychotherapists have suggested the importance of placing a child's parent or guardian in psychotherapy when a child is about to be treated. Still other therapists claim that the only way to successfully treat a child is to see that child in the context of his or her family where, again, the child's problems were born.

From these arguments, at least two other sets of arguments come forth. First, child psychotherapists do not agree on the basis of the child's problems. If so-called disturbed children come from so-called disturbed families, then how does one explain the fact that seemingly healthy and normal children emerge from some of these disturbed families? Even more to the point, how is it that the same family might produce, say, one "normal" child and one seriously disturbed child? The answers to these questions have not yet been settled, although most child psychotherapists would probably say that no two children ever come from the same parents. There are always differences in the lives of first-born children, second-born children, and so forth. Besides, one must not overlook the genetic basis of behavior and personality. Surely people do not inherit an identical psychological make-up merely because they are siblings, or even twins for that matter. Nonetheless, we continue to find debate on the cause of a child's problems, a debate which takes its place alongside the earlier debate regarding the relative merits and liabilities of prescribing psychotherapy for the child in the first place.

Second, child psychotherapists have not yet reached accord in the debate over the meaning and purpose of child psychotherapy. In this debate we find at least three clear-cut positions. There is, first, that group of psychotherapists who say that when a child begins to reveal problems it is already too late to do all that much good. Thus, to yield the best results in the child's behalf, psychotherapy should offer preventive assistance. The second position says that child psychotherapy can be efficacious, no matter when it is instituted, if only because any form of therapeutic alliance—the special brand of friendship created in psychotherapy—can only prove beneficial to the child. Finally, the third position, what we might call the most conservative or cautious approach, argues that psychotherapy for the child should remain a last ditch effort. Not until every strategy to intervene in the child's life has failed should psychotherapy be recommended.

One sees in even this brief discussion some of the turmoil that surrounds the practice of child psychotherapy. But there is one more issue that should be mentioned in this context, although it is a matter relevant to all the issues we will be raising throughout the book: Who is to say that child psychotherapy does any good? Less severely, are the techniques now being used in the treatment of children truly suitable for children, or are they merely accommodations of techniques designed for the treatment of adults? For that matter, do we ever design special situations for children, or do we merely scale down features of adult life until they seem suitable for our smaller people?

14

In Defense of Child Therapy

**BRAULIO MONTALVO
AND JAY HALEY**

Traditional child dyadic psychotherapy can be viewed from a family systems point of view. Seen in this light it shows itself to have powerful family systems effects. There are often therapeutically effective, although unintended. The deliberate identification of the child as "sick" and the choice of an intervention format that avoids direct dealing with the rest of the family may make change possible where it might otherwise not have occurred. Child psychotherapy is shown to have important elements in common with recently developed symptom oriented treatment methods.

In their enthusiasm for a new orientation of therapy, many family therapists disregard therapeutic approaches that have a long and respectable history. As family therapy expands and new approaches proliferate, many beginning family therapists seem to argue that if the whole family is not in the room, the therapy is old-fashioned. They disregard any therapy in which only individuals are interviewed. In doing so, they may overlook the valuable contributions made by earlier therapeutic modes. A glaring example is the way many family therapists regard child therapy, or child analysis. This was once a legitimate form of therapy with many adherents; family therapists talk about it lightly, if not with levity. They assume that a child could not possibly change unless his family changes, and playing with a child will not change his family. Yet even though outcome studies of child therapy are almost non-existent, it is undeniable that children have changed by experiencing play therapy. How is this possible? An

Reprinted by permission from *Family Process*, 12 (September 1973), 227–244.

explanation of such an occurrence will be offered here with an emphasis upon what can be learned from child therapy that might correct the errors of many family therapists.

Discussing the individual treatment of a child could be setting up a straw man; when a child is given play therapy, his parents are usually also involved in some form of treatment. However, such a discussion is legitimate, since the theory of child psychopathology assumes that only the child has the problem. His parents and other relatives are a stress factor rather than the unit with the problem.

When focusing on the treatment of the child alone, we must discuss a situation that has never been fully described. No research data are available on what child therapists actually do with children and families. Our description, therefore, is in part what is supposed to be done in child therapy, as we try to clarify the process by which a child might change in such a situation. First we will emphasize the structure of the treatment context and later the way the therapist uses the child to intervene in the family.

THE STRUCTURE OF CHILD THERAPY

Often the treatment of a child takes place in a clinic where many factors in addition to the individual interviews are causal to change. A social worker typically sees the parents, and as the parents are helped to resolve some of the basic ways they use the child in their conflicts with one another, the child can change. For example, if a male child must struggle against behaving in effeminate ways so that mother and father can use him in the issue of father's masculinity, the child is able to recover when the issue between father and mother has been resolved. However, what of those cases in which a therapist appears to be treating the child alone?

Clearly, a child is never the only one involved in the treatment, even when he appears to be. A number of important factors are part of the total encounter that occurs in child therapy. To begin with, there is the situation that precipitates the child into treatment. A child must express a family problem in such a way that a limit of tolerance is passed and the family is driven to take action. Either the parents decide upon treatment because of internal stress in the family or because of their concern about a traumatic experience of the child, or they are pressured into such action by school authorities, the family physician, or friends and neighbors. Often, when the parents decide to follow through on a referral for their child, they confront each other with the seriousness of the problem for the first time. This in itself can be therapeutic, since the parents are mutually agreeing that something must be done and so readying themselves for a change. They must also tell the child that they are going to take him to a doctor. When the child realizes that this time it is not merely one of the previous ineffectual threats, he can begin to initiate new behavior. Usually the parents benevolently reassure the child about the nice qualities of the therapist, but he is aware of his parents concern and anger with him.

The parents make an appointment with the child therapist who arranges to see the child and also to see the parents to set the fee and agree to the contract for treatment. During the interview with the parents, he listens to their complaints about the child, and when he agrees the child is disturbed, he offers treatment. Sometimes he must deal with the parental conflict over treatment, if one or the other parent has arranged it against the opposition of the other. Although these "management" aspects of the case are not usually considered theoretically to be central to the treatment, they are obviously crucial issues. Under the rubric of "management," there exists a range of effective techniques for making an impact upon the family system.

The Effects of Focusing on the Child

One major effect on the family occurs when the child therapist simply agrees with the parents that the child is the problem; this major intervention into the family joins the parents against their problem child. Since the theory of child psychopathology suggests that the child is reacting to his past and to his introjects, the therapist's approach to the parents can be one that frees them from the blame for the child's current problem. Granted that the child therapist is often accused of condemning parents because he identifies with the child, he is still sufficiently guided by his theory to think of the current parental influence as less relevant than the "real" internalized problem of the child.

Some family therapists would argue that focusing on the child as the problem and, therefore, siding with the parents against the child would be disastrous for a good treatment outcome; they believe it is always unwise to join any family members against the others. In fact, family therapists argue that focusing upon the child in this way freezes the child in the pathological system so that change is not possible. However, experienced family therapists also recognize that family therapy is an orientation to a problem and not a method of treatment so that different approaches sometimes have different advantages.

Spontaneous Change

One advantage of the child therapist's approach to families is the "spontaneous" change that can happen. Although parents offer up a child as the problem and claim that all is well with the family, they know on another level that this is not so. In those cases in which the therapist agrees that the child is the problem, the parents must redress the balance by accepting some blame themselves. As an example, a child will not eat all his food but hides it in various places in the house. The child therapist who operates close to the basis of this theory circumvents parental resistance, as he assumes that this problem is related to the child's interiorized oral aggression and anal retention. He will imply to the parents that the problem is entirely within the child. However, the parents know that at the dinner table the father insists that the child eat everything on his plate and the mother insists he does not have to. To deal with this conflict, the child hides his food. Since the parents know they are participating in this situation, they must accept part of the blame themselves because the child therapist offers them none. Sensing from him an exonerating stance, they are indirectly freed to privately work on the conflict when they might not have done so if the therapist had taken an interest in it.

The parents can leave a first session with a child therapist reassured that the problem resides more within the child than in their parenting, and they can feel relieved that they have taken action to resolve their difficult problem. In some cases the child will immediately improve; it can be argued that this response occurs because so much has happened within the family just by the action of reaching agreement, seeking treatment, and being reassured that they have not been causing the child's problems. Also, one should not underestimate the ability of the child to affect the other members of the family. The child can be a pivotal force for change when he senses his referral to a doctor as parental rejection. Upon feeling himself expelled, he can recoil into attempts to regain his parents' affection. His efforts may be interpreted by the parents as the therapist's success. They bring therapy to an end, and the child is rewarded by reintegration with his family.

The amount of time and effort the family puts into organizing themselves to get the child to the therapy sessions at regular intervals is in itself of importance. Not only is this a concerted activity requiring more efficient family organization, but often parents and child are thrown together for an extended period during the trip. Some parents report this is the only time during the week when they are engaged in a common activity with the child. The parents also experience themselves as being helpful and doing something for their child after living through long periods of feeling hopeless and powerless to help him.

Confidential Interviews With an Outsider

The family also faces the fact that the child is now going to an outsider, an expert, and revealing things about the family. Because of the confidentiality of the sessions, they cannot know what the child is reporting nor can they rebut what he might be saying. This concern about the child "revealing the family" can lead to more concerted effort by the parents to change the family so that what is reported will be more complimentary. Some families report that their most determined efforts to modify their behavior toward the child (becoming more lenient, or firmer, or more respectful) come from a mutual concern over what the child is saying about them.

Another aspect of the structure of the situation is the healthy competition that emerges between the parents and the expert. Parents can feel compelled to recover their child when they suspect that the child is getting more fond of an outsider than of them. Often the child was never previously permitted a relationship with an outsider, and now he has a base outside the family for changing his position within the family. Part of the merit of this outside base is the opportunity he has to help expert and parents compete for his affection. An interesting process can develop in which the therapist becomes a "friendly contender" who lets the parents emerge the winners. (Supervisory sessions often include the problems of dealing with the jealous parent, and poor outcome can occur if the therapist becomes too jealous of the parents.)

At the same time that they are competing for affection, the parents find that the child's therapy also forces them in the opposite direction. As the child in his therapy sessions is given freedom to say and do anything he pleases, he finds that his therapist will try to put up with just about any kind of behavior. (Not only are many child therapists permissive, but to help the child express his fantasies they allow a wide range of undisciplined behavior.) Naturally, the child begins to behave in the same way at home thinking that his parents must approve or they would not have put him into that situation. Yet, even though a child therapist can be permissive with almost any kind of behavior for an hour in the office, no one living with the child twenty-four hours a day can tolerate such impulsive and undisciplined behavior. Therefore, the parents are driven to discipline the child in order to live with him. In many cases they have never effectively disciplined him before, so the child finds a more secure home life. Often, too, the parents could never agree with each other about discipline, and each attempt led to a quarrel. Now they must agree to survive when the child is behaving in such an extreme way. A fundamental rule becomes apparent in the situation—the more permissive the child therapist in the office, the more he provokes the parents to provide discipline at home. Consequently the child undergoes therapeutic change.

Related to questions of discipline and security is the change in the parental relationship with the child when he has been given over to an expert. Since the child has professional support, the parents feel more free to make mistakes and, therefore, more free to make decisions, because the therapist will make it up to the child and work it through with him. For example, parents may become free to expect the child to go to bed at the proper time, instead of having the usual evening battle, because they feel the treatment must be helping him to be more normal. As they expect proper behavior from him, the child delivers it, with consequent changes throughout the family. In this instance, the parents usually find that if they are not quarreling with the child at bedtime, they are quarreling with each other. Now they must resolve their conflicts, because the child won't rescue them as he has done in the past by making trouble in the evening.

Therapist as Extended Kin

Other structural changes occur in the family merely by the act of placing the child in therapy. If the treatment goes on long enough, the child therapist takes his place in the kinship structure by becoming a paid member of the extended family. He becomes built in as a helpful uncle or grandparental figure who emphasizes marital harmony and can, in time, offer advice to everyone in the family and not merely focus upon the child. Even at the start of treatment, the extended family structure is affected. When the parents take the child to an expert, they free themselves from the need to quarrel with their own parents about the child. The mother can say to her mother, "He's in treatment now, so I would rather not discuss his problems with you." Since the child's symptoms reflect not only the parental conflict but the conflict with extended kin as well, the introduction of the outside expert forces a change throughout the total family system. Once the child is shifted outside the focus of family conflict, he is free to change and respond more normally. The exclusion of the in-laws also fosters the cementing of the marital relationship and helps draw a boundary around the nuclear family.

When a child therapist interviews a child, he is inevitably intervening in the marriage of the parents. As one example, he replaces father as the person mother talks to about the child's problem. The complaints that used to go to the father are now directed toward the therapist; the father is displaced from the position of listening to a constantly complaining and harassing wife. With this structural shift, some of the bitterness of the relationship lessens and the spouses reach out to one another. Ultimately, the spouses can form a tighter coalition that puts pressure on the therapist for more success with their child.

As treatment continues, the influence of the child therapist upon the parents often becomes more direct, even though his contact with them is brief. One must emphasize the skill that is necessary to deal effectively with the parents while having only short contacts with them. When the mother delivers and retrieves her child, she must be influenced quickly, as must the father when he discusses the bill and joins his wife in receiving a report on the child's progress. Using what he has learned about the family from the child, the therapist has a series of brief encounters with the parents that have a cumulative effect over time. Full credit must be given to child therapists for their ability to do brief therapy and exert influence upon both the parent, child, and the marital relationship so that the child can change.

A child therapy orientation may prevent one of the most recent and common errors of family therapy—that of overfocusing on the couple and losing the child in the process. Buttressed by the popular theory that if the marital struggle is resolved, the child's symptomatic functions will disappear, some family therapists work unilaterally with the couple, failing to deal with the child as a necessary, integral part of the problem and its resolution. If they lose the child's contribution as regulator of the speed of therapy, as moderator of the pace of change (through his "when and how" of symptom increase or decrease), the child fails to change.

The Therapist's Influence on Parents

At first the child therapist may be influenced by his theory to treat the parents as only the ghosts of past introjects, but later he begins to deal with them as human beings, particularly as he becomes more fond of the child. If the therapist finds that his individual therapy sessions with the child are not effecting behavioral change, he usually feels an empathy and compassion for the parents' similar plight and thus develops a more positive relationship with them. The parents become more relaxed and flexible, and the child can have an atmosphere in which change is more possible.

As he begins to deal with the parents more directly, the therapist finds also that they ask more of him if the child is not changing. Feeling he must offer them something, he gives increasing amounts of advice about how to deal with the child. Sometimes the parents are willing to follow his advice at this stage, partly because the therapist is more friendly but also because they feel pride in their competence at having forced the advice from him. The advice is also more valuable than it would have been if freely offered.

The child therapist deals more directly with the parents when the child has begun to undergo change. The therapist becomes invested in protecting the changes he sees himself as having created. To do this, he is subtly but surely compelled to move into the larger system. This move can dovetail with the changes the child is producing in the system, sustaining and reinforcing them.

The Function of "Play"

Granting the child therapist's skillful use of brief therapy with the parents, his influence on the family does not confine itself to direct contact with the parents. He not only uses the child to gain information about the family, but he effectively uses the child to bring about change in the family. In this sense, child therapy is similar to the approach taken by some family therapists who select a key member and interview him individually, using him as a lever to bring about family change. However, child therapy has developed a unique method of influencing a family with its use of "play" with the child. It is significant that the vehicle used to enter the complicated organization of family life is the child, the most innocent and directly perceptive member.

The private playroom of the child therapist and the child is like a safety zone for both of them, although the content of the play may appear to be about unmastered experiences and the resolution of internalized conflicts. To the extent that play and fantasy mirror the actions of the family, the child learns to deal with harmful family interventions by coping with them in miniature; the therapist, who may have been appalled by the destructiveness evident in the family, becomes more inured to these patterns in play form. The child and his play become the child therapist's way of entering a family on a familiar path, with the play therapy like a decompression chamber that permits the therapist to approach the family later without too much risk and uncertainty.

Play is one of the most important factors in human life, but in child therapy, "play" is a peculiar and deviant form. By definition, play is something that occurs between voluntary participants and has no purpose except the pleasure of the action. This generally accepted definition of play is clearly not applicable to "play therapy." When play is used as a therapeutic tool, it is given a purpose and so by definition becomes something other than play. There is also a question as to how voluntary the play is in therapy; the child is sometimes brought to it unwillingly, and the child therapist is paid money to participate. Clearly it is not a spontaneous occurrence but an arrangement made with an ulterior motive—to induce change in one (or both) of the participants. Another aspect of it is also unusual; although adults sometimes play with children, it is rare to find two people playing with dolls when one of them is old enough to have a moustache.

Seen in this way, play therapy is less play in form and more of a special communication that has different rules from ordinary life. Like other forms of therapy in which patient and therapist can play with ideas and words that would not be proper in other settings, child and child therapist can play with objects in ways that would not be appropriate outside the room. For example, if the child picks up a toy truck and throws it, an adult will ordinarily protest. The adult child therapist might pick up the truck and throw it himself, or if less active, he might at least make a permissive comment or interpretation. The usual rules of adult-child interchange are suspended or treated as a fiction in this setting.

With this kind of freedom established, there is also a suspension of the usual rules for directing someone to behave differently. The unstated task of the child therapist in the play room is to ease the child into behaving differently with adults and particularly with his parents and siblings. This persuasion is not accomplished by explicit directives to behave differently, any more than it is in most methods of therapy, but by indirection, which is more difficult to resist. As the child goes through searching behavior to define his relationship with the therapist and to find out how he is to behave the toys in the playroom become devices for trial-and-error experimentation. They not only become expressions of real family issues that can be resolved (as theory has it) in symbolic form, but more importantly, they can become a vehicle for the therapist's instructions as to how to deal with these family issues in reality. The way the child therapist responds to the child's handling of the family dolls, for example, can be an indirect instruction as to how he is to deal with adults and with the real family at home. In effect, they are remote, indirect communications to the adults as to how to deal differently with the child.

The most typical children's problems involve a contract between parent and disturbed child that the parents will demand certain behavior from the child, which he will not deliver. The child may not talk or he may not control his bowels and bladder, or he may not learn in school, and the parents put pressure upon him to do these things. Child therapy, with its format of a nonpressured atmosphere, an emphasis on play, a loosening of rules, and so on, not only offers the child a different adult response, and so a new contract, but also a directive for how to deal differently with the parents. For example, a young child is brought to a therapist because he is restless and "doesn't talk yet." At home the parents are locked in a struggle with the child to persuade him to talk. The therapist agrees with the parents that he will deal with the child's mutism, but actually he deals with it by offering other modalities of expression, such as drawing, plastics, and toys. With no pressure on him to talk, the child begins to speak in the playroom. The therapist also draws the parents' attention to these alternative ways of dealing with the child, and so the conflict over talking is reduced. When the withdrawn child is offered the opportunity to express himself with toys, he can be less withdrawn in a new modality and proceed to behave more aggressively, first with toys and later at home. As he knocks over the mother doll and survives it in the playroom, the therapist encourages this aggression against the doll. Implicitly he is encouraging more aggression with mother. When the child is then more outspoken with mother and does not deal with her by withdrawing, mother is forced to deal with him differently, and so a different pattern is set up in the family. Yet the therapist has never asked the child directly to assert himself more with mother, he has "merely" directed his play with a mother doll. He has never asked the mother to deal differently with the child either. With older children the therapist will use other devices, such as saying to the child, "Your bad side wants to fight with your parents all the time, but your healthy side wants to be happier." Dividing up the child this way, or joining the healthy part of the ego, is a way of directing the child to behave differently without making a "request" that can be refused.

In those cases in which the child is obviously responding negatively to parental pressures, the child therapist must help the parents deal with him differently. For example, the therapist might ask the parents to be less intrusive and not pump the child but, instead, to let him have some secrets. This is easy to do within his theoretical conviction about the need for confidentiality between himself and his child patient. However, the therapist does not merely make these requests to the parents, he also uses various arts of persuasion. One of his procedures is to explore briefly with the parents their own childhood, with a compassionate view of how it has influenced their behavior with their child in ways beyond their control. Finding themselves being forgiven for their current behavior, the parents are more willing to change it. If the child "regresses" because the loose and permissive setting of child therapy facilitates moments of controlled "regression," the parents become more dependent upon the therapist. This is reinforced by handling the child's regression as a phasic event, if possible even as proof of progress, reassuring the parents in their moments of increased stress. The disappointment of the parents, which initially made them seek treatment, is deepened and so is their need for the therapist's guidance and support. As they lean upon him more, he becomes more relevant to their family system and is more able to influence it.

One should also not overlook the importance of the play therapy setting for the therapist. In the standard therapeutic setting for adults there can be an illusion that people are rational or irrational (although dream interpretation helps overcome this myth), but the child therapist is under no such constraint and can use nonverbal communication, fantasy, etc. when dealing with his child patient. Unlike the modern family, with its emphasis on cognitive solutions to problems, or reasoning with the child, he is free to use means other than intellectual to contact the child. These nonverbal techniques also make him better able than the parents to monitor the child's pace of interpersonal development.

Because "play" is theoretically unacknowledged as a means of communication from the therapist through the child to the parents, and from the parents through the child to the therapist, child therapy respects and utilizes the family's defensive arrangement by its very definition of method. Pretending that the parents are not (through play) being given instructions and circumstances for behaving differently, child therapy avoids many current trends. It avoids frontality, explicitness, "getting to know where you are at," and any confrontative "reasoning out" of the problems. These trends are stressed as important to change in many therapies. But by using "play" and by claiming no direct influence on the parents, child therapy provides a "double masking screen" through which the proper freedom for indirect communications, so essential to outcome, is preserved.

A "modern" error of many family therapists is treating family members as if they are only behavioral contributions in unfolding interpersonal sequences. The possibility of family members feeling a measure of responsibility for their own behavior can be reduced in this format. In play therapy, the framework by itself allows family members to feel always that they are discrete and separate individuals, despite the fact that their behavior can be at the service of obscure forces, like larger multi-generational sequences or "childhood events." Because the framework of child therapy serves ostensibly to enable the child to come to terms with himself as a separate being, most processes through which the significant work occurs can only become incidental or implicit. Since the incidentals entail most communicational relays between parent, child, and therapist, a convenient situation of unguardedness develops; that is, all participants can keep out of the field of conscious preoccupation any rational checking of each other's intentions, while these are modified. The rethreading of parents and child into a different system proceeds then precisely by deemphasizing that they are a system at all.

One should note in passing that one of the dangers of individual play with the child is the possibility that the therapist will become too attached to the child and so threaten to detach him from his parents. As part of the wisdom of the child guidance movement, this effect was balanced by having a social worker deal with parents. Along with many other functions, the social worker could interpret the therapist's ideas and behavior to the parents and serve as a mediator while also influencing the parents to change.

When therapy fails to change the child, the child therapist who works alone becomes increasingly involved with the parents and requests certain kinds of changes in the parent-child relationship. If this does not produce results, the therapist raises the question of whether the marital relationship should be investigated and treated. This threat often is sufficient to force the parents to deal with each other differently to avoid going into their marital problems further, and consequently the child changes. The more the therapist is thwarted in his attempts to help the child change, the more he begins to inquire incisively into the nuances of the conflict between the spouses. The parents quickly shield themselves by changing their parenting, thus benefiting the child. The child himself can also initiate a fast bootstrap operation to modify his behavior sufficiently so that the parents have an excuse to withdraw him from treatment; thus the child helps protect his parents, with their marital difficulties, *by improving instead of by having symptoms as he did previously.* This kind of intervention is sometimes done by family therapists, who see the child's problem as largely a product of family conflict, but usually they help the parents work through the conflicts because they are seeking perduring changes in the child and not temporary ones. Obviously, change in the child can only persist if his family has changed.

The Contribution of the Child

Up to this point there has been an emphasis upon the parents' influence upon the child and the therapist's influence upon the family. The important influence of the child upon both parents and therapist should also be dealt with explicitly. An example can partially summarize the child's contribution. In a family with conflict between the parents over who was superior to the other, their child was caught between them as a vehicle for this conflict. The mother insisted that the child be outstanding in school as part of her attempt to set the child up as a competitor to her husband, whom she considered weak and unsatisfactory. The father responded to the child's achievement by indicating that the child was siding with the mother against him and humiliating him. The child responded to this situation by manifesting an acute fear of homework, thereby being unable to achieve in school for reasons outside of his control. When he entered child therapy and began to relate in a positive way to the therapist, his problem was increased. To please the therapist, he must lose the fear of homework in the context of play with this safe and significant person. As happens in many such cases, the child improves, but the family has not significantly changed. The child then either relapses or offers different symptoms, such as other fears, headaches, etc. Often the therapist sees the "regression" of the child as part of the transference aspect of treatment. However, in terms of his actions, the therapist shifts his strategy with the child and also becomes more involved in "management" interviews with the parents, partly to persuade them to deal differently with the child—"We mustn't rush him so much"—and partly to gather more information about the home setting in order to understand the child's difficulties. In the process of canvasing the field for more information, the therapist can seldom fail to insinuate a paradoxical situation as well. He can talk about the regression in such a way that its implications for signaling therapeutic gains cannot be ignored. Almost everything the child does and alarms the parents can turn out to imply the possibility of immediate or impending progress in an unfolding process. This keeps child and parents firmly bound to the situation. Either the therapist's "brief management" interventions then steer the parents in a radically different direction, or the regression so intensifies that it pulls the parents into behaving differently with the child, or eventually the child's maturation ushers in a new developmental stage changing the regressive behavior.

From the point of view we are describing here, "regression" can be seen as a progression of the child to a more effective way of communicating with the therapist. He is responding to the therapist's lack of understanding by trying other means to influence the therapist to modify his situation, particularly the parental behavior. Symptomatic behavior, and play, are the child's way of indirectly instructing the therapist to shift his strategy of therapy. If the therapist does not understand, the child will communicate by more severe symptoms, as if using a megaphone, until his influence is successful in activating the therapist and the parents to behave differently. His severe symptoms encourage the parents to seek counsel with the therapist and encourage the therapist to enquire further into what is happening at home. When the sensitive therapist picks up the child's cues and modifies his approach to child and parents, the conflicts in the family become resolved and the child is free to give up this form of communication. At this point, neither symptomatic behavior, which the child had learned to use in his family, nor the "play" therapy, which the child has learned from the therapist as a way of communicating, is necessary.

In terms of the relationship between therapist and child, a mutually regulatory pattern becomes established. When the therapist is flexible enough to heed the child's message, he demonstrates his respect for the child's autonomy. He communicates to the child, "Your communications have power." A level of respectful reciprocity within the interdependent relationship is attained, and autonomy is now feasible for both. The autonomy of the therapist, as well as of the child, is in this sense an eventual product of an underlying collaborative dimension. This dimension is achieved by child and therapist testing each other for impact of communications, without perceiving themselves in a complex relay system of more than two persons. Evidence that communicational cues beyond the two of them are being effectively relayed and received may show only in non-verbal indicators of collaboration. There is room for behavior shifts on the part of both—the therapist to modify his strategies, the child to change his deviant behavior, neither feeling necessarily conscious of dealing with more than one person.

The Family Orientation

It was once thought that perduring change in the child could occur only if in addition to child therapy, both parents were in individual therapy. Sometimes it was assumed that treatment could be coordinated by collaboration among the several therapists of the different family members. Such collaboration usually failed, and typically the individual treatment did not resolve the marital struggle in which the child was entangled. From the view offered here, it would seem that treatment can be most effective and efficient if the person treating the child also "manages" the parents so that change in the different parts of the family system at different stages are coordinated by a single person.

Many child therapists continue with the procedure of alternate interviews with child and parents, and this way of approaching families has many merits. In some cases parents can react with resentment and resistance if they are directly confronted with family conflicts the child is expressing. Advice offered by someone who is clearly not blaming them because he feels the child has a problem inside of himself can often lead the parents to accept directives and respond in new ways with less resistance. In this sense it is the very fact that the child therapist acts naive about family dynamics that sometimes makes his influence upon the family effective.

WHY CHILD THERAPY FAILS

What has been emphasized here are those aspects of child therapy that have merit if viewed from a family orientation. Yet, if one grants these merits, one must address the question of why child therapy and child analysis do not usually succeed in bringing about therapeutic change. It can be argued that the naivete about the context of the child helps the child therapist correct errors of family therapists who are overfocused upon the marriage and neglect the child's contribution to the problem and to the therapy. Yet being naive also causes change to come about inadvertently instead of predictably, and, therefore, treatment failure is as likely as treatment success.

There are two main handicaps for the child therapist, both of them related to the theory he is taught. The first handicap is, of course, the idea that the problem is within the child. Although this theory helps the child therapist be less blaming of the parents, it is also likely to cause him to neglect the parents after the fee is set. If his theory persuades him that he is trying to change something within the child, he will not communicate to the parents through the child but will merely pass the time playing with the child, and no change will take place.

The second handicap is based upon the child therapist's lack of understanding of the ways the child is responding to his interpersonal context. If the therapist takes the child's communicative behavior only as a report about his inner nature rather than a report about his social situation, the therapist will not direct his efforts toward deliberately influencing the social situation so that the child can change. While it is true that by not forcing the family to deal with the parental conflict, he may avoid the consequent bad feelings among the family members, he will be like the behavioral modifier who brings parents together around a new conditioning program without ever realizing that previously the parents were in conflict about how to deal with the child. Yet, by not knowing that the child is responding to a conflictual family structure, the child therapist will not be able to indirectly influence that structure in any *systematic* way. If he does have an influence, it will be a chance occurrence, and so therapeutic change will occur by chance.

When a social worker is dealing with the parents while the child therapist treats the child, there is a chance of an influence on the family through the social worker's endeavors. However, there is also a chance that social worker and child therapist will be in covert conflict with each other about the family, taking sides in family struggles, and will merely replicate the conflictual situation that has produced a disturbed child.

SUMMARY

Despite the many theoretically based factors that can cause treatment to fail, one should not overlook the fact that the child therapist approaches symptoms within the newer theoretical model developing in the field. Previously, it was assumed that a patient's symptoms should not be dealt with directly because they are supposed to have "roots." Child therapy offers an alternative view: focus on the child, or symptom, acknowledge the roots of pathology in the family, but do not deal with the roots directly. In the last few years this approach has been considered innovative in the treatment of symptomatic adult behavior, such as phobias or compulsions. Such symptom-oriented therapies as behavioral conditioning, the paradoxical intention approach (1), Milton H. Erickson's methods (2), or Stampful's procedure (3), all assume that the symptom should be dealt with directly. Some of these approaches emphasize not only focusing upon the symptom, but even encouraging it as a way of bringing about change.

Clearly child therapy has anticipated these innovations and is in the *avant garde* of the field. When the child therapist accepts and encourages the family's presentation of the child as the problem, he is accepting the scapegoat function of the child without arousing resistance in the family. This approach leaves him free to convey effective suggestions in his brief contacts with the parents. Whether he conveys those suggestions to bring about change in the family and consequent change in the child is partly determined by chance since in the nature of child therapy theory it must be unplanned.

REFERENCES

1. Frankl, V., "Paradoxical Intention: A Logotherapeutic Technique," *Amer. J. Psychother.*, 14: 520–535, 1960.
2. *Advanced Techniques of Hypnosis and Therapy: Selected Papers of Milton H. Erickson,* Haley, J., (Ed.) New York, Grune & Stratton, 1967.
3. London, P., *The Modes and Morals of Psychotherapy,* New York, Holt, Rinehart and Winston, 1964.

15

The Futility of
Child Therapy

LENA BLANCO FURGERI

The impetus for this paper resulted from the observation of a pattern which became evident after years of working with children in play therapy. In many instances, at times more so with children who tended to show severe pathology such as autism, the parent would terminate the treatment immediately or shortly after the therapist had established meaningful contact with the child. This paper will delineate and discuss how in some instances the standard child therapy model, where parent and child are seen separately, either by the same or different therapists, is contraindicated, considering the needs and problems of modern-day families and emerging communication theory. An attempt will be made to show how the family systems approach can be a viable treatment option.

A typical incident of abrupt and premature termination involved an autistic boy who had been with several former therapists. After many sessions, during which he remained mute, he responded verbally. The following week the mother called to say that she was "taking him to another doctor." There was the familiar overwhelming feeling of failure, but as the therapist looked beyond her personal feelings she thought of how confused the child must feel at having been suddenly cut off from another relationship and how threatened the parent was not to allow the child to continue. Some steps had clearly been missed in parent-therapist communication. This realization, together with many similar prior incidents, suggested the possibility of changing the treatment strategy by seeing children and parents together at least in the initial phases of therapy.

If we look back to the beginnings of psychotherapeutic thought, it's clear that Freud by no means neglected the family—the Oedipal theory involves an intricate network of family interrelationships. Moreover, his emphasis on the intrapsychic was influenced by his socio-cultural and political milieu. Likewise communication theory, as a link in psychoanalytic thought, has also emerged in relation to the socio-political construct of our institutions. A slow evolution from emphasis on the intrapsychic to emphasis on the interpersonal started with Sullivan's (1953) interpersonal theory, which was influenced by Ruesch and Bateson's (1951) book on communication. Sullivan (1954) was also one of the first to question the therapist's traditional role. In the child guidance movement, pathological behavior in children started to be viewed within the context of the family structure. No longer were disturbances seen strictly as intrapsychic problems. As Pollack (1952, p. 6) indicated, "what appears to be the social environment of one person is a combination of the intrapsychic problems of others. Correspondingly we have found that the intrapsychic problem of one person is part of the social environment of other persons." Haley (1962, p. 265) observed that "In the search for more satisfying ways of explaining differences between individuals, the emphasis in psychiatry and psychology has been shifting from the study of processes within an individual to the study of processes which occur naturally between people." Likewise Carroll (1964, p. 180) indicated that individual psychoanalysis focuses on illness within the patient or his disturbed intrapsychic structure whereas in family therapy the emphasis is on the disordered functioning processes within the group, but this does not mean that there is a denial of the maladaptation of individuals in it.

According to systems theory, families develop a network of communication in which individuals can maintain a psychological balance. In disturbed families, where the child is often the supposed focus of the problem, the evident symptomatology has become crucial to the homeostasis of the system. The family has learned to accomodate and adapt to such behavior as hyperactivity, acting out, phobias, and scapegoating so that this has become a way of life for the group. It was Watzlawick (1976, p. 13) who observed that

> From the studies of families containing a schizophrenic member, there can be little doubt that the existence of a patient is essential for the stability of the family system and the system will react quickly and effectively to any internal or external attempt to change its organization.

The family's adaptation to the disturbed behavior, which in the above example was autism, explains the termination of treatment once the child responded to the therapist. Although the motivations of parents and intentions of the therapist were consciously worthwhile, the families were not being helped. Parents did not willfully intend to sabotage treatment but they probably panicked when confronted with new behaviors which inhibited their ability to respond. The therapist thought back to the case of a nine-year-old chubby boy who was being treated for soiling. The therapist was treating parent and child conjointly at the time, as in those days the sessions were still on an intuitive hit-and-miss basis rather than out of any theoretical framework. In one session where the mother was talking of how her son had been verbally assertive during the week she became extremely upset and commented "you're making him worse." With both of them present it was possible to question why his verbal response towards her was more upsetting than his soiling. Rather than focus on the intrapsychic concomitants of his soiling by seeing him in play therapy sessions, much more was being observed as mother and son sat together. She would often feed him Lifesavers whenever he got close to any feelings during the sessions. The emphasis during the sessions was more on exploring how she needed him to soil as a way of protecting her shaky self-esteem and cover up her poor self-image. His soiling justified her controlling and nagging behavior as a means of expressing her anger towards him.

As the writer further considered the problem of termination at a crucial point in therapy, she also began to view it as a possible indication of how she was being caught up in the ongoing system of various double bind communications which occur in disturbed families. The double bind theory of Bateson, Jackson, and Weakland (1956) became crucial in understanding how individuals lock themselves in a closed communication system where there is a binder and victim who take turns in roles which end up by "producing conflicting definitions of the relationship and consequent subjective distress." (Bateson, et al., 1963). In dealing with the child alone, therefore, the therapist realized that often her effectiveness was hampered. On the one hand the child was given the message to come and relate and yet once this task was accomplished, the parent terminated giving the understanding that something inappropriate had occurred. Usually the therapist was also caught in a double bind. If she was ineffective then the parent wanted to terminate because nothing was happening. If she was instrumental in effecting any behavior change, particularly within the family, then the parent might terminate out of panic and anxiety. Either way the therapist was bound in her position, which was further compromised by the confidentiality clause, since she was not free to talk openly about what she was learning in the play sessions.

Additional roadblocks which presented themselves in varied ways were often exhausting and time-consuming. Parents would often greet the therapist with "I have something to tell you" or "Can I see you for a few minutes?" or "The guidance counselor wants you to call her." Usually the child would stand by fidgety and nervous. Initially this was handled in the perfunctory manner of "talk to your therapist about it" but this did not really get to the root of the problem. After the session the parent would usually ask, often within earshot of the departing therapist, "What did she say?" "Did you tell her what you did?" In this way the parent put more pressure on the child.

As the frustrations built up both for parent and therapist, the former would use one last resistance available, namely finances, usually justifying the termination of her own treatment because "the child needs it more." Once this occurred, therapy took a steady downhill course as the parent depended even more on the child's therapist who had made a commitment to the child as the patient. As a last resort, but again on a hit-and-miss basis, the therapist would ask mother to come in and discuss the matter in front of the child instead of chatting in the waiting room. The parent, still unsatisfied, terminated anyway. The amount of time spent on the phone with school personnel and the parent's therapist, especially if it was someone the therapist did not know, was exhausting and usually led to rather limited results.

Thinking about all the incidents where mothers waited anxiously to talk to their child's therapist, yearning for a direct contact with the one who had an intimate weekly relationship with their child, the awareness slowly emerged that behind every problem child was a frustrated hungry parent yearning for help but not able to ask for it directly. In getting the child to act out their unconscious wishes and urges they could then ask for help via the child as a way of gratifying themselves. In other words, on an unconscious level they needed to perpetuate the child's pathology as a way of gratifying themselves indirectly. Many parents feel guilty and selfish in asking for help directly for themselves, especially when culturally the child comes first. Lesoff (1975) writes about how the identified patient, usually the child, is acting out some aspect of the parents' unconscious. Ironically, therefore, once the child was treated for its behavior the mother would actually feel deprived on an unconscious level and would be strongly motivated, out of her anxiety, to terminate the child. Change of behavior was often experienced as a symbolic loss by the parent.

Taking all of the above factors into consideration, the therapist finally decided to try a personal experiment. She would shift treatment strategy by not seeing any child alone in beginning treatment but only together with one or both parents and the rest of the family. It needs to be stressed that the therapist had more leeway in her private practice than in a clinical setting. Haley (1975) describes the many paradoxes in attempting family therapy in a mental health clinic which follows traditional modes of therapy. The therapist decided to start with the case of a lovely, autistic nine-year-old girl.

This child would not speak outside the home. The therapist had been treating her and her mother for more than three years on a low-cost basis in alternate individual sessions, i.e., one week the mother and one week the child. During the years of contact there had been only one or two family sessions because her father, who was equally silent, and two older brothers were reluctant to attend. There had been extensive history-taking, all of the appropriate tests, referral for chemotherapy which she was receiving, and placement in a special school. In the meanwhile, she continued to stand in catatonic-like fashion, barely a few feet away from the office door, with her hat, coat, and gloves on and lunchbox in hand, responding only nonverbally by nodding yes and no, smiling, and twisting and contorting her body to relay different tensions and moods. The writer was aware that she was adhering to the classical model and resisting the idea of observing the system on an on-going basis. If this was really a system where mother and daughter would remain symbiotically tied even though they were being seen separately then the therapist was ready to risk change. She decided to start seeing them in joint sessions weekly. A major breakthrough occurred as the therapist restored full power to the mother, so to speak, who finally got her daughter to talk. As soon as the child started there was no stopping her. Shortly afterward she started talking in school. This was the first time the therapist had had success with an autistic child and the therapeutic relationship continued for several more years.

By seeing as many members of the family as possible in an initial interview, the therapist perpetuates a new communications system based on open expression of problems and feelings. The therapist serves as an active model in setting up the therapeutic contract, which takes on some of the following contours:

1. An alliance is made with the parents in terms of "your kid has you over a barrel." The therapeutic rationale for joint sessions is given. The therapist shares some of the futility involved in seeing the child alone, explaining that the parents deserve first-hand attention as they have worked hard. Their active participation in the session together with observing and listening will help them gain a better understanding of their child which can also benefit them in relation to others in the family. Parents feel directly acknowledged, accepted, and understood, especially if they have been asking for help via the child's problem.

2. The child or identified patient presenting the difficulties is not really the problem but is a symptom of something going on in the family which is contributing to unhappiness and tension for all. Since they are all living together and know something about this, it is important that they all participate and contribute towards the understanding of what is happening. This construct not only alleviates some of the tension for the identified patient but for all the members. Usually some of the other siblings have considerable guilt and have also felt rejected, since the focus of attention in disturbed families is on deviant behavior. This engages everyone in participating and becoming active allies in the therapeutic process. Therapy becomes a means of bringing the family together on a new level.

3. This is a place where problems are solved through *talking*. Each person is to remain in his seat and talk about his feelings. There is to be no hitting or striking out. In families with many children and much hyperactivity or where parents tend to automatically hit when angry it is important that this rule be stated and worked on during the sessions. Children will usually play into the resistance of working through difficulties by changing seats, hitting each other, or getting up for water, so it is important that a working atmosphere is structured into the session. At the same time, the therapist begins to act as an active model for the parents in terms of setting rules and getting them across. In many disturbed families the parents sit passively as their children disrupt and one sign of their growth is when they are able to step in and set rules and structures with the therapist. In rigid families where silence and conformity is the rule, the therapist works towards a more relaxed, open atmosphere.

4. Each person is to talk for himself. No person talks about the other or for the other. There are no secrets in the office and everything is to be said in words. These ground rules are discussed when the relevant situations occur. Invariably in the early sessions one will usually whisper in another's ear or parents will begin with "Tell Lena what you did."

5. The time and day is set for everyone's convenience by attempting to take into consideration school, play, and work schedules. Any person not able to come is to call personally since each person is responsible directly to the therapist and to himself. This takes the burden off the parents for reinforcing the appointment and helps children become more responsible for what is happening.

6. Any incoming or outgoing calls regarding any family member will be discussed. Any school action taken, whether it be a call, a letter, or a suggestion for a change of

class placement, is discussed directly with the person involved. Feelings and thoughts about the plan are discussed and cooperation is enlisted.

7. Parents are to stop running to the school when called. Often in disturbed families this has become a repetitive syndrome. Parents are called to account for and explain the child's behavior. Of course, if they could deal with the behavior they would not be seeking help. This instruction brings relief to some parents; they feel encouraged to have school personnel call the therapist in crisis situations so that she can make appropriate recommendations. This takes parents out of the school bind—and often may make the child anxious. Likewise, some parents react with apprehension because it breaks up their tie to the school and on a symbolic level is a separation from their child. These reactions, however, are readily observable when the family is present and they are noted and worked with during the session.

What occurs, therefore, is that the therapist becomes a new intervening agent in the system. The theoretical shift from the intrapsychic to the interpersonal implies that the therapist's role is affected as well. The posture of the silent therapist does not meet the needs of twentieth century man having problems with isolation, alienation, self-expression, and communication. As a result there has been a shift in the therapeutic model from a quiet, introspective position to a more overt, interactive system. It may not be wholly accidental that communication and systems theory has evolved in a culture where a free press and the free exchange and expression of ideas have been highly valued. Families are facing radical social change and intellectual insight regarding problems is not enough. With the interventive approach the therapist needs to shift from history-taking and analyzing the past to more immediate considerations involving here-and-now behavior. Erikson (1975) discussed how the therapist's role needs modification from the passive to the active model, especially in working with families. How the therapist intervenes via different strategies is actively described by Haley (1963). The form which the resistance takes and how it is played out by different members needs particular consideration. It's also important to note that the therapist assumes many diversified roles including that of referee, moderator, peacemaker, agitator, devil's advocate, rule-setter, analyst, etc. In playing out these roles in the parents' presence, the therapist can be a model so that parents can observe how they can use themselves in multifaceted ways. All family members develop feelings of trust and dependency toward the therapist. She is available to all members rather than being confined to just one person. In this way no one feels deprived or left out.

Since this paper is concerned with those situations in which the play therapy model was not particularly effective, the next question is: What types of situations call for the use of the family interview or parent-child session initially? Based on this therapist's experience the following are some examples of situations where initial joint sessions are in order:

1. In families who have previously been in treatment and are again requesting help either for a repeat of the original problem or for another child.

2. In families where a strong symbiotic tie exists between parent and child so that the separate play therapy session is a threat to the mother's attachment to the child. The separation will arouse such anxiety that the mother will eventually unconsciously

sabotage the treatment plan because she feels abandoned by the child and misunderstood by the therapist.

3. With parents who are referred by other agencies, such as the school, and who state that everything is just fine at home. Such parents don't understand what is going on and often feel that the problem is related to outside influences such as poor choice of playmates, the teacher, etc. At times these parents are rather unsophisticated analytically and may need a somewhat directive counseling approach.

4. When the child may be acting out repressed unconscious wishes and impulses of either or both parents. In seeing all jointly, one can slowly begin to point out to parents those externalized aspects of themselves which they are attempting to handle through the child (Lesoff, 1975).

5. With parents who may not be formally educated but who are very much in tune with their feelings. Often these parents tend to act impulsively on their feelings because they are unable to put them in any type of cognitive construct. These parents are usually eager to learn.

6. Where finances are a real problem and the family cannot afford a double fee or where finances are being used as an initial resistance.

Since the writer has been seeing families in beginning interviews there have been no terminations. Everyone feels they have a place to go to air out their feelings and everyone feels nurtured and taken care of. What usually happens is that the child's symptoms are arrested fairly early. Parents feel that they have been helped on a concrete level and they are usually ready and willing to work on more subtle problems involving the marital relationship or their own intrapsychic difficulties. Usually, once the children's symptoms diminish, parents start coming for themselves or more often than not, parents will go on to either group therapy, joint counseling, or their own personal analysis. Family sessions are usually called for as different developmental states are experienced. In many instances, families who have come when their children were in the latency age return to joint sessions as the children approach adolescence because the family needs to adapt to a new developmental life cycle problem.

SUMMARY

If one takes into consideration modern communication and family systems theory, it is apparent that the therapist's effectiveness may be greatly hampered in situations where she works with the child alone in a play therapy situation. Seeing a child alone in play therapy often tends to play into the already existing double bind situations in a family. The family aims at rejecting new behavior patterns which emerge because it has adapted to the problem behavior. By seeing the child and related family members, an open therapeutic contract can be established aimed at educating and preparing the family to be more receptive to new behaviors via new means of communication. The therapist becomes the active intervening agent in the system, available to all of the members. With the therapist serving as the nurturer which the family lacked, its members learn how to be available to each other in a new way. Once nurturance occurs, the family members feel strengthened to mature and respond differently to each other.

REFERENCES

Bateson, G., *et al.* A note on the double bind—1962. *Family Process*, 1963, 2 (1), 154-161.

Bateson, G., Jackson J., & Weakland, J. Toward a theory of schizophrenia. *Behavioral Science*, 1956, 1, 251-264.

Carroll, E. J. Family therapy and some observations and comparisons. *Family Process*, 1964, 3(1), 178-185.

Erikson, G. Teaching family therapy. *Journal of Education for Social Work*, 1973, 9(3), 9-15.

Haley, J. Family experiments: A new type of experimentation. *Family Process*, 1962, 1(2), 265-293.

Haley, J. *Strategies of psychotherapy*. New York: Grune and Stratton, Inc., 1963.

Haley, J. Why a mental health clinic should avoid family therapy. *Journal of Marriage and Family Counseling*, 1975, 1(1), 3-13.

Lesoff, R. Foster's technique: A systematic approach to family therapy. *Clinical Social Work Journal*, 1975, 3(1), 32-45.

Pollack, O. *Integrating sociological and psychoanalytic concepts*. New York: Russell Sage Foundation, 1956.

Ruesch, J., & Bateson, G. *Communication: The social matrix of psychiatry*. New York: W. W. Norton and Co., 1951.

Sullivan, H. S. *The interpersonal theory of psychiatry*. New York: W. W. Norton and Co., 1953.

Sullivan, H. S. *The psychiatric interview*. New York: W. W. Norton and Co., 1954.

Watzlawick, P., Beavin, J., & Jackson, D. *Pragmatics of human communication*. New York: W. W. Norton and Co., 1967.

16

The Child Guidance Clinic as a Center of Prophylaxis and Enlightenment

ANNA FREUD

As opening speaker of this convention I have the privilege of offering some general considerations concerning the role of the Child Guidance Clinic in the community as well as discussing the interrelations between child analysis and the allied field of child guidance work.[1]

CHILD ANALYSIS BEFORE THE CHILD GUIDANCE ERA

I begin with my personal recollections about the development of these relationships, recollections which make me feel that analysts and child analysts owe the child guidance clinics a debt of gratitude. Before such clinics existed, we analysts felt that we were in possession of much solid analytic knowledge potentially useful for the upbringing of children, their teaching, and the treatment of their problems. But there were no recognized channels of communication, neither with parents nor with the professional workers within the children's services. All that the analysts could rely on in this respect were chance contacts: parents while or after undergoing a therapeutic analysis themselves could not help but apply some of their newly acquired insight to the handling of their children; teachers who, for personal reasons, underwent analysis were expected to carry back to the teaching profession some analytic findings

[1]The content of this paper is based on material collected in the Hampstead Child-Therapy Clinic with the aid of grants by The Field Foundation, Inc., New York; The Foundations' Fund for Research in Psychiatry, New Haven, Connecticut; The Ford Foundation, New York; The Psychoanalytic Research and Development Fund, Inc., New York; and The Grant Foundation, Inc., New York.

concerning child development. It was a thrilling occasion when in Vienna (approximately in 1930) an inspector of nursery schools invited us to conduct a seminar for a small group of nursery school teachers to discuss their problem children; or when an inspector of municipal play centers invited me to give a series of introductory lectures to his workers. Actually, one of the first schools to make systematic use of analytic child psychology was the Walden School in New York, a fact which Dr. S. Ferenczi learned on one of his early visits to the States and reported on most enthusiastically after his return. But these hopeful signs of possible cooperation between analysis and work with children remained few and far between.

There was another side to the same picture which was no less frustrating. We knew that there was a large amount of child material near at hand from which we, as child analysts, could have profited greatly. There were all the initial states of mental disturbance, as they show up in childhood, the many transitional stages between health and illness, the common developmental difficulties of all young children, their relationship to the more circumscribed syndromes of the infantile neuroses—all this was potentially available in our environment and, still, we were denied access to it. The children brought to us in private practice or within the hospital services were those where mental illness had passed the initial phase of behavior disorder or symptom formation and had become ingrained in the personality in a massive way, causing severe breakdowns or permanent deviations of character. Again, there was little or nothing that we could do to alter the position.

But it is precisely this situation which has changed with the advent of the child guidance clinics. Since they have come into being, they have opened up a two-way traffic between parents and professional workers with children on the one hand and child analysis or child psychiatry on the other hand. It is the child guidance clinics which act at present as mediators between the two fields and serve as clearing houses between them: they receive material from the public to pass on to the child analysts and child psychiatrists, and conversely they receive information from child psychiatry (or analysis) to hand out to the public. This is an important and formidable assignment, and it seems worth while to me to investigate how far the child guidance clinics of our knowledge have been able and equipped to fulfill this double task.

THE CHILD GUIDANCE CLINIC AS A CLEARING HOUSE

Collection of Material

As regards the first side of the assignment, the collection of available case material, there is no doubt that the existing clinics are eminently successful. Probably on the basis of their status as public institutions they have done what the private child analyst had been unable to achieve: namely, to gain the confidence of the public.[2] As director of a child guidance clinic, or when talking to one of the directors, you will find that

---

[2]It was August Aichhorn who remarked first on this difference between private and public work with parents. When praised for the hold he had on parents and the amount of information he gathered from them, he would answer: "Don't forget what I represent for the parents. As official advisor, appointed by the authorities, I am backed up by the whole Municipality."

collecting the material presents no difficulty. If anything, trouble arises in the opposite direction: there is too much material. Clinics are swamped with the cases sent in to them by the parents themselves, by teachers, youth workers, general practitioners and pediatricians, almoners of hospitals, probation officers from the courts, child welfare organizers, etc. There is everything from the most common difficulties of management with which parents used to deal on their own (such as the early sleeping, feeding, and toileting troubles), to the severe retardations, borderline and autistic and atypical states. There is, indeed, more than the diagnostic skill of the child psychiatrist or child analyst can cope with at present. The bewildering variety of pathological, or seemingly pathological manifestations, seems to call for new diagnostic categories based not on symptomatology but on developmental considerations. But, however this may be, the case material is there to be looked at by the analyst, studied, sorted out for therapy, understood, and, perhaps in the future, to be newly classified.[3]

There is, as said before, no lack of confidence in the clinic on the part of the public; again, if anything, there is too much. With many people, the concept of treatment in a clinic has acquired a magical connotation. Little difference is made between children who suffer from environmental neglect, unsuitable parents, tragic bereavements, and those cases where something has gone wrong in the development and personality structure for internal reasons. In both instances to know that a child is in treatment seems to spell safety to parents, welfare agencies or public authorities, as if every non-organic disturbance were automatically suitable for psychological treatment, and as if treatment guaranteed a cure in all cases. Paradoxically enough, it will soon be necessary on the part of the clinics to disabuse the public, i.e., to induce people to lower their expectations of therapy to a level more justified by the conditions and limitations imposed by reality.

The Application of Analytic Knowledge

I find that the clinics have been less successful where the receiving and application of analytic knowledge is concerned. At least, there is in this respect a wide gap between the "analytic" clinics as they exist in some of the big European and American centers, usually in close collaboration with a local psychoanalytic society and training institute, and the ordinary, although frequently "analytically oriented" child guidance clinics as they exist in larger or smaller numbers all over the countries. The analytic clinic usually has a fully trained analyst as psychiatrist-in-charge with several younger staff members in analytic training. The analytically oriented clinic may base its whole connection with psychoanalysis on some contact with analysis which a senior staff member has had at one period of his career. What has been brought back from such contacts are often no more than single pieces of analytic findings which bear the hallmark of a certain phase of analytic thinking. I name as such the following: emphasis on the pathogenic role of repression of infantile sexuality (resulting in therapeutic emphasis on sex enlightenment, dealing with guilt arising from oedipal fantasies, masturbation conflicts, etc.); emphasis on the pathogenic repression of aggression

[3]In our Hampstead Child-Therapy Clinic, our Psychiatrist-in-Charge, Dr. Liselotte Frankl, is conducting a diagnostic study of this kind.

(with therapeutic emphasis laid on the discharge of the child's aggressive and destructive tendencies); emphasis on the mother-infant unity in the earliest years (treatment being directed toward the aftereffects of traumatic separations); emphasis on the pathogenic role of the mother's abnormal personality, emotional withdrawnness, severely neurotic or psychotic traits (with consequent inclusion of the mother in the child's treatment). Not that these findings do not represent all-important parts of the analytic knowledge of child development as it stands at present, but they have to be pieced together and fitted into the framework of analytic child psychology before their clinical application can be wholly useful. When they are used in isolation, the diagnostic as well as the therapeutic issues become distorted, a frequent occurrence for which psychoanalysis has had to take much blame. Perhaps in future our distinction between analytic child guidance clinics and others should be based less on the therapeutic time available for each patient (once weekly versus daily treatment) but on the fact whether the whole analytic knowledge of children is available for application or merely selected portions of it.

We are left with the question where to place the responsibility for this, to the analyst, unsatisfactory state of affairs and where to look for remedies. The fault may lie mainly with us analysts who are notoriously bad at public relations and known to publicize findings all too often in unsuitable language or with exaggerated emphasis on the most recent discoveries. On the other hand, the fault may lie with the clinics where people fail to sift, weigh, and integrate data before applying them to therapy and guidance work. The necessity for such discrimination in this field is not so different, after all, from the corresponding one in the medical field where knowledge of new findings, new methods or new drugs has to be pursued constantly and integrated with former knowledge before application.

The Distribution of Analytic Knowledge

For discussing the distribution of knowledge I turn once more to the experience of those clinics where a considerable fund of reliable and comprehensive analytic data is available for use. The points of contact with the public open to them are of various kinds.

(i) **Diagnostic assessment**   There are, for one, the constant demands for the assessment of children, as they are made on all child guidance clinics for purposes of the juvenile courts, or placement for adoption, with foster parents, in residential institutions, for selection of school, etc. Where the assessment is made not in terms of symptomatology but from the wider point of view of personality structure and development (as mentioned above), and where the language is nontechnical, more than the immediate practical purpose can be served. Here is a legitimate channel of communication which can be used to acquaint the referring agencies with the clinical (and theoretical) aspects on which the clinic's understanding of the child is based. In time these case histories will illustrate many of the main issues of analytic child psychology, such as the interdependence of environmental and internal factors, of body and mind, of emotional and intellectual capacities; the overriding importance of drive activity and its position in the personality structure; the role of anxiety and of defense activity leading to inhibition of function or to symptom formation; the developmental aspects of social or dissocial development, etc.[4]

(ii) Instruction of professional workers   A second and more direct channel of communication is opened up by the constant demands for instruction which arrive from the professional workers in the field, such as pediatricians, nurses, or teachers. It is true that many of us feel that the teaching role of the clinic is a very temporary one with regard to these. By rights, instruction in child development should be an integral part of the medical or nursing courses as well as of the teachers' training colleges. But while developments in these institutions have to be waited for, there is a gap to fill, and it may be worth while to discuss how to do this constructively, avoiding past mistakes.[5]

So long as the general knowledge of child development has to be introduced as an afterthought to the majority of the members of the medical, nursing, and teaching professions, the success or failure of such ventures will depend on three factors: (1) the selection of the right teaching method; (2) the selection of the right facts; (3) some over-all considerations which provide a framework.

To take the last point first: when working with doctors, nurses, or teachers, it is essential to remember that not all the psychological data which we can offer are suitable for immediate application, since the conditions under which they work are different from ours. It is only a short time ago that teachers learned that the child's intellect does not function divorced from his feelings and that, therefore, some connection with their pupils' emotional life is indispensable for teaching. For the medical world it is a similarly recent discovery that the child's body is not divorced from his mind and that, therefore, physical and mental matters are interrelated sufficiently to influence and interfere with each other. But schools and hospitals as institutions have antedated all these new findings. The application of the latter, therefore, implies a whole host of changes which range from the free entry of parents to schools and hospitals to the rota of changing nursing personnel and the very arrangements of schoolroom or ward, changes which especially for nurses and doctors may mean a more or less complete upheaval in the established conditions of their work.

As regards teaching methods, many of us agree that formal courses in child development remain ineffective before links have been established between the data offered in them and those contained in formal professional training on physical

---

[4]In the East London Child-Guidance Clinic Dr. Augusta Bonnard has carried out valuable work of this kind for a number of years. She has done an effective teaching job with the school and welfare authorities in her area through answering their requests for diagnostic assessment by means of elaborate and enlightening developmental pictures of the children referred to her.

[5]The next speaker in the Symposium, Dr. Grete Bibring, will report on the manner in which the analytic theory of child development is taught today already to pediatricians and other residents in the Beth Israel Hospital, Boston, Mass. Another participant in the Convention Dr. Anny Katan, might tell us about the way in which such knowledge is integrated with the medical course from the first year onward in Western Reserve University, Cleveland, Ohio.

matters. On the other hand, openings are provided by those patients or pupils who remain "problems" in medical practice or schoolroom, i.e., where the physical or intellectual data fail to explain the picture. Teaching "on the case" has been found satisfactory by many analysts for these reasons.[6]

As for the selection of facts for teaching, I emphasize, as before, that few analytic data are beneficial if applied out of context. Schools, for example, may profit greatly from applying the analytic concept of *sublimation* to the teachers' work. By deflecting libidinal energy from its original sources and harnessing it to school subjects much drudgery in school can be changed into activities pleasurable almost as play. On the other hand, progressive schools will come to grief if they base their schedules too consistently on this single piece of analytic knowledge. Psychoanalytic theory also has much to say about the essential differences between *play* and *work*, the first being governed by the pleasure principle, the latter by the reality principle. It is one of the main tasks of education to lead each individual child from the earlier to the later mode of functioning. Only the integration of the knowledge of sublimation with the more intricate knowledge of mental functioning on the various stages of development will be of real benefit to the psychological orientation of the modern schools.

Pediatricians might be similarly misled if they meet the present psychoanalytic campaign against hospitalization of small children unconnected with other facts. It is true that a first early separation from home for purposes of medical or surgical intervention may prove traumatic to the individual child and that the psychological damage done by it may go as far as outweighing the physical benefit in health. On the other hand, doctors should not be impressed exclusively with the fact, or the effects, of separation. It is equally necessary for them to learn what part physical illness as such even when undergone at home plays in the mental development of children. Again, it is only the combination and integration of both these lines of inquiry which will lead to beneficial application.[7]

(iii) Work with parents This leads us to the third and last channel of communication with the public, the work with parents which will remain the Clinic's domain, whatever the developments.

There is at present the widespread belief, held by all clinic personnel, that work with parents (or in the case of young children with their mothers) is effective only if directed toward changes in their personalities. Consensus on this point has been reached, I believe, on the rebound from earlier and outmoded attitudes toward the parents, attitudes which included much teaching of facts on a purely intellectual basis, advising in an authoritative manner or, at worst, preaching and exhorting. Our analytic discoveries have laid bare the intricate emotional relationships between child and parent, the role of internalization of the parents' personalities, and identification

---

[6]Our Hampstead Clinic is lending an experienced child therapist, Mrs. Bianca Gordon, to the Paediatric Department of the Woolwich Memorial Hospital for weekly consultations—an experiment which proves successful.

[7]For the effect on children of severe physical illness and (or) immobilization see the paper by Thesi Bergmann (pp. 139–148).

with their qualities, the consequences of love and hate, the subtle or crude forms of seduction, the overriding importance of any one of the developmental phases, whether libidinal or aggressive, being acceptable or repulsive to the parent. Once the parent-child relationship is seen in this light, work with a parent ceases to imply a teacher-pupil attitude and takes on the aspect of a therapeutic relationship.

Most analysts subscribe to these arguments, which are, after all, derived from their work, although with the proviso that experience in analytic practice also teaches to be modest in the expectation of personality changes through any but the most intensive therapy.

For my own person, I remain a heretic in some of these respects. I am far from denying the effect on a child from a beneficial change in the parents' attitudes. Still, I cannot help believing that this therapeutic approach to the parents is no more than one among a whole series of possible approaches, all of them serving the same ultimate purposes of beneficial change, prevention, and enlightenment. In what follows I shall try to justify this rather unpopular view of mine by outlining a number of these possibilities as I have learned to see them.

(a) *The Therapeutic Approach.*—I begin with those instances where I have no hesitation and no reservation in joining the popular demand for therapeutic dealings with the parents. There are the cases, by now known to most clinics, where the mother's and the child's pathology are completely intertwined. We believe that very young children have some primitive pathway of communication with their mothers' unconscious which render them sensitive and vulnerable for the latter's unconscious libidinal or aggressive impulses and fantasies. A young child may merely act out the mother's fantasy in play,[8] or may defend himself against it in some complicated way, or may build a complex pathological structure of his own on the basis of the mother's secret or manifest disturbance. In the most extreme instances the mental disorder of mother and child will be fitted together as if they were pieces in a jigsaw puzzle or—to compare it with adult disorders—as in a *folie-à-deux.*

In our Hampstead Clinic we have studied a number of such mother-child couples over the years by analyzing both partners simultaneously under different therapists and analysts and coordinating the results. Our aim is to determine the limits of dependence and independence in their disturbances and to assess the therapeutic chances for those other cases where only the child, i.e., the more passive factor in the partnership, is taken into treatment. On the basis of several of these investigations we have concluded that there is some hope in altering the condition by the child's analysis alone so long as the pathogenic agents from the mother's side remain in the realm of thought and fantasy; but that nothing except simultaneous treatment will alter the position where these mental influences are reinforced by actions of the mother which tie the child to her as a result of pleasurable or painful actual excitations.[9]

[8]As described by Dorothy Burlingham (1935).

[9]See in this respect Dorothy Burlingham et al. (1955).

The therapeutic approach to the mother is equally vital in those cases where young children show the various signs of deprivation of mothering, though in the mother's presence. This may be caused by a depression of the mother, or a period of actual mourning which causes withdrawal of feeling from the object world, including the child. Her incapacity to fulfill the task of mothering may be caused, equally, by the consequences of a pathogenic masculinity complex, etc. Again, nothing except therapy will have a chance of altering the position. But, since the therapeutic results are slow to come, we have seen repeatedly that the change in the mother comes too late for the child on whose handling the deficiency became apparent and that it is the next-born infant who benefits from the preventive measure.[10]

(b)   The Semitherapeutic Approach: Guiding the Parents through the Child's Analysis.—The close interdependence of mother and child at the beginning of life, and the exaggeration of this factor in some abnormal cases, should not make us ignore the fact that children are growing personalities in their own right with a wide range of possible disturbances and conflicts within their structure. But while they need treatment in their own right, their mothers will be severely affected by this procedure and will need to be helped and guided through the period.[11] To safeguard the child's future in the family after conclusion of treatment, the parents, and especially the mother, should be allowed or even urged to accompany the analytic process to some degree. This implies facing their own adult resistances against the repressed remnants of infantile sexuality and the cruder forms of infantile aggression, all the more so since the child's impulses are directed against their persons and become increased temporarily during treatment as a rule. The child's treatment acts as a threat to the defenses of the mother, quite apart from the violent feelings of jealousy and competition with the child analyst which are aroused by the young patient's positive attachment to the latter's person. Much human tact plus therapeutic skill on the part of the clinic's representative (whether therapist, psychiatrist, or psychiatric social worker) will be needed to handle these difficulties of the parents and to safeguard treatments.

(c)   The Therapeutic-Guiding Approach; Dealings with the Mothers of Handicapped Children.—The approach is different again where the mothers of abnormal children are concerned, i.e., those who are either born physically or mentally defective (blind, deaf, spastic, deformed, mongol, etc.) or have acquired such abnormalities in early life, or undergo some unusual experience or fate (traumatic separations, deprivations, adoption, fostering, motor, or dietary restrictions). There is no reason to expect that mothers are equipped automatically for the specialized task

[10]Mrs. Kata Levy, London, is responsible for drawing our Clinic's attention to the difference between the mother's disturbance being (a) a direct agent in the child's pathology through identification and excitation; (b) an indirect agent through incapacitating the mother for her task of mothering.

[11]See in this respect Dorothy Burlingham (1932).

of bringing up such a child in a manner calculated to minimize the handicap. On the contrary, the mother's natural hurt and despair concerning her child's defect, the injury to her pride and pleasure in the child, will all work toward estranging her from the task of mothering, thereby increasing the initial damage. There is here a specially difficult therapeutic task with the mothers which has been tackled in few places. But there is, besides it, also the need for expert advice, based on knowledge of the abnormalities concerned, such as the following: how to ensure with the blind infant that contact with the object world by sight is substituted for through other channels; how to provide motor outlet for the blind toddler, thereby preventing many of the abnormalities following on motor restriction; how to prevent necessary dietary restrictions from being understood by the child as punishments and experienced as intolerable deprivations; how to minimize the effect of inevitable separations from the mother; how to prepare for operations and meet their equally inevitable aftereffects, etc. There are a whole host of emergency situations of this kind in which the normal mother will feel helpless without guidance.

(d) The Guiding Approach; Treatment of the Young Child by the Mother.—A number of analytic clinics, besides ours, have devised a procedure recently in which an intuitive and willing mother, free from severe pathology herself, is helped to guide her own child through the phases of an average developmental disturbance or infantile neurosis.[12] Such work implies close contact with the mother, usually through weekly sessions, in which the child's difficulties, his tantrums, his behavior, his play or whatever other material has been elicited are discussed, assessed, and elucidated for the mother who then bases her next handling of the child on her understanding. Inevitably this implies also much reassurance of the mother, so far as the severity of the pathology, the comparison with other children, the confidence in her own ability as a mother are concerned. I have reported elsewhere personal experience with two cases of this kind, one a case of soiling in a two-and-a-half-year-old boy, the other an incipient but violent school phobia in a six-year-old girl. In both instances satisfactory results were achieved, in spite of the therapeutic aspects of the work being concentrated on the child alone. That the mother's attitudes during the cooperation have to be met with understanding, patience, and sympathy goes without saying. Also, the mothers suitable for this type of cooperation have to be selected carefully; but there are more than a few who will be able to respond positively to the appeal to their reason, common sense, and good will, who will cope with their own resistances and succeed in the task, helped by the satisfaction that their child need not be handed over to a stranger for therapy.

(e) The Indirect Approach by Way of Public Opinion.—It is not only on the basis of the foregoing considerations that I refuse to believe that mothers need to change their personalities before they can change the handling of their child. Assertions of this

[12]See in this respect Mrs. Erna Furman's report on work done in Western Reserve University, Department of Psychiatry (pp. 123–135).

kind, I find, are not based on facts, above all not on historical facts. Even in the last 30 to 40 years during which I was able to observe the methods of upbringing, changes have been remarkably great. *Breast feeding*, for example, has been adopted, given up, is being adopted again, and may be on the way out once more. *Feeding schedules* have been extremely strictly observed for two or three decades (with some disastrous results for the later feeding disturbances), have given way to feeding on demand (with other disturbing results), and show some indication at present of returning with more moderation. *Toilet training* before the war in England began with official hospital approval soon after birth, was delayed in the postwar period until the end of the first year, and is postponed now by many mothers until the second or even third year. To widen the picture we need think only of the question of *sexual enlightenment* now being accepted as a must by almost all parents; of the immensely increased freedom given to the child's *aggression*, even if directly expressed toward the parents; of the altered attitude to *corporal punishment* as a recognized tool of education, etc. Far-reaching developments of this kind are not due directly to personality changes in the individual mothers but indirectly to alterations in the social atmosphere to which the mothers cannot help but respond. My contention is, therefore, that in rearing their children mothers are not only guided by instinct and misled by distorting personal influences, but they are to an even larger degree dependent on tradition and public opinion, both of which are open to change.

For the child guidance clinic this opens up the possibility of playing a part in the setting up of new traditions. As described above, they have gained the confidence of the public already where the treatment of problem children is concerned. It should not be difficult for them to establish a similar position of trust with regard to the handling of normal children during the all-important first four or five years of life, very much in the manner in which the well-baby clinics have established their traditions with regard to the healthy infants' physical needs. This will be slow work, supplanting gradually what is left of religious, national, and class traditions, but it will be no less effective so far as influence on the mothers is concerned.

CONCLUSION

I foresee even a further role for the child guidance clinics. At present all the workers in the children's services, whether in schools, hospitals, courts, clinics, suffer from the effects of specialized training and lack of coordination and integration in the field. It is as rare for a teacher to deal with a sick child as it is for a hospital nurse to handle a healthy one, or a pediatrician to come in contact with the juvenile courts. This limits each specialist's outlook on childhood of which the various tasks show no more than a single aspect. I can envisage a future when a basic training in understanding all the developmental manifestations of childhood will become the rule for any worker in the field. Whenever this happens, the child guidance clinics as places of demonstration and instruction may be called upon to play a central part in the new scheme.

BIBLIOGRAPHY

Burlingham, D. (1932), Child Analysis and the Mother. *Psa. Quart.*, IV
——(1935), Die Einfühlung des Kleinkindes in die Mutter. *Imago*, XXI.
——& Goldberger, A.; Lussier, A. (1955), Simultaneous Analysis of Mother and Child. *The Psychoanalytic Study of the Child*, X. New York: International Universities Press.
Freud, A. (1954), In: Problems of Infantile Neurosis: A Discussion. *The Psychoanalytic Study of the Child*, IX. New York: International Universities Press, pp. 68–69.
——(1958), Child Observation and Prediction of Development: A Memorial Lecture in Honor of Ernst Kris. *The Psychoanalytic Study of the Child*, XIII. New York: International Universities Press, pp. 100–102.

Part Six

Psychotherapy in the Hospital

It may seem to some that the site of psychotherapy is only an insignificant aspect of the practice. After all, what happens in psychotherapy happens, irrespective of the envioronment. Clearly, this is hardly the case. The style as well as the intention is going to vary as a definite function of the site of psychotherapy.

On the one hand, these variations may be explained according to a cluster of so-called psycho-spatial or psycho-environmental factors. Take the same man and tell him he will be entering psychotherapy in a hospital setting or a private office setting or a home setting and very different images, expectations, and ultimately responses will come forth. For that matter, the mere decor of the setting may have an effect on the client, or even the psychotherapist. But this is not the major point. More precisely, hospital settings imply a certain attitude toward the patient, a certain conception of the patient's problems or illness, and a certain less easily defined quality that seems to affect all people who practice psychotherapy in hospitals.

Years ago a very important distinction about mental hospitals was advanced. On the one hand, certain hospitals were described as being essentially therapeutic, which meant their first order of business was to get the patient better, which in turn meant out of the hospital as quickly as possible. On the other hand, there were those mental hospitals classified as essentially custodial. That is, on close examination of the hospital, one found the staff working to maintain the patient at a certain level of functioning, but not to the extent that he or she was either improving or preparing to leave. In some instances, this custodial philosophy, and practice, was subtle—almost impossible to detect. One could look at the hospital and almost feel sorry for the staff for being saddled with such incurable patients. Last refuge places is what these hospitals seemed to be. In other instances, however, researchers discovered very explicit and hardly subtle custodial practices extant in some hospitals, which clearly indicated that the hospital's commitment was to keeping people committed. In the worst cases—and with publicity some of these hospitals were forced to close—the custodial philosophy bordered on a penal philosophy. Patients were conceived as and treated like prisoners, and as long as they made no trouble for their fellow inmates, their custodians, or themselves, they could stay—and no doubt would stay—for as long as they wished, irrespective of the cost of this form of custody to the individual or the state.

To some degree, a strong case can be made that the greater the economic resources of the hospitals, the greater the likelihood of the hospital furthering therapeutic aims and benefits. Conversely, the more meager the economic resources of a particular institution, the greater the likelihood of its perpetuating custodial aims and privations. Yet regardless of the reasons for these two prominent forms of hospital setting, psychotherapists of all ideologies, theoretical orientations and persuasions have been obliged to try to make some inroads in these hospitals, and some beneficial intervention in the lives of hospitalized patients. Often, the lack of resources facing a hospital face the psychotherapist as well. Accordingly, new therapeutic devices must be tried. Often, too, they must be quick, efficient, and cheap devices. Long term intensive psychotherapy requiring many hours a week may be just what a particular patient requires, but how will this be possible when there are wards filled with needy patients and only a handful of psychotherapists available to treat them?

With this very complicated and often saddening predicament as background, we might introduce the following selections by offering two points. First, given the special requirements of hospitalized patients, people whom society would just as soon lock up forever (even though in financial as well as human terms this is rarely a reasonable decision), new techniques have been tried. One of them, so-called behavior modification psychotherapy, has been shown to be especially useful. Predicated on a set of rather logical learning and re-learning steps, behavior therapy for a variety of reasons has been tried again and again in all forms of so-called rehabilitative institutions, and especially hospitals. Let us not conceal the fact that behavior modification therapy has some very outspoken critics. It is called manipulative, dehumanizing, a form of mental programming and deprogramming that implies an utterly mechanical conception of the human being. In addition, the critics would claim that its putative psychotherapeutic benefits are neither far-reaching nor long-lasting. In defense of the technique, its practitioners would offer the sort of argument found in the following readings, then claim as a final point that, at the very least, behavior modification works where other forms of treatment do not, and is being tried where other forms of psychotherapy are not.

Point number two involves the utterly complex social, legal, and fundamentally human question of whether or not a person's rights are being abrogated when he or she is involuntarily committed to a hospital or other institution. The point becomes even more serious when one considers the fact that every day people are being committed for being "crazy." In fact they have broken no laws, denied no one his or her rights, trespassed on no one's property, and invaded no one's privacy. Along with sociologists and lawyers, psychotherapists too are involved in this complicated and delicate matter. But there is also another side to the story. How can the psychotherapist, or anyone else for that matter, know whether a so-called voluntary commitment to being in a hospital or to undergoing psychotherapy is genuinely a voluntary act at all?

17

Psychiatry in the General Hospital and the Day Hospital

ASMUS FINZEN

Can psychiatry in the general hospital and the day hospital be realistic alternatives to the mental hospital? If so, should it be each of them separately, or both of them combined? What conception of the mental hospital is in our minds when the question of alternatives is raised? Is it an institution for those who are considered by psychiatrists or other medical professionals to be mentally ill or handicapped, or an asylum for all those who are too weak or too disturbing to live in or be carried by the community—a place where almost anybody showing deviant behavior could be sheltered? Probably it is this latter, more comprehensive function of the mental hospital we are to consider.

If we accept this concept, it follows that psychiatry in the general hospital and the day hospital cannot be adequate alternatives to the mental hospital as a whole, unless the idea is to construct small mental hospitals on the sites of general hospitals. They are only partial alternatives in a complex system of services—elements of a comprehensive psychiatric service. In fact, I regard these two elements as particularly closely linked. For day hospitals, as a recent NIMH analysis points out, are rarely independent institutions.

Day treatment services...are provided primarily within the program of a mental health facility offering also inpatient and/or outpatient care. In January 1972 only 3.4% of 989 day treatment services [were] free standing (NIMH 1973).

Reprinted by permission from *Psychiatric Quarterly*, 48 (1974), 489–495. Copyright © 1974 by Human Sciences Press, 72 Fifth Ave., New York, N.Y.

LEVELS OF SUSTAINING AND CORRESPONDING INTERVENTION
(Loeb, 1965)

I Intimates	II Case Finders	III Diagnosis and Treatment	IV Semi-Protective	V Total Care	VI Semi-Protective	VII Out-Patient Treatment	VIII Case Losers	IX Intimates
Family	Ministers	General Practitioner	Day Care Centers	Mental Hospital	Day Care Centers	General Practitioner	Non-psychiatric Agencies	Family
Friends	Doctors	Psychiatrist	Sheltered Workshops	General Hospital	Sheltered Workshops	Psychiatrist	Boarding Houses	Friends
Fellow Workers	Social Workers	Social Workers	Day Hospital	Private Sanitarium	Day Hospital	Social Worker	Self	Fellow Workers
Neighbors	Nurses	Psychologists	Night Hospital	Nursing Home	Night Hospital	Psychologist	YMCA-YWCA	Neighbors
Relatives	Social Psychologists	Nurses	Halfway House	Retreat	Halfway House	Counselors	Friends and Other Volunteers	Relatives
Self	Employers	Ministers	Group Care	Prison	Group Care	Clinics		Self
	Policemen	Counselors	Hostel	Colony	Hostel			
	Sheriffs	Clinics	Family Care in Foster Home	Enclosed Community	Family Care in Foster Home			
	Judges	"Quacks"	Alcoholics Anonymous and Similar Groups		Alcoholics Anonymous and Similar Groups			
	Teachers	Social Agencies						
	Dentists							
	Bartenders							
	Public Welfare							
	Bankers							

The proportion is similar in most other western countries. Although in Britain as well as in the U.S.A. and other countries, quite a number of day hospitals are attached to mental hospitals, the question of alternatives becomes an issue only with regard to new systems of psychiatric care—e.g., the community mental health center or any other type of comprehensive service with the psychiatric unit in the general hospital as a base.

The diagram, presented by Martin Loeb 10 years ago, marks the position of the psychiatric unit and the day hospital in a system of "Levels of Sustaining and Corresponding Intervention." Their allocation to the center of the scheme underlines the relative intensity of care they offer. The comparison with other services in the corresponding columns (e.g., day care centers, sheltered workshops, hostels, Alcoholics Anonymous, private hospitals, nursing homes, prisons, etc.) clearly emphasizes the psychiatric treatment given in both the unit and the day hospital.

The importance of clinical psychiatric aspects, the intensity of care, and a limited duration of stay make up the most important differences between day hospital and general hospital unit care and other services offering semi-protective or total care. They imply at once both their capacity and their limitations as alternatives to the mental hospital. As a result of these characteristics, they are selective and depend for their functioning on the availability of other elements of a comprehensive mental health service. What patients do they accept? Whom can they realistically take care of? And do they really meet the needs of the group of patients they are designed for?

Units at general hospitals mainly admit acutely ill patients suffering from schizophrenia and depressive syndromes, as well as a substantial number of neurotics, many of whom are referred from the medical departments following suicide attempts. They are hesitant about alcoholics and drug dependents, except for detoxification, and, where there are no special geriatric services, about accepting the senile demented. They generally do not admit the mentally retarded, nor any type of social dropout, to whom conservative psychiatrists would very much hesitate to apply the medical model of mental illness. This description of the patient population is confirmed by British and American national statistics, as well as by individual data on selected units in other countries. (NIMH 1973; Dept. Health, 1973; Finzen et al., 1974).

Although furnishing a marked minority of beds, they deal with a considerable majority of inpatient admissions in the U.S.A. and with a remarkable share in Britain. And the picture does not turn out too badly either, if we look at their share in terms of inpatient care episodes. If we keep in mind that we need special services for the aged, the mentally retarded, mentally ill children, and for other groups of the psychiatrically handicapped, British and American statistics suggest that it is realistic to hope that one day all patients needing acute psychiatric hospital care will be treated by units in general hospitals or in community mental health centers.

Taking the 1971 data as a base, the British plan of 120-bed units serving a catchment area of 250,000 inhabitants seems to be a realistic perspective—more realistic anyhow than certain megalomanic German tendencies to suffocate the general hospital by psychiatric departments of 400 or 600 bed units. Requests for psychiatric teaching hospitals with 600 beds have recently been heard. It seems uncertain whether such ideas are confined to German psychiatrists, or if they express a more general problem of transmitting the message to people used to working in oversized institutions that only patients in need of the full range of intensive services of a hospital should go or stay there for treatment. As Garrat, et. al. (1958) showed in the 1950's, this is definitely the minority of patients. I do not contend, however, that psychiatric units always work as they should, nor that they generally take the patients that are most in need of their care. Since by definition they are selective, within the setting of a comprehensive mental health service, they are open to abuse when certain links are missing or when they are not under obligation to serve a catchment area.

The region of Tübingen is an excellent, although I am afraid not an exceptional, example of what can happen in this way. The district of 150,000 inhabitants is served by a university psychiatric department of 120 beds and a state mental hospital, 40 miles away. In the course of an investigation, we found that the university department admitted almost three-quarters of the patients from the district, although it is not under obligation to do so. At the university department, we were quite proud of these data, until we looked at the differences between the university and the mental hospital patient population, which are quite revealing and have no medical justification of any kind (Table 1).

TABLE 1.
Admissions from Tübingen (N = 380)

	University Unit %	Mental Hospital %
Admissions...	73	27
First Admissions	55	40
Diagnosis:		
Schizophrenia*..................................	25	26
Affect. Psychosis	18	10
Neurosis...	30	1
Senile dementia................................	5	36
Alcoholism..	14	21
Lower Class	30	72

*Schizophrenia first admissions: *None* to the mental hospital.

Soon, however, a day hospital with 30 places was opened in Tübingen, and two years later the scene had changed completely. A preliminary analysis shows that except for geriatric patients, who are not taken by the day hospital, hardly any patients from the region are now admitted to the state hospital. In spite of this incomplete success, our colleagues from the mental hospital accuse us more heavily than ever of "skimming off the cream."

Although by no means representative, this example suggests that the day hospital is not only a possible alternative to mental hospital care, but also an important supplement to the psychiatric unit at the general hospital.

Notwithstanding the early optimism of its pioneers, the day hospital had had more difficulties in receiving general acceptance than the general hospital psychiatric unit or other elements of a comprehensive mental health service. These are reflected in the different proportion of day patients within total admissions in different countries— more than 20% (including psychogeriatrics) in Britain; 6% in the U.S.A., and 1/1000 in West Germany, where there are hardly any psychiatric units in general hospitals anyway.

One of the reasons is certainly that a completely new service offering neither in- nor out-patient treatment needs more than 25 years to become a matter of course. Another is somewhat of the day hospital's own making. As Glaser (1972) puts it:

> The overweening pride such programs demonstrated in the first flush of their youth was very certainly not likely to endear them to others. Even more fundamentally, any new notion that wishes to intrude itself into a well-established system ought to have some degree of unity of form, or function, or both. Partial hospitalization programs have tried to be all things to all men and have succeeded only in not being utilized. They serve vastly diverse patient populations in a bewildering variety of ways.

It is no exaggeration to say that day hospitals have often served to implement the personalities of the staff, rather than the needs of a comprehensive mental health service. On the other hand, in a rigid system of care, partial hospitilization programs are hard to fit in, because no real need for them is felt. Private psychiatrists frequently maintain that they can handle all patients who do not need inpatient care. (In our program, only three percent of the referrals come from private psychiatrists, although they do most of the outpatient work in the town). Professional staff in hospital, on the other hand, tend to feel uneasy about the open setting of the day hospital, about "the other 128 hours" which day patients spend on their own.

As expressed in a study by Herz et al. (1970), hospital staff prefer inpatient care, because they feel:

> Day patients are more difficult to treat because they spend a good deal of time in situations that the hospital staff has no knowledge of or control over, that they are more difficult to schedule for therapy sessions, that it is difficult to control intake of medication, and that more involvement with the family is often necessary. Furthermore, many clinicians believed that separation of the patient from his family is a necessary part of therapy or that more can be learned about the patient's pathological modes of behavior through the close observation possible on an inpatient service.

Whereas the first may be true, the latter must be disputed. It gives the impression that 24-hour care is identical with 24-hour treatment, and that day treatment is less intensive. This definitely is not correct. Different as day hospitals may be, they have in common a tendency to provide "intensive treatment, particularly in the areas of group treatment, therapeutic community treatment, family treatment and the provision of massive social assistance."

I agree with Glaser, who maintains (1972):

Thus, the assignment to provide intensive and prolonged service to individuals within a treatment system who need it would seem to be given most logically to the partial hospitalization services. Another way of conceptualizing this would be to consider the emergency service and the inpatient service as tools for the restoration of a disturbed equilibrium, and outpatient services as tools for maintaining that equilibrium at its current point. Partial hospitalization then becomes the tool whereby the attempt is made to lift the point of equilibrium to a higher level, if it is felt that there is any likelihood this may occur. It is in this sense that partial hospitalization services are special, rather than general services; they are not for everyone and they provide a kind of service not available elsewhere in terms of depth and intensity.

If you accept these arguments, day hospitals are primarily places for clinical and social rehabilitation. Therefore, they have to be selective and their selectivity is not an argument against the efficiency of day treatment services, but is a consequence of their locus in a carefully planned system of services.

In fact, many day hospitals seem to live up to these expectations. A British Pilot Survey of 1,927 patients attending day hospitals (Dept. of Health, 1969) revealed that nearly 60% of the sample suffered from functional psychoses, that less that 8% had no previous psychiatric treatment at all, and 28% no previous inpatient or day care. Glaser's survey of several day care programs in the U.S., however, shows a patient population described as highly impaired. The same view can be derived from reports of 10 German day hospitals, recently published. All of them concentrate on patients threatened by long-term hospitalization or other long-term protective measures (Finzen, 1974).

Thus, reconsidering the issue of alternatives to mental hospital, only a carefully planned combination of units in general hospital, day hospital, and outpatient services, as elements of a comprehensive mental health service, in the community, can guarantee a high degree of accessibility, flexibility, and continuity of care in a system, integrated and coordinated with the general health and social services.

We must keep in mind, however, that this will function only if, at the same time, we offer specific services to those groups of mentally ill or handicapped people who are not taken care of adequately by the general psychiatric unit, nor by the day hospital. And we must keep in mind that unit and day hospital must be supplemented by other institutions, offering protective living and working conditions, with special regard for chronic patients, both the old and the new.

If we do not succeed in doing so, the sophisticated plans for alternatives to the mental hospital will turn out to provide institutions for the socially privileged, the educated and acceptable patients. And the others will continue going into the mental hospital as they used to, or will go on disappearing into old or new hiding places, somewhere in the country (Cumming 1968).

REFERENCES

Cumming, E. (1968): Remarks prepared for a discussion of ASA Annual Meeting, Boston.

Department of Health and Social Security (1969): Statistical and Research Report Series No. 6 Psychiatric Hospitals and Units in England and Wales, Inpatient statistics from the Mental Health Enquiry for the year 1971. Her Majesty's Stationary Office. London.

Finzen, A. (1972): Gemeindenahe psychiatrische Krankenversorgung. Von der Asylierung zur Intergration. In: v. CRANACH, M. u. FINZEN, A.: Sozialpsychiatrische Texte, S. 94-96, Springer Verlag. Berlin/Heidelberg.

Grunewald, F.; Jantzen, F.; Wietholter, H., and Rempp, B. (1974): Ansatzmoglichkeiten fur eine gemeindenahe Psychiatrie. 3.Aufl., Werkstattschriften zur Sozialpsychiatrie, Heft. 1, Soziale Arbeitskreise im Tubinger Verein fur Sozialpsychiatrie und Rehabilitation; Tubingen.

——: (1974): Psychiatrische Praxis, S. 33-35, Heft 1.

Garratt, F.N.; Lowe, C. R., and McKeon, T. (1958): Lancet, i, 682.

Glaser, F. B. (1972) In: Progress in Community Mental Health, II. L. Bellak and H. Barten, eds. Grune and Stratton. New York.

Herz, M. I.; Endicott, J.; Spitzer, R. L., and Mesnikoff, A. (1970): Day versus inpatient hospitalization: A controlled study. Presented at the annual meeting of American Psychiatric Association, San Francisco, Calif.

Loeb, M.; Roberts, L.M.; Halleck, S. L., and Boeb, M., (1969) Community Psychiatry. Anchor Books. New York.

National Institute of Mental Health (1973): Mental Health Statistics, Series B, No. 5: Utilization of Mental Health Facilities, 1971. Washington, D.C.

18

Behavior Therapy in a Community Mental Health Center

ROBERT PAUL LIBERMAN
AND EDWIN BRYAN III

Behavioral principles offer an operational model for the services of a community mental health center. A demonstration and clinical research project adapted behavior analysis and therapy to the problems, patients, staff, and setting of a typical comprehensive community mental health center. Innovations in the day hospital included a credit incentive system, educational workshops for community adaptation, and a goal-attainment method of planning and evaluating individual treatment. Behavior therapy was introduced for outpatients with anxiety and depression, marital conflict, and deficits in social skills. Consultation and education programs were established for parents, schools, and other community agencies. Experimental and evaluative research has documented the effectiveness of these programs.

With contraction of funding and increasing criticism from political and professional ranks, the community mental health movement is entering a period when its practitioners and supporters will have to demonstrate achievement of its lofty goals, i.e., continuity of care, rapid restoration of vocational and social adjustment, reduction of time spent in hospitals, treatment for all including the severely disordered, inculcation of skills for primary care among indigenous nonprofessionals and community "gatekeepers," and involvement of the total community in program planning and evaluation. New therapeutic approaches, as well as evaluation methods,

Reprinted by permission from *American Journal of Psychiatry*, 134 (1977), 401–406. Copyright © 1977 by the American Psychiatric Association.

will have to be devised to provide effective community-based mental health programs.

Most current evaluation efforts focus on the descriptive, structural, and procedural aspects of programs, rather than on treatment outcome (1). Evaluation of outcome, a difficult and challenging undertaking, should be built into the mental health delivery system as part of its regular functions. Mental health services can be improved by clinicians demonstrating what does or does not work and which interventions lead to changes in the clients' functioning. Implementing evaluation is a constructive response to mounting pressures from funding agencies (2) and consumer groups (3) for accountability, and it will put community mental health on a firm empirical base, thereby avoiding the pitfalls of becoming another psychiatric fad.

Clinically meaningful and scientifically reliable and valid methods of outcome were developed during the course of an applied research project at the Oxnard (California) Mental Health Center. The objectives of this project were to introduce and evaluate behavioral approaches to the spectrum of clinical problems that are encountered in a typical comprehensive community mental health center. Outpatient, day-hospital, inpatient, emergency, and consultation and education services evolved from a behavioral framework, starting with specification of problems and goals. The project evaluates each treatment program and each individual's progress by a built-in, convenient, and clinically useful means of assessment. Novel applications of behavioral-learning principles have been used with a wide range of problems including chronic schizophrenia, marital conflict, anxiety and depression, life crises, conduct disorders of children and adolescents, child abuse, psychosomatic illnesses, and academic underachievement of schoolchildren. This article will present examples of studies carried out during this demonstration project. More detailed descriptions of the project and its programs can be obtained from other publications (4,5) or from the first author.

STAFF TRAINING

The behavioral approach offers administrators and clinicians in community psychiatry several advantages over more traditional schools of therapy.

1. The methods are suited to the brief therapy and time constraints found in community mental health centers. The goals of treatment are limited, functional changes.

2. Many methods have been developed and tested for their effectiveness with specific problem areas, symptoms, and well-defined target populations.

3. Behavioral procedures are sufficiently concrete and operationalized to be quickly learned by paraprofessionals and other personnel. They can be disseminated conveniently when found effective.

4. The directive and active techniques of behavior therapy can be applied to a wide range of community residents, including minority groups and the poor. Their usefulness is not limited to educated, verbal, and psychologically minded individuals.

5. Since the behavioral clinician prefers to work in natural settings, there is congruence with the emphasis in community mental health on providing treatment in real-life environments such as the school and the home.

6. The empirical orientation basic to behavior therapy facilitates evaluation. Because specification and measurement are intrinsic to behavior therapy, the evaluation of treatment outcome is a natural by-product. This promotes an evolutionary development of treatment procedures that are refined or discarded as experience dictates.

Thus behavior therapy can be viewed as potentially adding some "working muscles" to the "philosophical skeleton" of community mental health ideology.

The adoption of a behavioral approach to patient care in a community mental health center required reorientation of both staff and patients. Innovation produced discomforts and resistances that had to be overcome in both groups. The patients and staff had to be convinced that the new techniques could be effective despite their apparent simplicity. Both groups learned to rely less on supportive relationships that maintained the status quo. Patients as well as staff came to depend less on vague, general statements of improvement and more on their own data-based assessment of the extent of progress. Both groups learned to set short-term, objective, attainable goals for themselves rather than long-range, global, and ambiguously idealistic goals.

The discomfort associated with innovation was reduced at the Oxnard center by intensive training of the 25-member staff along the following 4 levels.

1. There was formal training in behavioral principles and techniques at a 3-hour weekly seminar and through a self-paced sequence of readings.

2. The clinicians received individual supervision from the project staff on their caseloads and community consultations.

3. The clinical staff engaged in their own behavioral self-management projects as a way of learning experientially.

4. The project staff conducted individual and group sessions with patients using various behavior therapies while the clinical staff observed, participated as cotherapists, and finally assumed primary therapeutic responsibility. Eventually they were able to use behavioral methods autonomously with only periodic supervision, positive feedback, and consultation from the project staff.

DAY-HOSPITAL PROGRAMS

The day hospital has an average population of 25 patients and a staff of 7 nurses and technicians, an occupational therapist, and a psychologist and psychiatrist who both work half-time. Most of the patients are from lower to lower-middle social classes, and about 25% are Chicano or black. The patients range in age from 15–75 years, with a majority in the 22–45 range. Over half are acutely or chronically psychotic and are receiving phenothiazines or lithium.

Credit Incentive System

The first behavioral intervention at the day hospital was the introduction of a token economy that uses credit cards as the medium of exchange. Patients earn credits by arriving promptly at the center, completing treatment goals (e.g., inviting a neighbor for coffee), participating in therapeutic activities, cooking lunch, washing dishes, and serving as a monitor or staff aide. Patients spend credits on lunch, coffee, drug prescriptions, time off from the center, and individual time with therapists and the psychiatrist. Each patient receives a credit card that is functional for 1 week. A number on the card is punched initially with a die having a small heart or club shape when the patient has earned credits by performing therapeutic or maintenance activities. The same number is overpunched by a larger, circular die when the patient pays for a reinforcer, such as lunch or coffee. The credit cards serve as permanent products of earnings and payments, which the clinic secretary computes on a weekly basis. The totals are then used to give feedback to the staff and patients at the weekly planning meeting.

When credits are dispensed, they are accompanied by praise and social recognition from the staff and other patients. In an open setting such as a day hospital, the liberal use of social reinforcement more closely approximates the natural environment of the patients and makes it possible to gradually discontinue the credit system as the patients prepare for termination. The credit system serves a cohesive function since all patients share in common their participation in earning and spending credits from the first day of orientation. The use of credits also facilitates the reestablishment of cognitive skills by recovering schizophrenic patients who learn to count, organize, and budget. Controlled experiments at the Oxnard day hospital have documented the value of the credit system and, more importantly, the systematic provision of social reinforcement in maintaining high performance levels among the patients (5).

Educational Workshops

The central part of the Oxnard program consists of educational workshops that teach groups of patients community survival and adaptation skills. Workshops are offered in consumerism and personal finance, personal effectiveness, grooming, use of public agencies, recreational and social opportunities, transportation, and vocational preparedness. Each workshop has a set of instructional objectives, lesson plans, and a built-in evaluation of attendance, spontaneous participation, and completion of homework assignments. Data from the record keeping are used to critique, reevaluate, and revamp the workshops at 10-week intervals.

A more systematic evaluation of the workshop model was conducted using a time-sampling method of assessing the social participation of patients (4). Randomly chosen samples of patients from the Oxnard day hospital and cohorts from a day hospital using eclectic milieu therapy in an adjacent city were observed 4 times each day during a 2-week period just before and 6 months after the implementation of the workshop format at Oxnard. Following the introduction of workshops at the Oxnard day hospital, the social participation of patients doubled over the baseline period, while nonsocial, isolate behaviors decreased by one-half. The level of social participation of Oxnard patients was significantly higher than that in the comparison setting only after the workshops were in progress ($z=3.69$, $p<.01$). Staff-patient interaction also significantly increased from 30.5% to 64.8% of time-sampled observations of staff behavior at Oxnard, but not in the comparison day center ($z=6.71$, $p<.01$).

Behavioral Goal Setting

A basic innovation in the operation of the day hospital focused on the patient's chart, previously an unwieldly manila folder buried in a file cabinet and used for occasional narrative notes. The chart is still kept, but all information necessary for a patient's monthly program is displayed on a single-page progress note (the behavioral progress record) on a clipboard posted on the office wall. Short-term goals are prepared and reviewed weekly by the day-treatment therapist together with the client and family members. Goals generally focus on areas of social, family, and vocational functioning since their achievement facilitates the patient's reintegration into the community. Setting goals with patients and their significant others requires the therapists to assess current assets and deficits and to reinforce small increments of behavior change on a week-to-week basis. For many day-care patients, the most important initial goal is that of attendance. As the benefits of the day program and psychotropic medication accumulate, attendance generally becomes less important and it sometimes becomes necessary to set *reduced* attendance as a goal in order to diminish the patient's dependency on the clinic and its staff. Goal setting is the most personal of the services offered at the day hospital since it leads to highly individualized treatment plans. Because the patients and their relatives share in the goal setting, they come to understand their treatment and progress in a direct, tangible way.

TABLE 1
Behavioral Goals Set for Day-Hospital Patients Over Two Consecutive Months

Goal Area	Percent of Total Goals Set
Socialization and interpersonal relationships	27.6
Attendance and credit earnings	20.4
Employment, education, and personal finances	15.2
Assertion and communication skills	8.1
Anxiety reduction	7.1
Home and recreational activities	4.5
Self-image	4.5
Self-care skills	3.6
Proper use of medications	3.6
Decrease in bizarre behavior, delusions, and hallucinations	2.7
Controlled alcohol intake	2.7

For program evaluation purposes, the number of goals set and completed in the day hospital are tallied at the end of each month. The results are sent to hospital administrators and are also publicly posted in the day-hospital office. Over the past 2 years an average of 2.5 goals has been set for each patient each week, with monthly attainment rates ranging from 66–88%. Table 1 illustrates the areas in which goals have been set. In addition to the continuous use of the behavioral progress record, we conducted a clinical experiment using goal-attainment scaling (6) to compare the outcome of patients undergoing behavior therapy at the Oxnard day hospital with the cohort of patients receiving eclectic milieu therapy at another day hospital. This formal evaluation was done on every third admission to each day hospital, with 3-, 6-, and 24-month follow-ups. A total of 56 patients was selected and evaluated. Goal attainment was greater for the Oxnard patients at the 3-month follow-up, and the differences between the groups increased to statistical significance at 6- and 24-month follow-up p <.05, chi-square test).

As a further evaluation of the specificity of behavioral techniques in the improvement shown by Oxnard patients, 15 randomly chosen patients served as their own controls in time series, experimental analyses of their treatment. Repeated measures were taken for up to 8 months on target behaviors such as rational versus delusional speech, social interaction, prevocational tasks, and phobias. Twelve of the patients showed marked improvement of 50% or more from the baseline periods as a result of interventions such as desensitization, social reinforcement, covert sensitization, and credit rewards (5).

OUTPATIENT PROGRAMS

For reasons of efficiency and cost, the project staff decided to introduce behavioral methods into therapy groups for outpatients since the mental health center's clinicians were faced with overwhelming demands for services. The focus has been on developing specialized therapeutic procedures for commonly encountered clinical problems. For example, structured therapy groups were developed and empirically evaluated for such problems as anxiety-depression, life crises, adolescent behavioral disorders, and marital conflict. In each of the groups a "package" of therapeutic procedures, termed "training in personal effectiveness," has been used to promote the learning of adaptive social and emotional behavior.

Training in Personal Effectiveness

Since competence in social relationships appears to mediate successful community adjustment as well as to mitigate symptomatic disturbances, the staff at the Oxnard center have placed emphasis on methods that aid the learning or relearning of social skills. The personal effectiveness approach involves a structured set of procedures, starting with goal setting and progressing through behavioral rehearsal or role-playing, modeling or demonstrating more appropriate ways of expressing feelings and communicating information and desires, positive feedback and coaching, and "homework assignments" to carry out in real life what has been practiced in the clinic (7).

As patients practice communicating to parents, spouses, friends, coworkers, and those manning public agencies and stores, nonverbal emotional expressiveness is targeted for improvement through a focus on eye contact, facial expression, posture, gestures, and vocal tone, loudness, pacing, and fluency. Other levels of interpersonal communication are also developed, such as semantic meaning, timing, and reciprocity. The therapist helps the patient to formulate a series of interpersonal scenes or situations that evoke anxiety, frustration, helplessness, withdrawal, aggression, or avoidance. A wide range of situations are employed in the sessions, including using basic conversational skills (e.g., introducing oneself, asking open-ended questions), expressing affection, asserting one's rights, going through a job interview, and giving compliments.

Each scene is role-played using therapists or other patients as surrogates and as models for the practicing patient to observe and learn from. The therapist is active in prompting, cuing, and giving positive feedback for improvements. The critical measure of outcome is the *effect* that the patient has on his social world, that is, the patient's ability to obtain his or her personal, social, instrumental, and emotional needs. Thus reporting back to the group and the therapist on real-life success in completing "homework" is a crucial part of the training process. As individuals master their day-to-day problem situations, they gradually develop subjective comfort, naturalness, and self-esteem.

In an evaluation of training in personal effectiveness, the patients and observers reported that 80% of 100 consecutively rehearsed scenes were successfully performed in community and home settings. Ratings of videotapes made "blindly" by trained observers indicated that schizophrenic as well as neurotic patients can significantly improve their nonverbal components of affect and social competence. The personal effectiveness approach has been adapted for use with individuals, families, and groups for crisis intervention, divorce counseling, latency-age children who are overly shy or aggressive, adolescents, marital therapy, and for anxiety and depression. It has also been used in consultation with organizations, such as the U.S. Navy, for managerial and supervisory training.

Married Couples Group

A 9-session format for time-limited marital therapy was developed, using the personal effectiveness procedures, to improve communication of positive and negative feelings between marital partners. Homework was assigned to the couples in the form of practicing the communication exercises demonstrated and role-played in the sessions. Each spouse was also expected to note the occurrence of pleasing acts and statements made by his or her partner each day and to record these in a diary. In sharing the entries from each other's diaries and reporting these at the weekly group meeting, the couples gained greater awareness of reciprocity and were reinforced for increasing the frequency of pleasing interchanges. Couples also learned to distribute their recreational, social, and leisure time more equitably within such dimensions as doing things apart from one's spouse, within the marital dyad, with other couples, and with the family. A final intervention was the development of contingency contracts wherein each partner agreed, through a process of choosing desired changes in each other's behavior, negotiating their respective desires, and compromising their differences, to carry out certain responsibilities in exchange for which they could obtain desired privileges. Appendix 1 presents an example of a marital contract.

An outcome study was conducted comparing this behavioral marital therapy with a more nondirective, insight-oriented marital therapy that encouraged ventilation and abreaction of feelings. Data were collected on several levels, including "blind" ratings of videotaped marital interactions during problem-solving discussion before and after the group; direct coding of smiling at, looking at, and touching each other during the sessions; marital adjustment questionnaires; and client satisfaction. Results showed marked superiority of the behavioral format in both the videotaped and "live" codes of spousal interaction. Reciprocity, empathy, and congruence increased for the couples in the behavioral group but not for those in the comparative group (8).

Anxiety-Depression Management

Anxiety and depression were the chief complaints of over 16% of the patients at the mental health center, confirming estimates made by other investigators that 5% of the population suffer from chronic anxiety and 35% have experienced symptoms of severe depression (9, 10). Two groups of 10 patients each, which were led by the same cotherapists, were compared for their outcomes on symptom checklists; completion of homework assignments dealing with interpersonal relationships; verbal dysfluencies (an index of anxiety); and goal attainment scaling. One group was led in a nondirective, supportive manner. The members in the behavioral group were given training in deep muscle relaxation and imagery self-control for use in anxiety management, as well as training in behavioral rehearsal of problematic interpersonal situations with modeling and feedback. Comparisons at the time of termination (after 10 weekly sessions) and at 6-month follow-up indicated marked superiority for the behavior therapy group on all measures.

CONSULTATION AND EDUCATION PROGRAMS

Rather than assuming the responsibility of providing direct services for the myriad of individuals needing help with psychiatric illnesses or life crises, community mental health programs have emphasized the provision of indirect services through consultation and education efforts with community agencies, volunteers and nonprofessional therapists, schools, and other gatekeepers. At the Oxnard Mental Health Center behavioral principles have been flexibly applied to the development of indirect services for parents, schools, community workers, a probation department group home for delinquent boys (11), and operators of community care facilities for ex-patients (12).

Parent Workshops in Child Management

More than 50 educational workshops have been held for small groups of 6–12 parents who have sought help for their children's behavioral and emotional problems. Typical problems include disruptiveness, restlessness, and hyperactivity; fears; disobedience and lack of discipline; aggression; tantrums; crying; shyness; lack of self-confidence; and bed-wetting. Parents of problem children referred from schools, social agencies, and by the parents themselves are offered the "Parent Workshop" as a first line of service for the children. In these workshops the parents learn to become "therapists" for their own children. The workshops, consisting of 9 weekly meetings lasting two hours, are led by paraprofessionals under the supervision of a psychologist. The curriculum includes readings in social learning principles (13), observing and graphing behavior, pinpointing and reinforcing desirable behaviors, token economy, and contingency contracts. Demonstration videotapes have been used to model correct parental responses, and role-playing with feedback is used to give parents practice in improving their relationships with their children. For example, parents are taught to praise their children's desirable behavior by looking and smiling at the child, using a positive gesture or "pat" in close physical proximity, and verbalizing approval within 5 seconds of the occurrence of the behavior.

Testing the parents' conceptual knowledge of child management principles before and after the workshops revealed an average 34% improvement in their scores. Role-playing evaluations before and after the workshops indicated a 100% improvement of the parents in using praise for positive behavior and ignoring or using mild social punishment for disruptive behavior. Fifty-eight percent of the participating parents carried out at least 1 intervention that led to an observed, documented change in their child's behavior. Seventy-five percent reported significant behavioral improvement in at least 1 of their children. In follow-up phone calls 2 months to 1 year after the completion of the workshop, 65% of the parents reported that they were still using behavioral techniques successfully.

Consultation with Schools

As parents, teachers, and counselors increasingly referred children with behavioral and academic problems to the mental health center for treatment, it became evident that neither the schools nor the center staff could provide the volume of services necessary to meet the demand. In response to this pressing need, Project Friendship was established, in which college students, senior citizens, and other community members volunteered for training as paraprofessional counselors or "friends" for grade-school children with problems.

The core of Project Friendship is the intensive training and supervision provided by mental health center staff. Thirty volunteers have received training in 5 weekly seminars lasting 2 hours. During these seminars the trainees discuss reading assignments in behavior therapy and programmed instruction, learn to apply reinforcement methods to the classroom and home, and role play situations involving teachers, parents, and students. The training goals, to inculcate skills in relating to children and in the use of reinforcement and shaping, have been achieved, as measured by pretesting and posttesting use of quizzes for knowledge and role-playing scenes (14). After the training period each volunteer works on an individual basis with 1 or 2 students and serves as a model, a reinforcer for academic accomplishments, an advocate for the child's needs, and an active consultant with the child's parents and teacher. The training format was extended to Chicano community workers who were involved in a large-scale delinquency prevention program in Oxnard's barrio.

Results have been encouraging: two-thirds of the children have shown marked improvement as rated by teachers and parents. Project Friendship has demonstrated the potential of paraprofessionals in community mental health. Thorough training and careful evaluation ensure that quality of treatment is not sacrificed when larger numbers of people receive professional help.

CONCLUSIONS

The research and development project at the Oxnard Mental Health Center has provided evidence that well-structured behavioral programs can contribute to the realization of the laudable but ambiguous ideology of community mental health. Through careful training and supervision of clinical staff and paraprofessionals, improvements were achieved in day-hospital and out-patient services, with parents' efforts at child management, with elementary school children, and with other indirect services. The methods developed at Oxnard, a busy, typical, and comprehensive mental health center, are practical, convenient, and relevant. The intervention strategies that survive the rigors of a mental health center mandated to provide treatment, rather than training and research, are likely to be useful and appropriate for other service-oriented settings. However, behavior therapy is not a panacea. Many problems have not been dealt with adequately, and the temptation to magnify the importance of successes with specific problems should be resisted.

The community mental health approach to mental illness has the advantage of limiting disruption to the patient's life and increasing the probability of treatment generalizing over time and from clinic to home and work settings. The behavioral approach offers the additional advantage of empiricism that is embodied in a goal-oriented, monitored system of treatment. With evaluation methods built into the treatment services, continuous feedback to therapists and administrators regarding effectiveness and quality control is enhanced and decisions related to starting, stopping, and modifying services are facilitated.

REFERENCES

1. Feldman S. Windle C: The NIMH approach to evaluating the Community Mental Health Center program. Health Serv Rep 88:174–180, 1973.
2. Ochberg F: Community mental health center legislation: flight of the phoenix. Am J Psychiatry 133:56–60, 1976.
3. Chu FD, Trotter S: The Mental Health Complex. Part 1: Community Mental Health Centers. Washington, DC, Center for the Study of Responsive Law, 1972.
4. Liberman RP, DeRisi WJ, King LW, et al: Behavioral measurement in a community mental health center, in Evaluating Behavioral Programs in Community, Residential, and School Settings. Edited by Davidson PO, Clark FW, Hamerlynck LA. Champaign, Ill, Reseach Press, 1974, pp 103–139.
5. Liberman RP, King LW, DeRisi WJ: Behavior analysis and therapy in community mental health, in Handbook of Behavior Modification and Behavior Therapy. Edited by Leitenberg H. Englewood Cliffs, NJ, Prentice-Hall, 1976, pp 566–603.
6. Kiresuk TJ, Sherman RE: Goal attainment scaling: a general method for evaluating comprehensive community mental health programs. Community Ment Health J 4:443–453, 1968.
7. Liberman RP, King LW, DeRisi WJ, et al: Personal Effectiveness: Guiding People To Assert Their Feelings and Improve Their Social Skills, Champaign, Ill. Research Press, 1975.
8. Liberman RP, Levine J, Wheeler E, et al: Marital therapy in groups: a comparative evaluation of behavioral and interactional formats. Acta Psychiatr Scand, Supplement 266, 1976, pp 1–34.
9. Raskin M, Johnson G, Rondestvedt JW: Chronic anxiety treated by feedback-induced muscle relaxation. Arch Gen Psychiatry 28:263–269, 1973.
10. Zung WWK: How normal is depression? Psychosomatics 13:174–178, 1972.
11. Liberman RP, Ferris C. Salgado P, et al: Replication of the achievement place model in California. Appl Behav Anal 8:287–299, 1975.
12. DeRisi WJ, Myron M, Goding M: A workshop to train community-care staff to use behavior modification techniques. Hosp Community Psychiatry 26:636, 641, 1975.
13. Becker WC: Parents are Teachers: A Child Management Program. Champaign, Ill, Research Press, 1971.
14. Aitchison RA, Merrill J: Emphasis on environment: the partnership between home, mental health services, and school. Exchange 2:13–19, 1974.

APPENDIX 1
Example of a Contingency Contract Agreed Upon by a Couple

HUSBAND'S CONTRACT

Responsibilities: To ask about wife's feelings twice a day; to spend three hours a day doing something with the whole family.

Privileges: Wife will say something nice or nothing at all about my friends: wife will initiate sex three times a week.

WIFE'S CONTRACT

Responsibilities: To clean one room of the house to husband's satisfaction each week; to massage husband three times a week.

Privileges: Husband will express approval of work at shop once a day; husband will initiate sex three times a week.

The terms of this contract were monitored weekly and were completed satisfactorily 80% of the time over a six-week period.

19

When is a
Voluntary Commitment
Really Voluntary?

HOWARD OWENS

Cognitive disorganization limits a person's capacity to act voluntarily, because such action requires a significant degree of attention and comprehension. The compliance of a psychotic person who fails to understand his own actions may be construed by clinicians as voluntary behavior. This possible misuse of voluntary hospitalization is examined, and the employment of categories other than voluntary and involuntary is suggested.

In the continuing debate over involuntary psychiatric hospitalization relatively little attention has been given to defining the central concepts "voluntary" and "involuntary." Yet some clarification of the meaning of these terms is crucial, especially for those who espouse the so-called "medical model" of psychiatric disorders. Many psychiatrists reject the contention of Szasz[6] that every hospital admission should be voluntary. Those who take issue with Szasz often incorporate in their argument the notion that certain patients cannot be considered voluntary because they are lacking in autonomy or will. Peszke[5] noted that it is characteristic of severe mental disorders to interfere with a person's autonomy. Chodoff[2] presented clinical examples of patients who seem incapable of the effort of will necessary to control their behavior; calling their behavior "involuntary," he suggested that they require involuntary treatment. Both Peszke and Chodoff argued that, with such patients, the need for treatment provides the grounds for involuntary hospitalization.

Reprinted by permission from *American Journal of Orthopsychiatry*, 47 (1977), 104–110. Copyright © 1977 by the American Orthopsychiatric Association, Inc.

Neither Peszke nor Chodoff, however, amplified further on what is meant by "autonomy" or "effort of will."

Olin and Olin[4] brought the issue sharply into focus with their finding that even many *voluntary* patients have a very limited understanding of the terms of their own admission to a hospital: nearly one-third of their sample of voluntary patients from two Massachusetts hospitals had no apparent information about or understanding of their legal status and rights. These authors observed that little attention has been given to the voluntary patient's understanding of his contract with the hospital, and they argued that the value of such a contract is questionable if the patient does not understand it. Having described the "massive lack of comprehension" shown by their patients, however, their conclusion remained ambiguous. They suggested that it would be a step backward to deny any patient the opportunity to sign a voluntary, and they concluded with a question: "How can a patient participate in his treatment as a voluntary patient without a full understanding of his voluntary admission contract?"

This paper will attempt to demonstrate that the answer, in simple terms, is that some patients cannot. The question continues to arise, in part because of a misunderstanding of what voluntary action is, and of the particular difficulties voluntary choice may present to a psychotic person. In practice, a person whose thinking is highly disordered may be incapable of deciding for himself whether to give or refuse consent to treatment. Any attempt to *make* such a person be autonomous only creates a conundrum. (It becomes merely cruel to insist that a person be endowed with a right that he lacks the capacity to exercise.) Clinical examples will be offered to show what can happen when a person is presumed to be autonomous who in fact is not. These will be followed by an attempt to clarify what voluntary action entails, and why it makes no sense to consider every patient voluntary.

CASE REPORTS

The following examples of dubious "voluntary" admissions are taken from the records of the emergency room of one municipal hospital during a three-month period. Because each of these patients did sign a voluntary, their cases are especially revealing with regard to the ways psychosis can impinge on personal autonomy.

Case 1

A 30-year-old West Indian woman was brought to the emergency room because of bizarre behavior, including uncontrolled praying and preaching to strangers in the street. She had a history of two previous psychiatric hospitalizations. On admission, she was disoriented to place and time, had poor attention and concentration, agitated and pressured speech, and extremely labile affect, alternating between tears and laughter. At one point, she climbed onto the windowsill while being interviewed. On being presented with a voluntary form, this woman wrote her name fairly legibly but added the words "love god" and some other unintelligible letters afterward. On her Notice of Status and Rights, she did not sign her name; below the statement, "I have read, or had read to me, and understand the contents of the above notice," she wrote,

"WCCPMPPBSG rest know Thank he know goods." (The patient's name began with "W").

Case 2

A 44-year-old Irish Catholic woman was brought to the emergency room with a history of extremely disorganized behavior at home, including setting fires, not eating or sleeping for several days, stuffing bits of paper into her vagina, and conversing with the TV and radio. The admitting resident noted that she had loose associations and pressured speech. She was able to sign her name quite clearly on a voluntary form. Under the "statement of reasons for requesting hospitalization," however, she proceeded to draw two clusters of pencil marks which ran across both the printed type and the lines of the form. These did not appear to be attempts to write words but bore more resemblance to Chinese caligraphy.

Case 3

A 50-year-old Puerto Rican woman was brought to the emergency room with a three-week history of strange behavior and speech. She had recently lost her job and was unable to keep up the rent payments on her apartment. In the emergency room she was described as "delusional" and thought to have "extremely tangential and loose associations." This patient also wrote her name in a legible fashion on the voluntary form. Under the "reasons for requesting hospitalization" she simply scrawled across the page in large capital letters the word "VICTORY."

Case 4

A 54-year-old woman was admitted to the hospital in an acutely psychotic state; she reported hearing the voice of Satan speaking to her and communicating with her dead husband. Her thought processes were characterized as "very concrete." This patient signed her name to a voluntary form but left blank the space for reasons for requesting admission. When presented with a Notice of Status and Rights, she quite legibly wrote the name of the admitting psychiatrist in the space marked, "patient's signature." Upon inquiring, I found that the psychiatrist had signed the form first and had not noticed that the patient rewrote the same name.

Case 5

A 19-year-old black man was brought to the emergency room by the police who had been called because he was staring at a neighbor and tried to kiss her. The patient had had one previous hospitalization. On admission, he was intermittently mute; he would speak a few words, sometimes talk to himself, and then suddenly fall silent. The admitting resident suspected that he had hallucinations. The patient signed a voluntary form. Under "reasons for requesting hospitalization," he wrote "nothing."

Case 6

A 20-year old black man was brought to the emergency room by the police, who had removed him from the subway tracks. He had had no previous psychiatric treatment. He was able to report that he had recently lost his job and, when asked why he was on the tracks, referred to the incident as "a learning experience." He also complained that he was confused, and he was described as disoriented, concrete, circumstantial, delusional, and perhaps hallucinating. The interviewer considered his judgment and reasoning poor. This patient signed a voluntary form and wrote as his reason for hospitalization, "I need help." Two weeks later, when the patient was able to reflect on his state of mind at the time of admission, he clearly recalled that he had thought he was signing the papers as a way of obtaining help to kill himself.

These cases illustrate why it is questionable to consider "voluntary" to be merely a synonym for "agreeable" or "compliant." We often confront psychotic patients who appear to agree to be hospitalized, but who are also clearly so impaired as to be unable to understand what their admission means. Patient 1 seems to be unable to concentrate on her own name long enough to write it. Similarly, Patient 2 cannot attend to the task of giving a "statement of reasons" for admission. Patients 3 and 5 write in as "reasons" for admission single words that are completely cryptic. (Patient 5 is also perhaps unable to retain a thought long enough to write it.) The response of Patient 4 suggests a problem in identifying herself; one might sensibly ask whether she could differentiate herself clearly from the doctor or know who was admitting whom. Patient 6 is perhaps most interesting of all, since he appears to give an understandable reason for hospitalization but keeps its meaning private, so that he and the doctor are actually agreeing to two different contracts.

ASSESSING COMPREHENSION

Making an assessment of what a patient can understand is a necessary step in deciding whether he can be considered voluntary, and such an assessment must be made *before* the patient is offered forms to sign. The admitting psychiatrist in each of the reported cases presumed that the patient was rational and "voluntary," even though obviously psychotic. It is important not to underestimate the cognitive capacities implicit in the language of the papers the voluntary patient signs. In New York, for example, the patient is required to sign a request for admission which contains the statement:

I hereby apply for voluntary admission to . . . . . . , a hospital for the mentally ill. My reasons for requesting care and treatment are stated in part C below. I have been notified and understand the nature of the voluntary status and the provisions governing release or conversion to involuntary status.

If such a statement is to mean anything, a minimum of intact cognitive functions must be in evidence, including perception, comprehension, reality testing, and a sense of the reality of the self and the world.

In other words, the patient must have (at least) a sense of who he is, where he is, what he is reading and what he is doing in signing the paper. Moreover, he must even have a sense of *why* he is doing it. The requirement that he give a reason for hospitalization apparently represents documentation that the patient really does want to be admitted. In addition, it is a deduction of the form "I want X because I am Y." Besides correctly perceiving the referents of "I" and "X" and "Y," the patient must comprehend the whole thought and its relevance to his signing his name. It is clearly not the intent of the law that "voluntary" should mean no more than "signs his name to form 472DMH." Yet it is quite possible for a psychotic person to be able to write his name on a paper when it is suggested to him to do so, without any concept that such an action is logically connected with "illness" or his own state of mind, his behavior, or his need for hospitalization.

The pressures of an emergency room often militate against a proper evaluation of which patients can be considered voluntary. The resident on duty knows that he is held responsible for the patient's safety. He may decide that he is going to admit the patient no matter what the patient's wishes are; he may still offer the patient voluntary status, preferring to think the patient can maintain his autonomy, even if he has much evidence to the contrary. This maneuver creates the illusion that the patient is not being detained but rather is choosing to be admitted. In effect it becomes expeditious to treat the patient as if he were the relatively rational person delineated by the forms (*i.e.,* one who is "notified" and "understands"). The decision to place the patient on voluntary status is then made only on a dimension of compliance versus hostility, to the exclusion of the dimension of rationality versus irrationality. Angry and paranoid patients are then certified for involuntary admission, while passive though perhaps *more* disorganized patients are persuaded to sign "voluntaries." In this way the admitting psychiatrist reaches the point where his criterion for which patients are considered voluntary becomes "anyone who will agree to sign."

This is not, however, what "voluntary" means at all. William James[3] provided us with a psychological concept of voluntary action that emphasizes the purposeful mastering of conflicting motives. According to James, a person who thinks about something before doing it is necessarily inhibited by contrary alternatives. The type of decision that James considered most voluntary (as opposed to impulsive, automatic, or compulsory decisions) occurs when a person weighs the evidence, seeing both his alternatives at once, and makes an effort to choose between them. In such a case, the person is aware both of what he will do and also what he loses forever by taking one alternative; therein lies the necessity for effort. James considered other types of decisions to be more akin to the actions of an infant who has no mental inhibition to delay any wish or impulse. He concluded that

...attention with effort is all that any case of volition implies. The essential achievement of the will, in short, when it is most "voluntary", is to ATTEND to a difficult object and hold it fast before the mind. (p. 561)

Further on he added:

> The difficulty is mental; it is that of getting the idea . . . to stay before our mind at all. When any strong emotional state whatever is upon us the tendency is for no images but such as are congruous with it to come up. (p. 563)

This difficulty is precisely what a psychotic person has the greatest trouble with, distracted as his thinking is by every fleeting emotion. Faced with hospitalization, he must hold to his intention to be admitted over a prolonged period of time (more than a few seconds, certainly), if his admission is to be considered voluntary. James even provided us his own example of this problem in a patient reported by Pinel; the man underwent an examination that seemed at first to indicate that his reason was restored, but then signed "Jesus Christ" on his discharge papers and "went off into all the vagaries connected with that delusion."[3] Such a patient would today be characterized as schizophrenic, in part because of his peculiar tendency to lose his hold on who the "I" is who signs the papers. If we consider James's ideas about volition in the light of the Bleulerian concept of schizophrenia, it becomes clear how our patients can lack the capacity for voluntary actions.

Patients whose associations are disjointed enough will not "attend with effort" to anything. Bleuler[1] described the extreme case of a patient trying to sign her name:

> A hebeprenic wishes to sign her name "B. Graf" in the customary position at the end of a letter. She writes "Gra", then another word beginning with "Gr" comes to her mind; whereupon she changes the "a" to "o", affixes "s", and then repeats the word "Gross" twice over. Thus the whole complex of concepts which was at the root of the purpose of signing her name has all at once become completely ineffective . . . In this way the patients may lose themselves in the most irrelevant side associations, and a uniform chain of thought does not come about.

Similarly, if a patient is intensely ambivalent, it becomes impossible to know what his intention may be. One of Bleuler's patients stated the problem succinctly:

> When one expresses a thought, one always sees the counterthought. This intensifies itself and becomes so rapid that one doesn't really know which was the first.[1]

Another patient is quoted as saying, "I am Dr. H. I am not Dr. H." Such a patient seems to have no notion of the difference between one statement and its opposite. It is then hard to see what an assertion by this patient, such as "I hereby apply for admission," should be taken to mean.

Alternative categories

Perhaps at this point one caveat is necessary. It is certainly *not* being argued that *any* psychotic person is incapable of *any* voluntary action, merely by virtue of having a thought disorder. The ego functions (as well as their dissolution) represent graded phenomena, so that a given patient may be more or less de-differentiated, having more or less sense of his own reality as a person. But the radical point of view, which maintains that every patient should have the opportunity to sign a voluntary, necessarily implies a willingness to ignore what is known about the psychology of disordered thinking. Szasz seems unaware of the irony of his own words when he asserts that

> ... mental hospitals, both public and private, should be restricted to the care of consenting, voluntary, adult patients. Both the hospital and the patient should be treated as independent, contracting parties.[6]

Treating the patient this way unavoidably entails making certain psychotic people be what they demonstrably are not.

To say that it would be good if all patients were admitted as "voluntaries," though it sounds benign, is really to say no more than that it would be good if there were no psychotic people in the world. Each of the six patients reported above responded in writing to the opportunity to sign a voluntary; each of them was also indulged in a charade, treated as if he understood what he was doing and as if the doctors also understood his thinking. Most likely each patient had been through this kind of collusion before, having the confusion in his mind matched by the equally confusing response, "Yes, I understand." The psychiatrist in fact does not understand an autistic slogan like, "VICTORY," and may do his patient a disservice by appearing to. A discussion of the therapeutic implications of accepting such a misunderstanding would go beyond the scope of this paper. It is sufficient to note that the patient's difficulties are painfully obvious, and cannot be defined out of existence.

Finally, we should not be misled into an artificial dilemma by the idea that any patient who cannot be considered voluntary must be involuntary. "Voluntary" and "involuntary" do not provide us with an exhaustive set of categories with which to describe human actions. Apathetic or indifferent people, for example, do not clearly belong to either category. New York law in fact recognizes a third type of case—the "informal" admission—which has the same legal status as a medical admission. In essence, "informal" here means that the patient is agreeable to admission and that no one will detain him if he insists on leaving. (Insisting, of course, is an action that requires some attention and effort.) None of the six patients described above actively objected to hospitalization, and that fact has more meaning than all their signatures as "voluntaries." For some of them, informal admission might have been a reasonable alternative and would not have required them to go through the motions of signing a contract that they did not understand. When the psychiatrist finds no basis for detaining a patient but feels that hospitalization might be of benefit, he can propose admission on informal status. In any case, his obligation is to make a sensible evaluation; should he decide to detain the patient, the psychiatrist must be prepared to explain his decision in a court hearing. But the psychiatrist cannot, by any legal maneuver, convert a patient's passivity and confusion into understanding and autonomy.

REFERENCES

1. Bleuler, E. 1950. Dementia Praecox or the Group of Schizophrenias. International Universities Press, New York.
2. Chodoff, P. 1976. The case for involuntary hospitalization of the mentally ill. Amer. J. Psychiat. 133:496–501.
3. James, W. 1950. The Principles of Psychology, Vol. 2. Dover Publications, New York.
4. Olin, G. and Olin, H. 1975. Informed consent in voluntary mental hospital admissions. Amer. J. Psychiat. 132:938–941.
5. Peszke, M. 1975. Is dangerousness an issue for physicians in emergency commitment? Amer. J. Psychiat. 132:825–831.
6. Szasz, T. 1963. Law, Liberty, and Psychiatry. Macmillan, New York.

Part Seven

Economics, Ethics, and Psychotherapy

It should not be inferred from what has been said up to this point that the basic variations in psychotherapy or in the allocation of psychotherapeutic services may all be traced directly to money. The common axiom that says the rich get good medical care, and thereby good psychotherapeutic care, masks all too many significant issues. Still, there is a certain abiding truth to the common belief in the powerful influence not only of money, but of social class on theories and procedures of psychotherapy.

One of the more usual approaches to the field of mental health generally is to explore both the forms of psychological stress and the quality of psychotherapy among various social classes. Can we say with authority, in other words, that the classes reveal or indeed may be distinguished by the psychological stresses and illnesses they exhibit, or the variety and tenure of psychotherapeutic intervention? Studies by social scientists seem to suggest that the members of the higher social classes consult psychotherapists more readily and frequently than members of the lower social classes. This means that the more affluent members of the society will think about consulting a psychotherapist sooner than less affluent members of the society. Said differently, psychotherapy has been seen to make inroads into the daily lives of affluent people to a far greater extent than it has in the lives of less affluent people. This fact has led some observers to characterize the contemporary affluent classes in terms of their weightier psychological awareness, or their preoccupation with shrinks. The same fact has led other people to direct their attention at "enlightening" lower class communities on the value of psychotherapy. Naturally, one finds all too many people of various social classes perfectly willing to consult a psychotherapist only to discover that they cannot afford it, or that their medical insurance policy does not adequately cover expenses incurred in psychotherapy. But more on this point in a moment. For now, let us stress the fact that the different social classes appear to hold characteristic attitudes toward normal and abnormal psychological functions, which in turn relate to their attitudes toward psychotherapy. These attitudes, however, are far more complex than one might imagine at first glance.

If we speak about a particular attitude toward psychotherapy held by a member of the working class, for example, are we speaking of some abstract thought or image, or are we in fact making reference to some genuine experience members of the working class have had in regard to psychotherapy? Even more to the point, is the attitude held by that hypothetical working class person founded on abstract principles, or on the fact, say, that psychotherapy essentially is practiced by more affluent members of the society? Thus an attitude toward psychotherapy may turn out to be an attitude toward members of other social classes as well as their customs, conventions, and styles of friendship. We begin to see, then, just how complex are these relationships between social class, economics, and the theory and practice of psychotherapy. But let us make the point even more boldly.

We would assert that economic and social class phenomena play a very significant role in the development of both the theory and the practice of psychotherapy. After all, people are earning their living from doing psychotherapy, and no one can deny the extraordinary emergence of psychotherapy as a viable profession. Can we overlook, then, given present health care features of our society, the effect of a potential client's economic standing on whether a psychotherapist will accept the person as a client in the first place? Notice, we are not yet alluding to certain problems in relating and communicating that people of different social classes may encounter as the psychotherapeutic process evolves. We are speaking here only about the matter of who gets admitted to psychotherapy in the first place. Now, if this idea seems too radical, then perhaps we should inquire into the matter of whether or not the more affluent members of a society have first crack at the best psycho-therapeutic procedures and psychotherapists. Do we make anything of the fact that the rich tend to see psychiatrists, whereas the middle class consults psychologists, the working class social workers, and the poor so-called mental health workers? Do we not find these patterns operating in most hospital settings? What do we make of a psychotherapist's comment to a prospective patient: "If you don't want to pay fifty dollars for each session then you obviously don't want to be in treatment with me"? The word want in the statement is, of course, the pivotal one, for it implies not that a person cannot afford the "best" psychotherapy, but that the person at a conscious or unconscious level is resisting psychotherapy.

The psychotherapist's statement may seem preposterous and easily dismissed, but consider the following remark made less than two decades ago about a certain *population of prospective patients for psychoanalysis. Negroes, a psychotherapist remarked, do not make good psychoanalytic patients (analysands is the technical term), essentially because they either don't dream enough or cannot remember their dreams. The utter stupidity of the statement cannot be missed. If a certain population does not enter a particular form of psychotherapy, how could anyone possibly know whether or not they dream or remember their dreams? But that is not the point. Rather, we must stress the fact that various forms of psychotherapy cost a great deal of money. And rather than admit that by dint of the practice they have chosen, certain psychotherapists are automatically excluding large sections of the population, they would only naturally prefer to claim that scientific evidence demonstrates that these sections of the population cannot partake of psychotherapy on intellectual grounds, rather than that they cannot afford to partake on purely economic grounds.*

The relations between social class or economics on the one hand, and the practice of psychotherapy on the other demonstrates again the enormous influence of social and cultural factors on that intimate human involvement known as the therapeutic alliance. We have also seen how these influences are hardly mere abstract or theoretical issues; they represent very real and pragmatic issues. For example, will psychotherapists keep affluent clients in treatment longer than less affluent clients? Will psychotherapists gradually turn away from the less well-paying jobs in hospital and neighborhood clinic settings and find sanctuary in the more luxuriant confines of private practice? And one more question: Can a culture which already shows a dangerous shortage of mental health workers, irrespective of their orientations, credentials, and status, survive the ever increasing move toward private practice on the part of psychotherapists?

20

Psychiatry and Social Class

GUIDO CROCETTI, HERZL R. SPIRO AND IRADJ SIASSI

Summary. The role that patients' social class plays in the diagnoses that they are given and the treatments that are recommended for them, has been of continuing interest to the mental health profession. Charges of "bias" have not been infrequent. Examination of this issue was the primary focus of this study. Thirty psychiatrists in private practice and thirty-eight experienced clinicians from a community mental health center were presented with four psychiatric case descriptions. They were asked for their diagnoses and treatment recommendations. Each case description contained upper class or lower class cases. This paper reports on the diagnoses that were made and the treatment modalities that were recommended by private and public practitioners, using social class as the independent variable.

Does the psychiatric profession discriminate against the impoverished mentally ill? Is social class an independent variable in the diagnosis made and the type treatment recommended when a patient seeks help? In 1950, Hollingshead and Redlich held a mirror to the state of practice of psychiatric art at that time in the New Haven community. Their findings received wide dissemination in the 1950's culminating in the publication of Social Class and Mental Illness (Hollingshead and Redlich, 1958). They demonstrated in devastating detail that the deck was stacked against the mentally ill from lower classes, thus raising a troublesome moral question. The social foundations of psychiatric and medical diagnosis and prescriptions are based on a

Reprinted by permission of Springer Verlag New York Inc. From Social Psychiatry 11 (1976), 99–105.

'universalistic' nondiscriminatory approach. Yet, the New Haven findings suggested that psychiatrists operate in such a way as to restrict their 'best' treatment to the upper social classes (Miller and Mischler, 1959). This was the harbinger of many attacks on psychiatry both from within and without the profession. These attacks have been somewhat tempered in their intensity, but they have certainly persisted in the general consciousness, above all in community and social psychiatry. In this paper we shall 1). review a few studies of the role of social class in diagnoses and treatment of the mentally ill, and 2). present data from a comparative study of a survey of psychiatrists in private practice and mental health professionals in a community mental health center.

A BRIEF REVIEW OF LITERATURE

The literature reveals a variety of studies and discussions of role and social class in psychiatric evaluation and treatment, with contradictions in both findings and conclusions. Mischler and Scotch (1963), e.g., reported that patients admitted to state mental hospitals were more likely to receive the diagnosis of schizophrenia than those admitted to private psychiatric hospitals, while criticizing other studies that relate schizophrenia to social class.

Siegel et al. (1962), undertook an eighteen months study of the hospitalized patients in three major psychiatric hospitals in an effort to test the Hollingshead and Redlich hypotheses that patients from lower classes are more likely to receive the diagnoses of psychoses and to be administered organic forms of treatment than those from higher classes who would be more likely to be called non-psychotic and to receive psychotherapy. They found no correlation between social class on the one hand, and diagnosis, treatment selection, or length of hospitalization on the other.

Haase (1964) reported that greater psychopathology was found from Rorschach protocols when they were attributed to lower class patients. He postulated that middle class norms are used as criteria for "mental health" by all mental health professionals. He noted this middle-class bias as an occupational trait of the mental health profession and found it to be independent of group origin, employment, experience or theoretical orientation. Routh and King (1972) submitted case histories to fifteen clinical psychologists and thirty-two college students for class bias and found the reverse of the findings by Haase. Routh and King attributed their findings to higher expectations for middle-class persons; they also presented the possibility of the subjects allowing a wider latitude of behavior to lower class persons. Kurtz et al. (1970) reported that lower-class case histories received more serious diagnoses only from those mental health students who scored high on an objective test measuring authoritarianism. Lerner and Fiske (1973), however, in their study of fourteen clinicians working with lower class patients, reported that lower-class "attitudes" of the patients were the determining factor in evaluation and treatment.

Myers and Bean (1968), in a partial replication of the Hollingshead and Redlich study ten years later, reported that social class differences had continued to exist in the same New Haven population. Tischler et al. (1975), however, in their extensive study of essentially the same population, and by application of multivariate analyses to their data, demonstrated that social class was of little importance as bias or barrier to the allocation of mental health services in that community. And, Rushing (1971) in his study of three state hospitals in Washington, although finding many class distinctions, could not find any relationship between class bias and rate of hospitalization.

Psychiatrists have been accused of bias in administering too much organic therapies to patients from lower classes (Avnet, 1962). They have also been admonished for forcing psychotherapy on patients from lower classes and of not being sensitive to the patients' needs and preferences for organic therapies (White et al., 1964; Detre and Jarecki, 1971).

METHODOLOGY

This study was carried out among a sample of CMHC professionals and a separate sample of private practicing psychiatrists during 1974. The study was based on case descriptions or vignettes developed by Star (1952). Each of these case descriptions depicted symptoms of one category of mental illness. The symptoms do not overlap categories of illness. Packets of four vignettes, two with upper-class social cues and two with lower-class social cues were selected from six possible packets, each with four forms of mental disorders. These were handed to thirty-eight mental health center clinicians and mailed to thirty East-coast private psychiatrists. Through extensive follow-up, a response rate of 100% was obtained for both groups. Each clinician was asked to evaluate each vignette as to the presence of a mental illness, the appropriate diagnosis, the degree of severity and the preferred treatment modality. Cues to social class were occupation and residence. The four diagnosable disorders were classified as in the original Star vignettes: Juvenile Character Disorder, Simple Schizophrenia, Compulsive Phobic, and Anxiety Neurosis. The category "other" was also available. A total of 264 vignettes were offered for evaluation. Of these 133 had upper class cues, and 131 had lower class cues. Private psychiatrists saw 124 vignettes (61 upper class and 63 lower class). CMHC clinicians saw 140 vignettes (72 upper class and 68 lower class).

RESULTS

The results are presented in two sections. Section 1 examines the differences between the diagnoses given the upper and lower class patients by private psychiatrists and by the CMHC clinicians. In section 2, the recommendations for treatment are studied.

I. Diagnosis

Table 1 illustrates that no significant class bias exists in diagnosis of psychiatric disorders contained in these vignettes. Neither is there any significant difference between diagnoses given for upper and lower classes by private psychiatrists and those given by community mental health center clinicians.* Both groups appear to

*Occupations of the fathers of CMHC clinicians were obtained and compared to diagnoses and treatment recommended. There was no differential according to socio-economic backgrounds of these clinicians.

TABLE 1.
Diagnoses for 4 disorders by social class of vignette and by private practitioners and community mental health center clinicians (Total N = 264)

		% Correct Diagnosis	
	Total	Private Practitioners	MHC Clinicians
Schizophrenia N = 66			
Total percent correct dx 48%			
Social class of vignette:			
Upper	50	58	45
Lower	47	39	57
p 0.5			
Juvenile Character Disorder N = 66			
Total percent correct dx 44%			
Social class of vignette:			
Upper	39	50	32
Lower	50	31	63
p 0.20			
Compulsive Phobic Neurosis N = 66			
Total percent correct dx 73%			
Social class of vignette:			
Upper	62	71	93
Lower	65	56	72
p 0.30			
Anxiety Neurosis N = 66			
Total percent correct dx 30			
Social class of vignette:			
Upper	30	41	19
Lower	30	31	29
p 0.4			

have extreme difficulty in arriving at "correct" diagnoses. In 28% of the vignettes (74 of 264) no diagnosis was offered. "No mental illness" and "insufficient information" were equally frequently given as the reason in these cases. Overall, "correct" diagnoses were given only 49% of the cases. Private psychiatrists arrived at "correct" diagnoses in 46% of the vignettes and the CMHC clinicians in 52%. This finding is all the more surprising since permissive standards were employed in assessment of the results: All diagnoses of schizophrenia were accepted as "correct" for simple schizophrenia; all character disorders were accepted as "correct" for juvenile character disorder; obsessive compulsive neurosis and phobic neuroses were accepted as "correct" for compulsive phobic neurosis; and depressive reaction, depressive neuroses, as well as anxiety reaction were accepted as "correct" for anxiety neurosis.

As can be seen in the table, the upper- and lower-class patients do not differ significantly in receiving correct diagnoses. Overall, 50% of the former and 47% of the latter were correctly diagnosed.What can be said about the table is that the private psychiatrists diagnose the upper-class patients "correctly" more frequently than lower-class patients in every category. This finding, however, does not attain statistical significance in any of the categories. The CMHC clinicians on the other hand, diagnose the lower-class patients "correctly" more frequently in three of the four categories, but again not significantly in any category. These trends may indicate that CMHC clinicians have more experience dealing with lower-class patients and private psychiatrists are more experienced with upper-class cases. Further analyses of the responses (not shown in the table), disclose the great reluctance of both groups to use the diagnoses of psychoses, correctly or incorrectly. Both groups tend to use less severe diagnoses of the "situational reaction" type when misdiagnosing. (Detailed breakdown of the data will be made available upon request).

II. Recommendation for Treatment

In 20% of the vignettes (52 of 264), the recommendation was "no treatment." Upper- and lower-class patients did not significantly differ in receiving this recommendation. Results pertaining to recommendations for treatment for the remaining 212 vignettes are shown in Table 2 on the following page. As can be seen in the table, only in 10 cases hospitalization was the recommended modality. Of these, 2 were upper class and 8 lower class, with identical breakdown for private psychiatrists and CMHC clinicians. The numbers in each cell are too small for statistical analysis.

Long-term psychotherapy was the single most frequently recommended treatment modality (N = 81). More upper-class than lower-class patients were recommended for this type of treatment (61% vs 38%). The difference, however, does not reach statistical significance. The apparent trend is primarily accounted for by the recommendations from CMHC clinicians who recommended long-term psycho-therapy for an almost significantly (P<0.1) greater proportion of the upper-class patients (25%, N = 21) than of lower-class patients (13%, N = 11).

In terms of short-term psychotherapy, the recommendations (N = 52) were equally divided between upper- and lower-class patients. The CMHC clinicians tended to recommend this modality more frequently for lower-class patients and the private psychiatrists for upper-class patients. In neither situation, however, does the trend reach statistical significance.

Marital therapy was recommended for 31 cases, with no difference between the practitioners or patients' class.

Group therapy was the next recommended modality in terms of frequency (N = 26). The trend shows that this treatment is more often recommended for lower-class patients, but not significantly so.

TABLE 2.

Recommended treatment by social class of vignettes and by private practitioners and community mental health center clinicians (N = 212)

		% of Recommendations	
	Total	MHC Clinicians	Private Practitioners
Hospitalization N = 10			
Upper	20	10	10
Lower	80	40	40
Long-Term Psychotherapy N = 81			
Upper	60	35	25
Lower	37	24	13
Short-Term Psychotherapy N = 52			
Upper	49	26	23
Lower	48	12	36
Family Therapy N = 31			
Upper	48	19	29
Lower	50	12	38
Group Therapy N = 26			
Upper	34	11	23
Lower	65	19	46
Drugs and Supportive Therapy N = 12			
Upper	41	08	33
Lower	57	16	41

Drugs and supportive therapy was, except for hospitalization, the least favored modality of treatment (N = 12). In its recommendation, no differences were found between the practitioners or in terms of the social class of the patients.

The true serendipity coming from these findings (not shown in the table) is that the recommended treatments in no way correlate with the diagnoses. This is true for both groups of practitioners, for both classes of patients, and is independent of whether correct diagnosis is or is not arrived at. In 74% of cases where clinicians declined to diagnose, they proceeded to recommend one or the other treatment modality.

DISCUSSION OF RESULTS

First, the diagnosis is not affected by class bias. This is true for both private psychiatrists and CMHC clinicians.

Second, no evidence of class bias could be found in the recommendations for treatment modality given by either private psychiatrists or CMHC clinicians.

Third, long-term psychotherapy is the most frequently recommended and hospitalization the least frequently recommended treatment modality for both upper- and lower-class patients.

Last, the true serendipity coming from this study is that the record of correct diagnosis is woefully poor for both groups of practitioners. Whether the reason for this is that definitions of disorders are unclear or diagnostic practices have changed in the twenty years since these profiles were developed is uncertain. It is crucial, however, that the problem be defined and remedied if diagnostic classifications are to continue to have any value or meaning. The implications of the results of this study call upon mental health professionals to bring definitions of disorders up to date, as well as to review the grounds on which they base their decisions for recommending treatment for their patients.

COMMENT

The spectrum of the consequences of social inequality range from the significantly greater risk of infant damage and death in the lower class families (MacMahon and Feldman, 1972) through impoverished intellectual development (Smith et al. 1972), lower academic potential (Hess and Shipman, 1965), lower school achievement (Baldwin, 1958), and higher rates of juvenile delinquency (Conger et al. 1965; Derbyshire, 1968; Glueck and Glueck, 1950). It would be odd, indeed, if the lower classes were spared a similar disproportionate toll in severe mental disorders, with or without bias in diagnosis. The difficulties inherent in working with lower-class patients are not confined to psychiatry. Many have discussed the barriers between physicians and low-status patients in other branches of medicine, stressing the lesser likelihood of meaningful doctor-patient relationship with lower compared to the high status patients (Rosengren and Lefton, 1969; Freidson, 1961; Osofsky, 1968). Bias, however, denotes the premise of unequal human worth between one patient and another, or between classes of patients. It has an underlying destructiveness and irrationality clearly out of keeping with our professional credo.

To assess quality of psychiatric care, one needs to define it in relation to specified standards. To compare the relative quality of care provided for, say one class versus another class in the society, involves comparing the actual care provided for the majority of patients from each class with some criterion or standard of excellence. Differences between the real and the stated ideal are then analyzed in each case and deficiencies identified. The concept of standard-setting, therefore, is inherently necessary to the logic of quality assessment. For example, Hollingshead and Redlich raised the issue of class bias when their findings showed that the diagnoses made and the actual treatment provided were significantly affected by the class status of the patients. In the value system, implicit in their conclusions, the diagnosis of psychoneuroses and long-term out-patient psychotherapy were viewed more positively.

We have moved in the space of twenty-five years from a time when hospitalization was almost the only available treatment for the severely mentally ill to a time when the majority of these patients are treated as outpatients, when the concern has shifted from patients being kept in hospitals too long, to that of their not being kept there long enough. Reversing the old order of things, the state hospitals are now accused of "dumping" chronic patients on the community facilities, which complain of becoming overloaded (Gardener and Gardener, 1971).

The recommendation for treatment for a given patient by a clinician at any point in time is probably determined to varying degrees by a number of factors: the nature of the patient's psychopathology; the available resources within the community (and the clinician's knowledge of these resources); the financial resources of the patient and his family; the extent of the patient's need for supportive services; the determination of whether or not patient can or will be able to adapt to the schedules and other limitations of a private psychiatrist; and the appropriateness of the type treatment available for the patient at least as perceived by the clinician. It may very well be inappropriate for a private practitioner who has little contact with ancillary services in the community and little time to coordinate the treatment endeavor, to accept a severely disturbed patient from a multi-problem family into treatment. The appropriate treatment resource for such a patient may be a clinician who has available the ambiance of a large agency.

Furthermore, the role of scientific literature needs to be considered. For example, the pervasive influence of the many authoritative voices that have proclaimed that lower-class patients neither benefit nor are interested in psychotherapy (Riessmann, 1963; Baum and Felzer, 1964; Yamamoto and Goin, 1965; Beck, 1969) or those that recommend that the practitioners keep their patients out of hospitals at all cost should not be ignored (Group for the Advancement of Psychiatry, 1970-71). The difference between private psychiatrists and CMHC clinicians, in their recommendations for treatment, could reflect the differences in the literature they are primarily exposed to.

Today, a quarter of a century after the New Haven studies, mental health professionals and social scientists must ask anew some old questions about psychiatric practice and provide fresh answers which can guide policy suitable to the conditions of our times and for the decades to come. Many such questions pose themselves: 1. Who is to be hospitalized; what are the indications for psychiatric hospitalization; what are the implications of these characteristics for mental hospitals? 2. What should be taught to a student of mental health; what should a professional know about evaluation and optimal treatment? 3. How will uniform criteria of evaluation and treatment be established and who will do the teaching? 4. There are now conditions in the society affecting the health and mental health care systems profoundly—insurance coverage of varying forms, HMO's, the promise of national health insurance. What are the implications for the patients and how will the professionals adapt to these new conditions? 5. What will be the impact on the whole field of the increasing demands from governmental and other agencies for audits, peer review, guidelines, restrictions? In the urgently needed dialogue, pejoratives such as "bias" may neither be justified nor helpful.

REFERENCES

Avnet, H. H.: Psychiatric Insurance. New York, Group Health Insurance, (1962)
Baldwin, W. K.: The Social position of the educable mentally retarded child in the regular grades in the public schools. The Exceptional Children. 25, 106–108 (1958)
Baum, O. E., Felzer, S. B.: Activity in initial interview with lower-class patients. Arch. gen. Psychiat. 10, 345–353 (1964)
Beck, J. C.: Outpatient group therapy of the poor. Cur. Psychiatric Therapies. 9, 241–244 (1969)

Conger, J. J., Miller, W. C., Walsmith, C. R.: Antecedents of delinquency, personality, social class and intelligence. In: P. H. Mussen, J. J. Conger, and J. Kagan (Eds.), Readings in Child Development and Personality. New York: Harper and Row, 1965

Derbyshire, R. L.: Adolescent identity crisis in urban Mexican Americans in east Los Angeles. In: E. B. Brody (Ed.), Minority Group adolescents in the United States. Baltimore: Williams and Wilkins, 157-204 1968

Detre, T. P., Jarecki, H. G.: Modern Psychiatric Treatments, Lippincott, 1971

Freidson, E.: Patients' Views of Medical Practice. Russell Sage Foundation, 1961

Gardener, E., Gardener, M.: A community mental health center case study: innovations and issues. Seminars in Psychiat. 3, 172-198 (1971)

Glueck, S., Glueck, E. T.: Unraveling juvenile delinquency. New York: Commonwealth Fund, 1950

Group for the Advancement of Psychiatry: The crisis in psychiatric hospitalization. Intern. J. Psychiat. 9, 565-586 (1970)

Hasse, W.: Rorschach diagnosis, socio-economic class and examiner bias. Unpublished doctoral dissertation, New York University, 1956

Hess, R. D., Shipman, V. C.: Early experience and the socialization of cognitive modes in children. Child Development 34, 869-886 (1965)

Hollingshead, A. B., Redlich, F. C.: Social class and mental illness. New York: Wiley 1958

Kurtz, N., Kurtz, R., Hoffung, R.: Attitudes toward lower and middle-class psychiatric patients as a function of authoritarianism among mental health students. J. Cons. and Clinical Psychol. 35, 338-341 (1970)

Lerner, B., Fiske, D. W.: Client attributes and the eye of the beholder. J. Cons. and Clinical Psychol. 40, 272-277 (1973)

MacMahon, B., Feldman, J. J.: Infant mortality rates and socio-economic factors. National Center for Health Statistics: United States Public Health Service, 1972

Miller, M., Mischler, E.G.: Social class, mental illness and American psychiatry. Milhank Memorial Fund Quarterly 37, 174-199 (1959)

Mischler, E. G., Scotch, N. A.: Socio-cultural factors in the epidemiology of schizophrenia. Psychiatry 26, 315- (1963)

Myers, J. K., Bean, L. L.: A decade later: A follow-up of social class and mental illness. New York: John Wiley and Sons, Inc., 1968

Osofsky, H. J.: The walls are within. In: Among the People: Encounter with the Poor. Irwin Deutscher and Elizabeth J. Thompson, Eds. New York: Basic Books, 1968

Riessman, F.: New approaches to mental health treatment for labor and lower income groups. Mimeographed report, National Institute of Labor Education, Mental Health Program, 1963

Rosengren, W. R., Lefton, M.: Hospitals and patients, 197-198. New York: Atherton Press 1969

Routh, D. K., King, K. M.: Social class bias in clinical judgment. J. of Cons. and Clinical Psychol. 38, 202-207 (1972)

Rushing, W. A.: Occupation, income and mental hospitalization. Ment. Hygiene 52, 248-252 (1971)

Siegel, N. H., Khan, R. L., Pollack, M., Fink, M.: Social class, diagnosis and treatment in three psychiatric hospitals. Social Problems 10, 191-196 (1962)

Smith, A. C., Flick, G. C., Ferriss, G. S., Sellman, A. H.: Prediction of developmental outcome at seven years from prenatal, perinatal and postnatal events. Child Development 43, 495-507 (1972)

Star, S. A., What the public thinks about mental health and mental illness. Paper presented at the annual meeting of the National Association for Mental Health, November 19, 1952

Tischler, G. L., Henisz, J. E., Myers, J. K., Boswell, P. C.: Utilization of mental health services: II Mediators of service allocation. Arch. Gen. Psychiat. 32, 416-418 (1975)

White, A. M., Fichtenbaum, L., Dollard, J.: A measure predicting dropping out of psychotherapy, J. Cons. Psychol. 28, 326-332 (1964)

Yamamoto, J., Goin, M. K.: On the treatment of the poor. Amer. J. Psychiat. 122, 267-271 (1965)

21

Mental Health and the Disadvantaged

RAYMOND P. LORION

Conventional views about mental health approaches for poor people do not, in general, match what we actually know. It is not true, for example, that poor people are not interested in psychotherapy, nor are our treatment modes inapplicable to them. The goal of this article is to review treatment approaches which are of demonstrated effectiveness with the disadvantaged segments of the population. Further, for the purposes of this discussion, the "disadvantaged" will also refer to the "working class." Although they generally live under less financial pressure than the poor, the working class has historically shared the poor's difficulty in obtaining and remaining in psychotherapy.

Consideration of treatment approaches for the disadvantaged is of more than academic interest. The results of epidemiological surveys consistently reveal that the relative distribution of psychological disorders in the population is inversely related to socioeconomic status (Hollingshead and Redlich, 1958; Srole et al., 1962; Dohrenwend and Dohrenwend, 1969), while low-income status typically contraindicates psychotherapy as an intervention (Lorion, 1973). This is especially significant since these conclusions are frequently based on the records of public clinics in which the ability to pay was supposely *not* a treatment prerequisite (Bailey et al., 1960; Budner et al., 1964; D'Angelo and Walsh, 1967; Jackson et al., 1974; Krebs, 1971; Lee et al., 1974; Tischler et al., 1975a,b).

Reprinted by permission from *Social Policy*, 8 (May/June 1977), 17-27. Copyright © 1977 by Social Policy Corporation, New York, N.Y. 10036. Portions of this article are reproduced with permission of John Wiley & Sons. An extended version appears in S. L. Garfield and A. E. Bergin, eds., *Handbook of Psychotherapy and Behavior Change*, 2d ed., John Wiley.

Further, research evidence indicates that it is quite erroneous to assume that the disadvantaged cannot respond to psychotherapy (Albronda, Dean, and Starkweather, 1964; Lorion, 1973). Lerner (1972) provides carefully documented evidence of the potential efficacy of dynamic psychotherapy with the disadvantaged. In *Therapy in the Ghetto* she shows, very clearly, the positive impact of therapy—as measured by patient, therapist, and behavioral ratings—with low-income minority group patients.

Although we still do not have at our disposal means for responding prescriptively to all who seek treatment, recent experimental and clinical efforts suggest that we shall ultimately reach that goal. The strategies to be reviewed do not exhaust the range of alternative treatment approaches now in use with the disadvantaged. Of primary immediate concern is the identification of procedures for which there is available empirical evidence of effectiveness. Treatment strategies which, to date, have been justified primarily with clinical findings will not be discussed in this review. This is not to suggest that they are without merit, only that the extent and limitations of their impact have yet to be demonstrated through systematic means.

THERAPIST PREPARATION

Interviews with therapists have consistently showed that their attitudes toward the poor are not supportive of psychotherapy for disadvantaged patients (Lorion, 1974). While the research validity of these findings may be open to question, the significance of a therapist's negative attitudes on the course of treatment is reliably documented (Affleck and Garfield, 1961; Parloff, 1961). Indeed Goldstein, who has been a major contributor to the systematic study of the role of therapist expectations in treatment (Goldstein, 1960a, 1962a, 1966a, 1966b, 1971), has gone so far as to question whether, in fact, psychotherapy ends rather than begins with the intake interview. In this perspective, it is important that attempts to provide treatment for the disadvantaged address, in some way, the therapists' potentially negative set at the onset of treatment. Truax and Carkhuff (1967) alert us to the consequences of omitting this step:

> When the therapist pretends to care, pretends to respect, or pretends to understand, he is fooling only himself. The patient may not know why the therapist is "phony" but he can easily detect true warmth from phony and insincere "professional warmth." (p. 34)

In reviewing the available literature, I found only three studies which examine directly Frank's (1961) assumption that disadvantaged patients would respond more effectively to psychotherapy if therapists were trained to recognize and deal with their attitudes toward such patients. Baum and Felzer (1964) report that more than 65 percent of low-income applicants remained in treatment beyond six sessions when residents were carefully briefed about the lifestyles, needs, and expectations of these groups. Throughout the course of treatment, staff conferences dealt openly with therapists' reluctance to work with such patients. As similarities and differences in needs and communication patterns were discussed, Baum and Felzer report that therapists began to recognize and implement changes in previously inflexible treatment approaches. Discussion of actual therapy sessions revealed changes in communication patterns to insure maximum patient understanding of therapists' messages. Pains were taken to select analogies carefully. Conscious efforts were made to reinforce the patients' motivation to continue treatment. Bernard (1965) defined therapists' attitudes toward the disadvantaged as a countertransference topic appropriate to supervisory feedback. She reports increases in therapeutic effectiveness among psychiatric residents when supervision dealt openly with their misperceptions and resistance to serving the disadvantaged. Unfortunately, neither Bernard nor Baum and Felzer operationally define the criteria used to assess treatment effectiveness, nor do they report any attempt to compare supervised and unsupervised therapists.

The relative efficacy of modifying or ignoring therapists' pretreatment attitudes toward the disadvantaged was systematically assessed by Jacobs et al. (1972). These investigators simultaneously considered the treatment impact of therapist and patient preparation occurring prior to the first treatment session. The results of patient preparation will be discussed in the next section; therapist preparation is treated here.

Jacobs et al. randomly assigned 120 low-income outpatient applicants to one of four experimental conditions: (1) "prepared" patient seen by "prepared" therapist; (2) "nonprepared" patient seen by "prepared" therapist; (3) "nonprepared" patient seen by "nonprepared" therapist; and (4) "prepared" patient seen by "nonprepared" therapist. A total of 24 therapists participated in this study. The study involved a repeated measures design; all psychiatric residents treated patients in each of the four conditions. The therapist preparation, given by the chief resident at the time the case was assigned, consisted of a brief (15 minute) orientation to low-income life-styles, treatment expectations, and therapeutic problems. This information was incorporated into the regular case assignment procedures used by the chief resident. "Nonprepared" therapists did not discuss socioeconomic-status-relevant issues when they met with the chief resident. To insure that the observed findings do not merely reflect the therapists' recognition of the experimental conditions, all therapists were carefully interviewed once the last patient was seen. None gave any evidence that they were aware of the study's procedures or hypotheses, nor did they recognize any pattern in the chief resident's assignment discussions.

The observed findings demonstrate the merit of including therapist preparation procedures in clinical training and supervision. Treatment effectiveness was assessed by using a variety of indices including treatment duration, the development of a specific treatment plan, and improvement as rated by independent reviewers of care records. Prepared therapists retained disadvantaged patients in treatment significantly longer than the unprepared. Prepared therapists were also significantly more likely to propose a specific treatment plan and to perceive their patients as improving than those who were unprepared. Interestingly, disadvantaged patients seen by unprepared therapists were significantly more likely to have their psychiatric contact limited to evaluative sessions. On all outcome measures, patients seen in condition 3 (both patients and therapists nonprepared) had the least positive experiences.

Although nonsignificant, directional differences favoring the prepared patients were observed on attrition rates, the use of medication, and initial evaluation of treatment needs.

Although more refined outcome measures might have been employed, this study demonstrates that a relatively simple procedure which sensitizes therapists to their disadvantaged patient's needs can result in significant positive changes in therapists' responses to the disadvantaged. Undoubtedly, this study should be replicated and extended. Which therapists did or did not respond to preparation is unknown. Process analyses of actual treatment sessions could provide important insights into the ways in which "preparation" is translated into verbal and nonverbal therapist behaviors. Yet, even without these data, it is apparent that the negative self-fulfilling potential of therapists' attitudes and expectations toward the disadvantaged is reversible. Indeed, an even more promising finding reported by Jacobs et al. is their conclusion that more therapists, regardless of their economic or racial background, can become effective service providers to the disadvantaged.

Another way of influencing the professional's view of the patient is by adding nonprofessionals to the service delivery team. Both middle nonprofessionals and indigenous paraprofessionals have, more and more, provided additional and alternative humanpower resources for the mental health system.

Sobey (1970) reports the most comprehensive evaluation on nonprofessional performance, examining the efficacy of more than 10,000 nonprofessionals functioning in 185 different National Institute of Mental Health-sponsored programs. Her analyses suggest that nonprofessionals are utilized in traditional professional roles (e.g., providing individual and group therapy), in case work, in screening capacities, and in a general counseling role to assist peers' adjustment to the community. Undoubtedly, the number of individuals involved and the variety of functions in which they are employed support Sobey's description of the nonprofessional movement as a "revolution." Testimonials in behalf of the impact of these individuals are highly available (Cowen, 1973). Summarizing these, Sobey (1970) states:

> An untrained person can develop both skill and observation of symptoms and ability to deliver personal care for the mentally ill. One study project reported that 80 percent of the nonprofessionals trained as practical nurses seemed capable of functioning in therapeutic roles (individual, group, and milieu therapy) in the care of the mentally ill. Where nonprofessionals work with "normal" populations in the community, skills in community organization and reducing the distance between the professional and the community were frequently noted. For innovative roles which nonprofessionals have so often been asked to assume—the teacher-mom, home-visitor, reach-out aide, etc.—the flexibility and spontaneity of nonprofessionals make them ready and willing to learn and to undertake more than is expected of them. (pp. 177–178)

Unfortunately, however, the majority of data describing nonprofessionals' effectiveness evolves from relatively weak or nonexistent research designs (Karlsruher, 1974).

Indigenous paraprofessionals assume an equally varied set of roles (Gartner and Riessman, 1974). Their work ranges from providing escort service, home visits, receiving complaints and providing mental health information, to the organization of community meetings, the conduct of therapy groups, the design of aftercare services, and the provision of supportive psychotherapy to patients. Rieff and Riessman (1965) suggest that the use of indigenous personnel promises greater respect for and comfort with the low-income patient, since indigenous workers are part of the very community in which they serve. Given this, it is assumed that they can establish uniquely therapeutic relationships with clients. Beyond impressionistic and descriptive data, however, there is little hard evidence of the efficacy of their services. In reviewing indigenous roles, Sobey (1970) states:

> It is by now common knowledge that we have romanticized the indigenous worker, and that little hard data is available on the effective employing and training of this type of worker. . . .
>
> What happens to the indigenous person in the course of the training process? Can he retain assets for which he was originally selected or does he become socially distant like the typical professional? Many considerations need to be spelled out as we inquire into the effective employing and training of indigenous nonprofessionals. (pp. 187–188)

Directionally, however, the consistency of reported findings observed across a variety of settings and involving a wide variety of roles cannot be ignored. Nonprofessionals can make an important contribution to the delivery of mental health services for the disadvantaged. Effective utilization of their services, however, depends upon information collected in methodologically sophisticated studies. Thus, available data suggest not a turning away from the nonprofessional "revolution," but rather a sharpening of the experimental questions asked about nonprofessionals and an increase in the willingness to explore such issues.

PATIENT PREPARATION

Pretreatment preparation has not been used only with therapists. In fact, the majority of studies in this area have focused primarily on attempts to modify the treatment attitudes and expectations of patients. A variety of procedures to increase patients' understanding of the therapeutic process have been reported. Some rely on direct instruction; others on informational interviews; still others on modeling and role playing. The differential efficacy of these strategies has not been assessed and is as yet unknown. Overall, however, it appears that the majority of patient preparation techniques do significantly improve the mental health treatment experiences of the disadvantaged (Heitler, 1973, 1976).

Assuming that the disadvantaged patient's motivation for therapy could be enhanced early in treatment, Albronda, Dean, and Starkweather (1964) made available "pretreatment" informational interviews to these patients. Prior to the formal intake session, psychiatric social workers met with patients for one session to aid them in the formulation of specific treatment goals and to clarify for them the psychotherapeutic process. These meetings focused on the specific delineation of the therapist and patient roles. No control subjects (i.e., unprepared) were included in the experimental design. The investigators report significant increases (in comparison to prior case records) in the proportion of applicants who arrived for the formal intake and remained in treatment. Similar findings with a comparable procedure were reported by Baum and Felzer (1964).

Orne and Wender (1968) recommended a socialization procedure to prepare patients for psychoanalytically oriented psychotherapy. Prior to the onset of treatment, the patient participates in an individual clinical interview designed to provide: a justification of psychotherapy as an appropriate response to the patient's needs; a specific description of the role of therapist and patient in the treatment process; a general overview of the typical course of treatment and of the nature of transference and resistance.

In response to Orne and Wender's suggestion, investigators at the Phipps Psychiatric Clinic developed the *Role Induction Interview* (RII) and evaluated its treatment impact in a series of well-designed studies. Hoehn-Saric et al. (1964) report that patients who received the RII behaved more appropriately in therapy than did matched controls. Furthermore, the prepared group responded much more positively to treatment than did the controls, as assessed by a variety of outcome measures. Significant differences were found on three of these: therapist's ratings of change; patient's rating of change; and a "blind" interviewer's ratings of the patient's social effectiveness following treatment.

Careful review of these and related data indicates that an important consequence of utilizing the RII with patients is an increase in the perceived attractiveness of disadvantaged patients for the therapist (Nash et al., 1965). Furthermore, it appears that the RII's impact can be extended if someone from the patient's environment (e.g., spouse, friend, parent) participates in the RII and subsequently supports the therapeutic process (Stone, Imber, and Frank, 1966). The RII's positive contribution to the psychotherapeutic process was validated in a subsequent replication of the Hoehn-Saric et al. (1964) study by Schonfield et al. (1969).

Other attempts to assess the impact of patient preparation have been reported. In a partial replication of the Phipps Studies, Sloane et al. (1970) compared the differential impact of the RII's socialization and faith induction components. Their results demonstrate that the RII's socialization aspects (i.e. role clarification) were the major contributor to observed improvements in the course and outcome of treatment. Warren and Rice (1972) agreed with this conclusion in their evaluation of patient preparation *during* the course of treatment. In this study, patients were randomly assigned to one of three conditions: therapy; therapy plus "stabilizing" sessions designed to encourage discussion of transference issues; or therapy plus stabilizing and "structuring" (i.e., socialization) sessions. Significant positive differences were observed for the prepared versus unprepared patients on measures of treatment duration, involvement in the therapeutic process, and improvement as rated by therapists and patients. Warren and Rice's data demonstrate that structuring contributes significantly to the maintenance of the therapeutic alliance. This finding was also demonstrated in the Jacobs et al. (1972) study described earlier. These investigators demonstrated that prepared disadvantaged patients remained in treatment longer and showed more improvement than did matched nonprepared controls.

Since considerable emphasis is often placed upon group treatment approaches for the disadvantaged, a number of investigators have applied patient preparation techniques to group members. Using a university population, Yalom et al. (1967) used a modified version of the Orne and Wender socialization approach. They found that group members who participated in an initial preparatory session interacted more positively than did members of nonprepared groups. Heitler (1973) extended these findings by looking specifically at disadvantaged group members in an inpatient setting. He concluded that prepared patients

> tended to lower latencies for voluntary participation, to communicate more frequently, spend more clock time communicating, communicate more frequently on a self-initiated basis, to engage in self-exploratory efforts more frequently, and to do so in a greater percentage of their communications. (p. 349)

Furthermore, the therapist rated prepared patients as more involved, more similar to an ideal group therapy patient, more likely to engage in self-initiated collaborative efforts to explore personal difficulties, and having more hopeful purposes than control patients (Heitler, 1976).

It is important, however, to recognize that such similar positive treatment consequences accompany efforts to prepare therapists as well. The differential effect of these two approaches has been considered by Jacobs et al. (1972) in an interesting although not conclusive study. The Jacobs et al. data suggest, and I concur, that the crucial target may be the therapist. Given the tentativeness of their conclusion, further research is definitely needed to determine the optimal target for treatment preparation (therapist, patient, or both). Future psychotherapy research must also be designed to identify the process mechanisms through which preparatory procedures influence the conduct and outcome of psychotherapy.

INSIGHT-ORIENTED APPROACHES

Available data suggest that traditional insight-oriented approaches have not been made available to the low-income segments of the population. It is also true that disadvantaged patients assigned to traditional approaches have, for the most part, been unwilling to remain in that form of treatment. One cannot, however, on the basis of these facts conclude that insight-oriented approaches have not been and cannot be effective with these segments of the population (Lorion, 1973).

In seeking to identify effective treatment approaches for the disadvantaged, mental health researchers must not ignore the potential utility of traditional approaches. Rather than simply rejecting insight-oriented approaches as inappropriate for the disadvantaged, it seems reasonable instead to attempt to identify the effective components of these strategies so they can be modifed to fit more comfortably into the life-styles of the disadvantaged without significantly altering the primary therapeutic aspects basic to these strategies.

Some evidence is available concerning the positive treatment effect for disadvantaged patients of receiving less rigid traditional therapy. Gould (1967), for example, states that assembly-line workers responded quite well to his less formal analytic approach. His treatment was offered in a direct, simple manner with minimal emphasis upon the social distance between patient and therapist. Early sessions focused upon the patient's misconceptions about the nature and goal of mental health treatment (i.e., patient preparation). Whenever possible, psychological jargon was avoided and everyday language was used to communicate salient concepts to the patient. Gould focused on the patient's concern with specific issues as a means of encouraging discussion of dynamic issues. Gould reports that occasional sessions held while walking in a nearby park greatly facilitated discussions at certain critical points. He also reports that session length was modified in relation to productivity. At times, treatment lasted 20 to 30 minutes; at other times the full 50 minutes. Where appropriate, problems were treated at face value and direct advice was offered to the patient. Gould suggests that his proposed modifications of traditional therapy increased patient comfort and motivation without negatively affecting consideration and resolution of dynamic material.

Unfortunately, Gould did not systematically evaluate his efforts. He reports only his impressions of the results of his efforts. Obviously, a more controlled evaluation of his proposals is necessary. Support for Gould's conclusions, however, is provided by Hacker, Illing, and Bergreen (1965) who observed similar degrees of improvement in working-class patients participating in analytically oriented therapy. These investigators observed a 50 percent reduction in attrition rates as their therapists responded to patients in an increasingly flexible manner. Yet even these data can only be interpreted suggestively. Their ultimate confirmation depends upon their replication in a carefully controlled study.

Therapy in the Ghetto is the single systematic evaluation of insight-oriented psychotherapies for ghetto residents presently available in the literature. In this book Lerner (1972) reports the results of five years of research on outpatient psychotherapy with nontraditional patients. Forty-five patients were seen by 15 different psychotherapists (psychologists and social workers). Of these, eight were highly experienced and seven were relatively less experienced. All therapists emphasized insight-oriented approaches in their treatment methods. The 45 patients included 23 Black and 22 white outpatients ranging in age from 16 to 57. No specific procedures were used in selecting patients for the study. Outcome measures included a variety of patient and therapist self-description and symptom-education measures. Additionally, Lerner describes the psychometric development of the *Rorschach Psychological Functioning Scale* (RPFS). This measure assesses two specific dimensions of adaptive functioning. First, "structural soundness" relates to the patient's gross reality contact, perceptual accuracy, emotional control and integration, and cognitive balance. Second, "functional richness" refers to the patient's contact with and access to internal processes. This is assessed along two dimensions—affective richness and cognitive richness.

Of the 30 patients who completed treatment prior to the end of the study, 23 showed significant gains in psychological functioning following treatment. No significant racial differences in outcome were observed. Nor did same-race and cross-racial patient-therapist dyads differ on any measure. These results were supported on the majority of patient and therapist outcome measures used. Lerner emphasizes the extremely significant relationship found between assessed democratic attitude of the therapist and patient improvement. She interprets this finding as evidence of the fact that democratic or nonauthoritarian attitudes on the part of the therapist

> create an ambience which helps clients avail themselves of their own resources, but it may also be that such values make it easier for the very confused and needy people to avail themselves of other good things the therapist has to offer, such as warmth, support, acceptance, protection, understanding, and clarification. (p. 141)

Finally, it should be noted that Lerner's positive results were achieved in less than nine months and required fewer than 30 sessions. The actual cost per client was somewhere between $200 and $300 for the entire treatment process. Thus, she argues that insight-oriented therapeutic approaches, with understanding and open therapists, are both potentially effective and economically feasible for the disadvantaged.

BRIEF TREATMENT APPROACHES

Time-limited therapeutic approaches should be very appropriate for many of the disadvantaged. Not only are their economic and occupational realities inconsistent with long-term treatment (Frank, 1961; Garfield, 1963; McMahon, 1964; Storrow, 1962) but, in fact, most patients remain in treatment for only a brief period as evidenced by reports of *actual* national treatment duration averages. Depending upon the clinical setting, 30 to 60 percent of psychotherapy patients terminate within the first six sessions with or without their therapist's consent (Rubenstein and Lorr, 1956). Fewer than half of over 11,000 patients from 53 clinics remained in treatment beyond the eighth session (Rogers, 1960). For 1966, the National Center for Health Statistics reports an average of fewer than five contacts for almost one million patients seen in psychiatric treatment during that year. Thus, median treatment durations range from three to 12 sessions and, if only those patients who actually begin treatment are considered, median durations are between five and six sessions (Garfield, 1971). Given actual practices, it appears that rather than dropping out in the middle, patients leave treatment at phenomenologically defined end points.

A variety of time-limited approaches have been described for the disadvantaged (Bellak and Small, 1965; Sifneos, 1972; Small, 1971). McMahon (1964), Reiff and Scribner (1964), Riessman (1965), and Schlesinger and James (1969) recommend that time-limited contracts be established immediately to respond directly to presenting symptoms. As these problems are resolved, the therapeutic contract may be renegotiated to deal with more complex intrapsychic difficulties. Evidence of the efficacy of short-term approaches is available (Wohlberg, 1967). For example, Avnet (1962) reports that the Group Health Insurance Corporation surveyed 1,200 mental health professionals. Following time-limited treatment, 76 percent of their patients were rated as improved. A follow-up study two and a half years later demonstrated that short-term treatment effects continue over time (Avnet, 1965). Unfortunately, the criteria defining improvement were not reported, nor were control groups included in these studies. Levy (1966) reports similar findings. Only nine of 493 patients seen in time-limited treatment (four to six sessions) required any subsequent treatment. Levy interprets their reluctance to seek further treatment as evidence of symptom reduction. Yet, without clear evidence of symptom reduction, the actual impact of brief approaches cannot be assumed. That so few patients sought further treatment may, in fact, reflect the failure of time-limited approaches. Patients may have been reluctant to continue with what they experienced as an unsatisfying treatment.

A more rigorous assessment of brief therapy with the disadvantaged is provided by Koegler and Brill (1967). These investigators compared brief contact therapy with or without medication where indicated, and traditional long-term insight-oriented psychotherapy. Patients were randomly assigned to treatment conditions and double blind procedures controlled for therapist bias in evaluating the drug treatment. Patients having minimal contact met with their therapist for a limited number of sessions to discuss practical aspects of their problems and to receive medication (or placebos). Koegler and Brill report no differences in symptom reduction between the brief and traditional treatments lasting beyond six months. This finding is particularly noteworthy given the probabilities that disadvantaged patients would remain in treatment for as long as six months.

Additional support for time-limited treatment with the disadvantaged is provided by Goin, Yamamoto, and Silverman (1965) and Yamamoto and Goin (1965). These investigators report that a sizable number of their disadvantaged patients showed noticeable reductions in symptoms following participation in brief problem-oriented treatment. Since many low-income applicants often fail to arrive for intake, Yamamoto and Goin (1965) scheduled 10 to 15 patients for each 10 therapist hours. At times, several patients were interviewed together in a group intake session. All patients were seen within a few days of contacting the clinic. Some patients responded so well to these streamlined intake procedures that they required no further treatment. Others continued for up to six sessions during which the therapist participated actively and directly advised the patient. Rapid ongoing access to followup clinics was available. Stone and Crowthers (1972) also found significant decreases in drop-out rates following the introduction of crisis-oriented time-limited psychotherapy. These investigators found that blue-collar families utilized psychiatric services much more comfortably and frequently when they were available on a prepaid rather than a fee-for-service basis and when they provided direct immediate problem focusing.

Unfortunately, there presently are far too few systematic evaluations of short-term treatment approaches with the disadvantaged even though they are being used extensively. One cannot, therefore, rule out the possibility that while the disadvantaged are currently receiving more treatment they are not necessarily receiving more effective treatment.

BEHAVIORAL APPROACHES

Unfortunately, little data presently exist demonstrating the relative effectiveness of behavioral (i.e., psychotherapy approaches based upon learning theory, which emphasize the identification and direct manipulation of the reinforcement contingencies underlying the problematic behavior or symptoms) approaches with the working class and the poor. Most recently, Sloane et al. (1975) have completed a well-designed, carefully controlled comparison of traditional expressive and behavior therapies. In this study, 94 patients suffering from moderately severe neuroses and personality disorders were randomly assigned to traditional, behavioral, or a waiting-list control condition. To insure their involvement, control patients were promised therapy within four months, provided a contact to call in case of crisis, and telephoned irregularly during the four-month waiting period. At the end of the experimental period, Sloane et al. observed that all three groups had improved significantly and that the behavioral and traditional therapy groups had improved significantly more than their waiting-list controls. No differences, however, in amount of improvement were found between the therapy groups. At the end of one year, behavior therapy patients were significantly more improved on reduction of target symptoms than were the controls. There was no evidence of symptoms substitution in any group. In fact, improvement in target symptoms was accompanied by improvement in other symptoms as well.

The results of the Sloane et al. (1975) study are relevant to this discussion for several reasons. First, the results demonstrate that behavior therapy can be at least as effective as expressive psychotherapy with the problems typical of clinic paitents. Second, and perhaps most important, Sloane et al. demonstrate that behavior therapy can effectively serve more heterogeneous patient populations than can traditional psychotherapies. In this study, the behavior therapists were equally effective with patients from all socioeconomic backgrounds. Finally, this study exemplifies the level of design sophistication appropriate to the complex issues involved in prescriptive analyses. As will become evident later, the Sloane et al. study closely approximates the "ideal" design.

MARITAL AND FAMILY APPROACHES

Throughout this article I have emphasized the importance of identifying treatment approaches for the disadvantaged which are salient to their life-styles. Numerous discussions of the working class have stressed the importance of family to the attainment and maintenance of mental health (Gans, 1962; Giordano, 1973; Miller and Mischler, 1959; Miller and Riessman, 1968; Riessman, 1965). Although its composition may differ somewhat, the family is also an important parameter of emotional functioning among the poor and minority groups (Miller and Riessman, 1968; Rainwater, 1966).

Increasingly, therefore, the disadvantaged family is perceived as a viable target for mental health services (Chaiklin and Frank, 1973; LaVietes, 1974). Mannino and Shore (1972), for example, report on a program which aims to assist low-income families in their interaction with other social systems. The goals of their "ecologically oriented family intervention" include increases in the family's effectiveness as a unit and in its capacity to relate to and effectively deal with relevant social systems (e.g., schools, welfare, medical facilities.)

Yet, low-income families appear to be hesitant to use and respond to family services. Rosenblatt and Mayer (1972), for example, reviewed interview data collected from some 6,200 parents who participated in project ENABLE, a national demonstration program to help socially and economically deprived persons solve family and neighborhood problems. Rosenblatt and Mayer report that Black and white women show a marked difference in their willingness to approach professionals for family services: 61 percent of white women used professionals as compared to 45 percent of Black women. At the same time the interview data suggest that those least willing to use expressive family services (i.e., Blacks and members of the lowest income segment) are most satisfied with the help they receive. These observed satisfaction ratings suggest that increasing the availability and attractiveness of such services can have very positive effects on these segments of the population.

Speer et al. (1968) support this conclusion in reporting that individuals from low-income families had significantly more difficulty regularly attending sessions than did middle-class patients. They did not differ, however, in terms of continuing in treatment. In a well-designed comparative analysis of child psychotherapy, parent counseling, and "informational feedback" Love, Kaswan, and Bugental (1972) have demonstrated that expressive family-oriented approaches are most effective in serving the needs of the disadvantaged. In this study, a total of 91 referred families having a child experiencing serious school-related difficulties were assigned to one of three treatment conditions. Additionally, a "nonreferred" control group was used as a "normal" comparison group to provide baseline data on family and school measures. Dependent measures used in this study included school grades, behavioral ratings by objective observers, and ratings of family interaction and communication patterns from videotape recordings. The results clearly indicated that parent interventions were significantly more effective in improving their children's performance than was child psychotherapy. Socioeconomic analyses of subjects revealed that the disadvantaged responded most to procedures providing direct information and advice. Heinicke (1976) also evaluated the effects of family treatments on the parents of 112 children experiencing developmental lags. Consistent with other studies, she found a positive response to family approaches on measured ratings of effectiveness and on specific measures of adjustment.

The general findings reviewed thus far suggest that family-oriented approaches can be appropriate for the disadvantaged. However, evidence of their effectiveness is not readily available. Framo (1969) provides a thoughtful anecdotal description of a Black ghetto family in treatment. Although he does not evaluate objectively the results of this case, his report provides heuristically valuable insights into problems associated with that approach. Further grist for the subsequent evaluation of family therapy with minority patients is provided in an intriguing conceptual analysis by Sager, Brayboy, and Waxenberg (1970). They describe a laboratory exercise in which five Black staff members assumed the roles of members of a ghetto family and four distinguished family therapists (Nathan Ackerman, Thomas Brayboy, Robert MacGregor, and Carl Whitaker) individually confronted this "family" in a first interview. The major value of this book lies in its heuristic rather than empirical contribution. Mental health researchers who read this book will identify a variety of meaningful questions which merit immediate and systematic analysis. They will also recognize patient and therapist variables which must be controlled in a methodologically sophisticated study.

A somewhat less subjective evaluation of family therapy with the disadvantaged is provided by Minuchin et al. (1967). In their report of an "exploratory" study, the investigators compared 12 ghetto families having a delinquent child with 10 matched "control" families not having a delinquent child on a variety of objective-type family interaction tasks. Following treatment, posttesting was conducted with the experimental but not control families. In the absence of posttesting for the control group, the reported pre and post changes may reflect the impact of the treatment or simply the passage of time. The investigators report that seven of the 12 experimental families were judged to be clinically improved on all of the interactional measures after treatment. Although suggestive, these results must be verified in a systematic, methodologically sophisticated way. Wells, Dilkes, and Burckhardt (1976) conclude that this caution holds true for much of the available family therapy research.

If, as Rainwater (1966) suggests, low-income family life is characterized by unstructured marital roles, strategies focusing specifically upon improving the marital relationship should also be relevant to the disadvantaged. A fair amount of evidence exists which demonstrates the efficacy of these procedures. Gurman (1973) analyzed 15 studies which meet basic methodological criteria and concluded that across a variety of marital therapy approaches and outcome criteria, more than 66 percent of treated patients improve. The majority of these studies used clinic populations made up primarily of disadvantaged families. Moreover, the average treatment duration was fewer than 20 sessions. Gurman notes that marital therapy, like other therapies (e.g., Bergin, 1971), can have deleterious effects on some clients. In roughly 2 percent of the cases treated, the referral problem was worse after treatment.

The effectiveness of marital counseling with the disadvantaged is demonstrated by Beck and Jones (1973). Their report summarizes follow-up data (secured by interviews and mail questionnaires) on approximately 2,000 marital cases served by the Family Service Association of America. Criterion outcome measures included global ratings of patient improvement, indices of change in presenting problem, skills, and family relationships, and measures of improvement in specific family members. Independent ratings were secured from counselors and clients in each of these areas. Overall, 60 to 70 percent of the clients returning the questionnaires (N=985) reported improvement across the criterion measures. Beck and Jones attempted to compensate for the absence of a control group by assessing the relationship between change measures and the total number of sessions attended. Patients who had a single marital interview (which the investigators perceive as an approximation of a no treatment control group) had significantly lower improvement rates than patients attending between two and 20 sessions.

Further evidence for the efficacy of marital counseling with the disadvantaged is provided in a recent review of outcome studies by Beck (1976). Consideration of eight studies without control groups involving some 500 marital couples demonstrates improvement rates in the 65 to 70 percent range. Additionally, Beck reports that the combined results of eight studies (mostly reported in *Dissertation Abstracts*) which included a control group reveal significantly higher improvement rates in experimental over control subjects. In six of the eight controlled studies, half or more of the outcome measures showed gains which were significant at or above the .05 level. Marital counseling approaches which focused exclusively on improving communication patterns between the marital partners were considered in 12 studies. Nine of these showed statistically significant positive increments on half or more of the measures used to compare treatment and control groups (Beck, 1976).

One of the important findings included in the Beck review is the relatively stronger impact of structured, communication-oriented treatments. A variety of these approaches are reported in a recent work by Olson (1976). Some have been developed specifically with disadvantaged clients; others, although apparently generalizable, have yet to be proven effective generally and specifically with the disadvantaged.

Stuart (1976) describes a structured family program to improve communication skills between marital partners. Although a major evaluation of this program used with 750 couples over a 10-year period is still under way, Stuart reports interim findings on 200 couples. In 87 percent of the couples treated, at least one spouse met the initial behavioral objectives (i.e., improved communication among family members); in 81 percent of the cases, those objectives were met by both partners. One year after treatment there were only five divorces; five years later, 174 of the 200 couples remained married and reported reasonable satisfaction with the relationship. In view of these preliminary findings, Stuart's operant approach at improving communication skills merits further consideration. Stuart explains that treatment is very behavioral and focuses directly on the resolution of transactional problems between the partners. Couples proceed systematically through an orderly series of eight steps, each of which includes operationally defined criteria for moving on to succeeding stages. Initially, couples must identify specific problems and develop contractual arrangements for resolving them. The final stages involve direct efforts to resolve the identified problems and include "a set of specific instigations and criteria for determining whether the technique produced the expected behavioral change and whether the change has led to increased commitment." (Stuart, 1976, p. 122).

Blechman and Olson (1976) describe a "gamelike" treatment approach for improving the communication and problem-solving skills of family members. Data available thus far on the effectiveness of this approach were collected with single-parent families, which made them relevant to many disadvantaged families. The family contract game includes four basic problem-solving components: (1) the selection of a target problem; (2) the selection of alternative satisfying behaviors to replace problem behaviors; (3) the identification of appropriate rewards for pleasing behaviors; and (4) the acceptance of specific contractual agreement. Each step occurs within the game context. Evaluation of the game's effectiveness with four single-parent families has been reported. Each subject family serves as its own control in an *a-b-a* reversal design which includes repeated measurements of appropriate (problem-solving) and inappropriate problematic behaviors. Subject families were evaluated in two pretreatment baseline sessions, six pretreatment sessions, and two posttreatment sessions. Problem-solving behaviors were assessed by trained raters viewing videotapes of family functioning. Additionally, parents rated individual children's behavior before and after treatment. Blechman and Olson report highly positive and significant results in assessments of problem-solving behavior. Subjects proceeded through the game without difficulty and were able to form effective contracts with each other. These investigators recognize that considerably more research is necessary before the utility of their approach is firmly established. They point out, however, that the game's structure should increase its appropriateness with the disadvantaged.

Considerably more research will have to be done before the relative benefits and cost of marital and family approaches for disadvantaged clients can be identified. At the present time we are far too dependent upon clinical and/or poorly evaluated results to assume the efficacy of these procedures for the disadvantaged or other segments of society with any degree of certainty. The trend of available findings, however, is consistently positive and suggests that these procedures are worthwhile.

CONCLUSION

I believe that we have made significant progress during the past decade in our attempts to provide for the mental health needs of the disadvantaged. Viewed from a historical perspective, it is apparent that we have identified the existence of a problem, delineated some of its most salient parameters, and have begun to design and, to a limited degree, assess a variety of alternative solutions. Our efforts thus far have been unsystematic and inefficient, but is that not the typical pattern of the early stages of scientific pursuits? As we attempt to provide simple solutions to complex problems, the inadequacy of our knowledge base becomes evident and the limitations of our findings apparent. Nevertheless, recognition of the parameters involved in the delivery of services to the disadvantaged has increased significantly during the past two decades and further progress in this area is inevitable. I hope that the material reviewed in this article will contribute to a renewal of interest in the design and conduct of systematic clinical, observational, and empirical efforts focusing on the mental health of the disadvantaged.

REFERENCES

Affleck, D. C. and Garfield, S. L. 1961. "Predictive Judgments of Therapists and Duration of Stay in Psychotherapy." *Journal of Clinical Psychiatry* 17: 134–137.

Albronda, H.F.; Dean, R.L.; and Starkweather, J.A. 1964. "Social Class and Psychotherapy." *Archives of General Psychiatry* 10: 276–283.

Avnet, H.H. 1962. *Psychiatric Insurance: Financing Short-term Ambulatory Treatment.* New York: Group Health Insurance Co., Inc.

———1965. "How Effective is Short-term Therapy?" in L. R. Wohlberg, ed., *Short-term Psychotherapy.* New York: Grune & Stratton.

Bailey, M.A.; Warshaw, L.; and Eichler, R.M. 1960. "Patients Screened and Criteria Used for Selecting Psychotherapy Cases in a Mental Hygiene Clinic." *Journal of Nervous and Mental Disease* 130: 72–77.

Baum, O.E. and Felzer, S.B. 1964. "Activity in Initial Interviews with Lower-class Patients." *Archives of General Psychiatry* 10: 345–353.

Beck, D.F. 1976. "Research Findings on the Outcomes of Marital Counseling." in D.H.L. Olson, *Treating Relationships.* Lake Mills, Iowa: Graphic Publishing Co.

Beck, D.F. and Jones, M.A. 1973. *Progress on Family Problems: A Nationwide Study of Clients' and Counselors' Views on Family Agency Services.* New York: Family Service Association of America.

Bellak, L. and Small, L. 1965. *Emergency Psychotherapy and Brief Psychotherapy.* New York: Grune & Stratton.

Bergin, A.E. 1971. "The Evaluation of Therapeutic Outcomes." In A.E. Bergin and S.L. Garfield, *Handbook of Psychotherapy and Behavior Change: An Empirical Analysis.* New York: Wiley.

Bergin, A.E. and Garfield, S.L. 1971. *Handbook of Psychotherapy and Behavior Change: An Empirical Analysis.* New York: Wiley.

Bernard. V.W. 1965. "Some Principles of Dynamic Psychiatry in Relation to Poverty." *American Journal of Psychiatry* 122: 254–267.

Blechman, E.A. and Olson, D.H.L. 1976. "Family Contract Game: Description and Effectiveness." in D.H.L. Olson, *Treating Relationships.* Lake Mills, Iowa: Graphic Publishing Co.

Budner, S.S.; Escover, H.; and Malitz, S. "The Relationship of Social Personality and Psychiatric Factors to Choice of Psychiatric Therapy." *Comparative Psychiatry* 5: 327–333.

Chaiklin, H. and Frank, C.L. 1973. "Separation, Service Delivery, and Family Functioning." *Public Welfare* (Winter): 2–7.

Cowen, E.L. 1973. "Social and Community Interventions." In P. Mussen and M. Rosenzweig, eds., *Annual Review of Psychology* 24: 423–472.

D'Angelo, R.Y. and Walsh, J.F. 1967. "An Evaluation of Various Therapeutic Approaches with Lower Socioeconomic Group Children." *Journal of Psychology* 67: 59–64.

Dohrenwend, B.P. and Dohrenwend, B.S. 1969. *Social Status and Psychological Disorder: A Casual Inquiry.* New York: Wiley.

Framo, J.L. 1969. "In-depth Family Therapy with a Black Ghetto, Intact Family." Unpublished manuscript, Temple University, Philadelphia, Pa.

Frank, J.D. 1961. *Persuasion and Healing: A Comparative Study of Psychotherapy.* New York: Schocken Books.

Gans, J.H. 1962. *The Urban Villagers.* New York: Free Press.

Garfield, S.L. 1963. "A Note on Patients' Reasons for Terminating Therapy." *Psychological Reports* 13: 38.

———. 1971. "Research on Client Variables in Psychotherapy." In A.E. Bergin and S.L. Garfield, eds., *Handbook of Psychotherapy and Behavior Change.* New York: Wiley.

Gartner, A. and Riessman, F. 1974. "The Performance of Paraprofessionals in the Mental Health Field." in G. Caplan, ed., *American Handbook of Psychiatry,* Vol III. New York: Basic Books.

Giordano, J. 1973. *Ethnicity and Mental Health.* New York: National Project on Ethnic America of the American Jewish Committee.

Goin, N. K.; Yamamoto, J.; and Silverman, J. "Therapy Congruent with Class Linked Expectations." *Archives of General Psychiatry* 13: 133–137.

Goldstein, A.P. 1960. "Patients' Expectancies and Non-specific Therapy as a Basis for (Un-) Spontaneous Remission," *Journal of Clinical Psychology* 16: 339–403.

———. 1962. "Participant Expectancies in Psychotherapy." *Psychiatry* 25: 72–79.

———. 1966a. "Prognostic and Role Expectancies in Psychotherapy." *American Journal of Psychotherapy* 20: 35-44.

———. 1966b. "Psychotherapy Research by Extrapolation from Social Psychology." *Journal of Counseling Psychology* 13: 38–45.

———. 1971. *Psychotherapeutic Attraction.* New York: Pergamon.

Gould, R.E. 1967. "Dr. Strangeclass: Or How I Stopped Worrying About the Theory and Began Treating the Blue-collar Worker." *American Journal of Orthopsychiatry* 37: 78–86.

Gurman, A.S. 1973. "The Effects and Effectiveness of Marital Therapy: A Review of Outcome Research." *Family Process* 12: 145–170.

Hacker, F.J.; Illing, H.; and Bergreen, S.W. 1965. "Impact of Different Social Settings on Type and Effectiveness of Psychotherapy." *Psychoanalytic Review* 52(3): 38–44.

Heinicke, C.M. 1976. "Change in Child and Parent: A Social Work Approach to Family Intervention." *American Journal of Orthopsychiatry.*

Heitler, J.B. 1973. "Preparation of Lower-class Patients for Expressive Group Psychotherapy." *Journal of Consulting and Clinical Psychology* 41: 251–260.

———. 1976. "Preparatory Techniques in Initiating Expressive Psychotherapy with Lower-class, Unsophisticated Patients." *Psychological Bulletin* 83: 339–352.

Hoehn-Saric, R.; Frank, J.D.; Imber, S.C.; Nash, E.H.; Stone, A.R.; and Battle, C.C. 1964. "Systematic Preparation of Patients for Psychotherapy: 1. Effects of Therapy Behavior and Outcome." *Journal of Psychiatric Research* 2: 267–281.

Hollingshead, A.B. and Redlich, R.C. 1958. *Social Class and Mental Illness.* New York: Wiley.

Jackson, A.M.; Berkowitz, H.; and Farley, G.K. 1974. "Race as a Variable Affecting the Treatment Involvement of Children." *Journal of Child Psychiatry* 13: 20–31.

Jacobs, D.; Charles, E.; Jacobs, T.; Weinstein, H.; and Mann, D. 1972. "Preparation for Treatment of the Disadvantaged Patient: Effects on Disposition and Outcome." *American Journal of Orthopsychiatry* 42: 666–674.

Karlsruher, A.E. 1974. "The Nonprofessional as a Therapeutic Agent." *American Journal of Community Psychology* 2: 61–78.

Koegler, R.R. and Brill, N.Q. 1967. *Treatment of Psychiatric Outpatients.* New York: Appleton-Century-Crofts.

Krebs, R.L. 1971. "Some Effects of a White Institution on Black Psychiatric Outpatients." *American Journal of Orthopsychiatry* 41: 589–596.

LaVietes, R.L. 1974. "Crisis Intervention for Ghetto Children: Contraindications and Alternative Considerations." *American Journal of Orthopsychiatry* 44: 720–727.

Lee, S.H.; Gianturco, D.T.; and Eisdorfer, C. 1974. "Community Mental Health Center Accessibility." *Archives of General Psychiatry* 31: 335–339.

Lerner, B. 1972. *Therapy in the Ghetto.* Baltimore: Johns Hopkins University Press.

Levy, R.A. 1966. "Six-session Outpatient Therapy." *Hospital and Community Psychiatry* 17: 340–343.

Lorion, R.P. 1973. "Socioeconomic Status and Traditional Treatment Approaches Reconsidered." *Psychological Bulletin* 79: 263–270.

———. 1974. "Patient and Therapist Variables in the Treatment of Low-income Patients." *Psychological Bulletin* 81: 344–354.

Love, L.R.; Kaswan, J.; and Bugental, D.E. 1972. "Differential Effectiveness of Three Clinical Interventions for Different Socioeconomic Groupings." *Journal of Consulting and Clinical Psychology* 39: 347–360.

Mannino, F.V. and Shore, M.F. 1972. "Ecologically Oriented Family Intervention." *Family Process* 11: 499–505.

McMahon, J.T. 1964. "The Working-class Psychiatric Patient: A Clinical View." In F. Riessman; J. Cohen; and A. Pearl, eds., *Mental Health of the Poor*. New York: Free Press.

Miller, S.M. and Mishler, E.G. 1959. "Social Class, Mental Illness, and American Psychiatry: An Expository Review." *Millbank Memorial Fund Quarterly* 37: 174–199.

Miller, S .M. and Riessman, F. 1968. *Social Class and Social Policy*. New York: Basic Books.

Minuchin, S.; Montalvo, B.; Guerney B.G.; Kosman, B. L.; and Schumer, F. 1967. *Families of the Slums: An Exploration of Their Structure and Treatment*. New York: Basic Books.

Nash, E.H.; Hoehn-Saric, R.; Battle, C.C.; Stone, A.R.; Imber, S.D.; and Frank, J.D. 1965. "Systematic Preparation of Patients for Short-term Psychotherapy II: Relation to Characteristics of Patient, Therapist and the Psychotherapeutic Process." *Journal of Nervous and Mental Disease* 140: 374–383.

Olson, D.H.L., ed. 1976. *Treating Relationships*. Lake Mills, Iowa: Graphic Publishing Co.

Orne, M. and Wender, P. 1968. "Anticipatory Socialization for Psychotherapy: Method and Rationale." *American Journal of Psychiatry* 124: 88–98.

Parloff, M.B. 1961. "Therapist-Patient Relationship and Outcome of Psychotherapy." *Journal of Consulting Psychology* 25: 29–38.

Rainwater, L. 1966. "Crucible of Identity: The Negro Lower-Class Family." *Daedalus* 95: 172–216.

Reiff, R. and Riessman, F. 1965. "The Indigenous Nonprofessional." *Community Mental Health Journal*, monograph #1.

Reiff, R. and Scribner, S. 1964. "Issues in the New National Mental Health Program Relating to Labor and Low-income Groups." in F. Riessman; J. Cohen; and A. Pearl eds., *Mental Health of the Poor*. New York: Free Press.

Riessman, F. 1964. *New Approaches to Mental Health Treatment for Labor and Low-income Groups: A Survey*. New York: National Institute of Labor Education.

Rogers, L.S. "Drop-out Rates and Results of Psychotherapy in Government Aided Mental Hygiene Clinics." *Journal of Clinical Psychology* 16: 89–92.

Rosenblatt, A. and Mayer, J.E. 1972. "Help-seeking for Family Problems: A Survey of Utilization and Satisfaction." *American Journal of Psychiatry* 128: 1136–1140.

Rubenstein, E.A. and Lorr, M. 1956. "A Comparison of Terminators and Remainers in Outpatient Psychotherapy." *Journal of Clinical Psychology* 12: 345–349.

Sager, C.J.; Brayboy, T.L.; and Waxenberg, B.R. 1970. *Black Ghetto Family in Therapy: A Laboratory Experience*. New York; Grove Press.

Schlesinger, B. and James, G. 1969. "Psychiatry and Poverty—A Selected Review." *Canadian Medical Association Journal* 101: 470–477.

Schonfield, J.; Stone, A.R.; Hoehn-Saric, R.; Imber, S.R.; and Pande, S.K. 1969. "Patient-Therapist Convergence and Measures of Improvement in Short-term Psychotherapy." *Psychotherapy: Theory, Research, and Practice* 6: 267–272.

Sifneos, P.E. 1972. *Short-term Psychotherapy and Emotional Crisis*. Cambridge, Mass.: Harvard University Press.

Sloane, R.; Cristol, A.; Pepernick, M.; and Staples, F. 1970. "Role Preparation and Expectancy of Improvement in Psychotherapy." *Journal of Nervous and Mental Diseases* 150: 18–26.

Sloane, R.B.; Staples, F.R.; Cristol, A.H.; Yorkston, N.J.; and Whipple, K. 1975. *Psychotherapy Versus Behavior Therapy*. Cambridge, Mass.: Harvard University Press.

Small, L. 1971. *The Briefer Psychotherapies*. New York: Brunner/Mazel.

Sobey, F. 1970. *The Nonprofessional Revolution in Mental Health*. New York: Columbia University Press.

Speer, D.C.; Fossum, M.; Lippman, H.S.; Schwartz, R.; and Slocum, B. 1968. "A Comparison of Middle- and Lower-class Families in Treatment at a Child Guidance Clinic." *American Journal of Orthopsychiatry* 38: 814–822.

Srole, L; Langer, T.S.; Michael, S.T.; Opler, M.K.; and Rennie, T.A.C. 1962. *Mental Health in the Metropolis: The Midtown Manhattan Study*. New York: McGraw-Hill.

Stone, A.R.; Imber, S.D.; and Frank, J.D. 1966. "The Role of Non-specific Factors in Short-term Psychotherapy." *Australian Journal of Psychology* 18: 210–217.

Stone, J.L. and Crowthers, V. 1972. "Innovations in Program and Funding of Mental Health Services for Blue-collar Families." *American Journal of Psychiatry* 128: 1375–1380.

Storrow, H.A. 1962. "Psychiatric Treatment and the Lower-class Neurotic Patient." *Archives of General Psychiatry* 6: 469–473.

Stuart, R.B. 1976. "An Operant Interpersonal Program for Couples." In D.H.L. Olson, *Treating Relationships*. Lake Mills, Iowa: Graphic Publishing Co.

Tischler, G.L.; Henisz, J.E.; Myers, J.K.; and Boswell, P.C. 1975a. "Utilization of Mental Health Services I: Patienthood and the Prevalence of Symptomatology in the Community." *Archives of General Psychiatry* 32: 411–415.

——. 1975b. "Utilization of Mental Health Services II: Mediators of Service Allocation." *Archives of General Psychiatry* 32: 416–418.

Truax, C.B. and Carkhuff, R.R. 1967. *Toward Effective Counseling and Psychotherapy*. Chicago: Aldine.

Warren, N.C. and Rice, L.N. 1972. "Structuring and Stabilizing of Psychotherapy for Low-prognosis Clients." *Journal of Consulting and Clinical Psychology* 39: 173–181.

Wells, R.A.; Dilkes, T.C.; and Burckhardt, N.T. 1976. "The Results of Family Therapy: A Critical Review of the Literature." In D.H.L. Olson, *Treating Relationships*. Lake Mills, Iowa: Graphic Publishing Co.

Wohlberg, L.R. 1967. *The Techniques of Psychotherapy, Part II*. New York: Grune & Stratton.

Yalom, I.D.; Houts, P.S.; Newell, G.; and Rand, K.H. 1967. "Preparation of Patients for Group Therapy: A Controlled Study." *Archives of General Psychiatry* 17: 416–427.

Yamamoto, J. and Goin, M.K. 1966. "Social Class Factors Relevant for Psychiatric Treatment." *Journal of Nervous and Mental Disease* 142: 332–339.

22

Professional Ethics and Social Values

ROBERT MICHELS

Men try to influence and control each other's behaviour. This has always been true and always will be. One of the unique characteristics of the species is that the biological predetermination of behaviour is incomplete and that the actions of an individual are largely shaped by experience, particularly social experience. Although in recent years there has been considerable interest in biological means of behaviour control, most control is still mediated by social and psychological methods. Every parent, teacher, salesman, politician, or psychotherapist is a behaviour controller.

The exercise of control or power over another individual raises important ethical considerations and it is to these that we address ourselves here. A full exploration would require discussion of who is controlling whom, the motives of each for participation in the process, the tactics and strategy of influence, the goal, the actual effects of the intervention, and the social context in which it occurs (see Michels, 1973). I shall speak largely to this last issue, that of social context, and specifically focus on one aspect of that context—whether the behaviour controller is a member of a profession.

Some behaviour controllers are professionals, i.e. they belong to groups that are viewed by society as having certain abilities, skills, rights and obligations because of their knowledge and their moral commitment to use it in particular ways. Medicine is the prototype profession in modern society, and many professional behaviour controllers think of themselves as part of the medical profession or following a model

Reprinted by permission from *International Journal of Psycho-Analysis*, 3 (1976), 377-384.

exemplified by the medical profession. Many psychotherapists are in this category.

However, most behaviour controllers are not members of professions; neither themselves nor anyone else would consider them to be. Parents, salesmen and many teachers would be examples. Increasingly, some psychotherapists are also in this category. They are practitioners, but consciously avoid identification with the social institutions which a profession implies. More prominent are therapists who admit to their professional ties only with embarrassment and remain as peripheral as possible to the organized profession. This position is particularly popular among students and younger practitioners but leadership is offered by prestigious elder statesmen who have large followings both within and without the discipline. They often attack the professional 'establishment' and suggest that the existence of an establishment, or even of a profession, is antithetical to both the scientific quest for truth and the ethical pursuit of good.

Thus psychotherapists are engaged in acts that have great ethical significance, the intentional control of others and they operate both as members of professions and outside of professional contexts. An inquiry into the significance of the professional identity of psychotherapists offers an opportunity to explore the role of professions in our society.

PROFESSIONS

The Oxford English Dictionary defines a profession as 'a vocation in which professed knowledge of some department of learning or science is used in its application to the affairs of others or in the practice of an art founded upon it'. Traditionally the term has been applied to divinity, law and medicine. Freidson, the medical sociologist, points out the dual meaning of profession as a special kind of occupation and as an avowal or promise. He defines (Freidson, 1973, p.xvii) a profession as 'an occupation which has assumed a dominant position in a division of labour, so that it gains control over the determination of the substance of its own work'. Goode (1960) identifies the core characteristics of a profession as 'a prolonged specialized training in a body of abstract knowledge, and a collectivity or service orientation'.

These two themes, relating to knowledge on the one hand and its application in practice on the other, place professions in an intermediate position between sciences and trades, but differentiate them from both. Trades do not stem from abstract knowledge but from commercial interest, and they make no pretence at an ethic which places the general good or public service above their parochial concerns. Perhaps it would be more accurate to say that when they do make such pretences, few take them seriously. In recent years some social critics have urged trades to be more professional, to show more concern with broad social issues. Interestingly, they are often the same critics who have attacked professional organizations for pretending to moral leadership, arguing that their appropriate function is that of a trade union.

Pure science is the pursuit of knowledge without regard to its application. There is a critical difference between professional and scientific activity. Science is radical or revolutionary, forever trying new methods, questioning accepted views and rejecting arguments from established authority. Professions are inherently conservative, preferring the tested and traditional. Thus our standards for accepting a new drug are more rigorous than those with which we test a familiar one, while our standards for new or old models of atomic structure are identical. We admire an astronomer who announces that he is testing a new theory concerning the atmosphere of Venus, but regard with mistrust a surgeon who is experimenting with a new method for treating schizophrenia. When our lives or our bodies are at risk, the dangers of error are so great that we are likely to be most cautious before taking the risk of being wrong. The dangers associated with a new idea in science may also be great, but there is usually little difficulty separating them from the mere exploration and testing of the idea. This difference extends to the psychological set of the scientist and the professional while they carry out their daily activities. We expect a good scientist to understand why he is using a certain concentration of reagent in his test tube, and are not overly concerned if he makes an occasional error calculating the formula, as long as he understands the theory behind the calculation. We expect a good physician not to make errors in dosage of a drug, they are too dangerous; although we might not be overly concerned if he has forgotten the theoretical basis for calculating the dosage, as long as he remembers the result.

Professions, like fields of scientific inquiry, are concerned with developing new knowledge and providing their members with a forum for exchanging new information. Like common trades, they are involved in guild activities, encouraging some forms of monopolistic practice, such as price setting and fixing, protecting inept, borderline or incompetent members from exposure and punishment, promoting positive attitudes in consumers, and attempting to increase the more profitable aspects of their business while diminishing the less lucrative ones.

Professional organizations perform a number of functions. They set standards for selection, training and socialization, and then for membership or entry into the profession. When governmental review or licensure boards are involved, these are dominated by members of the profession. The standards concern scientific and technical competence, but often include explicit ethical criteria aspects of virtue such as 'fitness and character'. Professional groups also set standards for practice, and explicit codes of ethics, such as the Hippocratic code, relate primarily to practice. Professions are involved in self evaluation and policing, a sort of ethical quality control. Codes also perform another basic function of the profession, formulating the implicit standard contract which governs the relationship of each professional with his clients. Thus a client's expectations in such issues as confidentiality, continuity of care, disclosure, etc. are not negotiated anew in each contract with a professional but are assumed on the basis of such governing codes.

The public education functions of professions extend beyond publicizing their codes and contracts, and include informing the public about behaviours and practices which relate to those values which the profession is charged to safeguard. For example, the medical profession educates about such health-related issues as sanitation, preventive innoculations or nutrition, while the psychological professions might advise on child rearing or sex education, the clergy on virtue and salvation, and the law on threats to our liberty or social order. At times these efforts extend beyond education and the profession becomes a lobby, a faction in the political process advocating policies which will protect and extend the values which it represents. This may bring the various professions into conflict with each other, as when law and psychiatry fight over the relative importance of personal liberty and public health in their debates concerning commitment procedures and involuntary treatment (Himmelstein & Michels, 1973). At other times, professions may collaborate when their interests overlap, as when psychiatry and law join to formulate criteria for criminal responsibility or competency.

The profession's code of acceptable conduct for its members delineates the limits of professionally acceptable practice, and therefore if there is to be innovation or experimentation beyond these limits, there must be procedures for defining the conditions or circumstances under which the limits may be violated. This is a critical difference between professional and non-professional practitioners. The non-professional has to answer to his client and to the general society, but within these two constraints he is free to innovate or experiment as he deems appropriate. The professional has accepted a third set of constraints, usually more powerful than either of the others. For example, gifts from the client to the practitioner, or sexual contact between them, might seem acceptable or even desirable to both client and practitioner, and might be unobjectionable to the general society. If the practitioner is a professional, however, he has been socialized to subordinate his own feelings to standards that are accepted by his colleagues and the behaviour becomes unacceptable.

The control of professional education by professionals has been a matter of concern to the academic world. However, Edward Levi, the legal scholar and president of the University of Chicago has observed (Levi, 1971) that 'the notion that professional education has somehow forced its way into university education is a kind of Americanism. But as a matter of history, if we trace the modern university to the medieval university, then the point should be made that professional education was the reason for that university. . . . There is a sense in which the best university education, and the only real university education, is professional. One has to remember that the liberal arts themselves were training for the profession of a public citizen.' The recent concern of students with the 'relevance' of their education can be seen as a return to the professional origins of the university.

In a sense, a profession can be seen as a group of people to whom society has delegated power and authority based on the assumption that they have certain knowledge and skills which are not generally available and which are required for decisions in a certain area. Since many of these decisions involve values as well as scientific or technologic considerations, the profession becomes, in effect, a group of ethical as well as scientific specialists. Generally these ethical functions are concealed and there is a pretence that the decisions are really technical or scientific. For example, decisions concerning the distribution of scarce life preserving resources, such as artificial kidneys or rare medicines, are usually rationalized in biotechnologic terms. The reason for this is clear: scientific knowledge itself does not confer ethical sensitivity, and this 'generalization of expertise' (Veatch, 1973) from scientific to moral, when it is exposed, is an important source of anti-professionalism. I believe that this complaint is often reasonable but the problem is more complex than this brief outline would suggest. It is true that scientific knowledge does not confer ethical expertise, but it may make possible the life experiences which can lead to a refinement of ethical sensitivities. For example, the physician has no special claim to skill in deciding who shall live or who shall die because of his knowledge of anatomy or physiology. However, his knowledge of these fields may have led him to an unusual amount of experience in caring for dying people and may have allowed him that special privilege and responsibility of making scientific or technical decisions which lead to life and death results. Experiences such as these can lead to ethical expertise.

Professionalization therefore entails a moral as well as a physical division of labour. Further, every profession involves both licence and mandate, and practitioners 'by virtue of gaining admission to the charmed circle of the profession, individually exercise a licence to do things others do not do, [and] collectively they presume to tell society what is good and right for it in a broad and crucial aspect of life' (Hughes, 1959). Professionals are expected to exercise their moral authority not only as individuals, but also as a group when they promote those values for which society has assigned them responsibility.

ANTI-PROFESSIONALISM

There has been a recent rise of feeling against professions and in fact the question of whether the advantages of professionalization outweigh the disadvantages would hardly have been raised only a few years ago. These feelings are complex and have multiple roots. In part they derive from an anti-rational, anti-intellectual, anti-scientific *Weltanschauung* which has become popular in recent years. Science and reason once seemed to promise all of the answers and man temporarily turned his hopes away from magic and mysticism but, with the failure of reason to deliver its promise, many have returned to a prescientific search for meaning.

A second element of anti-professionalism is a general anti-elitism. Professionals are privileged, have high status and are therefore among the obvious symbols of the inequitable distribution of power and resources in our society. This basis of anti-professionalism is reinforced by the frequent collusion between professions and other elite groups to retain their privileged position.

A third basis of anti-professionalism relates to the generalization of expertise from scientific to moral areas, to which we have already referred. The public claim of professions is to expertise in an area of knowledge and its application. Their moral expertise is usually concealed and when its exercise is exposed, there may be an angry clamour. For example, psychiatrists who are familiar with a wide range of deviant people and with the effects of various types of institutionalization may be the most appropriate persons to decide which criminals should be treated in which way. However, this essentially ethical decision is usually disguised as a technical one and if this disguise is removed, the experts are usually accused of unreasonable exercise of personal power. This criticism may be valid, but the fact remains that technical knowledge may lead to an unusual range of life experiences, and moral sensitivity is based on life experiences.

A fourth basis of anti-professionalism is anti-conservatism, with the recognition that professions are inherently conservative (while, as we have said, science may be radical). Again this is aggravated when the essential conservative interest of the profession, protecting the value which society has assigned to it, becomes generalized to a diffuse protection of all current values and standards. For example, a conservative attitude towards the use of new foods or drugs is inevitable if the medical profession is to take its responsibility for health seriously, while a conservative attitude towards capitalism or private ownership of property has no inherent relationship to health.

A fifth basis of anti-professionalism stems from feelings about the monopolistic practices of professions. Professions are powerful trade unions and particularly when this function is concealed as a concern with the public good, as in the medical profession's fights against various health delivery systems, the sophisticated public is likely to become annoyed.

Finally, many feelings against professions are based on the failures of professionals, both as representatives of professions and as practitioners. For example, since professions monitor standards, those who are excluded from membership tend to turn against the profession, and while patients who recover rarely complain about their doctor's mistakes, those who get worse may attack the system that failed to help them.

Bernard Shaw said that 'every profession is a conspiracy against the laity' and many agree.

PROFESSIONS AND THE ETHICS OF BEHAVIOUR CONTROL

What is the relationship of professions to the ethics of behaviour control? If one man helps another to overcome disabling fears or coerces another to perform evil acts, do we care whether the controller is a member of a profession? Do professions make ethical behaviour on the part of practitioners more or less likely? Do they make it more likely that practitioners will be virtuous, will do desirable things and that the general social good will be promoted?

Psychotherapy can be seen as a paradigm for studying behaviour control. The simplest model for exploring the ethics of the psychotherapeutic relationship considers two participants, the patient and the therapist, and their interaction. It invites discussion of the explicit or implied contract between them and brings into focus many of the traditional contractual issues in the ethics of therapy, such as full disclosure of information to the patient and the requirement for informed consent.

A slightly more complex variation of this model adds a third participant to the therapist-patient interaction: the larger society. It recognizes that every contract implies not only two contracting parties but also a social order which defines the potential terms of all contracts and enforces them when necessary. This expanded formulation is helpful in looking at the problems that emerge when there is a potential conflict between one of the contracting parties and society. Conflicts between the patient and society are illustrated by governmental intrusions into the patient's confidentiality, or enforced and involuntary treatment. Conflicts between the therapist and society are illustrated by legal constraints on practice, malpractice, and regulation of innovative therapies. A further complexity is added when we recognize that in a sense there are two patients involved in many courses of therapy, the person who enters treatment seeking change and, if the treatment is successful, the one who emerges. Their desires may not be identical and the good therapist may have to anticipate the interests of the second patient at a phase of treatment when only the first is present, just as a good parent must anticipate the interests of the adult into whom the child will mature. This formulation makes explicit conflicts between what the patient wants and what might be best for him, and raises such ethical questions as the definition of health or normalcy and the criteria of success in therapy.

Finally, we can make the model still more complex by returning to our central topic, the role of the profession for those therapists who are professionals. All therapists have multiple roles and allegiances (class, caste, nationality, politics, religion, taste, etc.) but many consider the ability to minimize the impact of these personal value systems on the treatment situation a mark of technical skill. However, one value system, that of the profession, is forcibly brought into the therapist's work and this calls our attention to a new set of ethical questions. These are often experienced as conflicts between the narrow goals of a specific therapy and broader social goals, such as the interests of future or potential patients, the evaluation of methods of treatment, the prevention of illness, or even political and economic values: peace, justice and equality. Further, the professional identity of the practitioner has an influence on the problems which we have already described in the simpler models of the therapeutic contract, since it creates another influential factor in a dynamically balanced system. We will discuss the ethical impact of professional identity in these two areas; first, the problems which can be formulated as conflicts between therapeutic and other professional or extra professional values and, second, the impact of the profession on the conflicts which exist in the patient-therapist-society interaction.

(a) Conflicts between therapeutic and other values

From an economic point of view, therapy can be seen as an exchange between the patient and the therapist, with the patient getting help with his problems and the therapist getting some reward for his efforts. However, there are aspects of the therapeutic process which cannot be explained by this simple model and which must go on if the system is going to work properly. Research and evaluation of therapy is of no particular benefit to either patient or therapist and it may actually interfere with therapy, but it is obviously desirable. The training and education of new therapists falls into the same category. Any profession of therapists will place high value on these activities and will assist its members in setting priorities and in the ethical cost accounting which is necessary to balance the interests of the patient at hand against other future or potential patients. Without a generally recognized model for such decisions, they are likely to be left to the whim of the individual practitioner and may force him into value conflicts which impair his functioning. Most often long-term goals will be sacrificed for immediate ones. For example, it could be argued that any patient who is cared for by a student or trainee is receiving less than optimal care, but if students had no experience with patients, there would soon be no new practitioners. The therapist is far more comfortable if decisions concerning the participation of students in therapy are made by professional institutions rather than determined by the therapist anew in each therapeutic relationship.

Conflicts between therapeutic and other values may extend to values which are not only extra-therapeutic but also outside the realm of the profession. Some would argue that peace, civil liberties, social justice or a particular political doctrine are of superordinate value and that when they conflict with therapy, the therapy must retreat. Therapists may be attacked for pursuing their narrow therapeutic aims without regard to the impact of their work on this ultimate value. How does one regard the therapeutic problem represented by a Russian poet who is afraid to attack his government because of neurotic conflicts, a Nazi guard who has anxiety attacks when victims scream, an American G.I. who would rather shoot heroin than Vietnamese civilians, or the leader of a great country who experiences public criticism as an attack on his masculinity and equates resigning from office with an admission that he has been castrated? More important, are political and social values relevant in deciding how to handle these problems? Does it make any difference whether communism or national socialism or capitalism or democracy are good or bad, or whether the therapist thinks that they are good or bad, in determining how each of these patients should be handled? Finally, does it make any difference whether the therapist is a member of a profession?

Non-professional practitioners may experience these conflicts as urgent issues in therapy. For example, an American soldier in the recent Vietnamese war who had neurotic conflicts which impaired his fighting effectiveness might have very different experiences were he to see two different non-professional practitioners, one of whom thought the war was just, the other who found it evil. Yet the soldier, who might not identify his problem as a value conflict and could hardly be expected to select a practitioner on the basis of political ideology, would have very little power to determine his own fate. His treatment would to a considerable extent be a function not of his problem, nor even of the therapist's understanding of that problem, but rather of the therapist's extra-therapeutic values. If the practitioner were a professional, we would expect a different result. He would have a series of values which he shared with other members of the profession and which were related to its central concern with health and therapy. These would be anticipated by the patient and explicitly stated by the therapist. In addition, of course, the therapist would have many other personal value preferences, relating in part to his many non-professional identities. However, one of his professional values would be to keep these non-professional values out of the treatment situation or, if he found this impossible, to identify himself as unable to function in a professional role in that situation. As a result, the patient could assume not that he had a therapist who was free from values (clearly impossible), but rather one who represented a set of values defined by a professional group and whose other personal values were kept relatively separate from the treatment process.

This professional therapist might find his treatment furthering a cause which he thought repugnant, or helping a political system which he despised. He yet might continue to do so because he found the values of the profession sufficiently important to act on them when they conflicted with other values. If his personal conviction were that some extra-professional value was so essential that the impact of the therapy on his patient's political beliefs or social action was ultimately more important than its impact on his health, he might try to change his patient for extra-therapeutic reasons. He would then be practising rhetoric, not therapy. This is not immoral, indeed, if one holds such beliefs, it would be immoral not to do so. However, I believe that it is immoral to disguise rhetoric as therapy, and such an individual should reveal the fact that he is no longer a member of the therapeutic profession and drop the symbols and titles which might suggest otherwise. Further, if individuals use a therapeutic screen to conceal political rhetoric, it can hardly be surprising that those with opposed political views will seek to reduce society's support of the now pseudo-therapeutic profession. If therapy is politics, then the public support of therapy is appropriately subject to political considerations.

The example I have selected relates to conflicts between therapeutic health values and political values, but the problem is essentially the same if the conflict is between health and salvation, with the therapist's religious beliefs intruding in the therapy, or between health and justice with the therapist's concern for the enforcement of the law interfering with therapeutic goals.

(b) The profession and the patient-therapist-society interaction

In our earlier discussion of conflicts in the patient-therapist-society interaction several of the 'standard' ethical problems of therapy were mentioned: disclosure, informed consent, confidentiality, involuntary treatment, licensure, regulation of experimentation, malpractice and the definition of health. What is the impact of the professional identity of the therapist on these problems? Each of them can be seen not only as a conflict of values, but also as a conflict of interests or desires between two parties. The resolution of such conflicts usually represents a compromise, with the relative strength of the conflicting parties determining their relative impact on the result.

Let us consider the problem of confidentiality as an example. In most situations society has little interest in the content of therapy and there is no problem. Occasionally society may become very interested. If the therapist feels that society's interest will promote the patient's health, as for example with an acutely suicidal patient, the therapist may ally himself with society and violate the patient's confidentiality in order to save his life. If the therapist feels that society's interest is not helpful to his patient, as in questions asked by potential employers or inquiries concerning private patterns of sexual behaviour or drug use, he may ally himself with the patient and refuse to divulge the information. In society-patient conflicts, society is usually much stronger, yet many of us would prefer that the patient win the vast majority of these conflicts. Occasional therapists may be heroic but, acting as individuals, they are likely to succumb to the pressures of the social system. The practitioner can be subpoenaed, his office burglarized and records invaded or he may even be jailed. The added strength of a professional code and ethic can redress this imbalance, reinforce the practitioners commitment to his patient's welfare, and in time even modify society's behaviour. For example, schools and colleges now widely recognize that mental health professionals must have records not available to the school administration, a principle which took time and professional activity to establish. Even prisons and military institutions are beginning to follow this practice and in time the government itself may grow to accept it! There was a time when practitioners were dismissed from employment if they did not open their records to their employers; now organizations may be ostracised by the profession if they even request such information.

The profession, in this example, enhances the power and autonomy of the professional who mediates in a conflict between the patient and society. This is analogous to the adaptive value of the autonomy of the ego in its mediating role. The introduction of the profession as an additional structure in a complex dynamic system reduces the determining authority of the remaining structures and increases the possibility of autonomous functioning.

Autonomy, of course, has its dangers as well as its virtues. These are most likely to appear when the conflict is between the patient and the practitioner, and the profession increases the power of an already too-powerful practitioner. For example, malpractice occurs, but if its detection and the patient's compensation are dependent on the co-operation of other practitioners, and if the profession is overly zealous in protecting its inept members, the net effect is to increase the practitioner's power over his patient. It is clear that a profession that is functioning well will see itself as representing patients, practitioners and society, not the practitioners alone. The autonomy of all can be enhanced by a stable and enduring value system, which protects each from intrusion by the others.

Perhaps the value of the profession emerges most clearly when it safeguards the interests of someone whose existence is clearly recognized only by the profession. Medicine's concern for the effects of genetic engineering on future generations is an example. We see a parallel in the psychotherapeutic profession's recognition that gratifying the patient's transference desires, no matter how pleasant for both patient and therapist, is inimical to the patient's future interests. Someone who does not yet exist needs a powerful lobby, and a professional ego ideal reinforced by membership in a group with shared values is the most powerful balance to the temptations of transference-countertransference collusions.

CONCLUSION

Psychotherapy is a form of behaviour control which is practised within and outside professions. It raises many ethical problems and the relationship of the practitioner to a profession affects these problems. The advantages of professions have been emphasized, although real and potential disadvantages have been noted.

Other forms of behaviour control, such as teaching or social engineering, are more likely to be practised by individuals who do not have a strong professional identity. In part this can be explained by the more public nature of these activities, along with the greater likelihood that the client will have a realistic view of the practitioner. There are more likely to be multiple forces in society outside the client and practitioner that will prevent an undesirable concentration of power in one of the principals. The private nature of therapy, together with the likelihood that the client will have little power in his conflicts with society, make the advantages of professional organization of the controllers particularly great.

Professions are recognized as having expertise in an area of knowledge. However, they also have moral expertise in those areas of human experience which are available only with their special knowledge. It is important that their moral expertise not be generalized beyond their areas of special experience, but it is also important that it be recognized within these areas. This recognition involves the delegation of certain social functions, including the authority to make moral decisions to the profession. This should be balanced by the practitioner's readiness to accept the profession's scrutiny and standards, and by the profession's exercise of its power on behalf of all of its constituencies, not only its members.

REFERENCES

Freidson, E. (1973). *Profession of Medicine*. New York: Dodd, Mead.

Goode, W. J. (1960). Encroachment, charlatanism, and the emerging profession: psychology, medicine, and sociology. *Am. sociol. Rev.* **25**, 908–914.

Himmelstein, J. & Michels, R. (1973). The right to refuse psychoactive drugs. *Hastings Center Report*. 3, (3) 8–11.

Hughes, E. C. (1959). The study of occupations. In R. Merton (ed.), *Sociology Today*. New York: Basic Books.

Levi, E. H. (1971). The place of professional education in the life of the university. *Ohio State Law J.* 32, 229–230.

Michels, R. (1973). Ethical issues of psychological and psychotherapeutic means of behaviour control. *Hastings Center Report*. 3, (2), 11–13.

Veatch, R.M. (1973). Generalization of expertise. *Hastings Center Studies* 1, 29–40.

Part Eight

Psychotherapy and Being

In the previous sections, we have examined various traditional and contemporary forms of psychotherapy; cultural and community influences on these forms; the economic and social class factors that directly influence the practice of psychotherapy; the settings of psychotherapy, both in and outside of hospitals; and the people, adults and children, who partake of psychotherapy. In great measure our discussion, while not technical, has revolved nonetheless around many of the mechanical aspects of psychotherapy, or what we might properly call the social, environmental, or even philosophical considerations of psychotherapy. Now, in concluding, we need to say a word about some of the human issues, if you will, of psychotherapy; for it goes without saying that we are dealing with a characteristically human phenomenon.

It is clear from the reports of clients as well as psychotherapists that many people seek out therapy because of their difficulty in handling clear-cut and even tangible problems. All sorts of these apparently well-delineated problems are presented to psychotherapists every day. Symptoms, as psychiatrists might call them, may include sexual dysfunction, depression, extreme anxiety, alcoholism, even uncontrollable urges to gamble. But in each of these cases, the client is able to articulate some discrete area or topic of disturbance. It is also true, however, that many people seek out psychotherapists for disturbances of a far more diffuse nature. Indeed, when they are obliged to present their problems—or more likely, fill out that part of the inevitable intake form on which one must describe one's symptoms—they feel at a loss. Their thoughts are tentative, ambiguous, unformed. In fact, one almost believes, in listening to people like this, that they have consulted a psychotherapist in order to determine for themselves just what it is that troubles them. Years ago, a series of studies seemed to suggest that women presented ambiguous symptoms in psychotherapy more often than men. The findings, therefore, suggested that whereas men struggle with more "real" issues of living, women struggle with existential dilemmas. It may be that recent transformations in men's and women's roles in our culture would cause shifts in the results of similar studies undertaken now. But a more significant point may be drawn from all this.

Psychotherapy plays a major role in helping people adjust to, or better withstand, the stresses that their environment causes them to experience, as well as those stresses that they seem to generate within themselves. In this way, psychotherapy plays something of a social control role, just as it plays an educational role for the client. Presently, in an era of heightened self-discovery, or at least a culture-wide expression of the need for, or fascination with, self-discovery, psychotherapy takes on new roles, and exhibits new emphases. But if it is to be genuinely valuable both to the client and the culture—which is the point at which we commenced this volume—then psychotherapy, both as a research and a treatment strategy, must help us to understand what precisely is the nature of human behavior, human personality, and the relationship between the personality and the society in which the person exhibiting it is formed and lives. This is no mean challenge. In fact, one of the supremely significant aspects of psychoanalytic theory, derived, as we know, from the practice of psychoanalytic psychotherapy, was its conception of the human mind, and indeed of man's and woman's destiny. We know too, that it was not a rather happy or optimistic picture Freud painted of Western industrial society. Still, optimistic or not, accurate or not, the theory which grew out of the practice of a specific form of psychotherapy was closely allied with or had implications for, the understanding of cultures and societies.

Said in dangerously simplistic terms, people continue to look to psychotherapy to help them understand and appreciate the nature of being alive, the nature of the mind, as well as aspects of their behaviour that seem uncontrollable, peculiar, or enigmatic. In learning about oneself, moreover, one learns about the nature of the species, and hence psychotherapy continues to offer the possibility of self-understanding in anthropological, social psychological, and even theological terms. As we said earlier, because of its very evolution, psychotherapy cannot help but enlighten us about ourselves and our culture. But it also has the possibility of doing something else—namely affecting our sensitivity to our lives and to our fellow beings. For psychotherapy is built upon cognitive or intellectual foundations as well as emotional or affective foundations. We learn, and we feel when engaged in the psychotherapeutic process. Not only that, we learn how to feel, how to feel about self-learning, how to feel about feelings. It all seems a rather dizzying adventure, but we might merely suggest in summarizing the point that, like a good novel, psychotherapy should enlighten us in the matter of our lives and living generally.

In light of this discussion, it is hardly surprising that people would consult *psychotherapists for both tangible and utterly vague reasons. In this manner, they appear to feel content dealing with their psychotherapists as though they were doctors, teachers, counsellors, parents, ministers, friends, or somehow, a rare combination of all of these. By the same token, this need for help, guidance, enlightment says something about the requirements of a culture as well as the needs of specific individuals. And it says something too about the natural confusion of identity, both professional and personal, experienced by many psychotherapists. Once again, it is a dizzying adventure, a gargantuan human challenge and responsibility. The question that remains is whether or not the men and women of our or any other culture are able ethically and humbly to accept the challenge and continue to keep their senses trained on both their individual clients and the culture which affects their clients as well as the theories, techniques, styles, and definitions of their trade. If openness to experience is one of the hallmark goals of the psychotherapeutic enterprise, then it must be subscribed to by practitioners and clients alike. We tend to believe, although some may not approve of the metaphor, that openness to experience implies growth, emergence, and that which is generally freeing and ultimately life-giving. If psychotherapy's great contribution could be the promise of hope for both the individual and an entire citizenry, we would all benefit from this most complex and delicate act.*

23

On Hope: Its Nature and Psychotherapy

HAROLD N. BORIS

If one searches the standard psychoanalytic literature (I have in mind, for instance, Freud, A. Freud, Fenichel, Fairbairn, H. Segal) one is apt to find little in the index between 'homosexuality' and 'hysteria' save 'hunger'. 'Hope' itself is nowhere to be seen.

This is no accident. Psychoanalysis is primarily a theory concerning desire and its vicissitudes. And contrary to its popular usage, hope is, as I shall attempt to show, something quite different.

The relatively scant attention paid to hope by the psychoanalyst[1] leads the would-be student of the subject to the poets, who do not overlook its significance in the affairs of mankind. Even so, one comes away from a rereading of the poets with the sense of hope's ineffability. Consider, e.g., the two versions of the lovely story of Pandora (as commented upon by Bulfinch, 1855).

The first woman was named Pandora. She was made in heaven, every god

---

[1]Erikson is one exception. He (Erikson, 1964, p. 115) defines hope as the 'enduring belief in the attainability of fervent wishes, in spite of the dark urges and rages which mark the beginning of existence'.

Reprinted by permission from *International Journal of Psycho-Analysis*, 3 (1976), 139–150. Copyright © 1976 by Harold N. Boris.

contributing something to perfect her.... Thus equipped, she was conveyed to earth and presented to Epimetheus, who gladly accepted her, though cautioned by his brother to beware of Jupiter and his gifts. Epimetheus had in his house a jar, in which were kept certain noxious articles... One day [Pandora] slipped off the cover and looked in. Forthwith there escaped a multitude of plagues for hapless man,—such as gout, rheumatism and colic for his body, and envy, spite and revenge for his mind,[2]—scattered themselves far and wide. Pandora hastened to replace the lid! but alas! the whole contents had escaped, one thing only excepted, which lay at the bottom and that was *hope*.

'So,' remarks Bulfinch, 'we see at this day whatever evils were abroad, hope never entirely leaves us; and while we have that no amount of other ills can make us completely wretched'.

There is, however, the other version of the myth:

Pandora was sent in good faith by Jupiter to bless man; she was furnished with a box containing her marriage presents, into which every god had put some blessing. She opened the box incautiously, and the blessings all escaped, *hope* only excepted.

Bulfinch comments: 'This story seems more probable than the former; for how could *hope*, so precious a jewel as it is, have been kept in a jar full of all manner of evils, as in the former statement?' (Bulfinch, 1855, pp. 16–17).

How indeed, unless hope is not the blessing Bulfinch takes it to be.

But whatever the case, hope has *some* role to play in human events and as such it promises to repay serious study.

The way I shall proceed is to precipitate out desire, with which, thanks to psychoanalytic theory, we are more familiar and, having subtracted the role of desire from various situations, see what may be left.

I. THE NATURE OF HOPE

Hope vs. desire

Here are three possible instances:

1. A hungry child sits glumly refusing to eat his bowl of cereal. His mother thereupon dips into the cereal, tastes it and elaborately pats her stomach, saying, 'Mmm..., good'. The child then eats the cereal hungrily.

2. A patient, who for various reasons is feeling quite overwhelmed at a new job, believes that the people she overhears in the corridor outside her office are

---

[2]The particular aptness of these three qualities, 'envy, revenge, and spite' will be taken up later. Professor David Belmont (personal communication) of Washington University supports Bulfinch's translation of these words from Hesiod's version of the myth.

trying to tell her something. Precisely what they are attempting to communicate is difficult for her to tell. She demands of me whether I believe that these conversations need not be random or coincidental or whether (here she becomes very angry) I believe her to suffer from paranoid delusions.

3. A young woman feels fat and flabby, though she is only several pounds overweight. She feels unfit to be interested in a sexual relationship with a man, though she experiences sexual frustration. She wonders if the trouble she takes to keep herself fat is not a way of avoiding men. Her life is going by; soon she will be beyond child-bearing age. This is a source of great misery.

In each of these instances one will find, I believe, something more or other than desire at issue. Desire itself, as we know from Freud, adheres to the pleasure principle. It wants gratification and it wants gratification now. Although desire will come to accept moderation to the reality principle in order that pain may be evaded or eased, its acceptance of delay and modification is reluctant and, at root, time is only a fair-weather friend to desire. Desire, moreover, wants a real object and real fulfilment. In its headlong coursing towards real fulfilment it will take the path of least resistance: if it's not near the girl it loves, it will love the girl it's near. When near, it will accommodate, going from active to passive or from one sensual modality to another, adventitiously. When still frustrated, desire will fissure from its aggressive component and dissolve into rage and frequently into jealousy. In the end, however, if desire continues to be thwarted, the object of that desire will be replaced with another object more available to it, as Freud (1917) observed.

Goethe epitomized desire in Faust who, meeting Mephistopheles, wagered that he would never be caught experiencing desire:

> Let that day be the last for me!
> When thus I hail the Moment flying:
> Ah, stay Moment—thou art so fair
> Then bind me in thy bounds undying,
> My final ruin then declare! (My translation).

Contrast Faust's situation with those represented in the three instances to which I have previously alluded.

In the first, the mother appears to have surmised that hungry as the child was, he nevertheless hoped for something better. Her elaborate pantomime said: This cereal is not only what you desire, it is all one could hope for.

In the second, that concerning the young woman who felt that the conversations she overheard were not random or coincidental, the patient is suggesting a view that two theories, hers and my own, appeared to her to be competing for facts on which to feed and grow strong. Indeed, each theory, if it could not acquire the good facts for itself, might be driven to spoil those facts lest the other theory profit from them. In her view, my hopes would be served by the idea that she had paranoid delusions: her hope was that she need not resort to the necessity of experiencing mistakes and going through the slow drudgery of learning from them. To serve the theory based on her hopes, it helped her to believe that the events in question were not random but rather were suffused with meaning and significance. Indeed, so ardent was her hope that she preferred remaining unable to decipher the import of these overheard conversations to making the possible discovery that they were empty of meaning.

The third instance shares with the second the preference for a degree of ambiguity. The patient fears that if it is not fat that is wrong with her body, it will turn out to be something else, about which there is a great deal less she can do. She hopes that it is flab and fat that is the matter and is prepared to enslave her desires to the ascendancy of that hope. Her feeling fat is thus considered a defect akin to a fault. The patient takes pains to keep this defect, for not only does it conceal the real defect, it preserves the ambiguity. I do not realize my hopes, she seems to say, because something is wrong with me and not because my hopes are unfulfilable.

In these comments I have already used the term 'hope' to speak of what I do not believe to be desire. Desire, I have suggested, is epitomized in Goethe's 'stay, Moment'. Hope, let me now propose, is epitomized by Dante, who placed at the gateway to the Inferno the sign: 'Abandon all hope, ye who enter here'.

Hope resides in time and it is lost, therefore, both to the timelessness of eternity and the instantaneousness of the moment.

These twin check-reins upon hope—eternity and the moment—reveal its paradoxical nature: hope is potential, and potentiality is lost both to actualization and to finality. As Bion (1961, pp. 151-2) puts it, 'Only by remaining a hope does hope persist'.

The stayed moment, the static situation, the constant object—these are the conditions propitious for desire. But for hope they are too finite, too unambiguous. Hope flourishes in change, uncertainty and flux. Clinically, for example one notices that when people begin to feel quite hopeless, they commonly begin to change almost everything that is not nailed down in their lives—job, spouse, locale and even health (cf. Jaques, 1965).

Such hopelessness is, of course, not the loss of hope itself. It is the losing of hope for one's hopes. The hopes remain, and it is the purpose of this hypomanic activity to rekindle hope for one's hopes. Should these bouts of change and flux fail to accomplish this, people may freeze into paralysis—depressive psychosis, autism and catatonia are instances of this—as if, by stopping themselves, they can stop unchanging time, which has now become the dreadful foe of hope.

An example of this is provided by Searles, one of whose patients responded to the various shifts in his demeanour or posture by experiencing 200 or 300 therapists in her room during any given session—'as if,' Searles remarks, 'in watching a motion picture, one saw it not as continuous motion, but as broken into a series of stills; the stills', he continues, 'remained on the scene and accumulated'. No one can surmise that this patient's hatred of time induced her to convert motion, which, of course, takes place through time, into 'stills' which she could instead distribute into space and so deny time's passage. Searles adds: 'She let me know also on another occasion that whenever I changed posture she identified me as some different person from her past.' (Searles, 1965, p. 307).

When a hope is genuinely abandoned, its renunciation is followed not by despair but by the burgeoning of desire; the child of my first instance, having let loose his hope of a superior sort of feeding, felt not hopeless but hungry.

This fundamental antagonism between hope and desire is crucial. Freud, I think was searching for this in 'Beyond the Pleasure Principle' (Freud, 1920) but came up awry by supposing that the antagonist to Eros, or what I have been calling desire, was a death instinct. Freud (1937) developed further his clinical conviction that something beyond the sources of the usual resistances ran counter to the lively, lusty emergence of the libido. Was not the time-limit he imposed upon the Wolf Man that death-knell for time which itself fuelled the hope that kept desire at bay?

But it was earlier, in 'Mourning and Melancholia' (Freud, 1917), that Freud drew the antagonism most sharply. In the face of loss, desire will take the path of least resistance and find a more accommodating substitute object. But, as we know, this does not always or even frequently happen. Instead, people elect to imagine that the object is within themselves, either as a part of the self, endowing them with various attributes, or as a somewhat separate figure remarking, cruelly or kindly, on their attributes—parts, that is, of the ego-ideal or superego respectively.

In this latter choice (internalization, introjection) I think we also see hope's hand at work, for where desire's aim is the giving and getting of pleasure, hope longs to have and possess.

But to make these and other distinctions between hope and desire plainer, I have to suggest something of the sources and origins of hope.

The genesis of hope

In attempting this I shall necessarily have to be very speculative indeed, taking facts from here, notions from there and assembling them all with an aura of coherence which belies the highly speculative nature of what I am about to say.

Piaget reports (Piers, 1972) the following findings from an experiment. Seven-year-olds are shown two balls of plasticene clay of the same size. The children examine them and agree that they are of the same size. The experimenter then rolls one of the spheres of clay into an elongated snake shape. The children watch this operation. But when asked which shape has more clay, they say the cylinder does. When the cylindrical shape is patted back into a sphere, they say that now both are equal again.

Similarly, children feel that a full narrow glass holds more water than a short squat glass, even when these vessels have been filled from an ordinary glass and poured back again so the children can see that the same volume of water has gone into the wide and narrow glasses.

To my mind, these experiments (among others) suggest that people have ideas about things which are powerful enough to induce them to disregard both empirical experience and their own good powers of inference. That is, they have a sense of how things *should* be and this sense of the seemliness or fitness of things prevails over actual experience.

Kant and Bion are among the relatively few who have dealt with this phenomenon.

Kant (1781) suggested that people have what he called 'empty thoughts' to which experiences with real events are more or less approximate. Bion (1963) holds that people have preconceptions for which experience more or less provides realizations. Such so-called 'structuralists' as Lévi-Strauss, the anthropologist, and Chomsky, the linguist, also find it logically necessary to infer that people have inherent ideas about experience. These ideas they call 'deep' or 'metastructures' and they view these structures as giving a shape to experience prior to, sometimes independent of, the influences of actual private or cultural experiences. (Chomsky 1972; Gardner, 1973; Leach, 1970; Lévi-Strauss, 1966, 1973; Lyons, 1970; Piaget, 1973, and Piaget in Piers, 1972.)

These metastructures, empty ideas, or preconceptions are like flexible containers into which experience, when poured, gives shape and substance. But they are not without their own shape, as Piaget's experiments show. Ethologists, for example, report countless instances along the following lines.

An experiment was done to investigate what qualities of the female attract the grayling butterfly (Tinbergen, 1958, 1965). Mock-ups, models, were made in which every conceivable variable—size, shape, colour, flying speed, flying pattern, etc.—could be systematically altered singly and in patterns in order to learn which ingredients proved to be the critical ones. Colour, as it happened, proved to be of vast interest: the darker the colour of the female mock-ups, the greater the number of males which would fly from their roosting tree in far-ranging pursuit. A jet-black colour had the greatest arousal value. But that colour does not exist in nature. It is as if the grayling butterfly has an idea of what the female of the species should look like and the closer the actual female approximates to that 'platonic ideal', the more satisfactory she is.

The room left over in the preconception after actual experience has contributed shape and substance appears to exercise a frustration no less painful, perhaps indeed even more redolent of danger, than the frustration of desire. As Piaget's experiments reveal, children, at least for some years, deny the teachings of experience in order to cling to a view of the world based on how things should be. Surely this same tendency was in evidence in the people represented by the instances I have given earlier.

If we take this idea of hopeful preconception as something inherent, we are able to put it side by side with traditional libido theory.

That theory begins with the infant and the breast. The infant is hungry and, more, he wants to suckle. Then there is, or is not, the breast. If there is, things go fairly well. If there is not, the infant has to cope with pain or terror, frustration and rage.

But now let us introduce into this situation the notion that the baby has an idea of what the breast should be like. If the idea is that it should be there and full and calm and it is, the actuality will exactly match the idea, the hope will be congruent with the desire and, as such, the hope will be, as it were, quite invisible. So let us suppose instead that the breast is full and there, but instead of being calm, as the baby we are imagining hopes, it is active.[3] Now the infant faces a conflict. His desires for milk and suckling

[3]Films or direct observations of infants feeding will not fail to illustrate sensitively such differences among mothers.

are fulfilable enough, but his hopes will be somewhat thwarted. It is easy to see from this very early situation how the relationships between hope and desire can be antagonistic, with hope going to the *quality* of the experience and desire to issues of satiation. But we can equally see that there exists not one but two sources of frustration. The one is the familiar frustration of desire. The other is the frustration of hope. Indeed, there are circumstances in which one frustration cannot be eased without at least in part incurring the other. An example familiar in psychoanalytic theory is this:

Another of baby's ideas for the breast—his hope—is that it is a breast that is his. His desire for the breast is that it feeds and nurtures him. When it occurs to baby that the breast, though provident and regularly nurturant, is nevertheless not his, a crisis—the so-called anaclitic depression—takes place. It is, however, a mistake to regard the crisis as one of desire, as weaning is. The crisis is one of hope; hence the depression. Patients are usually obliging enough to reveal that the depression, the emptiness, is precisely where on them the breast was supposed to be: the depression being literally that concave configuration left from where the breast was supposed to be, but is not. Baby is outraged not because his desires for nurturance and suckling are frustrated but because mother has a breast and he has not.

I am so far speaking of phenomena Freud and others have dealt with in terms of primary and secondary narcissism. But it will be clear that in thinking in terms of hope I am re-sorting matters such that hopes have not primarily to do with the self and only by projection or projective identification (Klein, 1957; Kohut, 1968) with others, but with what I think are more basic, i.e. metastructural, antitheses.

That is, the realization that mother has a breast may fulfil the infant's oral desire, providing him with pleasure and gratitude. But at the same time it fulfils his preconception that he should have a something-or-other of his own with evidentiary substance: The something-or-other now turns out to be a breast. This bite, as it were, of the apple of knowledge produces an 'Aha, so that's what I should have' and then a state of acute envy.

Later, the same sort of preconceptions will hold sway in the Oedipus complex. There will be not only desire for sensual satisfactions from the mother, but hope for satisfactions at least the equal of those which father is presumed to enjoy. Similarly, women who find satisfaction from their love-making with men may nevertheless feel depressed (again the concavity) by the presence of a penis which, however well it fills their desires, does not fulfil their preconceptions. The patient I mentioned who keeps herself overweight, frequently keeps herself from intercourse and almost always from orgasm. She is fearful that the gratification of her desires will undermine her hopes.[4] It is possible to speculate whether the stage of latency is similarly motivated more strongly by hopes, capitulating only when desires, rejuvenated by the well-springs of puberty, grow too strong for it.

The persistence of the attraction to the oedipal parent is, as we know, awesome indeed. Is this a function simply of desire? Or is it that the parent fits the preconceived

---

[4]I believe this fear that their desires will erode the strength of their hopes to be crucial in understanding the schizophrenic.

hope? It is so frequent clinically as almost to beggar mention to find such attitudes as 'if I can't have my parent, I don't want anyone' or 'whomever I can have can't be the right person because, by definition, the right person is the person I can't have'.

But lest we suspect 'imprinting', it is important to note that people maintain something akin to a lifelong shopping list of hopes, for which they collect 'evidence'. Surely any psychotherapist who has heard other therapists and other methods extolled by patients who feel their hopes languishing as a result of the therapy will be familiar with the pastiche patients form to feed and fortify their hopes.

Hope, to summarize this portion of my paper, arises from preconceptions of how things and experiences should be. These preconceptions at once structure and are shaped by their encounters with actuality. In so far as they are matched by actual experience, hope and desire can coexist and become co-terminous. But where preconceptions and actuality are too far apart, hope comes into being as separate from desire and in fact serves as a restraint upon desires more fundamental, in my view, than anxiety, the defences or other structures of the mind.

Biological, social and cultural considerations

To make this point concerning the function of hope in restraining of desire clearer, it may be useful to view matters against the background of man's biological evolutionary heritage. Present biological thought continues to offer strong ethological and experimental support for Darwin's thesis that species are not merely passively selected by the exigencies of their ecology. They also select among themselves and this too determines which genes survive to be passed down the generations.

For such active selectivity, e.g., that of mating partners, to occur, two factors must be present. There must be characteristics which distinguish members of a species not only from members of other species but from one another. And there must be a predilection to choose from amongst this varied array. Without such morphological characteristics as size, colour, age, shape or such acquired discriminates as territory or dominance position in a social hierarchy to choose from, the predilection for choosiness would be meaningless. But equally, were there not choosiness, were choice random or governed by such chance factors as proximity or propinquity, the significance and function of the characteristics to choose from (indeed, in all likelihood the characteristics themselves) would ebb away into the mists of time. Something to choose from and a predilection to choose are both, therefore, essentials.

As Mayr (1972) observes:

It is well known that the mating drive in the males of many species is so strong that they display not only to females of their own species, but also to females of related species. If the females were equally lacking in discrimination, an enormous amount of hybridization among closely related species would take place. Since hybrids are ordinarily of considerably lower fitness, natural selection will favor two developments: First, any genetic change that would make the females more discriminating, and second, any characteristics in the males that would reduce the probability that they be confused with the males of another species. Such characteristics are designated isolating mechanisms (p. 98).

Mayr notes that earlier, in 1942, he had 'called attention to the fact that the conspicuous male characteristics sometimes were lost in island birds when there were not other closely related species on the same island. The loss of these characters was apparently due to a relaxation of selection for the distinctive isolating mechanisms' (ibid).

The inhibition of the procreative drive pending the approximation of the object to the 'preconception' paradoxically facilitates the release of the drive. That is, the readier and more assured the capacity not to choose A, the easier and quicker the capacity to choose B. Though sexual selectivity involves this procedure, so too do feeding and parenting, eliminatory and aggressive actions and interactions. In all of these, inhibition until the 'right' conditions are present makes for greater ease of release once the 'right' conditions are present.

How far animal preconception represents a variation upon what I have been supposing to be human preconception is subject to the same uncertainties as the resolution of how far animal drives are variants of human drives, or what I have been calling desire. For myself, I find it reasonable to put forth, not as a substantive analogy but as a hypothetical construct, that preconception in man may be a residue of Darwinian processes of natural selection such that hope's effect upon desire can be viewed as having a species-specific survival value in carrying out nature's blueprints for man. Hope holds desire from taking its any old course of least resistance and it keeps desire from static satiety by calling it to 'finer' possibilities.

In proposing such a construct I do not intend in any way to minimize the role of man's social universe; man is born into a social order, the values, ideals and sanctions of which importantly shape his hopes, aspirations and expectations. But neither should it be forgotten that the social universe was no less born of man: he shapes and reshapes it, even while it does him.

By regarding man as the shaper of his social universe and not exclusively as its product, one is in turn able to see beyond the unique differences among particular societies to what all social systems were endowed with by man.

No known culture, for example, is without a system governing the relations of kin and hence non-kinship groups. And none is without a religion. The explanations for these facts are so complex as to be by no means in hand. But hope, as I have been regarding it, permits at least certain hypotheses to unfold.

When hope attains ascendancy over desire, future time takes on a correspondingly magnified importance. If hope is to be maintained against the erosions of hopelessness and desire, time needs to be conserved and preserved—the more so since the pleasures attendant upon the gratification of desire are not present to console or compensate for the loss of hope. Nor will they be until hope is renounced and desire given its head. The burgeoning importance of the future escalates the horror and fear of death,[5] clinically so central to the suicide (and illustrated so aptly by a patient who, even while seriously attempting to kill herself, was giving up smoking). As antidote to such fear, a future beyond death's limits upon hope must be devised, and maintained free of jeopardy.

The social order—family, group, tribe and nation—has, to this effort, a considerable contribution to make. The removal of personal hopes to the group—the sense, fantasied or real, of being part of something (or it of one) larger, stronger and more enduring than one's self—offers a powerful ameliorative to the incursions of mortality. But in return for the opportunity of vesting his hopes in the social unit, the individual must relinquish his desires of it: he eschews cannibalizing it; neither may he plunder or foul it: and he is constrained to follow its rules of exogamy and incest (Boris, 1970; Boris et al., 1975).

Religion, too, is ordinarily organized to afford reprieve from the fatal limits of real time through construction of an afterlife or one or another form of deathlessness. Although religion competes with the secular group for its use as a source of hope, as the story of Abraham and Isaac suggests, accommodations ('Render unto Caesar . . .') between the two are generally to be found.

Religion's offer of reincarnation or other versions of transubstantiation, like the group's offer of investiture, is not without its price: desires must be abdicated or taken only in symbolic form; but in return there is the proffer that hope may be realized without being lost to fulfilment. Indeed, lest hope be lost on the way towards the hereafter, certain remedies are available. Perhaps chief among these is the endeavour by the mystic to reassimilate hopes, with their specific preconceptions, into a global hope which has no preconception other than the direct and consummate apprehension of God (see in the list of references: St John of the Cross; also St. Augustine on the relation between hope and faith). Specific hopes are more vulnerable to fulfilment and renunciation; hope itself is more easily retained. Time, too, is transfigurable through altered states of consciousness induced by drugs or other means, so that time may be made more elastic while people await the ultimate. Finally there are more 'worldly' measures, ceremonies and rituals, employed to restore flagging hope.

Still, hopes and hope require other sources of nourishment, and these are built into other parts of culture. If, as Weisman (1965, p. 235) observes, 'The most comprehensive antithesis of a meaningless existence is to believe that whatever happens has significance', science (and, indeed, madness) shares with religion the task of rejuvenating hope with infusions of meaning.

But it is not alone the contents, the reassuring news that the universe is lawful and

[5]I use the words 'horror and fear' of death to refer specifically to the state of mind that obtains when hope is regnant over desire and hopes are propelled into the future. When desire is paramount, fear of losing the means and opportunity of taking pleasure in the object, e.g. the castration-death transformation, is pre-eminent. When hope is vested in the group or afterlife, the horror and fear are proportionately diminished and people, as in war, often face death with docility and relative equanimity.

fathomable, that restores hope. As in art, form (e.g. the 'elegance' of the scientific solution) has its contributions to make.[6] Both, in the Aristotelian proposition, imitate but improve on nature. Aesthetic pleasure, that sense of exhilaration and admiration, reflects this. In what is aesthetically pleasing that-which-is has been brought into closer identity with preconception. That is, there has been an 'improvement' in the sense of ownership of that-which-is and there has been a 'refinement' of its quality, for both ownership and quality appear to be intrinsic to the preconception of what is seemly and fit, and both, accordingly, inspire and sustain hope.

II. THE PSYCHOTHERAPY [7] OF HOPE

When life becomes nearly unbearable, and a being can change neither of those twin prongs of his nature—his hopes or his desires—any further, and yet the events conditions and people on whom he depends for the fulfilment of his hopes or his desires are also not to be changed, he ordinarily takes that one further, fateful option open to him: unable to change his experience, he changes what he experiences of what he experiences.

Much of psychoanalytic theory, as indeed much of everyday psychotherapeutic practice, is taken up with these alterations of the experience of what one experiences. These involve people's use of the mechanisms of defence. Perhaps the simplest way to review these for purposes of discussing the psychotherapy of hope is to recall Aesop's fable of the fox and the sour grapes.

In that fable, it will be recalled, the fox was unable to reach the good, sweet grapes. To relieve his intense feelings of frustration—the frustration of his desire and the frustrations of the hope he had that he was a fox who could reach grapes—he modified the terms of the experience. The original terms were something like this: I, a hungry fox, want to reach sweet, good grapes. The fox changed these in the simplest way possible. He used denial; the terms of condition then read: I, a hungry fox, cannot reach bad, sour grapes.

If that change were one which did not offer him the relief from his twin frustrations, the fox had still other options for changing the terms of the experience. He might, for example, have changed the idea that grapes themselves were involved. Or he might have changed the idea that he was hungry. Or, for that matter, he might have been driven to change the idea that he was a fox.

The use of denial, a subtractive procedure, is, however, not the only one open to beings. Indeed, it is often all too weak a solution to the pressing pain of frustrated desire or the anguish of thwarted hope. Accordingly, the fox may have used, in addition, the introduction of terms which might buttress his attempt to alter what he experienced of the experience. That is to say, in addition to denial, he might have constructed a cover story. He might, for example have said: I, a bad fox, cannot reach

[6]Greenacre's (1953) observation that the middle part of a three-part dream will always refer to the genitals is an example of the preconscious use of form as a source of hope.
[7]I use psychotherapy in its generic sense to include psychoanalysis primarily but not to exclude psychoanalytically 'orientated' modifications.

good, sweet grapes because I am bad. This is the sort of procedure that the patient in the third of the instances I previously presented employed by keeping herself somewhat overweight. She was saying, it is the palpable presence of my flab that is what is wrong. One can see from this the great value of elements taken into the superego and kept there as manic defences against the depressing realization that life may be simply what it is.

But whatever the precise fantasies employed to transform and transfigure the original experience into something more tolerable, the fateful results are inevitably the same: in exchange for his relative freedom from the pain of frustration or humbling of hope, the individual becomes prey to anxiety and insecurity.

If, however, as Homer observed, happiness consists in being able to make use of whatever the gods toss our way, the task for the psychotherapist is obvious. It is to enable our patients to experience—really re-experience—the original experience, to tolerate it, to learn from it, and thus be free to take such other experiences as they can fashion together with life and to derive benefit from these.

This is as true for the psychotherapy of hope as for that of desire. But having said that, one is close to exhausting the likenesses. Desire will be shy of frustration; it will be surrounded by an array of defensive manoeuvres and security operations, and will come screened and transfigured. But its nature is appetitive and urgent; if it takes time, it hates the time it takes. So sooner or later, via the transference, desire and its crises will unfold for therapist and patient to know about.

Hope, as we have seen, having a different sort of nature, does not ordinarily come to the fore. It is vested—e.g. in the very outcome of the therapy, months or years away—and, being vested, follows an almost Parkinsonian law: it spreads, elongates, permeates to fill the space and time and possibility available to it. As such, special measures are required if the analysis of hope is not to be left to that scant period of time between the establishing of the date for termination and termination itself.

I shall address myself to these measures, but I want first to set the backdrop in terms of which various approaches or procedures can be viewed. The ideal datum, the condition from which both patient and therapist can best work, is present when the patient is experiencing a crisis of hope in the here-and-now of a given session and will talk of it fully precisely as it occurs. This means that the crisis has to do with the therapy, the therapist and the patient in the instant. That is the ideal, and it is seldom realized. For one thing, when the patient is feeling hopeless, he is ordinarily not inclined to cooperate by communicating his experience; but he will convey it and, by certain procedures to which I will come presently, conveyance will cumulatively develop into communication.

Much stands in the way of this happening, however, and these impediments must be pared away as best one can.

First of all, as I have already implied, there is the fact of therapy itself which functions as a powerful source of hope. About this there is nothing one can do; but it is of no conceivable use to the patient to aid and abet his hopeful attitude towards therapy. Therapy is a basic research project, not unlike any in molecular biology or nuclear physics. Two—or more people when a group is involved—join forces to make 'a systematic investigation of self-deceptions and their motivations', to use Hartmann's (1959, p. 20) words. As in all such endeavours in basic research, one may learn something, but whether it will result in breakthroughs or indeed have applications is uncertain. I do not know what the figures are for successes in those other fields, (if a word like 'success' is applicable) but outcome studies of psychotherapy certainly would not engender general optimism in any save the sort of people who regularly buy the Brooklyn Bridge. No therapist has reason to 'sell' therapy—or even to recommend it. The only thing he can do is offer to share the attempt at research and discovery and, along with his patient, see what they shall see.

Of course this stance can be assumed only by that therapist whose own hopes are not dependent on the progress of his patients. Therapists also invest therapy with hope; as a supervisor, one frequently hears reports of progress or, alternatively, of stasis in terms that cause one to wonder how distinguishable the patient's hopes are from the therapist's. Perhaps the kinship of therapy to the religious systems of the preliterate peoples of the world, reported by anthropologists (Erikson, 1963; Mitchell, personal communication) needs closer attention. But psychotherapy is not a substitute for religion or, for that matter, for education or socialization, as people sometimes think. It has its own function. And as in the psychotherapy of desire the therapist ordinarily learns through his own analysis and supervision to become free of making his patients the object of his desire—his voyeurism, rescue impulses and the like; so in the psychotherapy of hope the therapist must recognize the force and play of what he hopes for, for or from his patients.

One way of doing so is for him to notice the verbs he uses in speaking of his work. If in making a therapeutic alliance he hopes to convert the patient to a psychodynamic viewpoint or if in making an interpretation he hopes to shed light, he is performing a religious function. Socialization functions will reveal themselves in hopes to instill or inculcate or to provide corrective experiences. Offering support to a patient or a faction in a patient is a socio-political activity, better left to affairs of state. Winnicott (1965) observed that he could tell when his doing of therapy slipped over into educating by his use of phrases beginning with 'moreover'. The function of sage or guru is in evidence when the therapist proposes a view of life: 'What did you expect?' or 'Do you think you're the only one?' or 'Who promised you a rose garden?' Schafer (1970) has identified several of these life-views. But the point to be made here is that the therapist's vicarious hopes for his patients or his need for daily rejuvenation of hopes of his own soon find him doing something other than psychotherapy. An interpretation given to get a patient to stop doing, thinking or feeling one way and get on to something else instead is not an interpretation; it is a legal brief. Bion (1970, p. iv) has remarked that it is important not only to understand a patient's communication, but the use to which it is being put. Much the same holds true for the therapist in regarding his own communications.

These divestitures of hope in therapy itself help the patient to become self-conscious of his own investments of hope in therapy and able then to deal with them when he is so inclined. But ordinarily before he will do so, he will shift his hope from his preconceptions of therapy to the person of the therapist himself. Flattering as this is, the fact remains that hope vested precludes crises of hope from being re-experienced. Once again, though the therapist cannot (nor should) do anything to repudiate this investiture directly, it will be important for him to determine whether he shares this charismatic view of himself. Some therapists do. They have a touching faith in their teachers, their reading, their ideas and for them therapy is a process whereby they await the opportunity to make revelations based on these. Whether or not the revelation is correct is not at issue here. What is at issue is that such a procedure orients the patient to the therapist as the font of insights and thus hope. Neither patient nor therapist are much interested in learning from the experiences they jointly have. The therapist has already learned all he wants to know from elsewhere and is impatiently (or even patiently) awaiting the opportunity to deliver himself of some portion of it. The patient, far from attending to himself and what he is experiencing, is behaving like a contestant in a quiz show—say the magic word and you receive the revelation. Therapists who can forget their preconceptions—and obviously this is tremendously difficult; one has after all invested so much hope in studying, learning, gaining wide experience—but, therapists who *can* forget their preconceptions *must* learn from each given patient.

However, even clearing away the therapist's hopes from and for therapy and in and of himself will not by itself bring crises of hope to the fore. The patient for whom hope is the matter will have his hopes deeply invested in activity. It is as if no sooner does he begin to experience crises of hope, he swings into actions designed to forestall these. And once he does that he cannot speak of his hopes because in the realer sense he does not experience them.

A patient tells of a fight with a girlfriend: he may be hoping—Now do you see what you mean to me?

A patient is silent: he may be hoping—Now do you see how bankrupt your methods are?

A patient tells a dream. What we should consider is not so much the meaning of the dream but what it is that induces this patient, having an experience, to express it in images and convey it in that form to us.

Similarly, here is a patient.

She struggles for hope. She is 'afraid to close any door'. She tries desperately 'to keep her options open'. She is afraid of closed spaces, of lifts and airplanes particularly. The lift will get stuck, the plane can crash. Even seeing a plane disappear behind a cloud fills her with panic. She imagines the people as shrinking to the proportion of the dwindled size of the departing plane—until 'they are small creatures inside this long tubular thing'. When she has to fly, she thinks to take tranquillizers or a drink or two. But then, once she has swallowed these, they are in her for good and there is no reversing the process. Thus both entering and being entered are torments of irrevocable finality.

The material here, a few minutes from a single session, is rich with symbols and unconscious equivalencies; knowing the patient one could interpret it with relative ease. But the material is narrative; its substance, so far, takes place outside the session. If one interpreted the penis—breast equivalencies, the castration fears or the fantasies about intercourse, conception and birth, the patient would gain insight but something of great momentum, not yet evolved, would escape the session. In fact, interpretation under the circumstances would probably serve to bind and make coherent something not yet experienced in all its incongruity and incoherence. In other words, interpretation would serve as a defence. Like the narrative of the patient, the interpretation would talk about an experience not present in the session.

Narration is spurious. It gives an order and meaning to experience which the experience is unlikely to possess. When Plato was pondering who should rule the Republic, he decided against the artist on precisely these grounds. The artist, he felt, gives a verisimilitude to nature that is meretricious. As Trilling (1971) says:

> It is the nature of narrative to explain, it cannot help telling how things are and even why they are. . . . But a beginning implies an end, with something in the middle to connect them. The beginning is not merely the first of a series of events; it is the event that originates those that follow. And the end is not merely the ultimate event, the cessation of happening; it is a significance or at least the promise, dark or bright, of a significance.

Narration then is the language of action; it presents not an experience but a semblance of an experience; it is told for effect. And while being told, it may hold such thrall for the therapist that he may become more taken with what is being told him than with how and why. Since, however, the object of the psychotherapy is to divorce hope from its various vestments and activations so that it can become an experience capable of being experienced, the therapist will do better to wonder to what purpose this is being told him than to succumb to the temptations of searching out the contents of the story and replying to these with an interpretation that, after all, is likely to be a narrative of his own.

So far I have suggested a series of renunciations—of hope in therapy, in one's prior knowledge, in one's person—followed by a series of restraints—from engaging with the meaning instead of the purpose of what patients communicate, of attending to narrated rather than currently experienced events. This is no easy prescription, partly because we are better trained in the psychotherapy of problems around desire. But if one recalls the peculiarly paradoxical nature of hope, namely that it fears fulfilment as much as frustration, for both produce hopelessness, one can see that fairly special measures are required.

Let me now assume that the therapist has managed all of this and that crises of hope have begun to evolve. As these crises of hope evolve, they must be worked with minutely. The aim now is not their emergence but their reconstruction. But little help can be expected from the patient, who is likely to have become outraged or spiteful, depressed or apathetic, mute or as changeless as he can be. It will be for the therapist to put things into words. Even so, the patient should be expected to adopt towards the therapist's words the aloof, haughty attitude of the suicide, a prospect which, of course, is never far distant. The therapist will accordingly need always to be mindful of how persecuting the patient finds his interpretations. For example with the patient whose session I have excerpted, I need to acknowledge that an exceedingly frightening part of periodic sessions is that out of envy I will ruin her enjoyment of her penis. Or, equally, that she will do so to mine and so will no longer have someone to acquire a less defective penis from.

The point to bear in mind is that when the patient has got past attempting to activate his hopes and has let the crisis evolve, the resulting experience is so immediate, so 'now', as to be veritably real. Interpretations, accordingly, need no longer be tutorial or explanatory: they need simply describe the experience that once, and now again, derived from the preconception involved, but which, to protect the hope, became transfigured out of recognition and recall.

When the total experience—the preconception, the experience and the untransfigured experience of the experience—is available to the patient, that portion of the therapy is complete: the research has been done, in *viva*, as it were, and the discovery made. In time, the task of the therapy will become the more familiar analysis of problems with desire.

SUMMARY

I do *not* split hope into good and bad hopes, normal hope or delusional hope, necessary hope or dispensable hope. To my mind, that would be like saying that hope is better than desire or desire better than hope or stars better than molecules. Stars are: hope is.

The preconceptions out of which hope arises concern the following:

> the quality of the breast; the ownership of the
> breast;
> the quality of the mouth; and the ownership of the
> mouth; ·
> the quality of the faeces; and the ownership of the faeces (or
> sphincters);
> the quality of the genitals (often their size); and the ownership
> of the genitals;
> the qualities of the parents; and the ownership of those
> qualities;
> the qualities of one's group; and the ownership by one's
> group;
> the quality of life; and the ownership of life.

Though several of these preconceptions conjoin with the familiar developmental orientations of desire, desire and hope are different. Desire is sensual; hope is not. Desire arises from the cyclic, appetitive passions of the body; hope appears to arise from preconceptions of how things should be. Desire seeks gratification and surcease—it is kinetic; hope is possessive and potential. Desire likes the here-and-now, the definite, the actual; hope likes the yet-to-be, the changeable, the ambiguous. When thwarted, desire tends to retreat, we call it 'regress', to its last best success, while hope goes forward, beyond even a lifetime or outwards beyond the confines of probability. Desire, frustrated, gives rise to rage and jealousy; hope—to outrage, and to envy and spite and revenge. When renounced, each, however, gives over to sadness; but desire changes its object while hope changes over to desire.

It follows that in the treatment situation, the therapist need neither a painter nor sculptor be: he need neither infuse hope (or desire) nor pare it away. But by revoking his own hopes, he will make it possible for his patient's hopes to move from being vested to being experienced and thus to being subject to analysis and reconstruction.

REFERENCES

Augustine, A. St. *Confessions; City of God; on Christian Doctrine.* Chicago: Encyclopaedia Press, 1952.

Bion, W. R. (1961). *Experience in Groups.* New York: Basic Books.

Bion, W. R. (1963). *Elements of Psychoanalysis.* New York: Basic Books.

Bion, W. R. (1970). *Attention and Interpretation.* New York: Basic Books.

Boris, H. N. (1970). The medium, the message and the good group dream. *Int. J. Grp Psychother.* 20, 91–98.

Boris, H. N., Zinberg, N. E. & Boris, M. (1975). People's fantasies in group situations: towards a psychoanalytic theory of groups. *Contemp. Psychoanal.* 11, 15–45.

Bulfinch, T. (1855). *Mythology.* New York: Random House.

Chomsky, N. (1972). *Language and Mind.* New York: Harcourt, Brace.

Erikson, E. (1963). *Childhood and Society.* 2nd ed. New York: Norton.

Erikson, E (1964). *Insight and Responsibility.* New York: Norton.

Freud, S. (1917). Mourning and melancholia. *S.E.* 14.

Freud, S. (1920). Beyond the pleasure principle. *S.E.* 18.

Freud, S. (1937). Analysis terminable and interminable. *S.E.* 23.

Gardner, H. (1973). *The Quest for the Mind: Piaget, Lévi-Strauss and the Structuralist Movement.* New York: Knopf.

Greenacre, R. (1953). Penis awe in relation to penis envy. In R. M. Loewenstein (ed.), *Drives, Affects, Behavior.* New York: Int. Univ. Press.

Hartman, H. (1959). Psychoanalysis as a scientific theory. In S. Hook (ed.), *Psychoanalysis, Scientific Method and Philosophy.* New York: Int. Univ. Press

Jaques, E. (1965). Death and the mid-life crisis. *Int. J. Psycho-Anal.* 46, 502–514.

John of the Cross, St. In K. Reinhardt (ed.), *Dark Night of the Soul.* London: Ungar Press, 1957.

Kant, I. (1781). *The Critique of Pure Reason.* Chicago: Encyclopaedia Britannica Press, 1952.

Klein, M. (1957). *Envy and Gratitude.* London: Tavistock Publ.

Kohut, H. (1968). The psychoanalytic treatment of narcissistic personality disorders. *Psychoanal. Study Child* 23.

Leach, E. (1970). *Claude Lévi-Strauss.* New York: Viking Press.

Lévi-Strauss, C. (1966). *The Savage Mind.* Chicago: Univ. Chicago Press.

Lévi-Strauss, C. (1973). *From Honey to Ashes.* New York: Harper & Row.

Lyons, J. (1970). *Noam Chomsky.* New York: Viking Press.

Mayr, E. (1972). Sexual selection and natural selection. In B. Campbell (ed.), *Sexual Selection and the Descent of Man.* Chicago: Aldine.

Piaget, J. (1973). *The Child and Reality; Problems of Genetic Psychology.* New York: Grossman.

Piers, M. (ed.) (1972). *Play and Development: A Symposium.* New York: Norton.

Schafer, R. (1970). The psychoanalytic vision of reality. *Int. J. Psycho-Anal.* 51, 279–297.

Searles, H. (1965). *Collected Papers on Schizophrenia.* New York: Basic Books.

Tinbergen, N. (1958). *Curious Naturalists.* New York: Basic Books.

Tinbergen, N. (1965). *Animal Behavior.* New York: Time-Life Press.

Trilling, L. (1971). *Sincerity and Authenticity.* Cambridge: Harvard Univ. Press.

Weisman, A. D. (1965). *The Existential Core of Psychoanalysis: Reality Sense and Responsibility.* Boston: Little-Brown.

Winnicott, D. W. (1965). The aims of psychoanalytical treatment. In *The Maturational Processes and the Facilitating Environment.* New York: Int. Univ. Press.

24

The Problem of Pointlessness—A Challenge for Counselling

JEREMY HAZELL

A sense of pointlessness is a deep problem which underlies many more familiar problems. Its origins lie in deeply-rooted feelings of personal insignificance which can only be resolved by a genuine experience of relationship. The possibilities of establishing such a relationship in a counselling setting are examined with reference to condensed case-histories and relevant psychodynamic theory.

This article is prompted by the frequency with which students complain of feelings of pointlessness in their activity. In six years as counsellor in a university college of 4,000 students, I have often found that in the course of stating his problem a student sooner or later complains of the pointlessness of what he is doing, and that this may become for him a matter of the deepest concern. It is this problem—which so often seems to underlie other problems—that I want to investigate here. I wish firstly to describe the phenomenon of pointlessness; secondly, to attempt to trace, with reference to psychodynamic theory, its emotional antecedents; thirdly, to ask how counsellors can help; and finally, to illustrate in two condensed case-histories my own attempts to deal with the problem.

CLINICAL DESCRIPTIONS

(a) A direct statement. If a client begins by saying that he feels no point in his activity, there are two possible interpretations: either that he has mistakenly chosen the wrong

Reprinted by permission from *British Journal of Guidance and Counselling*, 4 (July 1976), 156–170.

activity, or that he is in a seriously devitalised state which affects whatever he tries to do. The first possibility is easily checked. Genuine mistakes arise which throw individuals into confusion, so that they panic into a mistaken activity and feel trapped in it. If that is so the client will respond appropriately once he sees how the mistake arose, and the counsellor can then encourage him to achieve a solution. This is useful counselling and leaves no problems.

A deeper problem arises, however, if this line of enquiry ends in stalemate with the client demurring and showing that he feels counselling itself to be a pointless uncreative process. It is at this point, when the client becomes apathetic with the counsellor, that the deeper problem appears. It is both a crisis and an opportunity. The client has come to the counsellor, often with considerable courage, only to find his need stifled by an overwhelming sense of futility. He will be likely to say 'I don't know why I've come', or 'I'm here under false pretences', or, if the counsellor has tolerated an opening silence, 'My mind was full of things to say outside. But now I'm here, there is no point'. Or there may just be an awkward silence, which is hard for both counsellor and client to tolerate. If the counsellor does tolerate it, he may be rewarded in time by a tentative outreach. But meanwhile the client feels empty—a 'hollow person'—with little or no expectation of relationship. He cannot relate to the counsellor, and yet the counsellor's presence remains important to him. He does not need 'clever' interpretations, but a consistent grasp of his desperate need to be wanted and valued as a person. A direct statement of this kind is illustrated in case-history 2, later in the article.

(b) Indirect statements. Although the problem is sometimes stated directly, it often emerges through other problems, not obviously connected with pointlessness, which are revealed as arising from and denying that state. 'Excessive' states, for instance, are often kept in place by a fear of lapsing into the state of pointlessness, such as excessive ('manic') excitement or excessive mental or physical (obsessional) activity. These excesses quite often give way to states of exhaustion, for which some 'point' has then to be found—often in the form of severe head- or back-aches.

An urgent craving for sexual or aggressvie gratification may also indicate a sense of inner pointlessness: an attempt to impart 'meaning' to a relationship about which one has no real confidence. A student once told me that he was 'a typical male predator' who specialized in 'one-night stands' with women. Some weeks later he confided that he had no choice about this since, whenever a deeper relationship started to develop, he felt 'bored' and had to leave. This was his deeper problem, a feeling of pointless emptiness arising from a feeling of having nothing to contribute. Similarly, unless he had someone to hate and fight, he began to feel empty. Here again, although hating and fighting were real problems, they were not as deep or painful as the state they disguised: a deep feeling of not mattering as a person, and therefore of activity not mattering.

A pervasive problem here is the socially-reinforced excess of ruthless competitiveness within 'systems' of which human beings are mere 'components'. In such situations human beings may come to feel invisible as persons. This impersonality has an appearance of 'efficiency', but it is highly inefficient in terms of good personality functioning. From such systems a stream of anxious persons approach the counsellor. Their problem is that their 'selves' keep getting in the way of their activity. Their expectation is that the counsellor will also be a mere component of the system, predictably carrying out a prescribed activity. A medical student who found his sense of inadequacy in social groups affecting his very high academic performance was plainly astonished when I suggested that he was more important than his career.

In most of the above examples the client directly involves the counsellor in the indirect statement of his pointlessness. All his attempts to forestall and deny the state of pointlessness, which constitute the 'presenting problem', will be used with the counsellor for the same purpose. The state of pointless emptiness and alienation is unconsciously assumed by the client to be an inevitability, and at first he sees the counsellor at best as a conspirator helping him to avert it. When the counsellor fails to collude in this way, clients may complain that he is dull, ignorant or wanting in some other respect, in order to provoke a physical or mental battle, in order to feel 'somebody'. Or they may attempt to seduce him, or complain about limitations of time and space: 'I'm sure I could think of what I want to say if I could see you any time.' But further meetings usually bring about more pointless encounters, since it is not primarily time that is needed, but a solution to the feeling of the client that relations for him are hopeless and pointless since no-one would want or respect him unless they were tricked, bribed, seduced, stung or in some way forced into doing so. Since the client cannot trust, he must manipulate, and his manipulative behaviour is an indirect statement of pointlessness. The counsellor's interpretation of such statements must always constitute evidence to the client that the counsellor is on his side (Blake, 1968). Interpretations which fail to convey this message are experienced by this kind of client as intrusions or attacks (Balint, 1968).

EMOTIONAL ANTECEDENTS

There are three main emotional ingredients of the pointless state: (a) a deep and enduring internalised experience of alienation: (b) an experience of personal weakness or of unreality; and (c) a fear of life's demands, resulting in withdrawal of the self's core from activity, which is then carried on in a routine mechanical fashion. The theory which encompasses these phenomena most successfully is the 'object-' or 'personal-relations' theory of the personality originally conceived by Fairbairn (1952; 1963), and developed subsequently by Guntrip (1961; 1968). Winnicott (1965; 1971) and Balint (1952; 1968), who were contemporaries of Guntrip, also produced theories which—although they deal with the same phenomena—lack the systematic clarity of Fairbairn's original theory and Guntrip's development (see Morse, 1972).

Fairbairn's theory (1952; 1963) was evolved from clinical experience with patients whose schizoid or 'cut-off' state convinced him that human beings are principally person-seeking, and not pleasure-seeking as Freud had maintained. Fairbairn redefined 'libido' as the primary energy of the ego or core-self for personal relating. He regarded anti-social impulses as the results of frustration in achieving this primary aim, due to the emotional inconsistencies of the 'object' (i.e. the person who is the object of the infant's need). Fairbairn saw the core of the self as an original undamaged whole, and the therapeutic task as rescuing split-off parts of this original 'whole' from their unconscious preoccupation with 'bad objects' (i.e. unsatisfying persons or aspects of persons) in order to restore the wholeness of the ego.

Guntrip (1968), however, discovered with schizoid patients that releasing the ego from 'bad-object situations', while it resolves anti-social impulses, does *not* restore wholeness to the ego. On the contrary, it leaves the patient feeling weak and unreal, as the loss of actual parents would. Guntrip therefore describes the ego, or core of the self, as a 'latent potentiality in the psychic', dependent for its realisation upon a secure, loving, maternal relationship. The deepest problem is not that bad personal relationships in infancy damage an otherwise whole ego, but that without personal relations no ego is able to develop at all, and bad relations are better than none. The rescuing of the ego from preoccupation over relations with bad objects therefore tends to reveal a seriously weakened core, which feels unrelated and cut off. Guntrip termed this self 'the regressed ego' or 'lost heart of the self'. For him the therapeutic task was to locate the 'regressed ego' and impart to it a sense of relation in order to facilitate its development as a secure purposive social self. He writes that 'the human psyche is an incipient ego', needing an experience of 'being with' the understanding therapist, just as an infant needs to 'be with' a secure mother. When this happens, 'psychic energy' is released from anti-social struggles with bad objects, and is re-enlisted in the service of the self.

Elaborating these ideas further, Winnicott (1971) describes how an infant loses 'continuity with his personal beginning' when there is a serious break in the early love-relationship with his mother, occasioning the formation of primitive defences against a repetition of unthinkable anxiety. This means that the infant has to start again, divorced from his personal starting point. He does this by developing a 'false self' which both protects and hides a 'true self in cold storage' containing his innate potentialities and natural capacities. Winnicott's 'true self' (1965) is the equivalent of Guntrip's 'regressed ego', and he sees the major therapeutic task as bringing about the rebirth of the 'true self' by means of a facilitating relationship which releases and activates 'maturational processes' innate within the psyche.

It is however the 'false self' which initially confronts the counsellor: he has to understand and accept the 'coping behaviour' by which the client struggles to keep in touch with a world experienced by him as harsh or remote. Once the 'vital heart' is frightened into withdrawal, it is kept repressed so that the client feels that this 'false self' is all he has. Thus a client described her attitude to myself in sessions as 'a willing suspension of disbelief'. It is salutary to bear in mind that but for this 'false self' the client may be given over to a state of near-total apathy and would certainly be unlikely to approach a counsellor for help. Guntrip (1968) reminds us that the 'false self' or selves must be respected as a client's attempt to manufacture a feeling of being a 'somebody', while inwardly he feels a 'nobody'. When the 'false self' begins to fail, an individual can feel he has no self. Another client recently said to me: "There must be a block in most people to the idea that you don't have a self at all—I mean that it's possible not to have a "self" and still be around'.

But there has to be a psychic subject to experience anything at all, even hollowness and emptiness, and it is to this psychic subject with the innate potentiality for development as ego or 'self' that the counsellor seeks to import an experience of relationship: 'The ego in its earliest beginnings is the psychic subject experiencing itself as satisfactorily in being...the ego is the psyche growing to self-realisation and identity, in the initial experience of identification or shared emotional experience with the mother' (Guntrip, 1968). Winnicott believes that this hidden capacity for growth underlies the 'false self'. He writes (1971): 'One has to allow for the possibility that...even in the most extreme case of...the establishment of a false personality, hidden away somewhere there exists a secret life that is satisfactory because of its being creative or original to that human being. Its unsatisfactoriness must be measured in terms of its being hidden, its lack of enrichment through living experience'.

HOW COUNSELLING CAN HELP

The state of pointlessness presents a daunting therapeutic challenge since it represents a weakness at the core of the self. It demands from the counsellor a strong well-founded belief in the client as a person who has inherent value, with a unique nature of his own: this belief must be founded upon the intuitive perception of the counsellor, and reinforced by a strong, accurate and well-thought-out body of clinically-tested theory. Without this the counsellor is in great danger of colluding with his client's attempts to involve him in efforts to avoid the real problem of weakness and pointlessness and to reinforce the 'false self', for example, by conducting the relationship in terms of guilt over problems of sex or aggression, or in terms of detached intellectual discussion of his 'case'. The client will be likely to succeed in this unless he perceives that the counsellor, while taking each anxiety seriously, is also looking 'beyond' it in an attempt to understand how his client comes to be feeling it. Each problematical situation is therefore looked at from the client's point of view and in three ways: (a) in terms of its connection with his present-day external world; (b) in terms of its meaning for the client in his urgent but despairing search for a satisfying personal relationship; and (c) in terms of what the client is needing from the counsellor as a person in order to enable him to feel more deeply understood and valued.

Guntrip (1968) points out that for those without an adequate experience of 'self', the need for relation is pre-moral. He writes: "We are dealing with individuals who, however much they may have been trained to adult social and moral obligations and values at the ordinary conscious level of their personality of everyday living, are unable to maintain themselves on that level because the underlying, unconscious strata of their personalities are on the pre-moral level of infantile fear, ego weakness and flight from life'. Because of this situation in the unconscious, quite desperate measures seem necessary to manufacture a sense of relationship. The greater the despair the client felt originally over his relationships, the more unscrupulous he will be in trying to force a sense of relationship from the counsellor and others in self-defeating ways. For example, irrational outbursts of hate may be at source an attempt to wring love out of the counsellor, about whom the client now feels the same despair which he felt about his original 'bad object'. Approached in the three ways described above, this would be dealt with as follows: (a) a current difficulty, leading to unpopularity and isolation socially; (b) a despairing attempt to force love out of a remote or rejective needed person, e.g. mother, mother-substitute or father; and (c) an indication of urgent despairing need for reliable dependency in the counsellor with a view to resolving the underlying fear of personal insignificance. Mere interpretations of the 'transference' of the original despair are insufficient. The need is for the counsellor himself to become a 'real good object' in his client's experience. He can only succeed by continuing to be a genuinely caring person and thus outlasting his client's anxious manipulations.

An equally severe test of the counsellor is the client's apparent coldness when his inner fear makes him incapable of responding openly to the counsellor's warmth. This in turn can make the client so afraid that the counsellor will lose interest in him that he becomes manipulative again in a desperate attempt to hold on to the relationship. Much depends on the counsellor's understanding of the kind of interpersonal atmospheres which gave rise to his client's desperate state of mind. Dreams and fantasies often give valuable insights into the bad interpersonal situations in which the client suffered, and unconsciously still suffers, helping the counsellor to see 'how it was' with his client. By entering into his client's situations, both past and present, the counsellor may eventually become recognised as a true ally on whom his client may begin to depend. Angry hating impulses are not innate anti-social 'instincts' but can seem to be such when exploited by a weakened ego for the purpose of obtaining a relationship. 'Instinctive behaviour', writes Sutherland (1969), 'is always the person in action, and it is *how he is dealt with as a person "owning" this behaviour which is crucial*'. Understanding of the 'personal relations' origin of anti-social behaviour is vital when counselling those persons whose expressions of pointlessness are indirect (see case history 1 below).

Once the person is located at the centre of his behaviour, the extent of his weakness and the 'pointlessness' of his isolated existence become evident, and his need for a safe, undisturbed experience of relationship with the counsellor intensifies. The counsellor's task is now to 'be with and for' his client in order to facilitate and consolidate the latter's first experiences of being in a safe and trusted presence. Guntrip (1968) and Winnicott (1965; 1971) state that the secure nursing mother is the prototype for the abiding consistent maternal quality required of the counsellor at this stage, in order that his client may have an experience of 'being at one with' him. On the basis of this 'undisturbed oneness' the client may develop the experience of being a separate individual, of 'being alone in the presence of someone' (Winnicott, 1965). He develops an experience of identity which gradually becomes effective in other settings, as he develops a 'belief in a benign environment' *(ibid)*. He may thus explore his world afresh, in the light of his experience of belonging with the counsellor, who for the time being represents 'the world' to him, but who is, by degrees, taken for granted by the client as he develops autonomy.

My own experience suggests that it may be possible for counsellors to make a significant contribution at this level provided they have adequate access to those who are familiar with the issues. There are special advantages in settings where young men and women are resident (as at college or university), often some distance from home, for three to five years. Opportunities for therapeutic success in these settings seem more favourable than among persons of higher age groups in more structured settings where they incur financial, professional and family responsibilities, or among younger persons under the direct influence of their parents. Clearly much depends upon the support available to the individual counsellor. The problem is formidable, and yet because of its frequency and importance, cannot be ignored.

CASE-HISTORY 1: INDIRECT STATEMENT OF POINTLESSNESS

I now wish to introduce two condensed case histories which illustrate the problem more fully. The first concerns a female 18-year-old science student, seen for 156 sessions of an hour's duration over a period of three years and five months. The basic pattern of once-weekly sessions was altered to twice-weekly sessions at the stage of deepest dependence. There were also some emergency sessions as needed, and telephone contact where necessary.

The client presented in the sixth week of her first term at the college. She was so frightened and disorientated that she could only attend her first six sessions if escorted by a friend, who remained present throughout the sessions. The doctor who referred her and undertook medical responsibility for the case informed me that the client had received psychotherapy as a child, but had been withdrawn by her parents, who disagreed about her treatment. Although this background doubtless helped to account for her extreme nervousness in the sessions, she experienced great difficulty in all relationships; she could never look at people, and her speech was jerky and unco-ordinated. Physically she had good features, but was very thin. Her academic work was above average, but it often appeared to be achieved at the expense of other students in her lodgings upon whom she made exhausting demands. She also had recurring back trouble which rendered her prostrate for a week at a time and dependent on her landlady and fellow-students.

In sessions the client recoiled if I made any move to speak to her, so I simply remained alongside. Apart from my observations, I knew nothing of why she had come, since she had made no statement. She became openly hostile when I suggested she 'feel free' to speak of what was troubling her. 'Free is the *last* thing I feel', she snapped. I told her that I could see she was frightened, and she said that she felt coming to me was 'giving in'. It then emerged that she was 'terrified of going home' (for the vacation) and was afraid I would send her there. Her mother had told her she would not survive away from home, but that she need not expect to be able to come to her for comfort. It became clear to me that the girl's hostility represented her all-out attempt to keep going despite being in an exhausted and frightened state. Her 'bad backs' indicated the extent of her need for rest, and her viciousness indicated her fear of dependence. The weakened core of the self was thus discernible from the start, though masked for the present by hatred of herself insofar as she felt weak, and of me insofar as I recognised her weakness.

She warned me that she was 'a vicious little cat'. I pointed out that she was equally vicious towards herself. Every expression of need was countered instantly by a rebuke—'stupid little bitch'. I asked who had called her stupid like that for feeling needy, and with a shock she realised that this was her mother's usual way of dealing with her needs. She had thus become identified with the rejective aspects of her mother in an attempt to feel more of a person. Sutherland (1969) writes that 'identification... is really a relationship in which the identity of another is being borrowed to fill the despairing emptiness of the self, and associated with this feeling is the typical infantile dependence on the other'. This statement clearly refers to 'morbid' identification which has outlasted its value to the infant as a basis for individuation and so has become a problem. I therefore made a bid to replace the client's mother as the object of her infantile dependence so that she might grow an identity of her own. In doing this I was opposing her 'parent-influenced self' and, so to speak, 'answering' her own self-accusations on behalf of the weakened and fearful self being accused.

Gradually the internalised version of mother became differentiated as a frightening figure of enormous power urging her towards self-suppression and even suicide, and constantly sabotaging the therapeutic relationship. The client awoke at night on several occasions, terrified and sweating, certain that her mother was in her room. By degrees, however, she began to be more aware of myself as a potential ally. The 'fight with mother in my head' began to abate, and the client became less aggressive as the identification dispersed.

Here, however, we came upon the 'despairing emptiness' mentioned by Sutherland, and the onset of pointlessness. Describing the battle with 'psychic mother', the client said: 'Before long I feel she doesn't really exist and I feel confused and lost'. Guntrip (1968) has stated that the loss of internal bad objects feels like the loss of actual parents, so that they can only be released when replaced by a real good object of need in the person of the therapist or counsellor. In *session 24* the client reported a fantasy of being a baby in a wicker cradle surrounded by mothers among whom was her actual mother and myself. She said: 'I knew my real mother was the last I wanted, but I wasn't sure of your hand. I was afraid to reach out to you in case you either snatched me or slapped me away'. Later she put the same problem in other terms: 'I can't bear to be alone. But whenever there's any hint of a deep relationship developing I feel I must get out'. Here was the crucial dilemma: could the client allow herself to take advantage of 'therapeutic dependence' without being deterred by twin fears of being snatched at and possessed, or slapped away and rejected. The original problem with mother was now transferred into the counselling setting. The pointlessness of her existence, unmodified by the fight with mother, became undeniable.

Sessions 30-90 saw the gradual reaching of the client's exhausted and weakened core self. They also showed the extreme difficulty of resolving the state of pointlessness by reducing the client's isolation. Although an experience of relationship is urgently needed, it is equally feared. The client would feel exhausted and close her eyes, but then would instantly start up, terrified that I was leaving her. At other times she was afraid I was standing over her, and once when I got up quietly to close the window, she recoiled, thinking I was about to hit her.

Nonetheless my presence was vital. In *session 32* she said: 'In the morning I can't get up straight away. I need desperately to know you are there ... now I feel like a small child and want to curl up on your lap and sleep. I told her I realised she wanted that but that she was also afraid of it. This fear worked itself out over the next ten sessions, as the client felt fleetingly in touch and then instantly withdrew, or tried to control the relationship in terms of hate or sex. On one occasion she rushed out in mid-session in a frightened rage, only to phone me an hour later to know I was 'still there'. At the end of session 42 she fell into a profound silence, after which she said: 'I felt you were going but then looked at you to remind myself you were still there, and I felt safe'. At this stage I was needed simply to be beside her; interpretation would have been an intrusion.

In session 43, after making sure her anxieties were understood, the client dozed and then slept. When she came to she looked around confusedly saying she could not get going. I said: 'It's all here just as it was when you dropped off. You really have a self to get going in an easy natural way'. The client looked directly at me for the first time and smiled. The next two sessions represented a consolidation of this state of 'secure being at one with'.

It was important that the regressed state should be consolidated by the client without undermining too greatly her activities as a student. Her restless energy for these activities, which had previously been manufactured by self-driving, was no longer available. Therefore she had to change from a specialised to a more general course, and various planned social activities were abandoned as she sensed the possibilities of her new security. Anxiety over this loss of energy made her resistant to the regressive process, while keen to acquire its benefits: 'I have definitely experienced something real here and want more. But I am impatient and want it to happen now and quickly' (session 55). Also, the unfamiliarity of the new state made her anxious: 'Neither of us was saying anything and yet I felt in touch' (session 58).

In session 59 this theme continued. Having phoned me at home to allay her anxiety, she said: 'There is something in me which won't allow me to rest—but I know I'm exhausted'. She was then able to rest for a time, until the unfamiliarity of her state once more disturbed her: 'I feel safe but I've never had anyone there for me like this and it feels strange'. I replied: 'Feeling safe is strange to you—like coming upon an unknown part of yourself. But both are necessary if you are to live a full life'. After that, relaxed rest was possible.

But the feeling of pointlessness recurred in session 63: 'I keep feeling I haven't got a self and there's no point in bothering'. It was a matter of resolving her anxieties as and when they emerged and interrupted the developing state of 'being at one with'. For the most part I would sit quietly beside her while her mood ranged from deep security to anxiety and back again to the much-needed state of identification. 'Basic ego-relatedness' is the term which Winnicott (1965) uses to describe the state of primary identification through which an individual develops a sense of ego-wholeness and identity with characteristic self-feeling, so that he feels 'a profound sense of belonging and being at one with his world which is not intellectually "thought out", but is the persisting atmosphere of security in which he exists within himself' (Guntrip, 1968). Because of this, he can be 'alone' without anxiety for longer and longer periods.

By session 79 the client began to consider dispensing with one of her two regular weekly sessions. We agreed she should phone me if she decided to do so. At session 83 a situation occurred which represented the differentiation of an independently developing self. The client had unconsciously arranged to discuss an essay with her tutor at the same time when she was due to have her first session of the week with me. When she realised this she decided to come to the session, but for a moment she thought of phoning to cancel it. Her momentary forgetting had not been 'resistance', for at the next session she presented a dream: 'I was in my lodgings looking for you. But I kept stopping outside friends' rooms until finally a girl said "Hello, did you have a good sleep?" Then I felt warm and safe. I thought I'd contact you sometime and later would do'. This dream showed her growing confidence in my background presence as the basis of her own growing autonomy and capacity for social relationship. Shortly afterwards she did in fact dispense with the second session.

Sessions 90-156 were concerned with supporting and encouraging the client's fast developing self: 'being-with' developed into 'doing-with' (Guntrip, 1968), until finally the client left, after a series of dreams involving wounded men (what she feared she would do to me by her development). She obtained an excellent qualification and now, six years after presenting, she has had no recurrence of her back trouble, is highly successful in her career, and enjoys mutually satisfying social relationships. Her occasional letters are cheerful and informative.

CASE-HISTORY 2: DIRECT STATEMENT OF POINTLESSNESS

The second client was a male of 26, married, with a 3-year-old daughter. He presented mid-way through his first year in an arts course. I saw him for 86 weekly one-hour sessions over a period of 2½ years. In this case I took no family history since it seemed intrusive to do so. Winnicott (1965) has observed that in the treatment of schizoid persons the counsellor 'needs to know all about the interpretations which might be made on the material present, but he must be able to refrain from being side-tracked into doing this work that is inappropriate because the main need is for an unclever ego-supporting or holding'. In this case, the significance of poor relations with parents was tacitly observed and used to indicate what was needed by way of compensation in the therapeutic relationship.

The client was initially very silent, staring blankly ahead for long periods. He showed me some poetry in which he had tried to express his state of mind. It described a meaningless existence in an uncaring world. When he spoke he was barely audible, and he seemed to have great difficulty in moving at the end of a session.

In *session 4*, he felt ready to make a statement: 'This awful gap; I feel it with my wife and daughter, although I see they love me. My work is enough to keep me in being for now, but it really is a meaningless exercise and I dare not look into the future'. He said that when his work ended he knew he would feel a vacuum and be driven towards suicide. He was in despair about his own lack of warmth. Although his daughter evoked feeling in him, his wife encountered in him a 'cut-off point' beyond which he could not experience her as a person, but only as 'a phenomenon'.

After six sessions the client's work became more 'meaningful and he cancelled further sessions. But the 'gap' after examinations forced him to seek help again. He told me that he had attempted suicide at the end of his first term, and I was able to get in touch with the doctor who was still treating him medically.

In *session 7* the client described a recurring fantasy: "I feel I am someone born and nurtured in a wood, but I have crept out beyond the fringe. I can intrigue people with my accounts of their world from *my* viewpoint. *But I can't get back in and feel their world'*. He added that others, more healthy than he, could climb the tallest trees for their viewpoint. The dilemma expressed by this fantasy is similar to that of the client in the previous case: the client gets out but cannot get back. I began to feel that he had been born into a world without sufficient maternal love to enable him to feel a proper sense of emotional connection. If this was so, the therapeutic need was to establish such a connection by communicating accurate understanding in a loving relationship.

He, however, was experiencing nothing with which I could connect in this way. Any feeling of identity lay in his activities, which he described as 'odd bits with no centre'. At other times his statements would imply the existence of a 'centre' or 'ego' seriously isolated beneath his activities: 'I look at jobs in a catalogue way, with no sense that I am doing them. They have nothing to do with me'. His feeling of pointlessness regarding his university course was extreme. He said he felt quite unable to carry on if the next two years were to be 'another set of duties'. His extreme weakness led him continually to expect catastrophe whenever hope seemed to be entering a relationship. He told me that whenever his daughter had a slight temperature he could not help imagining her dead, and the funeral, and the 'empty feeling afterwards'. I said: 'You are used to that feeling of emptiness, and it feels safer than hope and the uncertainty for people who love you'.

During the course of the next few sessions I discovered that the client had an advanced addiction to alcohol, the extent of which he hid from his wife out of a powerful sense of fear and guilt, and which seriously threatened the financial stability of his family. The alcohol gave him a sense of 'space', an escape from the oppression of life's demands, in the face of which he tended to assemble a false but rigid structure. Drinking allowed him to 'destructure' without the absolute destruction of suicide, which he felt would otherwise result: 'Death would not be an effort, just forgetting to make the effort to survive'. Although demanding much time and attention as a formidable practical problem, it was possible to see alcoholism as the client's own attempted answer to the problem of ego-weakness and consequent pointlessness. I pointed out that counselling represented a rival strategy: An attempt at 'destructuring' the 'false self' by evoking and strengthening a potential 'true self'.

This proved to be a significant stage. The client began to express mounting frustration at being able to be anything but 'neutral' towards myself. This was in fact the first 'un-neutral' expression he achieved, and in *session 15* he said he felt that something real was occurring in *'this unique situation.'* The extent of his need of real relationship was expressed by an acute fear that the process might be seriously harmed when he left in two years' time. I told him that if he moved away there need not be an absolute end, and that periodic visits might be possible, even from a distance.

In his next session he produced a dream which he had experienced periodically in the interval between sleeping and waking and which I felt linked significantly with the stranded state suggested by the earlier fantasy: 'I felt enormous pressure: a great weight bearing on me and a loud continuous noise. I felt that if I moved my little finger the world would collapse. I felt that I was too solid for the setting in which I was placed. I feel it was to do with being born—the pressure after nine months' weightlessness. If I dared to move my head slightly on the pillow the noise was deafening'. Did this, I wondered, represent the unprotected sensitivity of a new-born child? 'Birth is mere separation', wrote Guntrip (1968), 'and speedily results in the snuffing out of the emergent ego unless good enough mothering restores connection of a kind which replicates the womb situation'. At any rate I took the client's feeling seriously. He did indeed look and sit as if he hardly dared move, and in the frequent prolonged silences I had the feeling of being in touch with a psychic centre of great fragility and sensitivity.

Counselling at this stage was frequently a matter of dealing speedily and accurately with external practicalities—alcoholic, financial or academic—so that the client's equally practical internal need for emotional 'holding' and understanding could be met. Growing acceptance of the need for 'destructuring', and his self-defeating attempts to achieve this alone with alcohol, led the client to share his burden more fully with his wife. I also saw her at the client's request, and she confirmed my impressions of the unsatisfactoriness of the client's relations with his parents. The client's wife was now able to feel and become a valuable ally in helping with his problem, which I attempted to explain to her. It was Christmas, and the family stayed with relatives of the client's wife. He reported a new feeling of being 'close to it all' (i.e. not withdrawn); there was no drunkeness. This experience of closeness was associated by the client with my 'ongoing being' for him established in sessions, and it brought about a new awareness of freshness and beauty in nature: 'a total revelation'. The client's sharing of delight was a considerable achievement. He had told me earlier of how he had wanted to share 'a more optimistic feeling' with me, but had assumed I would be too busy to listen, and had taken to drink.

Session 24 brought a swing back to sadness, and some early memories: stealing from his mother's purse; truancy from school; hatred of his sister (3½ years younger). The stealing and truancy appeared to be related to feelings of loss on the birth of his sister. Of his mother he said: 'She does all the right things, but it is as if she wishes it were all right but knows it never can be'. The client had been told that his mother considered it 'right' for babies to cry, so that when he was a baby she took him down to the ground floor of their block of flats and left him to have his cry in the mornings. The client's father appeared as a gloomy rigid man who responded to his son's signs of need with anger.

By *session 39*, half-way through the client's course at college, I felt that 'connection' between myself and the client was securely established. Sessions were looked forward to as the physical expression of a relationship already in being, instead of 'meeting a stranger each time'. The client became aware of a link between his own developing awareness and interest and his daughter's active exploration of her world. On one occasion he brought both his wife and daughter to a session to meet me. Things were happening with a 'first-time-ever' quality, he said. In one session, for example, he stretched and yawned; later he observed, 'I yawned before I noticed. I would never have been able to relax so completely a year ago'.

As the client's sense of rapport with his family and the outside world increased, the anxiety which underlay his addiction to alcohol decreased. He was able to take advantage of his GP's suggestion that he see a psychiatrist specialising in alcoholic problems. In fact he only paid one visit to the specialist, who confirmed that his condition was alcoholism and recommended abstinence. His development had reached a point where alcohol was not essential, and he abandoned it.

The client forgot to attend *session 68*. Later he reported that he had been engrossed in his revision for the final examinations, and had simply forgotten. I pointed out the he could not have done this when he first presented, and he said 'I don't feel isolated when working because I know you are there. Sometimes I actually hold mental conversations with you about what I am doing'. This ingestion of myself as a 'good object' was tested to the full by the pressure of final examinations. I had no doubt that the client's personality development was more vital than his academic success, and I simply concentrated on him as a person throughout this phase. His growing confidence in personal relating had also resulted in valuable contacts with his tutor, who provided added support.

An encouraging measure of therapeutic effectiveness was the way in which the client would come into the session after an examination, and simply sit quietly resting in his chair: 'Sitting here in the silence, a fly-wheel has stopped and I have begun to live' *(session 81)*. He obtained a very good qualification, and was able to acquire a new improved home for his family. Most important, perhaps, he has been able to move to a new town for further training, and to dispense with sessions. The relationship, of course, continues to be significant.

CONCLUSION

The most vital point in both these cases was the arrival of a state of 'communion', which Nacht (1964) describes as a 'pre-object' level of experience where the client experiences 'a kind of one-ness (in which) all opposition and all ambivalence lose their sense and their *raison d'être*'. The state of pointlessness indicates the abdication of the self's central core in search of this pre-object state of communion due to remote or harsh experience in personal relationships. Balint (1968) points out that although 'the withdrawn patient is running away from something, it is equally correct that he is *running towards* something, i.e., a state in which he feels relatively safe and can do something about the problem bothering or tormenting him'. Successful therapy consists of facilitating this search for primary identification (Guntrip, 1968) or 'basic ego relatedness' (Winnicott, 1965) or communion, with as little disruption as possible to the client's everyday self. Once this state is reached the counsellor will be rewarded by the rapid integration of the client's true personality, and the development of a spontaneous interest in his world.

The most crucial test for the counsellor is whether he can consistently *believe in the process* of his client's withdrawal, which runs counter to most social norms, as well as to his client's 'anti-needs self'. In such circumstances, the counsellor needs constantly to balance his client's 'everyday-life needs' against his need for 'communion,' and so control the regressive process. From the observer's point of view the client may be seen as most disturbingly incapacitated when he is nearest to his goal. At this point he needs the counsellor to divert all intrusion and simply, like the good parent, be with him in his ordeal. Jung (1931) recognised the dangers of impingement when he wrote: 'We must be able to let things happen in the psyche. For us this is an art of which most people know nothing, consciousness is forever interfering, helping, correcting or negating, never leaving the psychic process to grow in peace'.

It is my belief that, although much counselling must be concerned with day-to-day behaviour, the scale and depth of the needs of human beings to experience their living as meaningful and themselves as 'real' demand that counsellors combine behavioural skills and 'personalistic' counselling with deeper understanding. It is certainly possible for counsellors with adequate understanding and experience to manage 'controlled regression' with one or two clients along with their more general work. If they do not, society's dissatisfaction with treatment by drugs and ECT may well be paralleled by a contempt for psychological techniques which, like drugs, seek only to operate on aspects of individuals, and fail to relate to them as whole persons. And society will be justified in its view.

REFERENCES

Balint, Michael: *Primary Love and Psychoanalytic Technique.* London: Hogarth, 1952.
Balint, Michael: *The Basic Fault: Therapeutic Aspects of Regression.* London: Tavistock, 1968.
Blake, Yvonne: 'Psychotherapy with the More Disturbed Patient'. *British Journal of Medical Psychology,* Volume 41, 1968.
Fairbairn, W. R. D.: *Psychoanalytic Studies of the Personality.* London: Tavistock, 1952.
Fairbairn, W. R. D.: 'Synopsis of an Object-Relations Theory of the Personality'. *International Journal of Psychoanalysis,* Volume 44, 1963.
Guntrip, Harry: *Personality Structure and Human Interaction.* London: Hogarth Press, 1961.
Guntrip, Harry: *Schizoid Phenomena Object Relations and the Self.* London: Hogarth Press, 1968.
Jung, C. G.: 'A European Commentary', in Lu Yen: *The Secret of the Golden Flower.* London: Kegan Paul, 1931.
Morse, Stephen J.: 'Structure and Reconstruction: a Critical Comparison of Michael Balint and D. W. Winnicott'. *International Journal of Psychoanalysis,* Volume 53, 1972.
Nacht, S.: 'Silence as an Integrative Factor'. *International Journal of Psychoanalysis,* Volume 45, 1964.
Sutherland, J. D.: *Sexuality and Aggression in Maturation.* London: Institute of Psychoanalysis, 1969.
Winnicott, D. W.: *The Maturational Processes and the Facilitating Environment.* London: Hogarth Press, 1965.
Winnicott, D. W.: *Playing and Reality.* London: Tavistock, 1971.

25

The Secret

RUSSELL MEARES

The revelation of secrets lies at the core of much psychotherapeutic method and was the seed from which early psychoanalytic theory grew. The notion of "the secret" can therefore be regarded as critical to an understanding of the psychotherapeutic process. This paper puts forward a view which contrasts, in important aspects, with traditional concepts and which emphasizes the positive or creative value of certain hidden ideas and the importance of the social arena on which they are displayed.

SECRETS AS SUBSTANCE

Ellenberger has traced the origins of psychotherapeutic theory. Amongst them is the concept of what he calls the "pathogenic secret" (pp. 44–46), which derives from a long tradition of psychological healing. He gives examples from the practice of primitive healers, the priests of the early Christian church, and the animal magnetists, all of whom depended at times upon the extraction from their patients of concealed and intolerable experience. This was also the basis of early psychoanalysis and of Freud's "cathartic method." In these cases, the secret is regarded as harmful, as if it were a toxin. There is, however, a class of hidden ideas and experience which is fundamentally different from the "pathogenic secret." In this case, that which is concealed is not something alien, of which the bearer wishes to be rid, but something highly valued. This concept is imitated by the words of a twenty-six-year-old waitress, shy, ill-educated and somewhat depressed:

Reprinted by special permission of the William Alanson White Psychiatric Foundation, Inc. from *Psychiatry*, 39 (1976), 258–265. Copyright © 1976 by the William Alanson White Psychiatric Foundation, Inc. This article is the first chapter in Russell Meares, *The Pursuit of Intimacy: An Approach to Psychotherapy*, Thomas Nelson Australia Pty. Ltd., West Melbourne, Victoria, 3003, Australia.

I suppose I'm scared that if I talk there'll be nothing left to say. Say I told you all my thoughts ideas and whatsit, it'd be like me piled up beside us, with nothing left to say.

She seems to feel that she is composed of a series of ideas, and that should they be lost, she will cease to exist. It is as if she attributes concrete substance to her ideas, and experiences her thoughts as the stuff of her existence. Their loss implies the threat of dematerialization. She fears invisibility in the sense implied by Bob Dylan's song:

> You're invisible now
> You've no secrets left to conceal.[1]

As a consequence, at our first meeting, standing in a corner of the room, she told me that she did not want to speak. Subsequently in groups, she remained silent. For her, there could be no idle chatter, since conversation served only to reveal her inner world of "thoughts, ideas and whatsit."

She was aware that her sense of personal fragility had something to do with her relationships with others. She strove, in halting phrases, to describe this apprehension:

If I begin to speak—it's too big—like stepping on a merry-go-round—no, it's like stepping-stones across the sea—having to go on to the end. These stepping-stones are like situations, incidents more likely. I can't quite manage them. I scramble from one to the other. How I got from this morning to here is most unpleasant. I feel things are demanded.

Her inner world of thoughts and emotions is constantly "demanded" in the encounters of daily life, when a part of herself is shown to another person and momentarily occupies a precarious existence "outside" her. A reason for her unease in these situations was expressed by another patient, a quiet, solitary boy, who described his experience when speaking to a group:

Their faces watch me. My words seem to float away, and I'm unsure.

These two people both imply that to expose one's thoughts is to risk a kind of personal damage, through a faulty response of others. In the words of another patient,

The risk's not worth it. I'm not game to be real.

This degree of frailty is not shared by everyone. Nevertheless, it does seem that, for most of us, there are threads of thoughts and images which are felt as intensely

[1]Bob Dylan, "Like a Rolling Stone"; © 1965, M. Witmark.

"personal" and important. Not all thoughts are given the same value. Those concerned with things commonly sensed are frequently regarded as peripheral and passed about in small talk and gossip. Those most valued are perceived as a kind of inner core. They remain secret except under unusual circumstances.

TRANSACTIONS AND THE DEVELOPMENT OF SECRECY

Secrets are disclosed with care in a developing dialogue with others who can be trusted to share and respect them. They then become the coins of intimacy, and the currency of its transactions. This connection between thoughts and value is suggested by the evolution of certain words. For example, the "teller" not only counts and deals out things of material worth, he also tells his tale. In doing so, he draws on what the Anglo-Saxons called his "thought-hord," "hord" having the Old English meaning of "hidden inmost place" or "treasure." Furthermore, the word "dear" refers to both value and intimacy. "Worth" descends from the Old English "weorth," which is related to "weorthan," to become. "Weorthan" is also related to "verse," which is affectively laden speech. In the origins of our language, therefore, a relationship might exist between "worth," an emotional use of words, and "becoming."[2]

These suppositions suggest that the attainment of the notion of secrecy is an important feature of the child's development (or "becoming") and his growing ability to make personal relationships. Indeed, Piaget (1926) distinguishes between "adult thought which is socialized but capable of secrecy and infantile thought which is ego-centric but incapable of secrecy" (p. 39).

Secrecy is related to an increasing distinction between "inner" psychic life and the "outer" world, and a growing sense of a boundary between them. For the small child this boundary seems to be incomplete. Thus, one of Piaget's five-year-old subjects (1929) doubts whether his dream is secret:

> "Could I see your dream?"
> "No, you would be too far away."
> "And your mother?"
> "Yes, but she lights the light."[p.94]

As the child's egocentric monologues end, he learns that he can control his thoughts. They, like his toys, become "mine" but also "secret." There seems to be an age, perhaps two, when all the child's toys are "*mine*." But gradually he discovers that he can play games *with* someone. Rather than clinging to "*my*" toys, he can share them. In a similar way, he can exchange his thoughts. But, in sharing, there is a risk of losing that which is "mine." The phase of development during which a child comes to distinguish himself (his own body and his own experiences) from others is a critical milestone on the pathway toward mature relationships. It is accompanied by a conflict between a desire for sharing and fear of loss—a dilemma which persists, in varying degrees, into adult life.

[2]*Oxford English Dictionary;* Partridge; Skeat.

SECRECY AND SEXUALITY

The work of Virginia Woolf deepens our understanding of the significance of the "secret." Whilst immersed in writing her books she experienced a heightened sense of her existence. During the final stages of *The Waves*, she experienced "such moments of intensity and intoxication that I seemed to stumble after my own voice, or after some sort of speaker" (L. Woolf, Vol. 4, pp. 53-55). When each book was finished and exposed to the world, it was as if she had lost something, or at least, feared losing it. She waited for the critics' response in extreme and unreasonable agitation. She also fell into a state of blackest despair. Four weeks after finishing *Between the Acts*, she drowned herself (L. Woolf, Vol. 5, p.44).

Her husband, Leonard, suggested that her novels represented an inner self expressed in the outer world. He wrote:

> She seemed to feel their fate to be almost physically and mentally part of her fate.... Being so intimately a part of herself, a hurt to them was felt as a hurt to her, and their mortality or immortality was part of her mortality or immortality. [L. Woolf, Vol. 4, p. 205]

Her nephew, Quentin Bell, had a similar intuition.

> Her novels were very close to her own private imaginings.... Her dread of the ruthless mockery of the world contained within it the deeper fear that her art, and therefore, her self, was a kind of sham, an idiot's dream of no value to anyone.[Bell, p.28]

She herself wrote:

> Suppose one woke and found oneself a fraud? It was part of my madness that horror. [Bell, p. 28]

In contrast to this horror she received with delight a response which somehow confirmed her value. Her nephew wrote:

> I believe then that Virginia's gradual return to health in 1915 was helped by the favourable notices given to her first novel. [Bell, p. 29]

She faced a dilemma which is similar to that of the shy waitress. The following passage, however, intimates a further dimension to the notion of "secret"—an association with sexuality.

> Now the cool tide of darkness breaks its waters over me. We are out of doors. Night opens; night traversed by wandering moths; night hiding lovers roaming to adventure. I smell roses; I smell violets; I see red and blue just hidden. Now gravel is under my shoes; now grass. Up reel the tall backs of

houses guilty with lights. All London is uneasy with flashing lights. Now let us sing our love song—come, come, come. Now my gold signal is like a dragon fly flying taut. Jug, jug, jug. I sing like the nightingale whose melody is crowded in the too narrow passage of her throat. Now I hear the crash and rending of boughs and the crack of antlers as if the beasts of the forest were all hunting, all rearing high and plunging down among the thorns. One has pierced me. One is driven deep within me.

And velvet flowers and leaves whose coolness has been stood in water wash me round, and sheathe me, embalming me. [V. Woolf, pp. 151–152]

Beneath the ambiguous words runs a theme of lyric eroticism, remarkable in a woman accused of primness and an aversion to sexuality. This is not to say her writings refer directly to sexuality, or her own sexual behavior, about which she was able to talk without apparent difficulty. Rather, her writing, in being highly charged with emotion, *connected* with many experiences including the bodily and sexual.

A connection between "secret" and sexuality is suggested etymologically. Both "secretion" and "secret" are derived from the past participle "secretus," of the Latin verb "secernere," to separate, or set apart. "Secretum," the neuter form of "secretus," had the Latin meaning of "a secret place," while the Old French word "secretion" meant "a thing separated, set apart" (Partridge; Skeat). Furthermore, in the last century, "secret" in slang referred to the vagina or copulation (Gittings, p. 452).

It has already been suggested that the core of self may be felt as a series of hidden ideas. Their connection with sexuality is made concrete in a characteristic Malaysian psychosis, koro, in which the core of self is believed to be seminal secretion, the loss of which has destructive bodily effects.

An awareness of the intimate nature of her writing may have evoked in Virginia Woolf a feeling of exposure akin to bodily nakedness. She once wrote:

"Is the time ever coming when I can endure to read my own writings in print without blushing—shivering and rushing to take cover?" [Quoted in Lynd, p. 28]

To be uncovered evokes "shame." Lynd makes this clear in tracing the origin of the word.

Adam and Eve felt shame in becoming aware of their own nakedness. Throughout our Western civilization, shame is related to the uncovering of nakedness. The terms *Scham* and *Schamgefuhl* in German carry the implication of uncovered nudity, and Scham is part of the compound words referring particularly to the genitals. [p. 28]

The possibility of being harmed through exposure is implied in the root meaning "shame," which has the alternative meaning of "wound" (Skeat). Lynd emphasizes the similarity between the feelings evoked by bodily and genital exposure and those engendered through "exposure of particularly sensitive intimate and vulnerable aspects of self" (p. 28).

These sentiments are reminiscent of those of the shy waitress, who spoke as if her ideas and thoughts were part of her material existence.

THE FALSE SECRET

The images and thoughts which Virginia Woolf "stumbled after" were felt as part of her substance. Images and thoughts of this kind are also to be exchanged in intimate relations. Their exposure involves risk, which is nevertheless necessary to personal growth. What can be done by someone who is afraid to take this risk? One strategy is silence, in which case the themes of hidden images and ideas are pursued in solitude. An example: A man, a homosexual, was suspicious of all close relationships. He had been conceived during his mother's menopause, and he never really knew his drunken father. He hated the nagging of his domineering mother. At 16 he was taken to court for mutilating library books. This destructive behavior consisted of cutting out all the information he could find about Catherine Howard, the young queen killed by her husband, King Henry VIII, for infidelity. The magistrate asked for an explanation, but the boy looked out of the window and refused to speak. He told me afterward that Catherine Howard was more real than he was himself. His life was spent in finding out about her, wandering round museums, the Tower, and Hampton Court—anywhere that reminded him of her. He meticulously wrote and rewrote the chronicle of her life, but refused to publish it. It was his own sacred and personal mystery. No other eyes, or hands, were permitted to sully it. Yet his strategy was self-defeating. The theme became circular, and through his fear of interchange with others, it could no longer grow.

Another man described a second strategy. Highly valued thoughts revolved in his mind, as he said, like a series of beautiful and colored constellations. In order to express them properly, he required emotive language. He avoided this, however, so that when the ideas were presented to others, they appeared, as it were in disguise. Any attack on the grey prose which carried them was deflected, since he could reassure himself that what others saw was not the *real* idea.

Perhaps the most interesting strategy, however, is the transmission of "false secrets." An example was given by a 45-year-old housewife, with a diagnosis of "mixed anxiety/depression." She vowed that every man in her life had betrayed her, yet simultaneously declared a desperate wish to convey her secrets. She repeatedly asked her therapist for assurance that everything she said would remain absolutely confidential. As soon as the therapist walked from the room he became a potential betrayer. In order to defeat what was to her an inevitable betrayal, she continued to maintain that there was always "something else," another secret which remained inviolate. She also remained untouched in another way. As far as could be gathered, her secrets, which generally had a sexual basis, were not descriptions of fact, but fabrications. She deceived her therapist but remained safe. She could maintain that what she had told him was not "really" herself. Such falsifications are of particular theoretical interest.

The diaries of Anaïs Nin are helpful in understanding this curious behavior. They are remarkable not only as pieces of writing, but also for the story of her relationships with major figures in modern literature, especially Henry Miller. They are particularly interesting from the point of view of psychotherapy. We have many descriptions of the process from therapists, but few from patients. She was treated successively by René Allendy, founder of the French Psychoanalytic Society; Otto Rank, for many years Freud's special protege; and then Martha Jaeger, a Jungian analyst. Their methods were very different, and her lucid and sensitive reporting of these encounters is uniquely valuable.

In despair and confusion, she chose to seek help from Rank. Yet, before she visited him, she planned to tell him lies. This she told him:

> I must confess to you the mood which preceded my talk with you. I made this note on the train. 'On my way to see Dr. Rank I am planning impostures, cheatings, tricks.' I begin to invent what I will tell Dr. Rank, instead of co-ordinating truths. I begin to rehearse speeches, attitudes, gestures, inflections, expressions. I see myself talking and I am sitting within Rank, judging me. What should I say to create such and such effect? I meditate lies as others meditate confessions. Yet I am going to him to confess, to get help in the solution of my conflicts, which are too numerous, and which I do not succeed in mastering by writing. I prepare myself for a false comedy. [Nin, p. 272]

This phenomenon, the confession of false secrets, was discovered by Freud in his work with hysterics, the class of patients upon whom he based his early theories. His initial conclusion was that "at the bottom of every case of hysteria there are *one or more occurrences of premature sexual experience,* occurrences which belong to the earliest years of childhood but which can be reproduced through the work of psychoanalysis" (1896, p. 203, Freud's italics). The occurrences included assaults and brother-sister incest. The most common story, however, was of a nursery maid or similar person who "has initiated the child into sexual intercourse and has maintained a regular love relationship with it ... often ... for years" (1896, p. 208). A short time after this, however, Freud "wrote Fleiss a startling confidence" (Ellenberger, p. 446). The stories of infantile seduction told to him by his patients had not, in fact, taken place.

Freud's interpretations of his experience are well known, but the phenomenon admits to an explanation which, if not alternative, is at least complementary. It is intimated by Anaïs Nin, whose journals convey a sense of personal fragility, and also a wish to remain "unknown":

> I love the idea of anonymity for the journal. It fits my earlier desire to remain unknown. It is wonderful the secrecy, again and always. [pp. 204–205]

> ... because my happiness with human beings is so precarious, my confiding moods rare, and the least sign of non-interest is enough to silence me. In the journal I am at ease. [p. 224]

It seems possible that her awareness of the "precarious" nature of human relationship caused her to commit what was most intimate to her journal, and when forced to share these feelings, for example with Rank, she considered subterfuge rather than risk the consequence of "non-interest," or worse. It may be that Freud's patients did the same. Certainly, the biographies of present-day patients who present with conversion hysteria show evidence of a sense of the fragile nature of a human interaction and a marked difficulty in making and sustaining important relationships. Though they long for intimacy, to share their inner world is to risk destruction. One way of coping with this impossible situation is by giving the other person invented "secrets," especially those which seem to be appropriate or desired—for example, sexual ones.

BETRAYAL

The theme of betrayal is necessarily linked with that of "the secret." The person who reveals secrets is afraid that in some way the recipient will betray this trust. When "false secrets" are conveyed, however, the fear of their purveyors is such that the other is betrayed in order to avoid the betrayal of themselves. A variant of the latter form of betrayal is described in the novels of Jean Genet. The person who reveals false secrets is aware not only of the intimacy which arises when secrets are shared, but also of a quality of this sharing which approaches the erotic. In the case of Genet, perhaps since the secrets are not real and are dispensable, it is his betrayal of the other which itself takes on the flavor of eroticism. In *The Thief's Journal* he wrote:

> Betrayal, theft and homosexuality are the basic subjects of this book. There is a relationship between them which though not always apparent, at least, so it seems to me, recognizes a kind of vascular exchange between my taste for betrayal and theft and my loves. [p. 141]

and again:

> ... saying of them, "They're treacherous" softened my heart, still softens me at times. They are the only ones I believe capable of all kinds of boldness. Their sinuousness and the multiplicity of their moral lines form an interlacing which I call adventure. They depart from your rules. They are not faithful. Above all, they have a blemish, a wound, comparable to the bunch of grapes in Stilitano's underpants. In short, the greater my guilt in your eyes, the more whole, the more totally assumed, the greater will be my freedom. The more perfect my solitude and uniqueness. [p. 68]

Genet implies that through betrayal of others he is inured against harm. By dealing in falsehood and giving out ideas which only *seem* to come from his innermost self, he avoids the risk of damage. At the same time, he realizes that others will judge this behavior as immoral, so that the more immoral and guilty he is in the eyes of society, the freer he is from the harm of others. Nevertheless, in giving to others things he does not feel as part of himself, he becomes dehumanized, as expressed in this passage from *Our Lady of the Flowers*:

> He liked selling out on people, for this de-humanized him. De-humanizing myself is my own most fundamental tendency. [p. 82]

SOME IMPLICATIONS

This account has concentrated on a notion of the secret which is similar to that of the sociologist George Simmel, a man two years younger than Freud. He gave a positive value to the development of secrecy, believing it produced an immense enlargement of life. Furthermore, rather than viewing its effects within the confines of a single person, as a self-contained system, he saw its significance in the sociology of human relations. This concept might be called the "creative secret," which is usefully contrasted with the "pathogenic secret." The concept of the pathogenic secret was first formulated by the Viennese physician Moritz Benedikt (Ellenberger, p. 46). His ideas were central to the embryonic theory of psychoanalysis, and Freud acknowledged his debt to Benedikt in a preliminary paper on hysteria published in 1893 (pp. 7–8n).

It is in the confessional where the "pathogenic secret" is to be found in its purest form. It has a negative value and is often related to guilt. The bearer wishes to be rid of the experience, since it is not tolerably compatible with the self system. In the case of the guilt-laden secret, the fear attached to it is not that some inner core of self may be damaged, but rather that the individual may be excluded from relationships with others as a consequence of his evil. A second difference between the two concepts of secret may be that the pathogenic secret is relatively static. The creative secret, on the other hand, invites elaboration. It is exposed in a relationship so that the other may add to it, modify it, or in other ways nourish it. It is not exposed in order to be lost.

Although two forms of secrecy can be distinguished, it should not be supposed that they do not co-exist. In the case of grief, for example, the two may mingle. Furthermore, they can be regarded as similar in one important respect. In the early days of psychoanalysis, it seemed that the discharge of a traumatic experience was the essential feature of the cathartic method, and interpersonal effects were relatively neglected. In later years, however, Freud reversed the emphasis, writing:

> .... the personal emotional relation between doctor and patient was after all stronger than the whole cathartic process.... [1925, p. 27]

Thus, the consequences of revelation of hidden ideas will be influenced by the social context of the revelation, whether the secret is to be regarded as "creative" or "pathogenic." In both cases, certain appropriate responses are required of the other. Nevertheless, despite Freud's statement, the early psychoanalytic ideas continue to have an influence. An example is the notion of the therapist as a blank screen. It is feasible that adherence to the earliest psychoanalytic ideas, which implicitly concern a one-person system, may lead to the production of persecutory feelings in the patient.

This is likely to occur when the therapist treats the experiences of his patient's inner world in a way which threatens their validity (Meares, 1975). In these ways he is seen as violating them and enhances the patient's sense of frailty. I am here, in contrast, orienting psychotherapy toward an appeal to "the secret" and its creative possibilities. Winnicott described this orientation:

> Even in the most extreme case of compliance and the establishment of a false personality, hidden away somewhere there exists a secret life that is satisfactory because of its being creative and original to that human being. Its unsatisfactoriness must be measured in terms of its being hidden, its lack of enrichment through experience. [p. 68]

In conclusion, I suggest that certain hidden ideas, which are laden with affect, are sometimes experienced as if they were the substance of self, and that the person to whom they are shown may inflict a sense of damage upon them, akin to bodily harm. On the other hand, their expression is necessary to intimacy. The need for intimate relations and the "enrichment" which others give is therefore counterbalanced by a fear of damage. It is suggested that particularly fragile people solve this dilemma by a confession of false secrets, and that this offers a complementary explanation of the confessional behavior of Freud's hysterics.

REFERENCES

Bell, Q. *Virginia Woolf,* Vol. 2; Hogarth, 1972.

Ellenberger, H. F. *The Discovery of the Unconscious;* Basic Books, 1970.

Freud, S. *Standard Ed. Complete Psychol. Works;* "On the Psychical Mechanisms of Hysterical Phenomena: Preliminary Communication (1893)" (with Breuer), Vol. 2; "The Aetiology of Hysteria (1896)," Vol. 3; "An Autobiographical Study (1925)," Vol. 20; Hogarth, 1955, 1962, 1959.

Genet, J. *Our Lady of the Flowers;* Panther Paperback, 1966.

Genet, J. *The Thief's Journal;* Penguin, 1967.

Gittings, R. *John Keats;* Heinemann, 1968.

Lynd, H. M. *On Shame and the Search for Identity;* Harcourt Brace, 1958.

Meares, R. "The Persecutory Therapist," submitted for publication (1975).

Nin, A. *The Diary of Anaïs Nin,* Vol. 1; Harcourt Brace, 1966.

Partridge, E. *Origins: A Short Etymological Dictionary of Modern English;* Routledge, Kegan Paul, 1958.

Piaget, J. *The Language and Thought of the Child* (1926); Routledge Paperback, 1959.

Piaget, J. *The Child's Conception of the World;* Routledge, Kegan Paul, 1929.

Simmel, G. *The Sociology of George Simmel,* Part 4, trans. and ed. K. H. Wolff; Free Press, 1964.

Skeat, W. *An Etymological Dictionary of the English Language;* Oxford Univ. Press. 1882.

Winnicott, D. *Playing and Reality;* Tavistock, 1971.

Woolf, L.: *Downhill All the Way: An Autobiography of the Years 1919 to 1939,* Vol. 4; Hogarth, 1967.

Woolf, L.: *The Journey Not the Arrival Matters: An Autobiography of the Years 1939 to 1969,* Vol. 5; Hogarth, 1969.

Woolf, V. *The Waves* (1931); Penguin Paperback, 1951.

Index